Kitchen Princess

2

Natsumi Ando

Story by Miyuki Kobayashi

Translated by Satsuki Yamashita

Adapted by Nunzio Defilippis and Christina Weir

Lettered by North Market Street Graphics

Ballantine Books · New York

Kitchen Princess volume 2 is a work of fiction. Names, characters, places, and incidents are the products of the author's imagination or are used fictitiously. Any resemblance to actual events, locales, or persons, living or dead, is entirely coincidental.

A Del Rey Trade Paperback Original

Published in the United States by Del Rey Books, an imprint of The Random House Publishing Group, a division of Random House, Inc., New York.

Publication rights arranged through Kodansha Ltd.

First published in Japan in 2005 by Kodansha Ltd., Tokyo

ISBN 978-0-345-49659-1

Printed in the United States of America

www.delreymanga.com

9 8 7

Translator: Satsuki Yamashita
Adaptor: Nunzio DeFilippis and Christina Weir
Letterer: North Market Street Graphics
Original cover design by Akiko Omo

Contents

Honorifics Explained

Throughout the Del Rey Manga books, you will find Japanese honorifics left intact in the translations. For those not familiar with how the Japanese use honorifics and, more important, how they differ from American honorifics, we present this brief overview.

Politeness has always been a critical facet of Japanese culture. Ever since the feudal era, when Japan was a highly stratified society, use of honorifics—which can be defined as polite speech that indicates relationship or status—has played an essential role in the Japanese language. When addressing someone in Japanese, an honorific usually takes the form of a suffix attached to one's name (example: "Asuna-san"), as a title at the end of one's name, or in place of the name itself (example: "Negi-sensei," or simply "Sensei!").

Honorifics can be expressions of respect or endearment. In the context of manga and anime, honorifics give insight into the nature of the relationship between characters. Many translations into English leave out these important honorifics and therefore distort the "feel" of the original Japanese. Because Japanese honorifics contain nuances that English honorifics lack, it is our policy at Del Rey not to translate them. Here, instead, is a guide to some of the honorifics you may encounter in Del Rey Manga.

-*san:* This is the most common honorific and is equivalent to Mr., Miss, Ms., or Mrs. It is the all-purpose honorific and can be used in any situation where politeness is required.

-*sama:* This is one level higher than "-san" and is used to confer great respect.

-*dono:* This comes from the word "tono," which means "lord." It is an even higher level than "-sama" and confers utmost respect.

-*kun:* This suffix is used at the end of boys' names to express familiarity or endearment. It is also sometimes used by men among friends, or when addressing someone younger or of a lower station.

-chan: This is used to express endearment, mostly toward girls. It is also used for little boys, pets, and even among lovers. It gives a sense of childish cuteness.

Bozu: This is an informal way to refer to a boy, similar to the English terms "kid" and "squirt."

Sempai/
Senpai: This title suggests that the addressee is one's senior in a group or organization. It is most often used in a school setting, where underclassmen refer to their upperclassmen as "sempai." It can also be used in the workplace, such as when a newer employee addresses an employee who has seniority in the company.

Kohai: This is the opposite of "sempai" and is used toward underclassmen in school or newcomers in the workplace. It connotes that the addressee is of a lower station.

Sensei: Literally meaning "one who has come before," this title is used for teachers, doctors, or masters of any profession or art.

[blank]: This is usually forgotten in these lists, but it is perhaps the most significant difference between Japanese and English. The lack of honorific means that the speaker has permission to address the person in a very intimate way. Usually, only family, spouses, or very close friends have this kind of permission. Known as *yobisute,* it can be gratifying when someone who has earned the intimacy starts to call one by one's name without an honorific. But when that intimacy hasn't been earned, it can be very insulting.

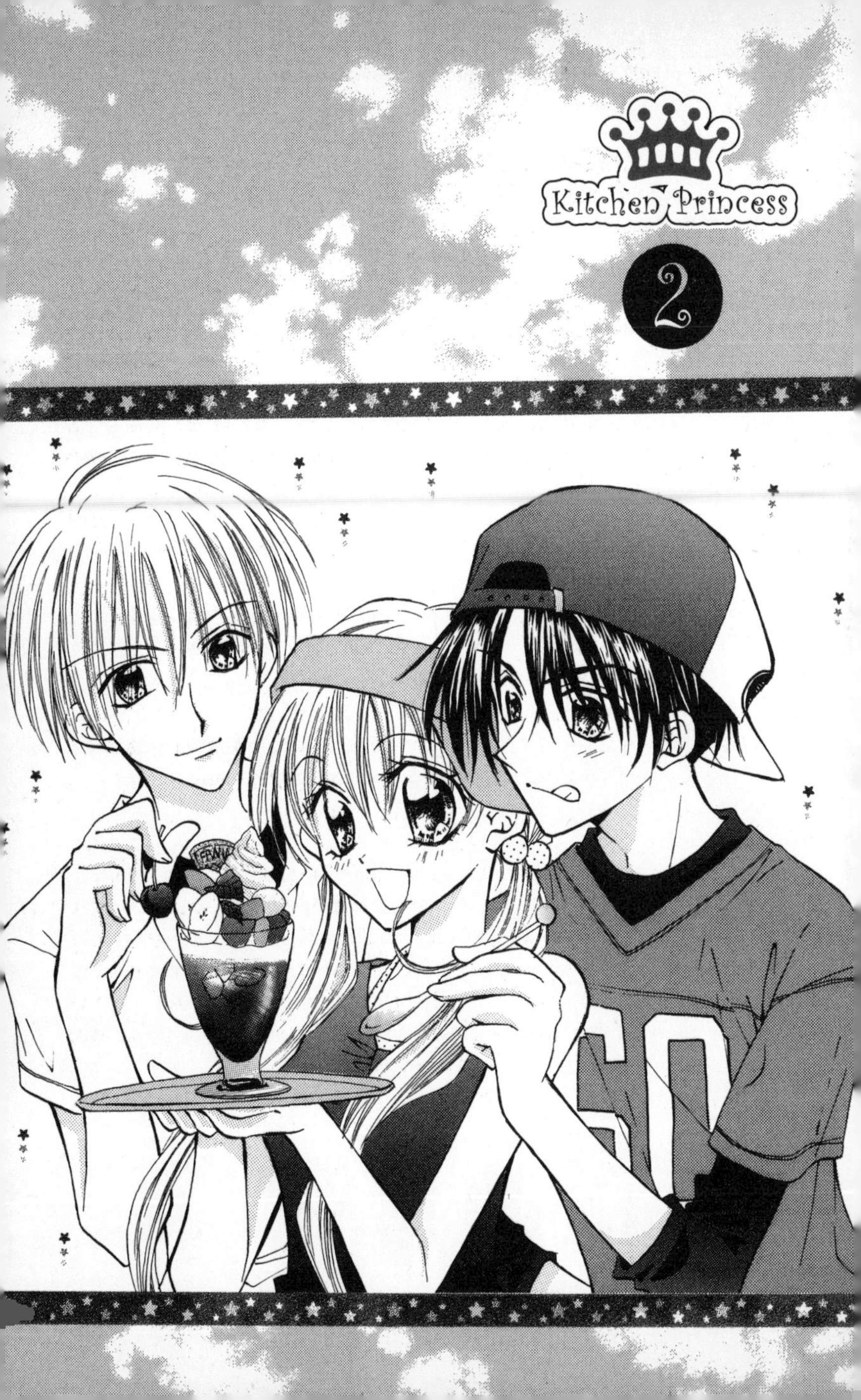
Kitchen Princess
2

Kitchen Princess

Table of
Contents

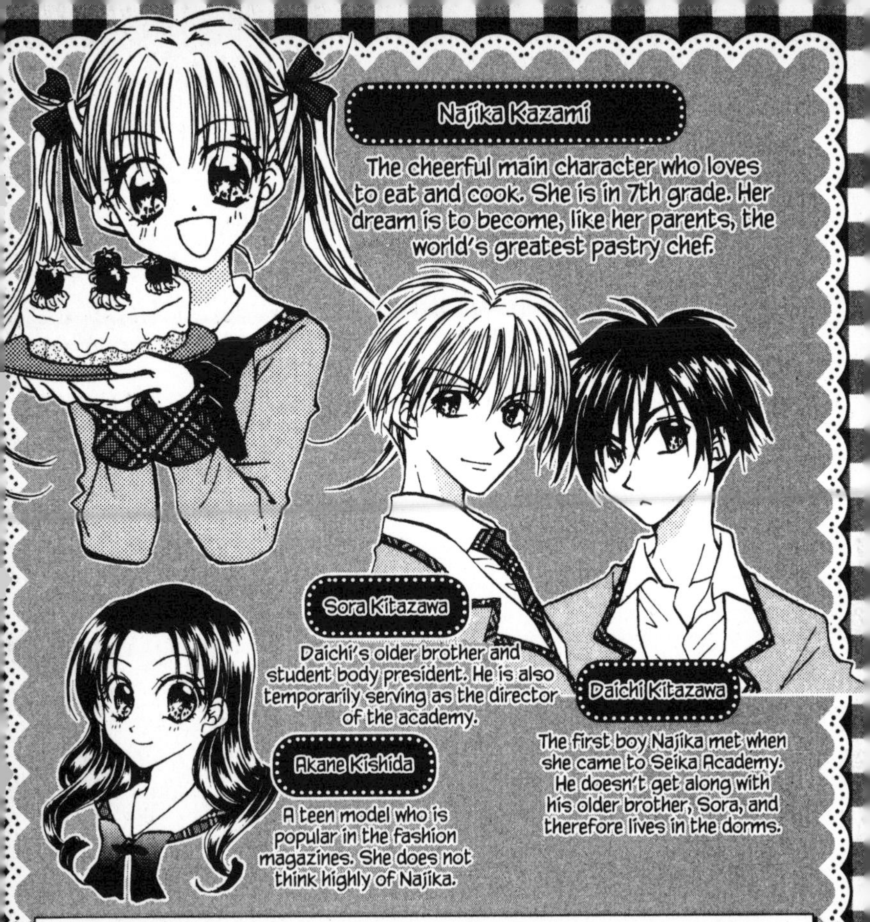
Najika Kazami
The cheerful main character who loves to eat and cook. She is in 7th grade. Her dream is to become, like her parents, the world's greatest pastry chef.
Sora Kitazawa
Daichi's older brother and student body president. He is also temporarily serving as the director of the academy.
Daichi Kitazawa
The first boy Najika met when she came to Seika Academy. He doesn't get along with his older brother, Sora, and therefore lives in the dorms.
Akane Kishida
A teen model who is popular in the fashion magazines. She does not think highly of Najika.

Kitchen Princess

The Story So Far...

Najika lost her parents when she was young and then moved to Lavender House, an orphanage in Hokkaido. She joined Seika Academy in Tokyo to find her Flan Prince, a boy who saved her from drowning when she was young. However, she failed to get along with her classmates because they saw her befriending Sora and Daichi, two popular boys at the academy. Even Akane, who had been nice to her, turned her back on Najika. Depressed, Najika tried to go back home, but Daichi and Sora stopped her.

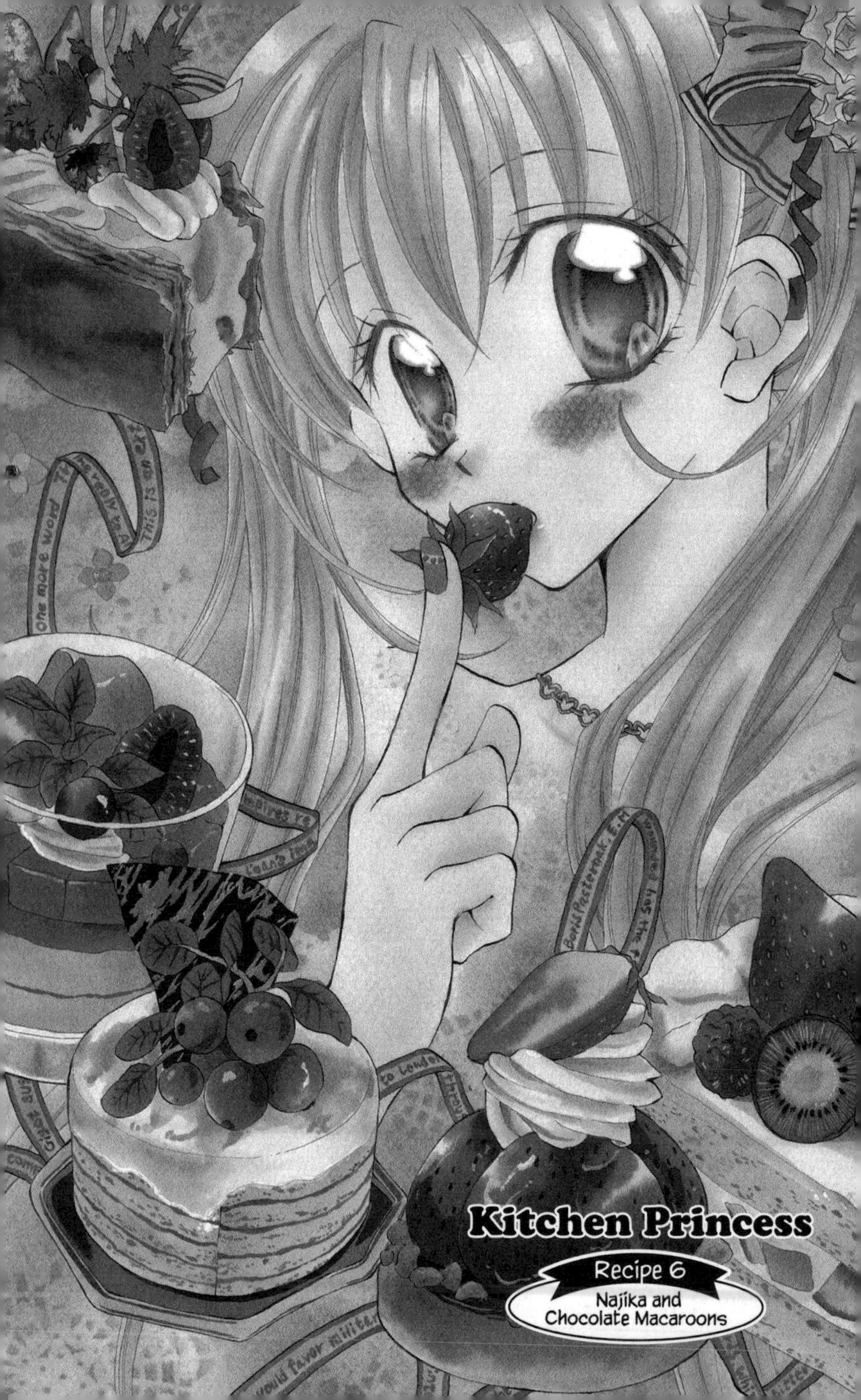
Kitchen Princess
Recipe 6
Najika and
Chocolate Macaroons

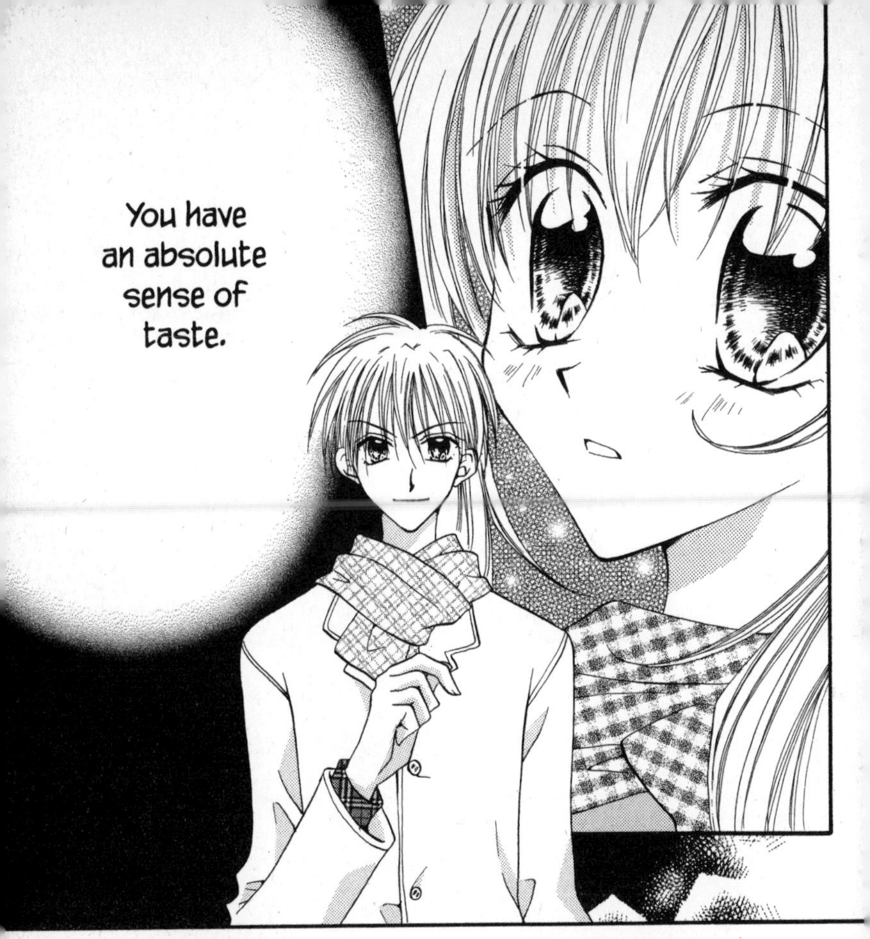
You have an absolute sense of taste.

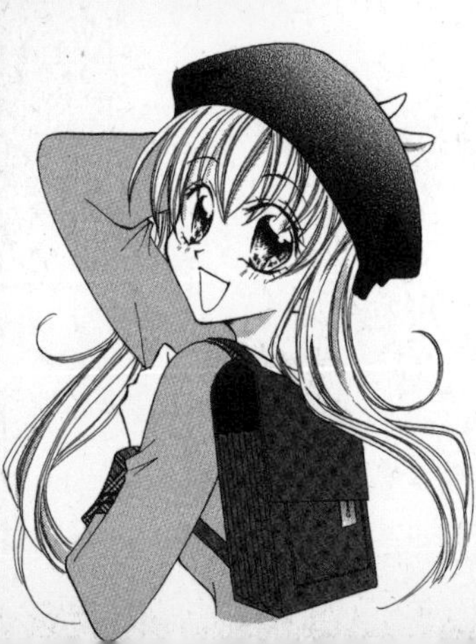

About Recipe 6's Splash Page

You can't tell because it's black and white in the comic, but I wanted to draw a lot of strawberries and used a lot of pink to draw a bunch of sweets ♪

Getting the right color for food is so hard... It usually takes longer than drawing the people.

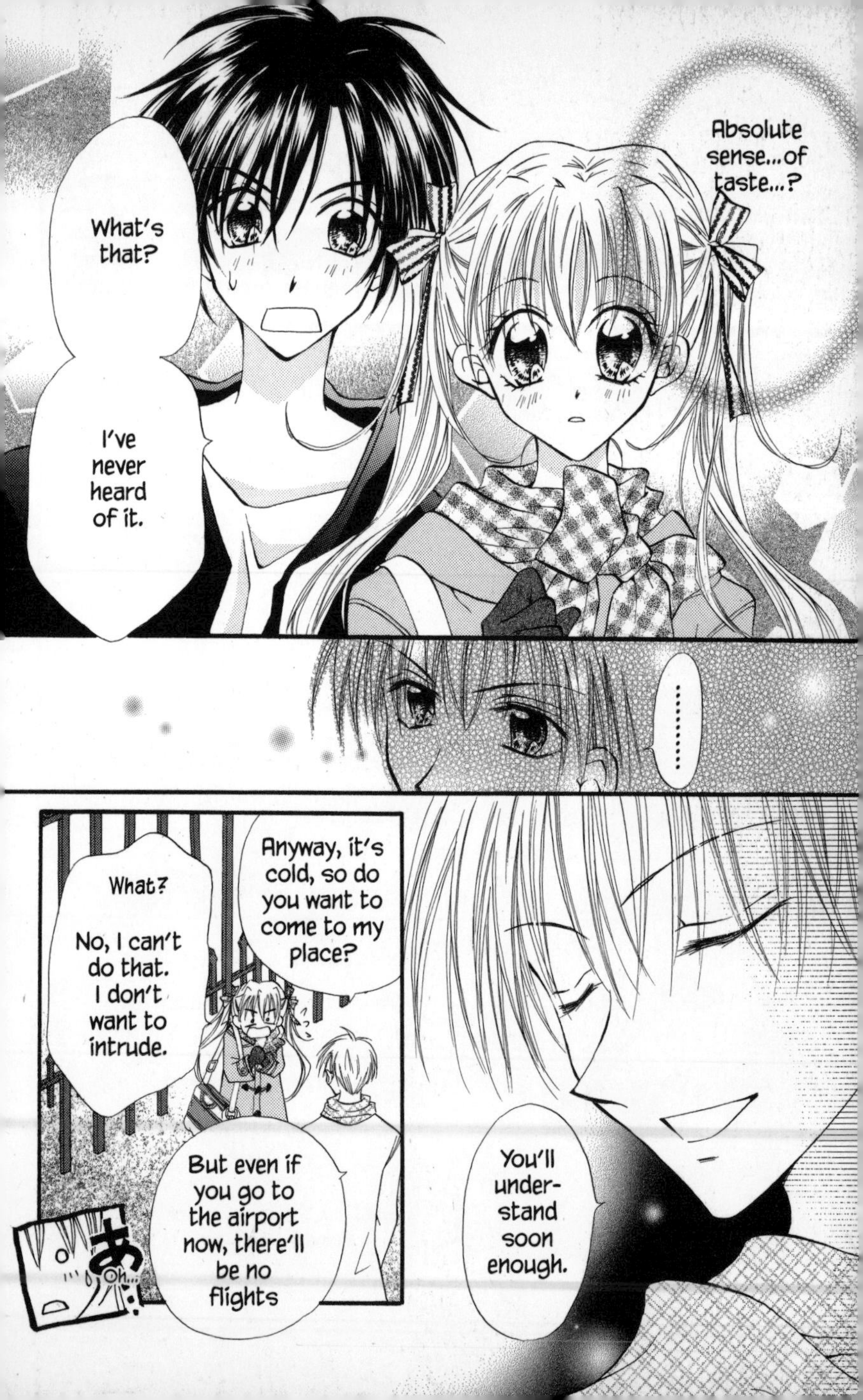
Absolute sense...of taste...?
What's that?
I've never heard of it.
......
You'll under-stand soon enough.
Anyway, it's cold, so do you want to come to my place?
What?
No, I can't do that. I don't want to intrude.
But even if you go to the airport now, there'll be no flights
あ
Oh...

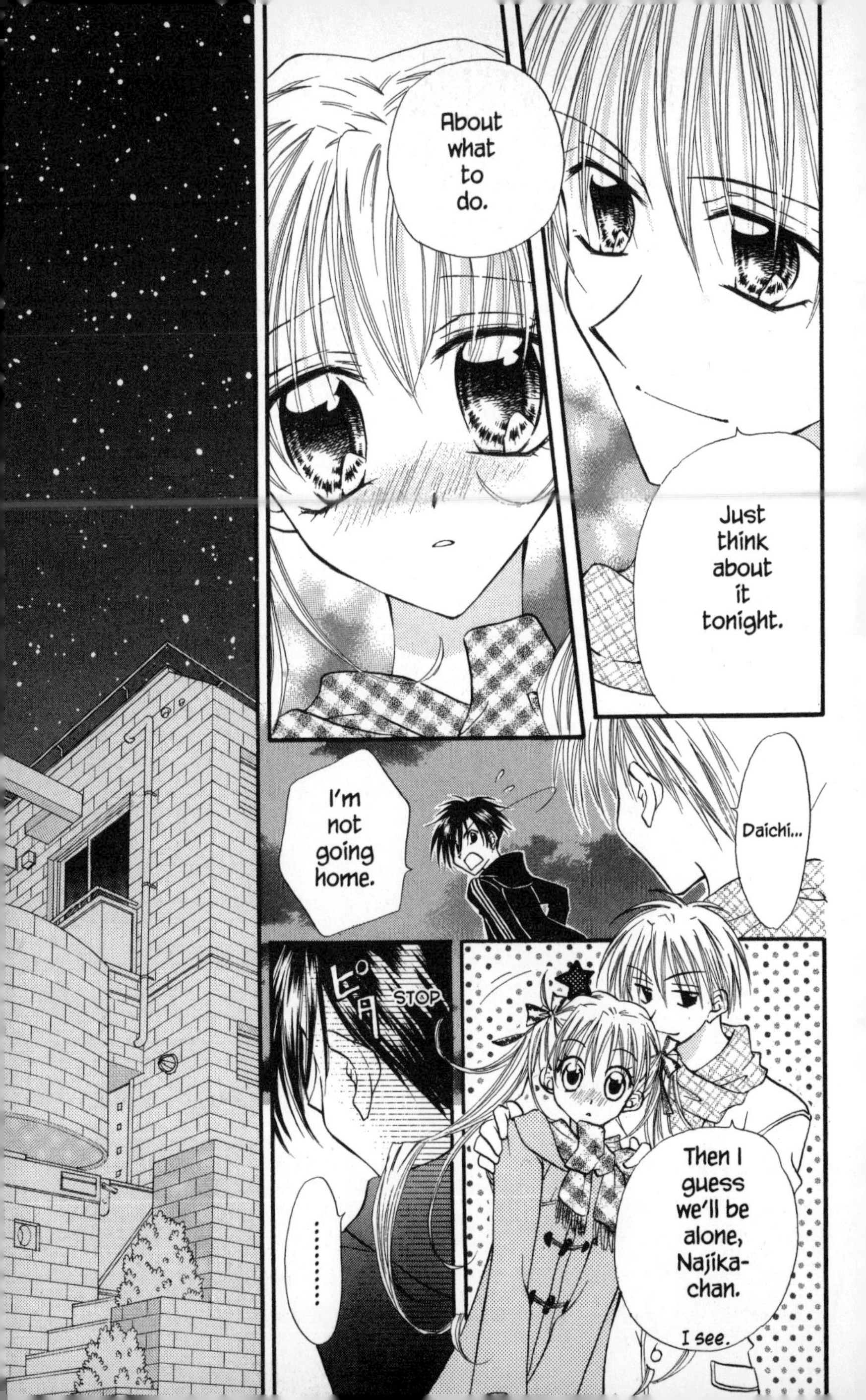
Just think about it tonight.
About what to do.
Daichi...
I'm not going home.
Then I guess we'll be alone, Najika-chan.
I see.
STOP
......

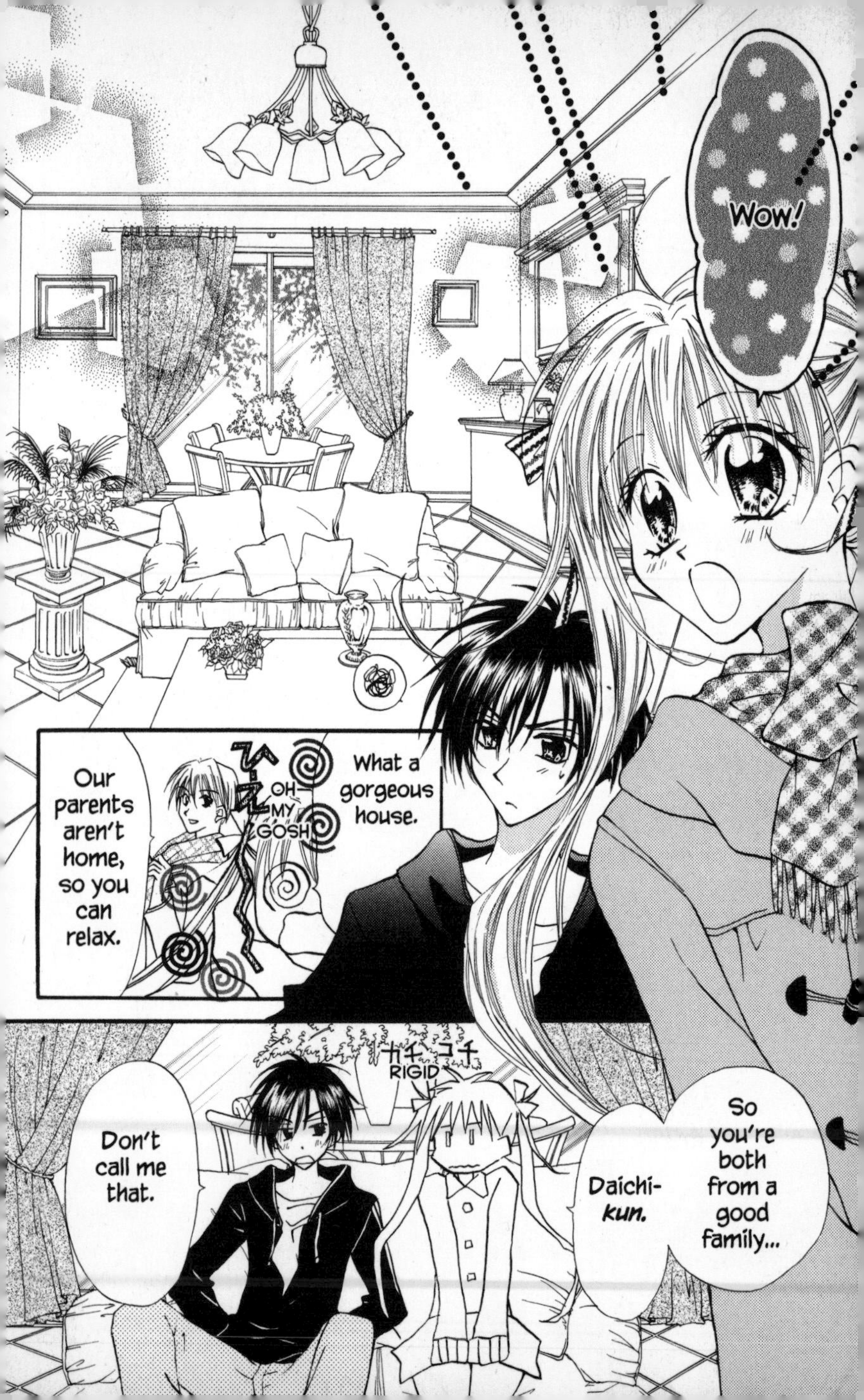
Wow!
What a gorgeous house.
OH-MY GOSH
Our parents aren't home, so you can relax.
So you're both from a good family...
Daichi-*kun.*
カチコチ
RIGID
Don't call me that.

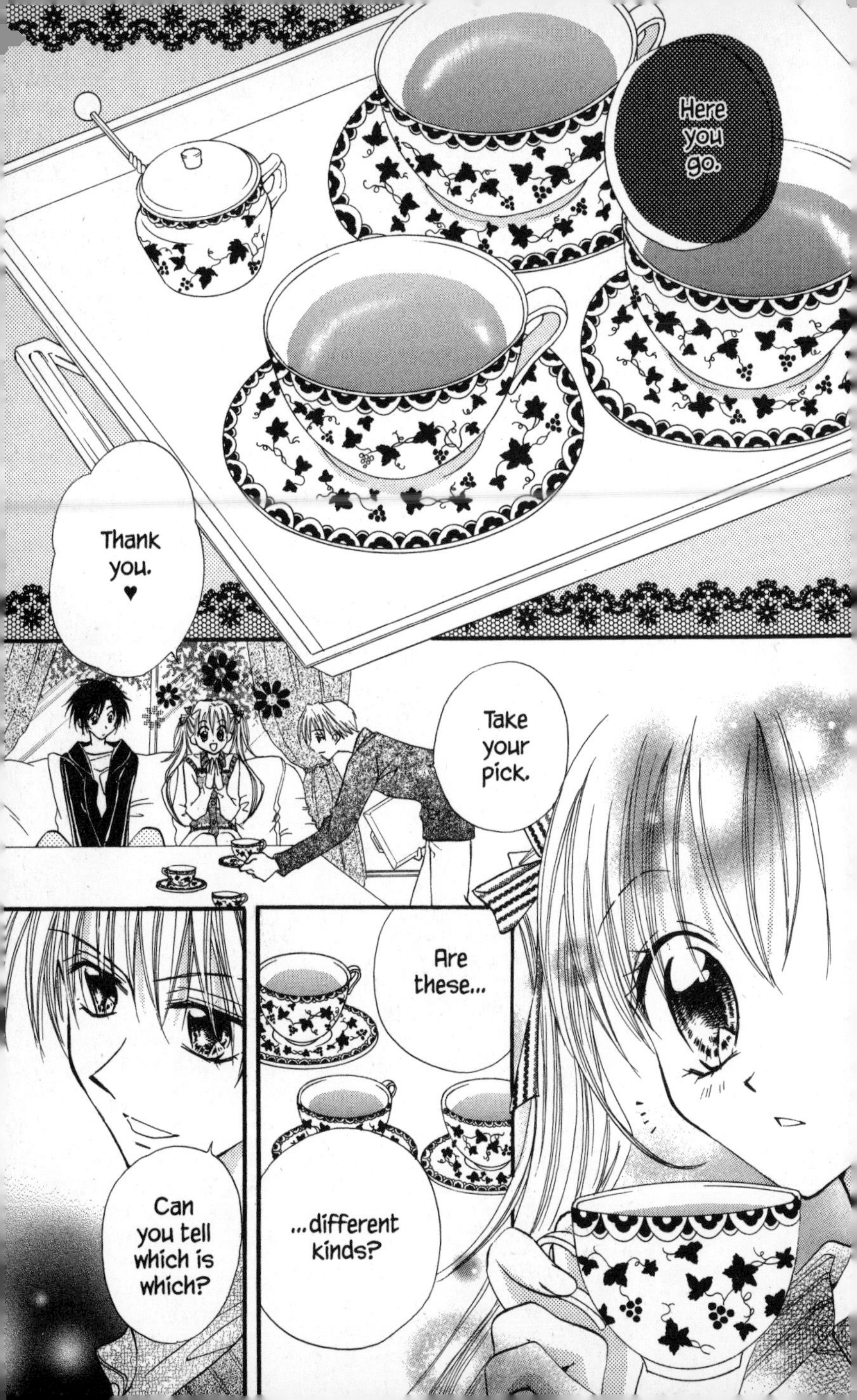
Here you go.
Thank you. ♥
Take your pick.
Are these...
...different kinds?
Can you tell which is which?

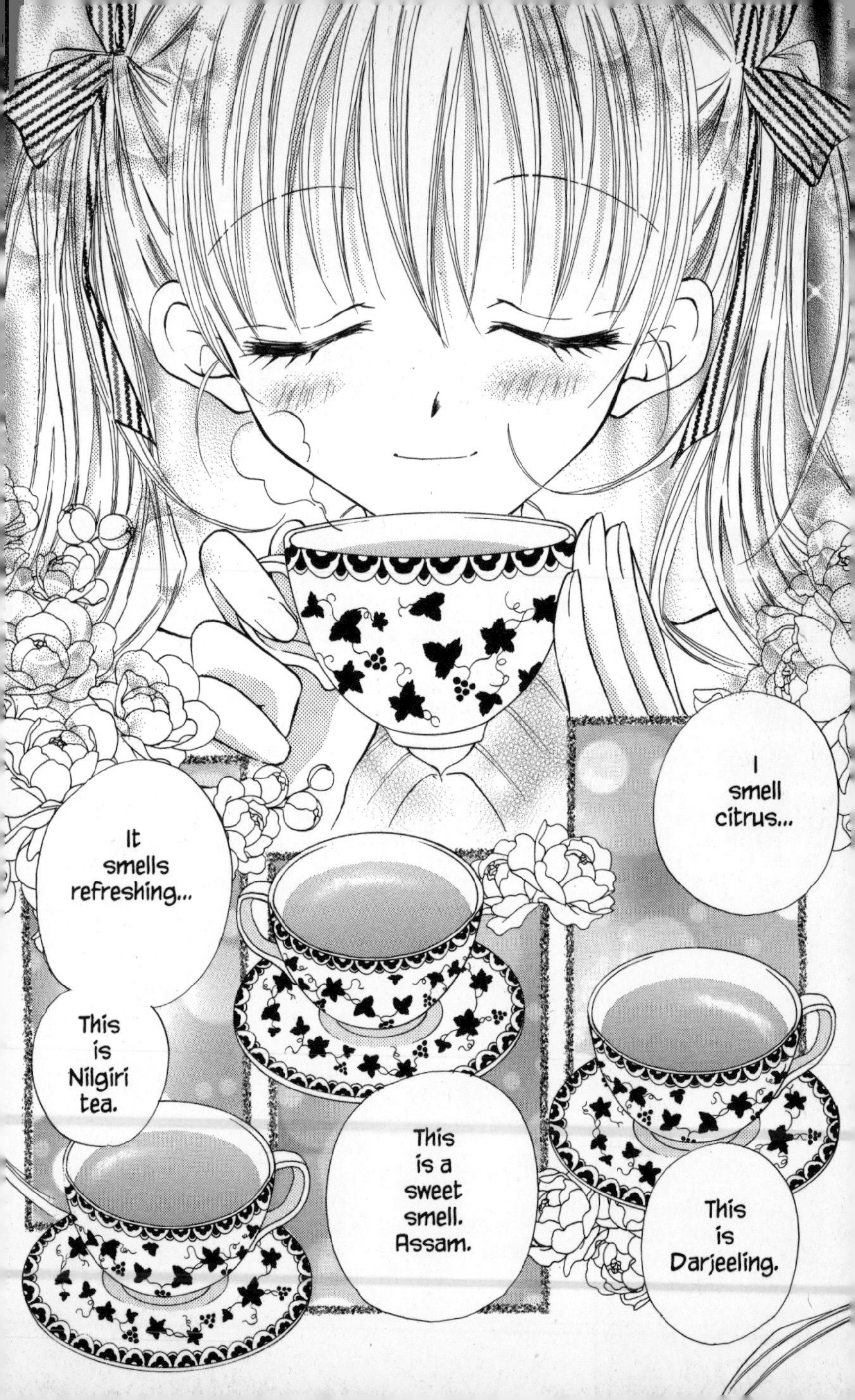
I smell citrus...
It smells refreshing...
This is Nilgiri tea.
This is a sweet smell. Assam.
This is Darjeeling.

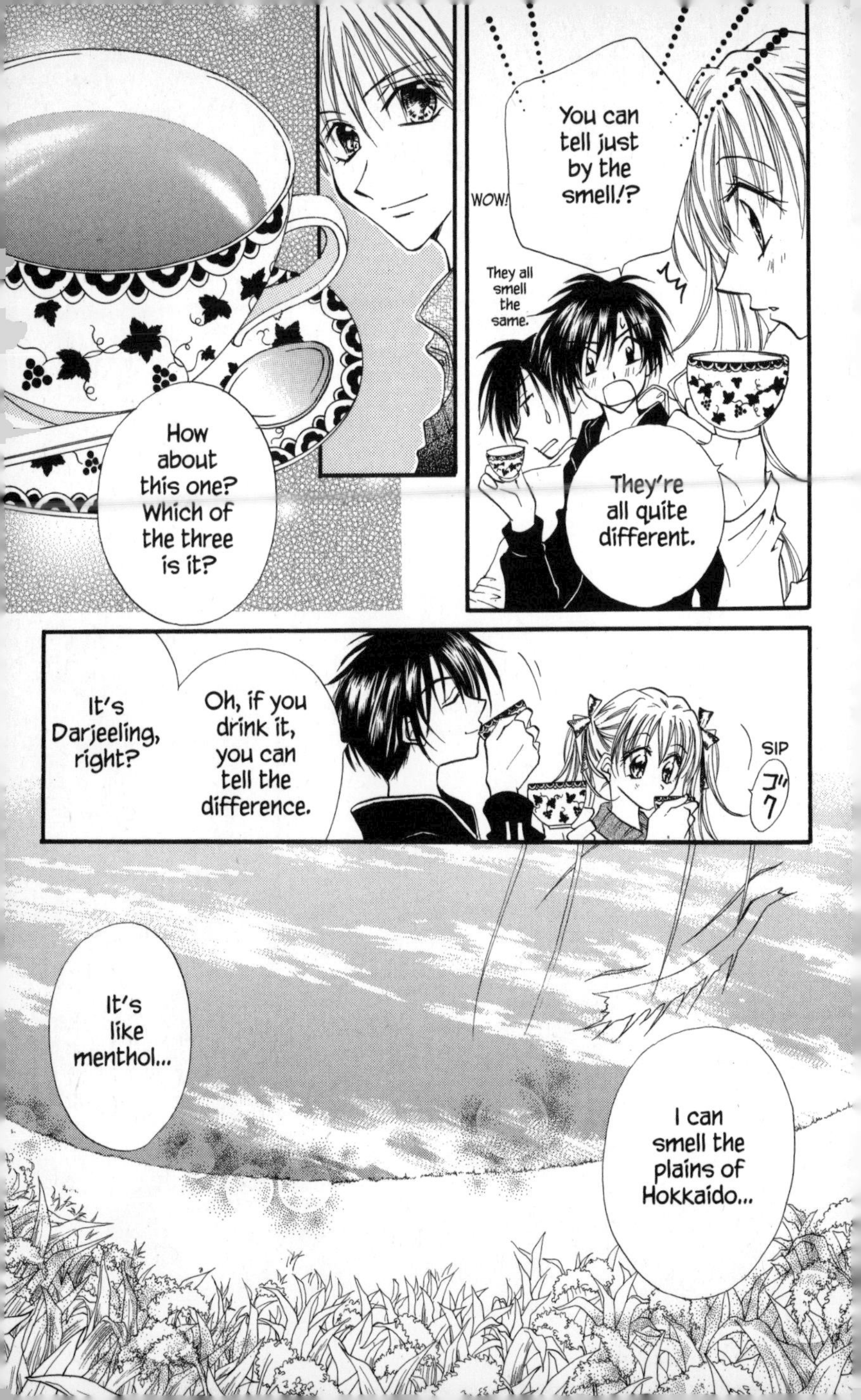

You can tell just by the smell!?
WOW!
They all smell the same.
They're all quite different.
How about this one? Which of the three is it?
SIP
ゴク
Oh, if you drink it, you can tell the difference.
It's Darjeeling, right?
I can smell the plains of Hokkaido...
It's like menthol...

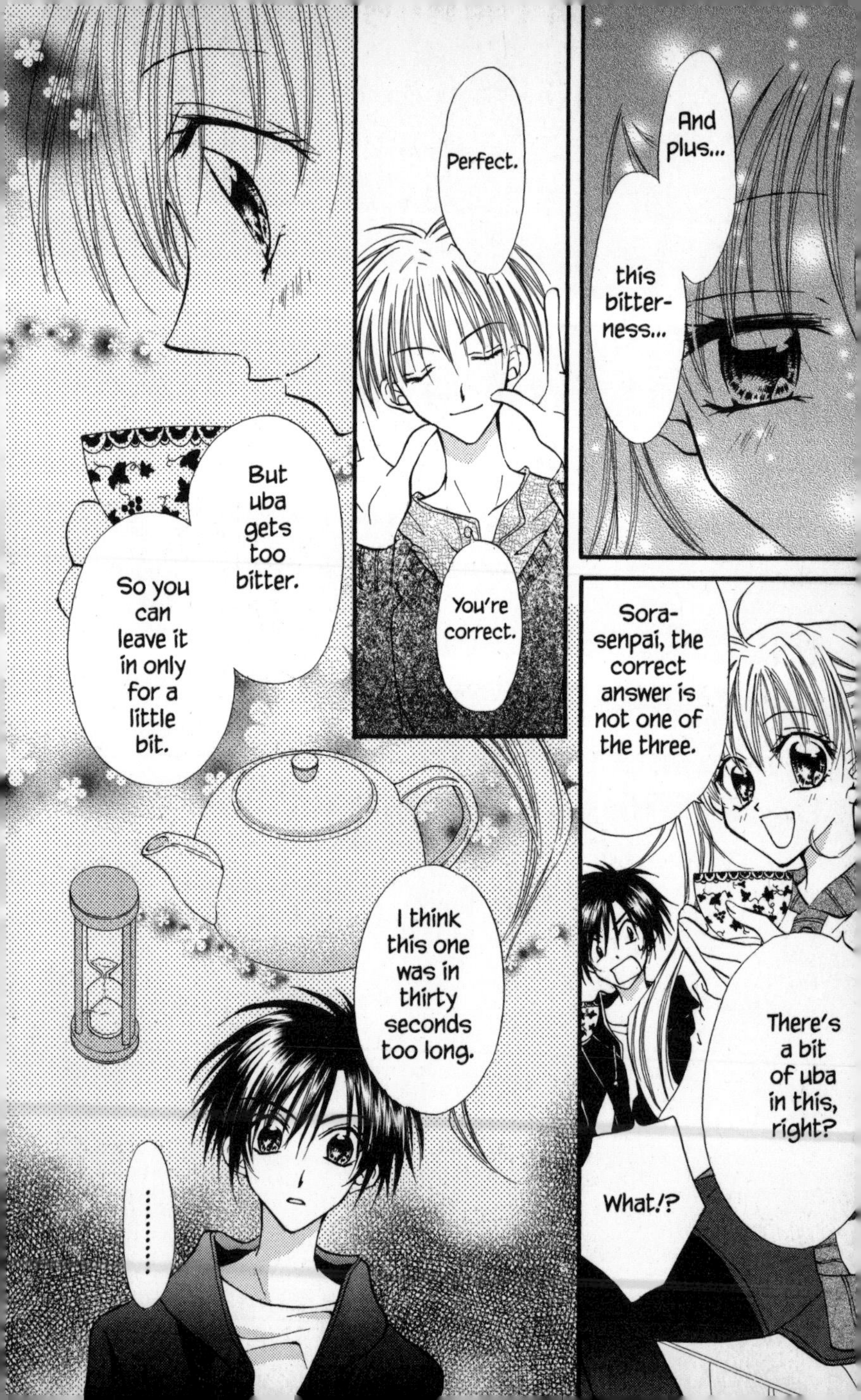
And plus...
this bitterness...
Sora-senpai, the correct answer is not one of the three.
There's a bit of uba in this, right?
What!?
Perfect.
You're correct.
But uba gets too bitter.
So you can leave it in only for a little bit.
I think this one was in thirty seconds too long.
......

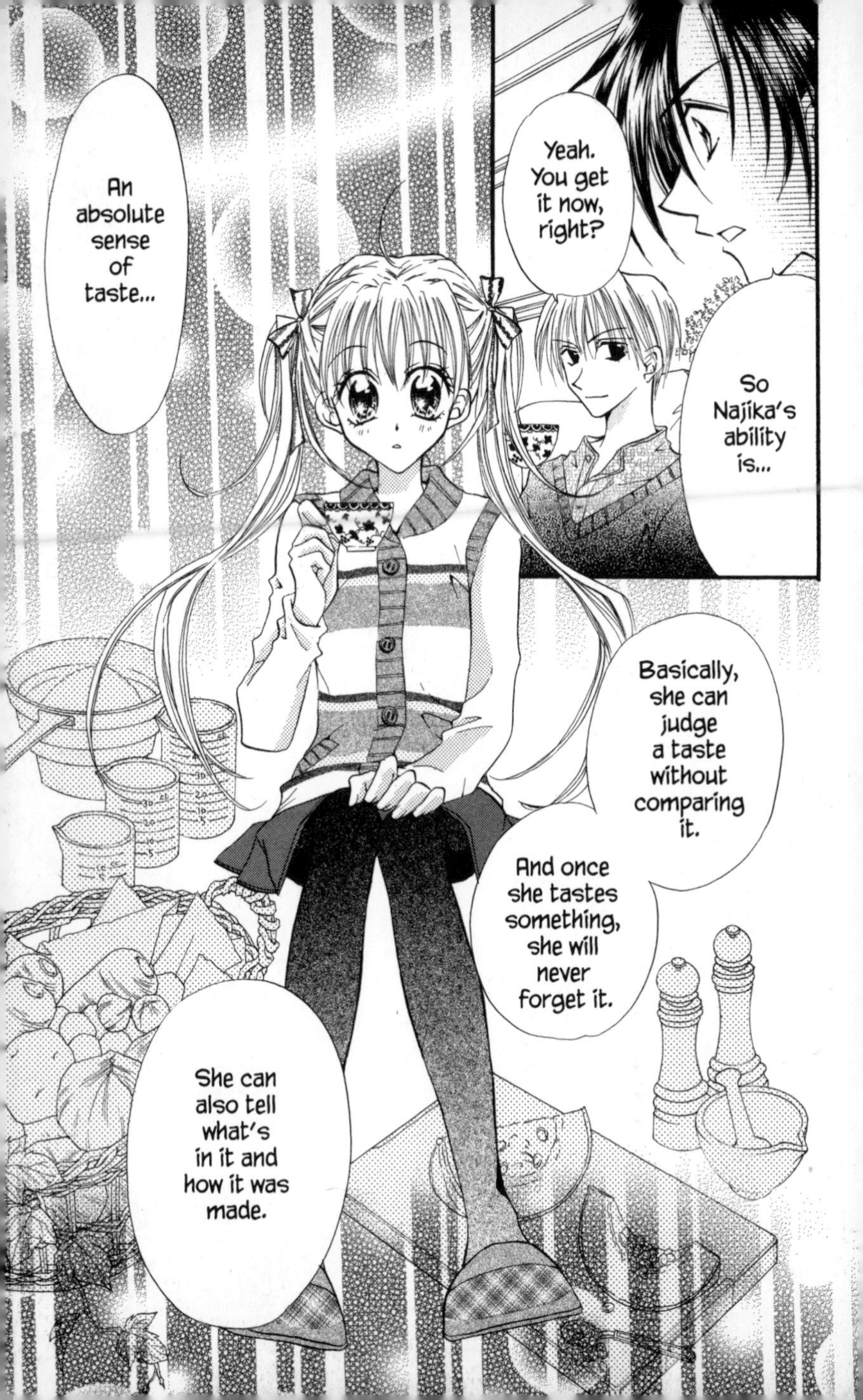
Yeah. You get it now, right?
So Najika's ability is...
An absolute sense of taste...
Basically, she can judge a taste without comparing it.
And once she tastes something, she will never forget it.
She can also tell what's in it and how it was made.

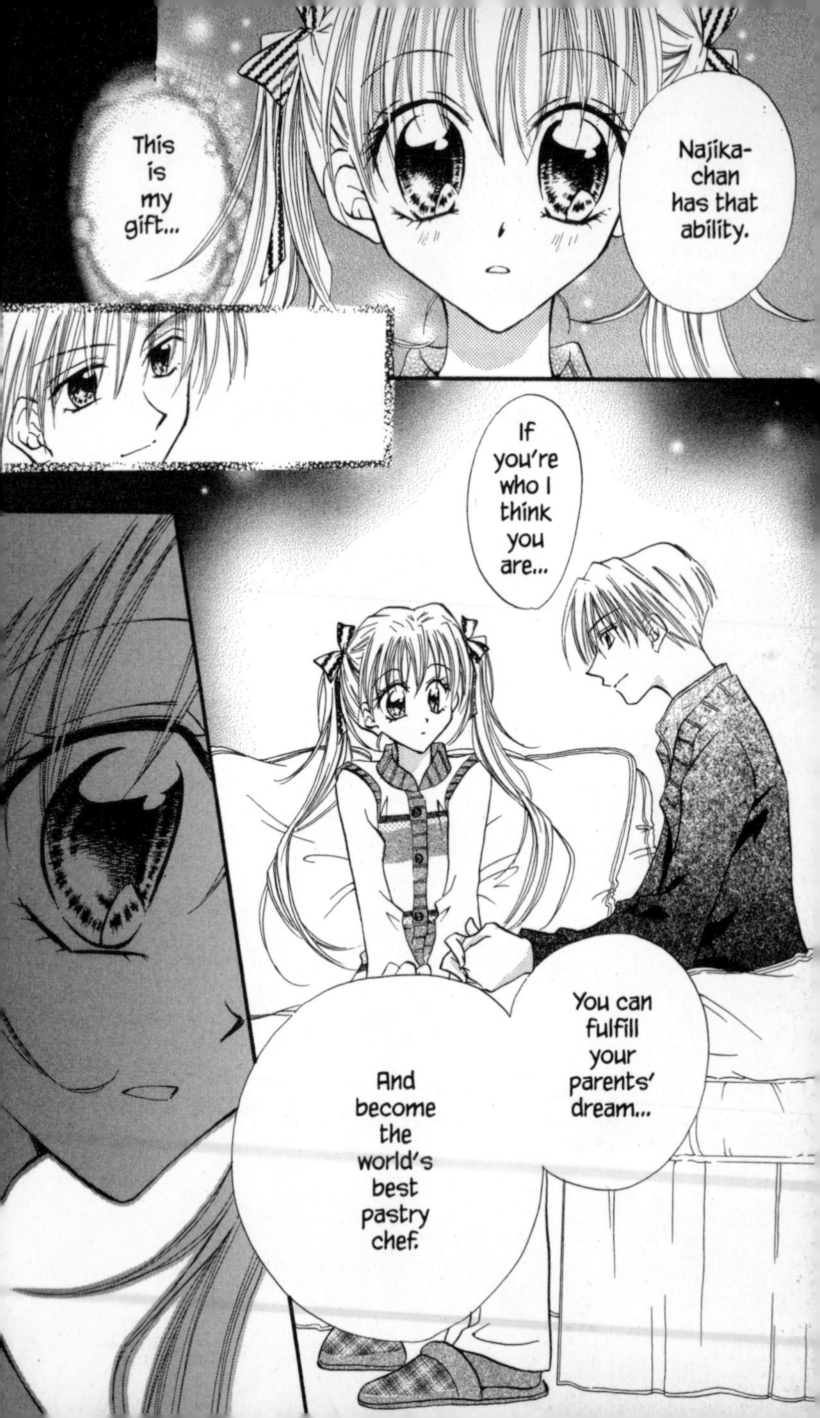
Najika-chan has that ability.
This is my gift...
If you're who I think you are...
You can fulfill your parents' dream...
And become the world's best pastry chef.

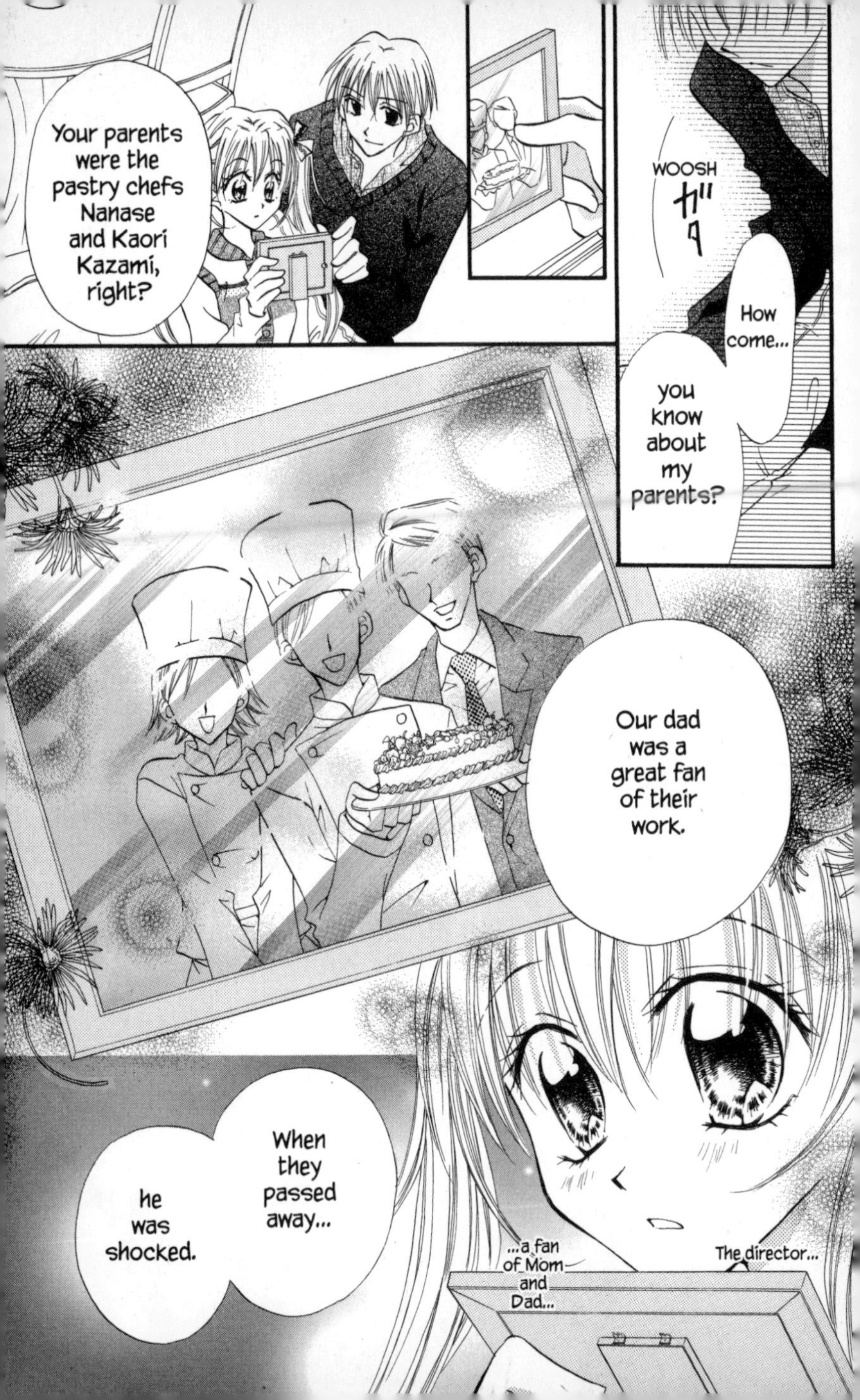
WOOSH
ガバ
How come...
you know about my parents?
Your parents were the pastry chefs Nanase and Kaori Kazami, right?
Our dad was a great fan of their work.
The director...
...a fan of Mom and Dad...
When they passed away...
he was shocked.

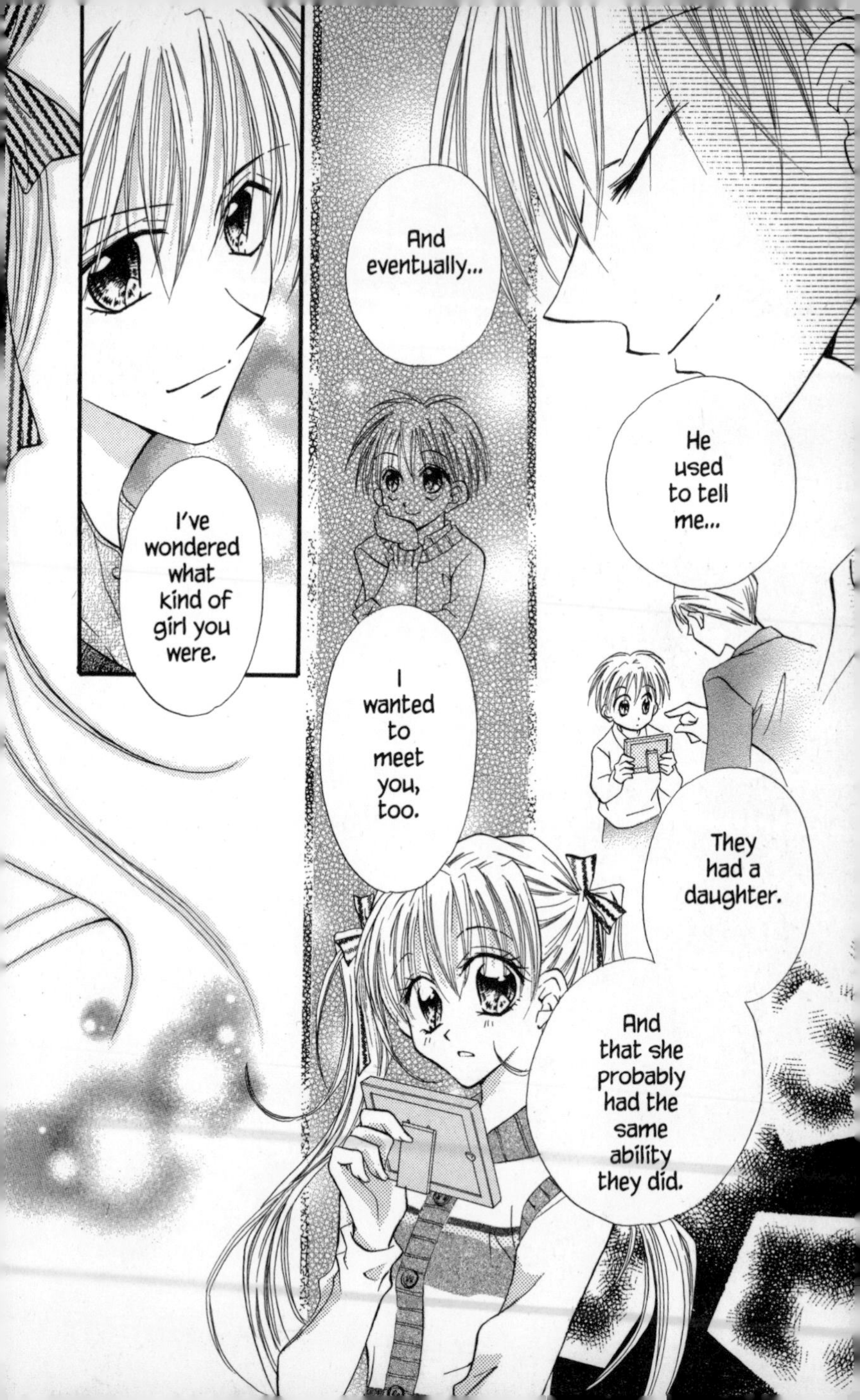
He used to tell me...
They had a daughter.
And that she probably had the same ability they did.
And eventually...
I wanted to meet you, too.
I've wondered what kind of girl you were.

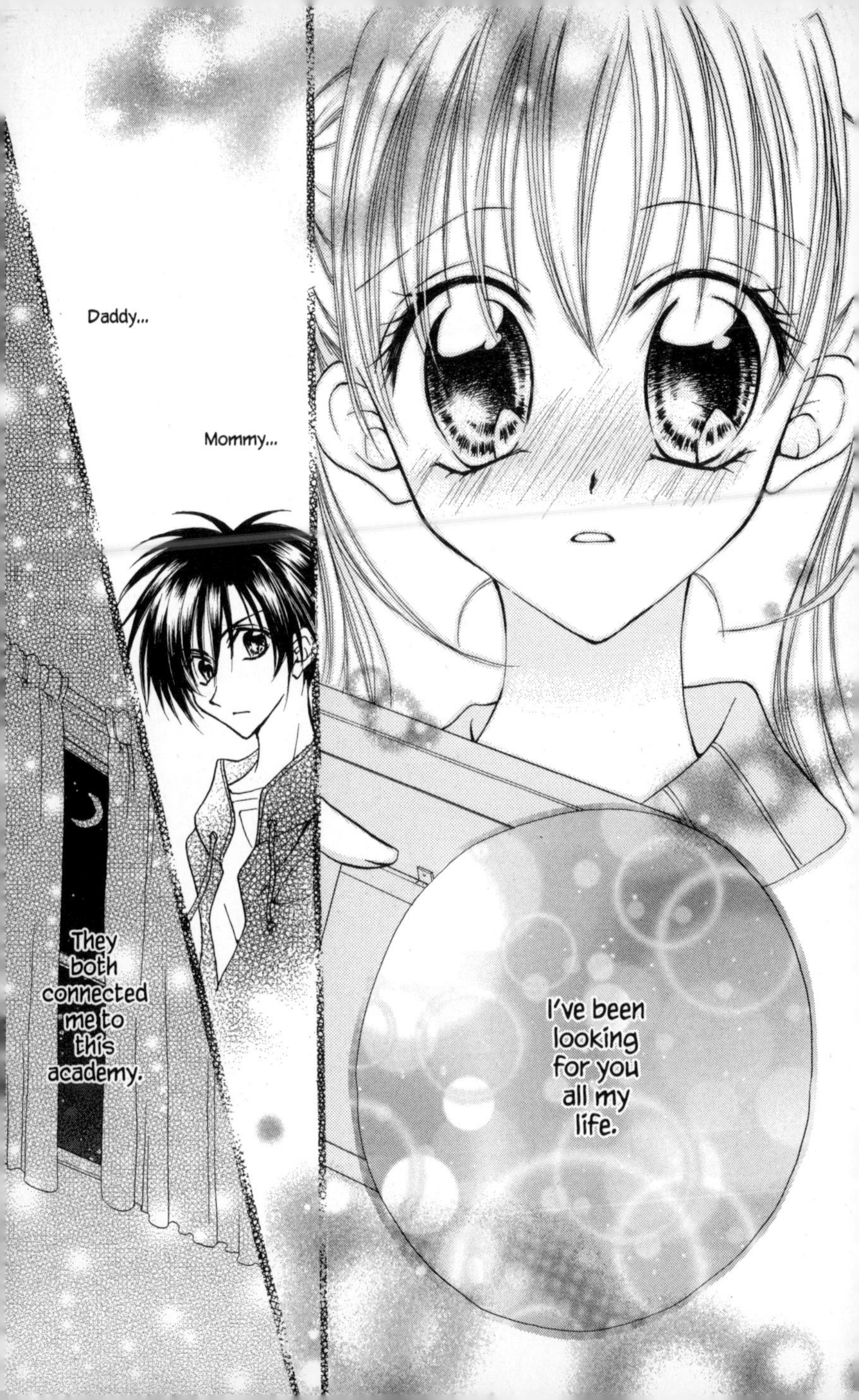
I've been looking for you all my life.
Daddy...
Mommy...
They both connected me to this academy.

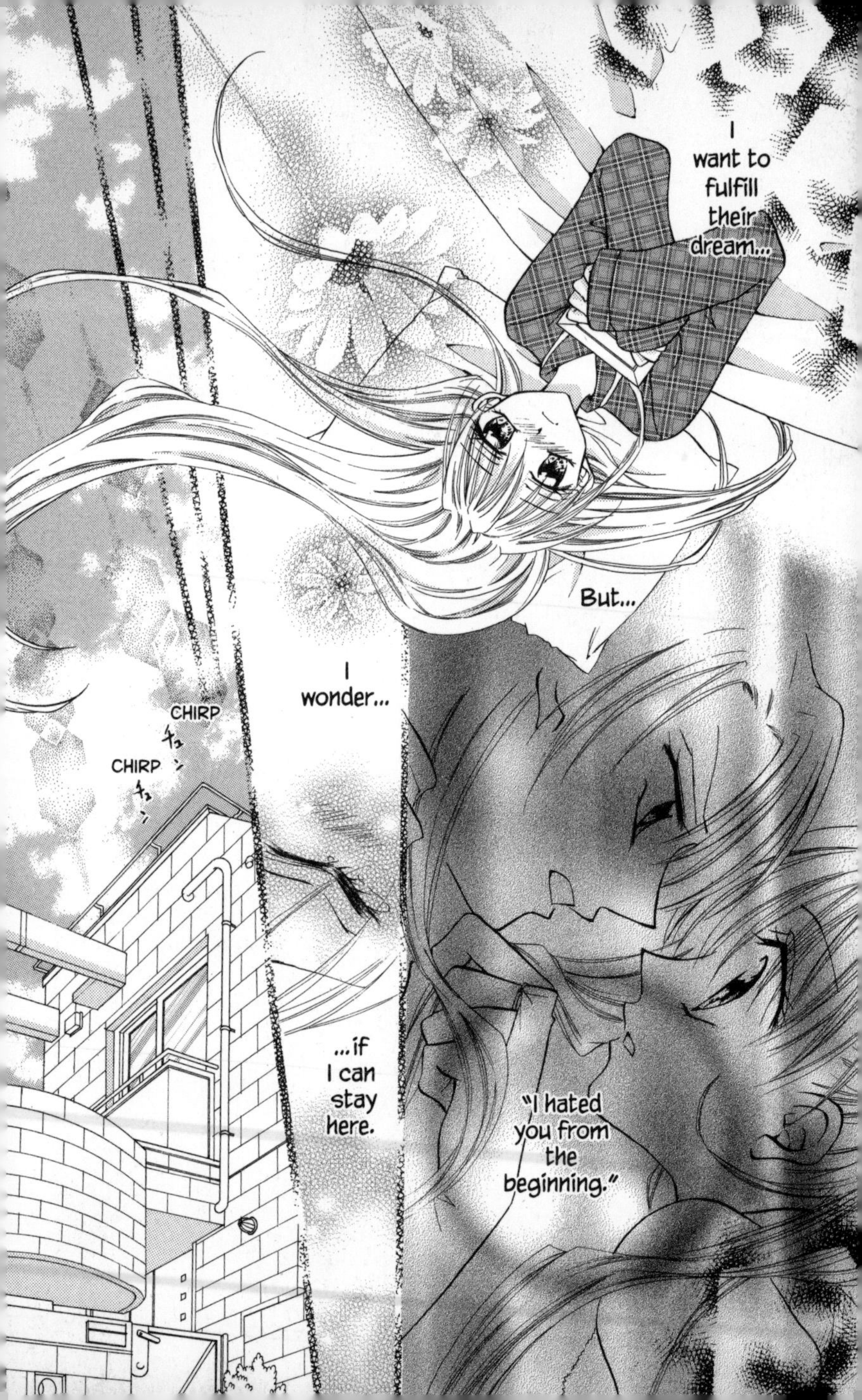
I want to fulfill their dream...
But...
"I hated you from the beginning."
I wonder...
CHIRP
CHIRP
...if I can stay here.

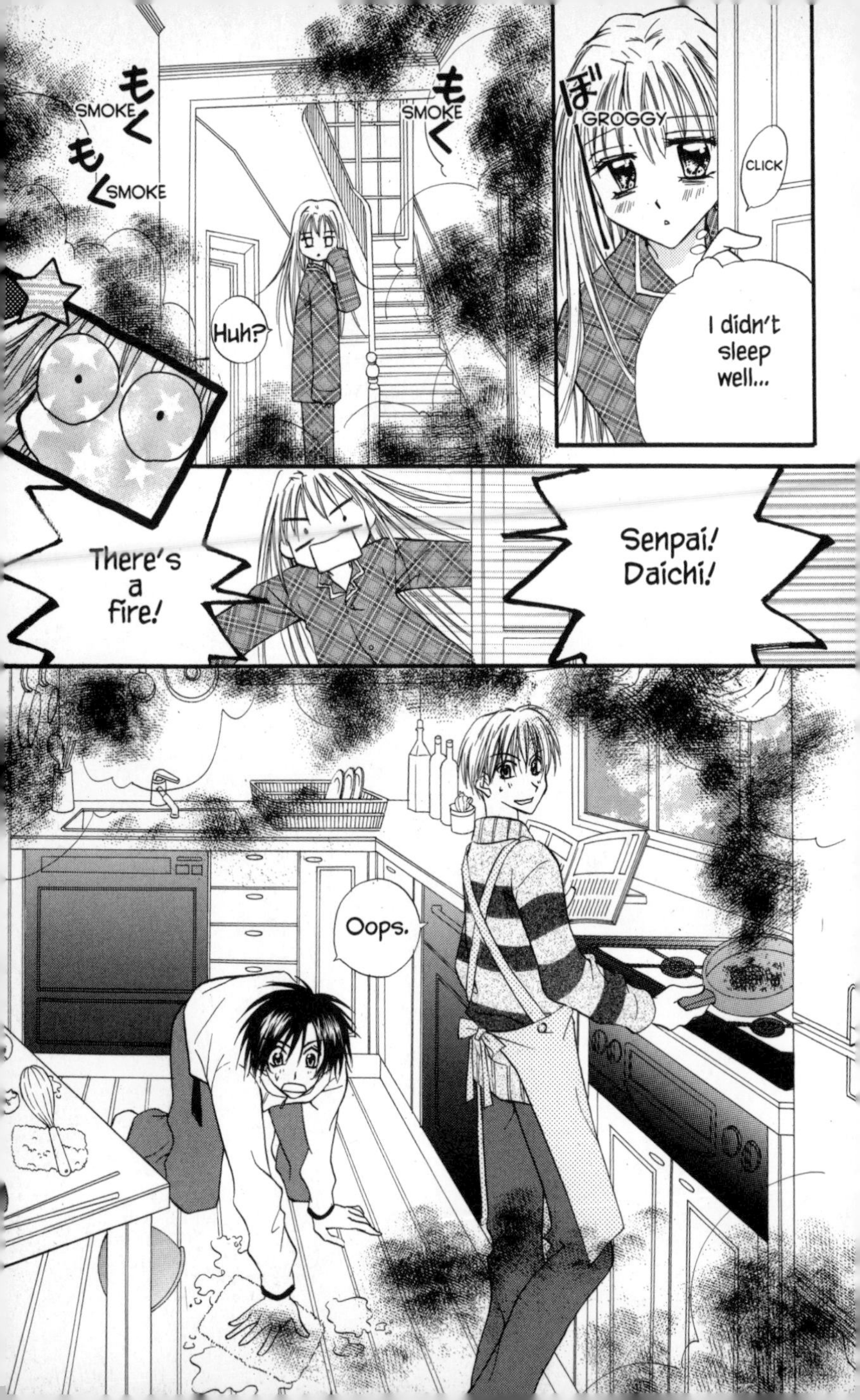
ぼ GROGGY
CLICK
I didn't sleep well...
もく SMOKE
もく SMOKE
もく SMOKE
Huh?
Senpai! Daichi!
There's a fire!
Oops.

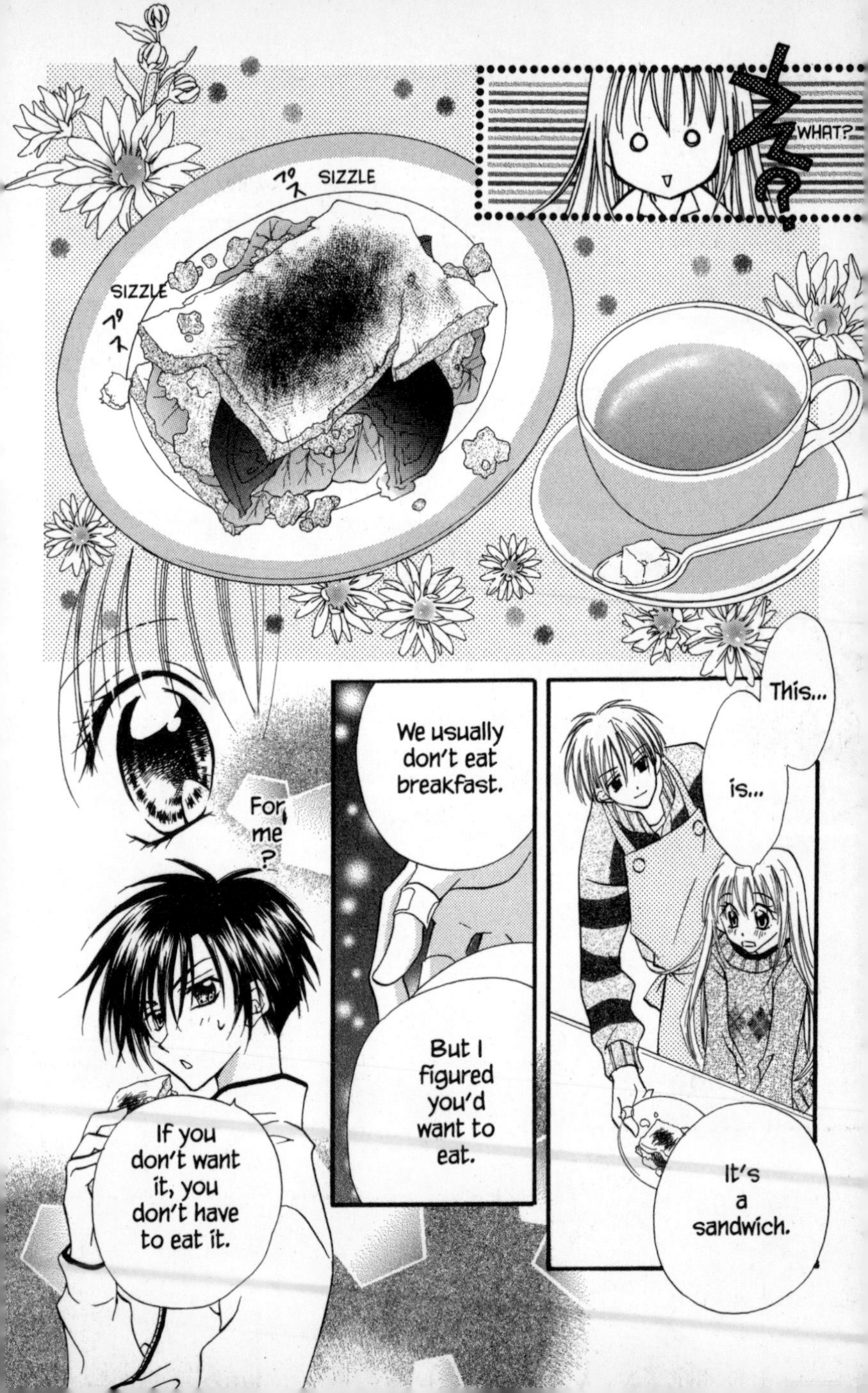
WHAT?
プス SIZZLE
SIZZLE プス
This...
is...
It's a sandwich.
We usually don't eat breakfast.
But I figured you'd want to eat.
For me?
If you don't want it, you don't have to eat it.

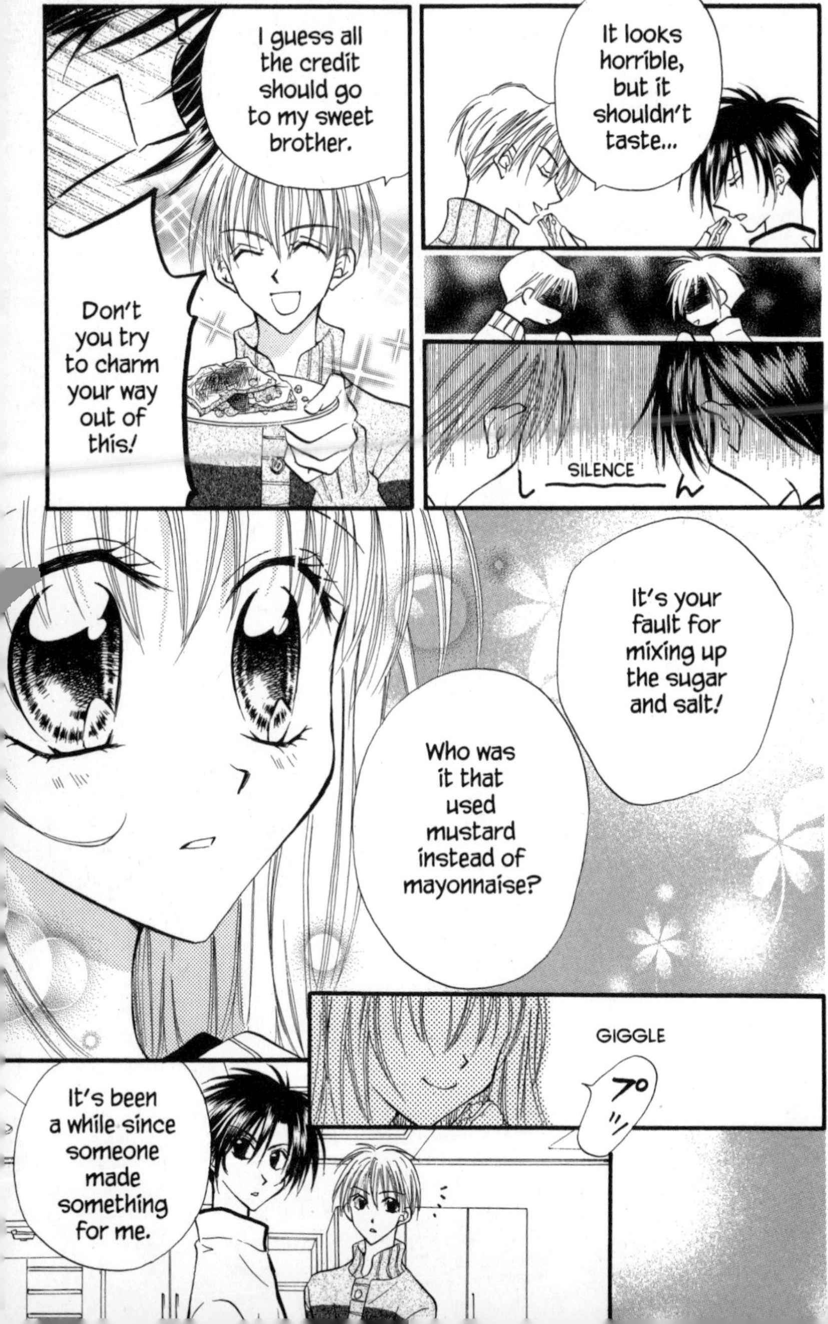
It looks horrible, but it shouldn't taste...
SILENCE
I guess all the credit should go to my sweet brother.
Don't you try to charm your way out of this!
It's your fault for mixing up the sugar and salt!
Who was it that used mustard instead of mayonnaise?
GIGGLE
It's been a while since someone made something for me.

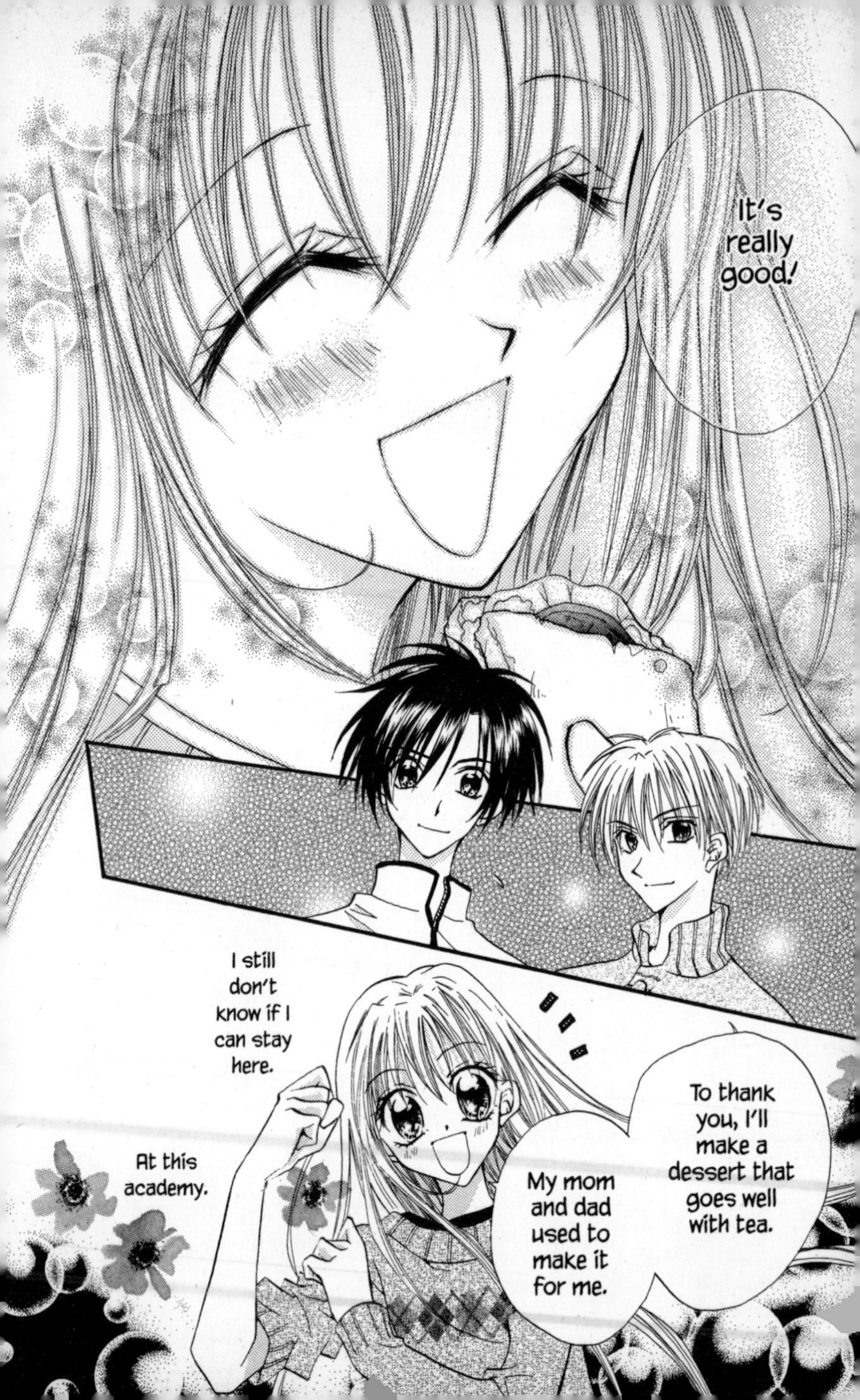

It's really good!
To thank you, I'll make a dessert that goes well with tea.
My mom and dad used to make it for me.
I still don't know if I can stay here.
At this academy.

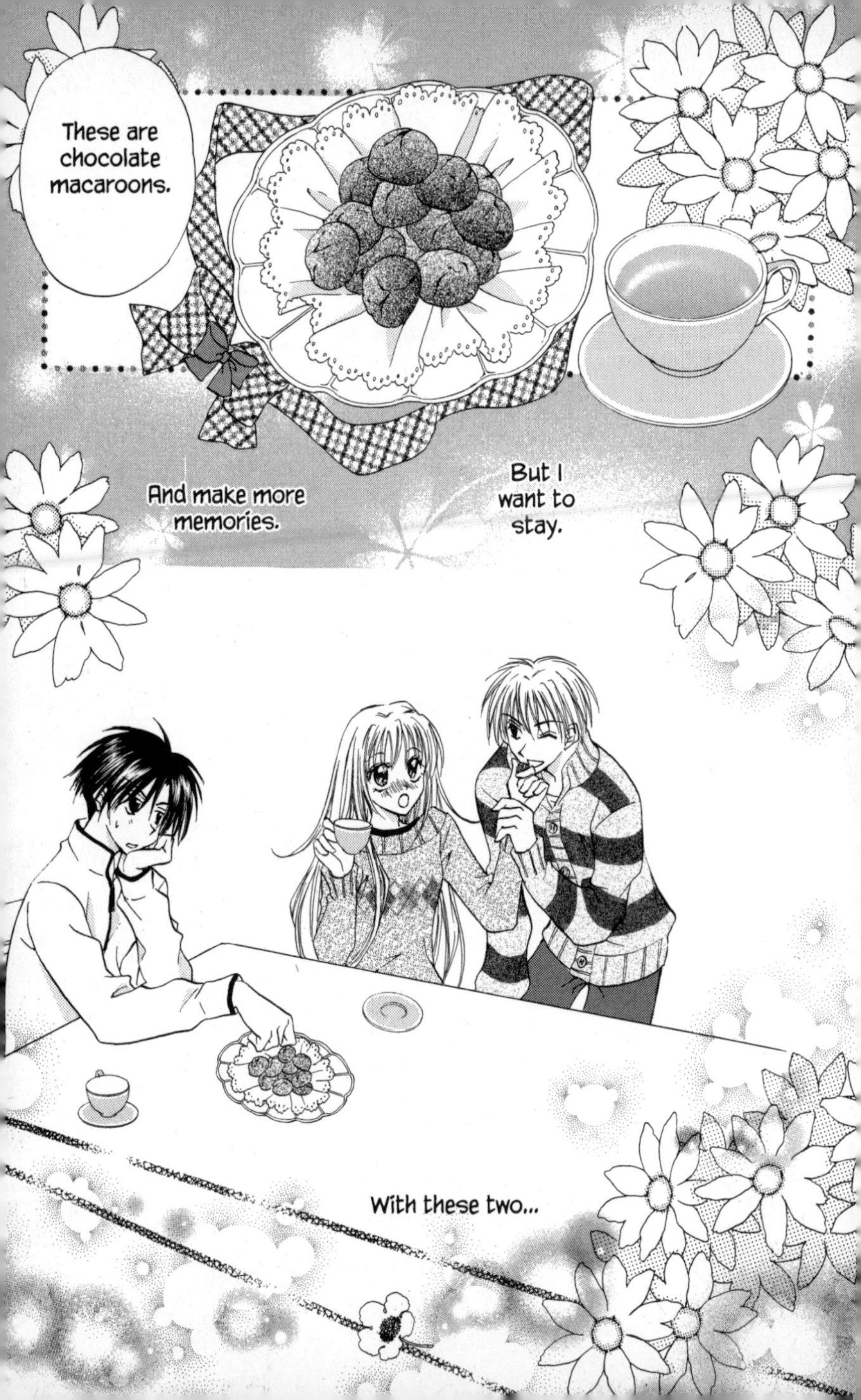
These are chocolate macaroons.
But I want to stay.
And make more memories.
With these two...

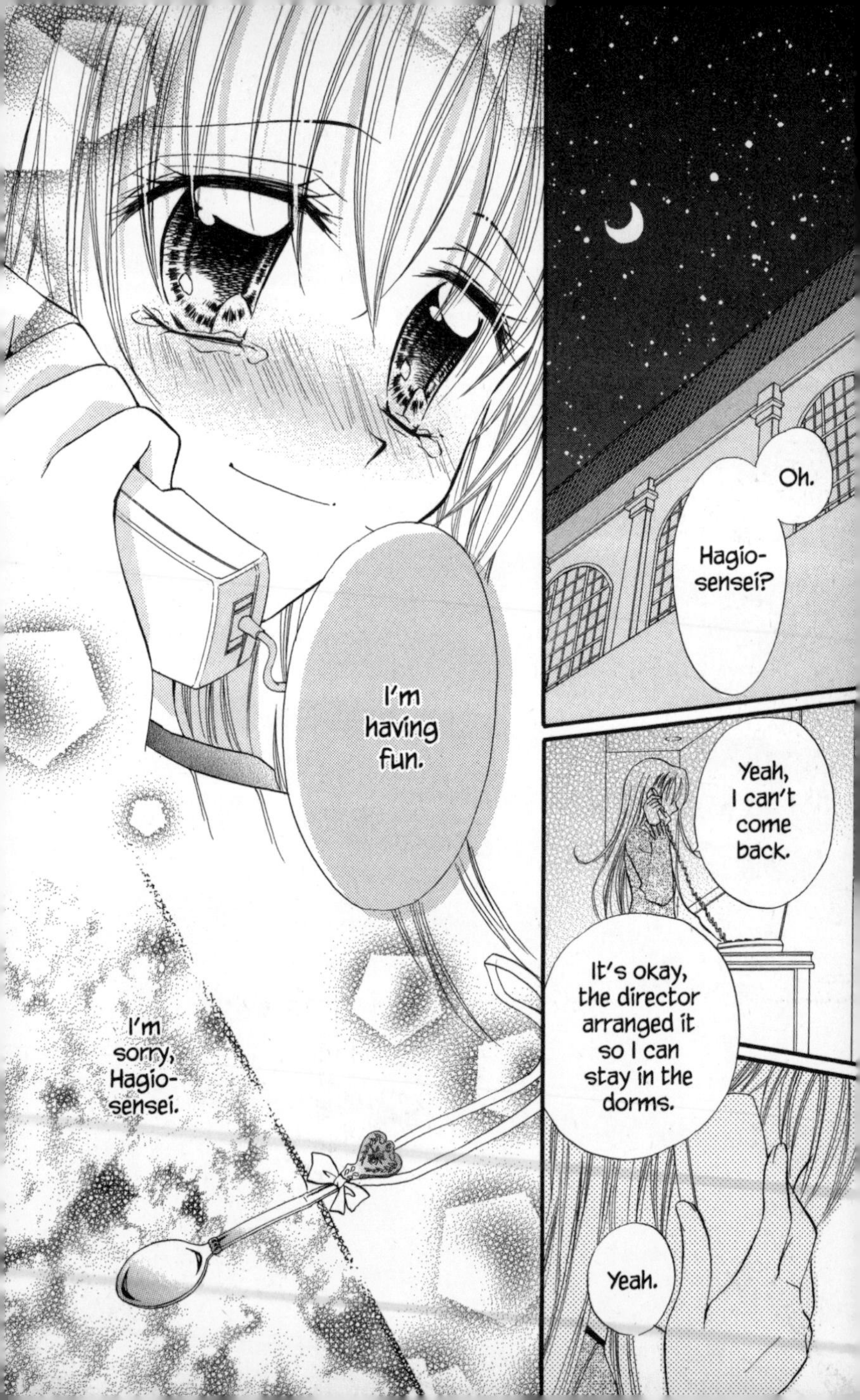
Oh.
Hagio-sensei?
Yeah, I can't come back.
It's okay, the director arranged it so I can stay in the dorms.
Yeah.
I'm having fun.
I'm sorry, Hagio-sensei.

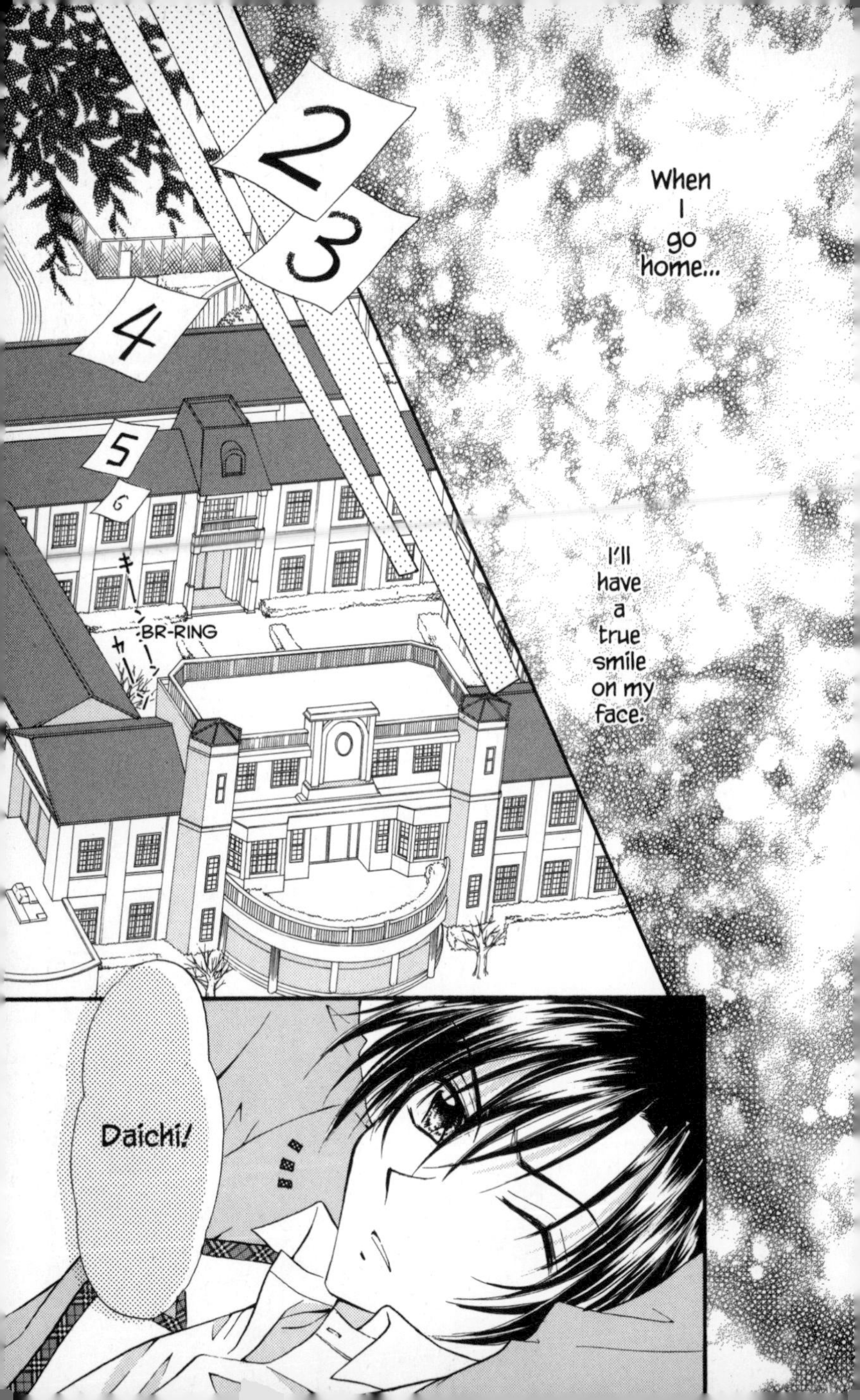
When I go home...
I'll have a true smile on my face.
2
3
4
5
6
BR-RING
Daichi!

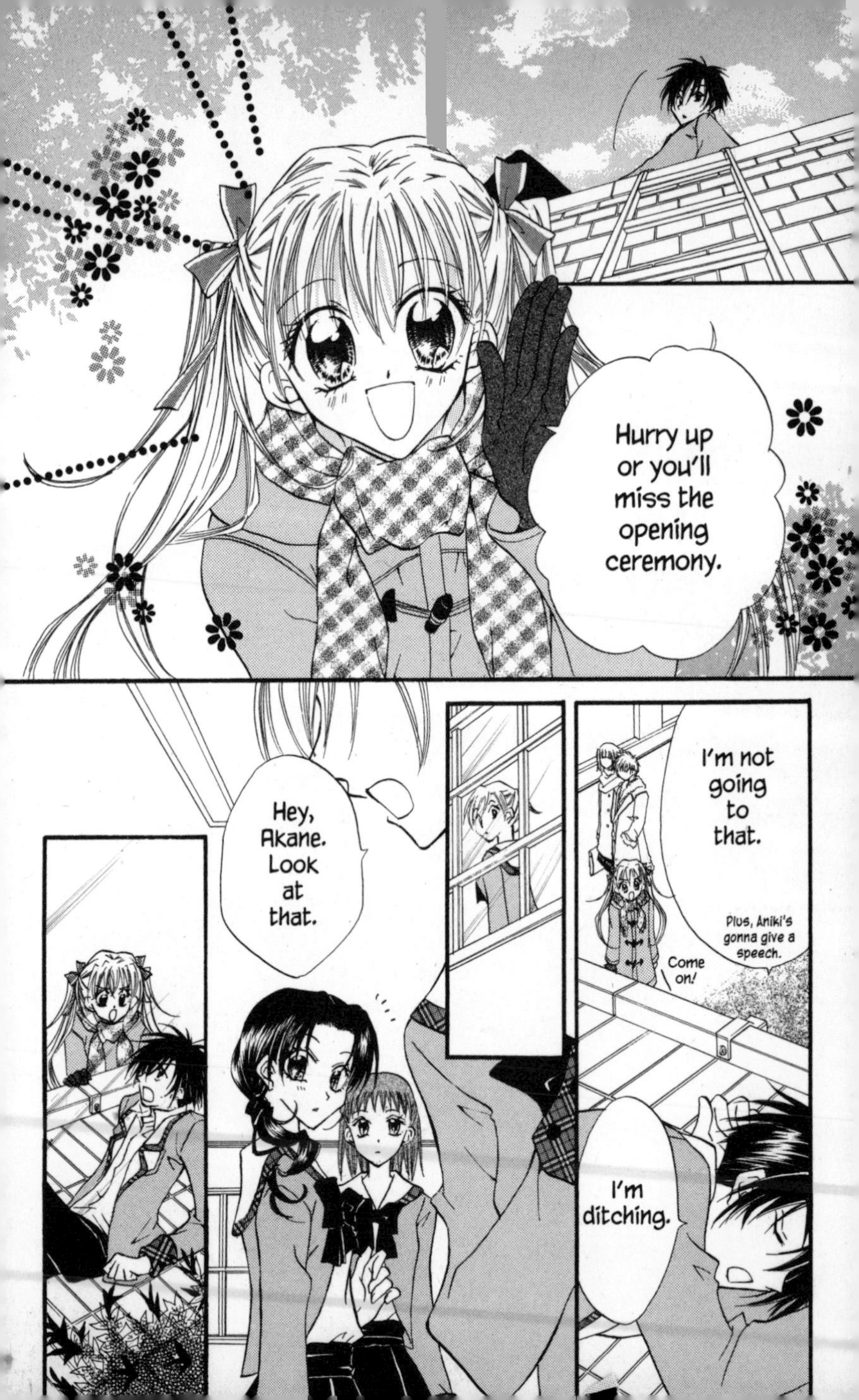
Hurry up or you'll miss the opening ceremony.
I'm not going to that.
Plus, Aniki's gonna give a speech.
Come on!
I'm ditching.
Hey, Akane. Look at that.

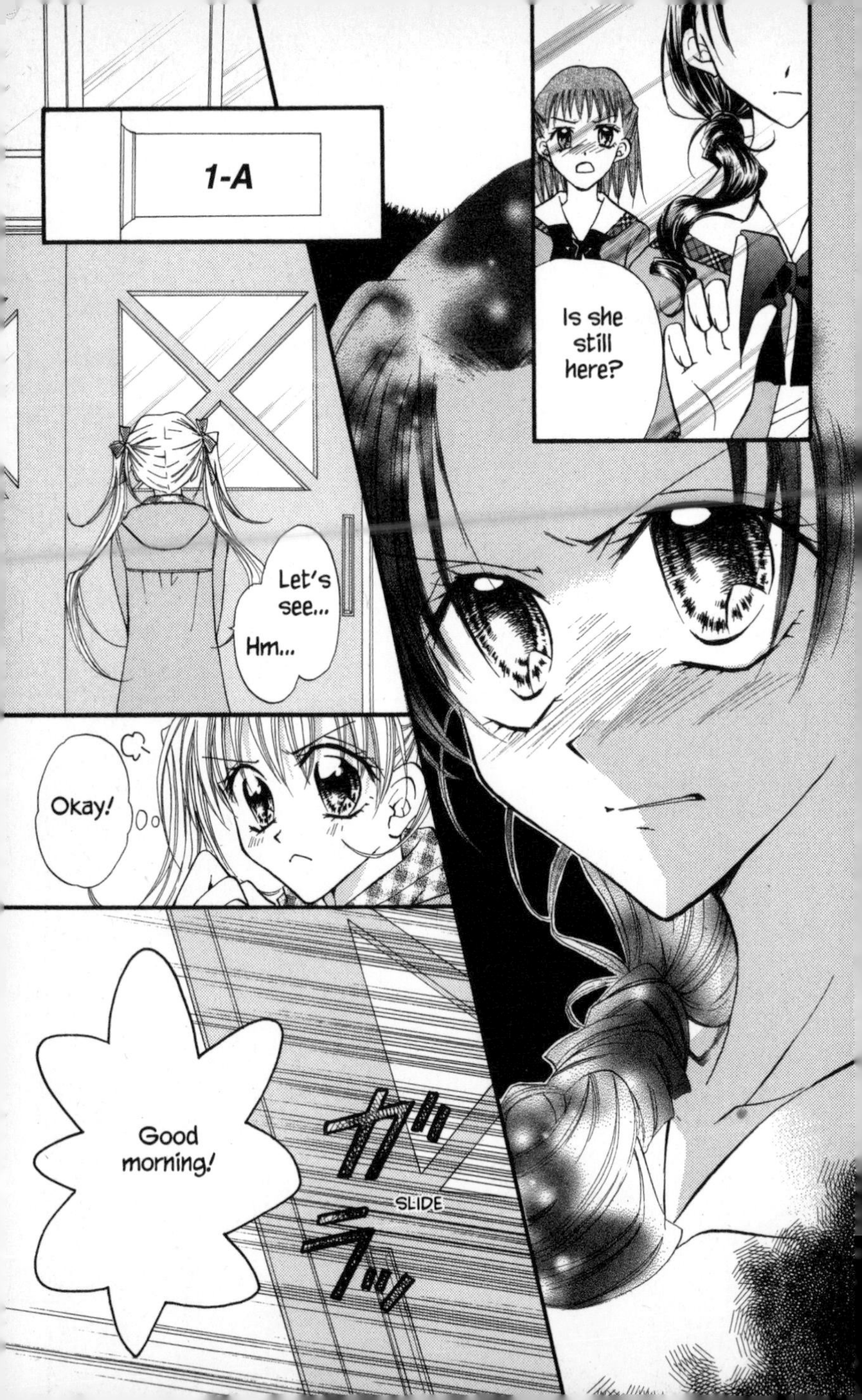
Is she still here?
1-A
Let's see...
Hm...
Okay!
Good morning!
SLIDE

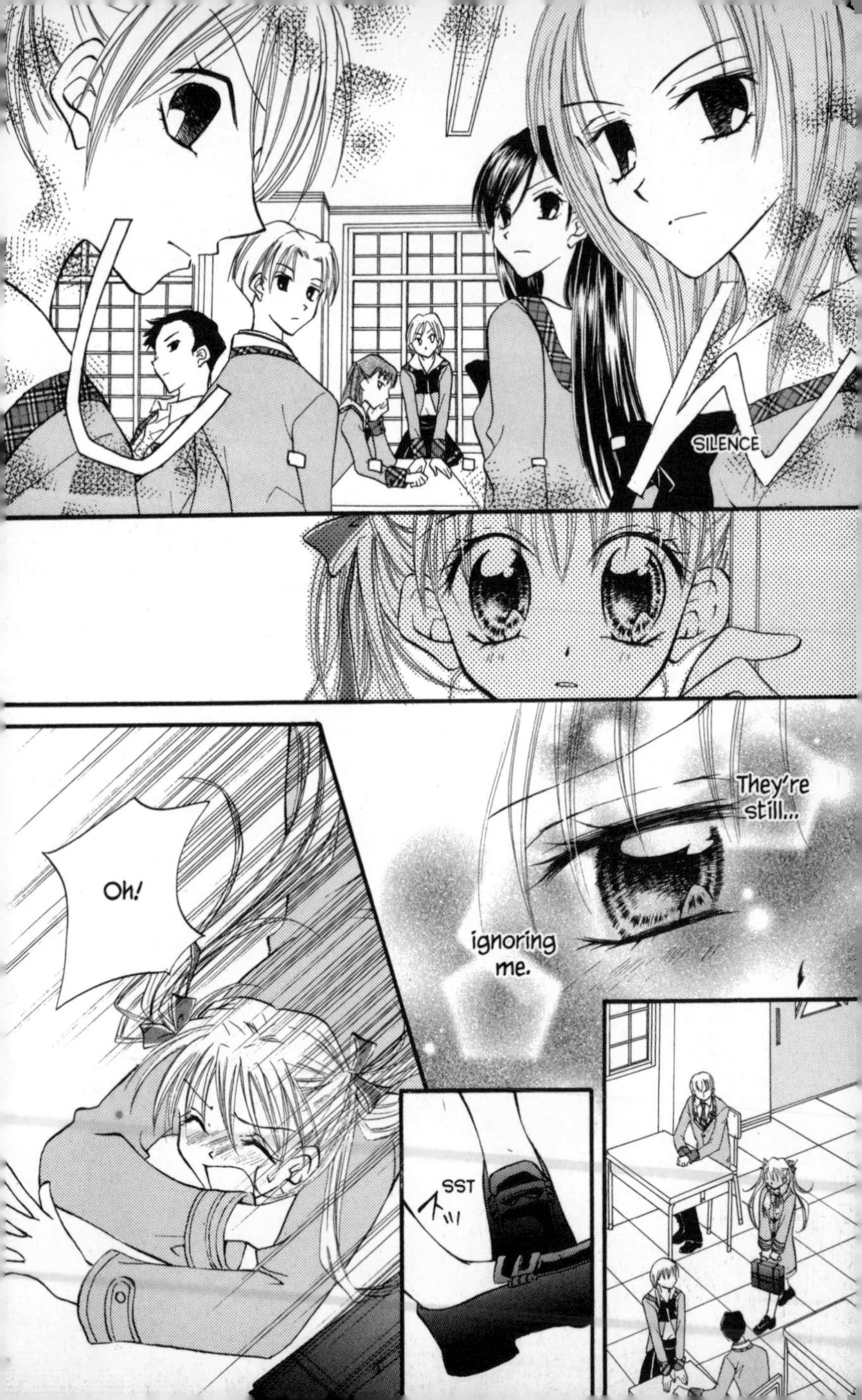
SILENCE
They're still...
ignoring me.
SST
Oh!

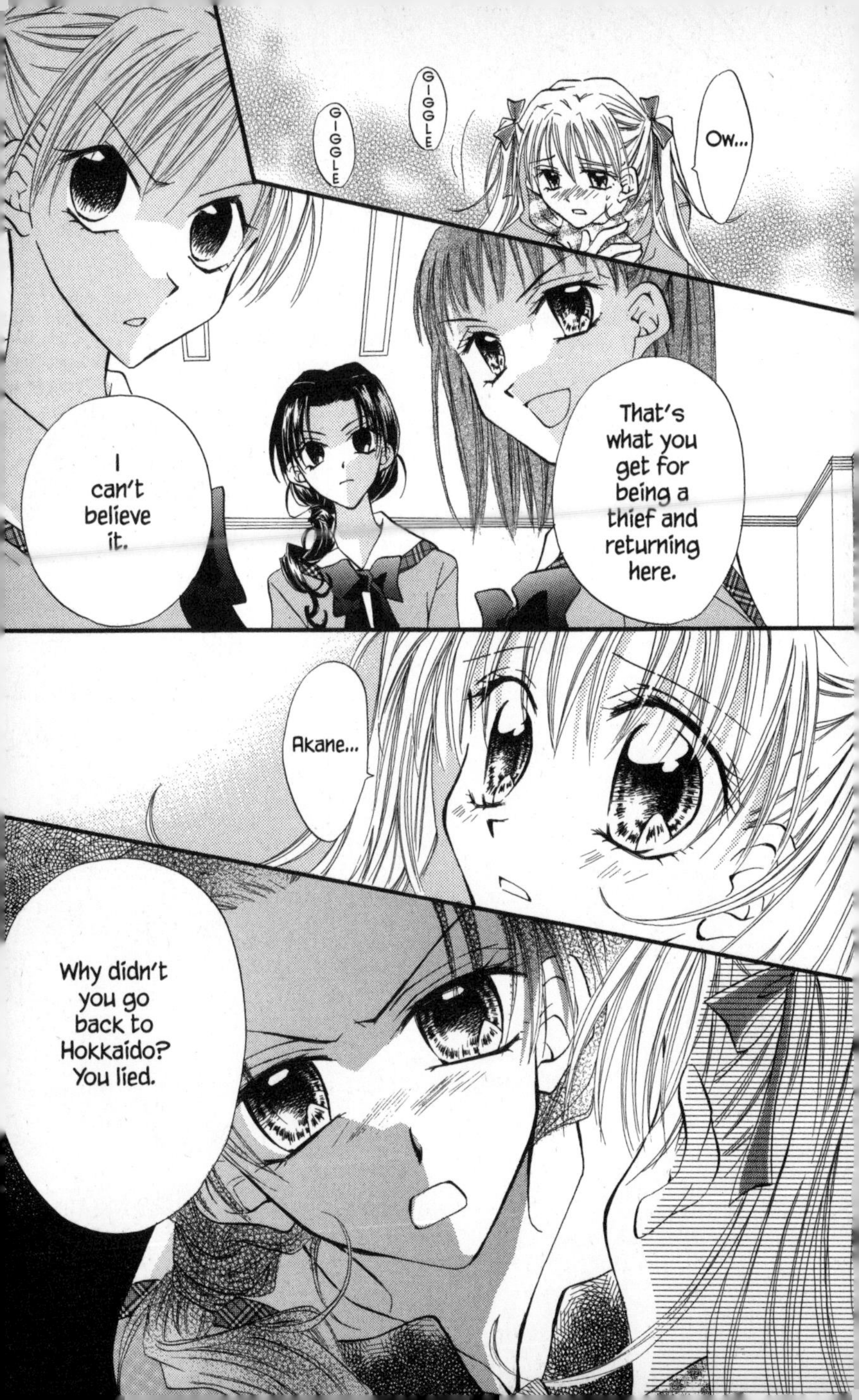
Ow...
GIGGLE
GIGGLE
That's what you get for being a thief and returning here.
I can't believe it.
Akane...
Why didn't you go back to Hokkaido? You lied.

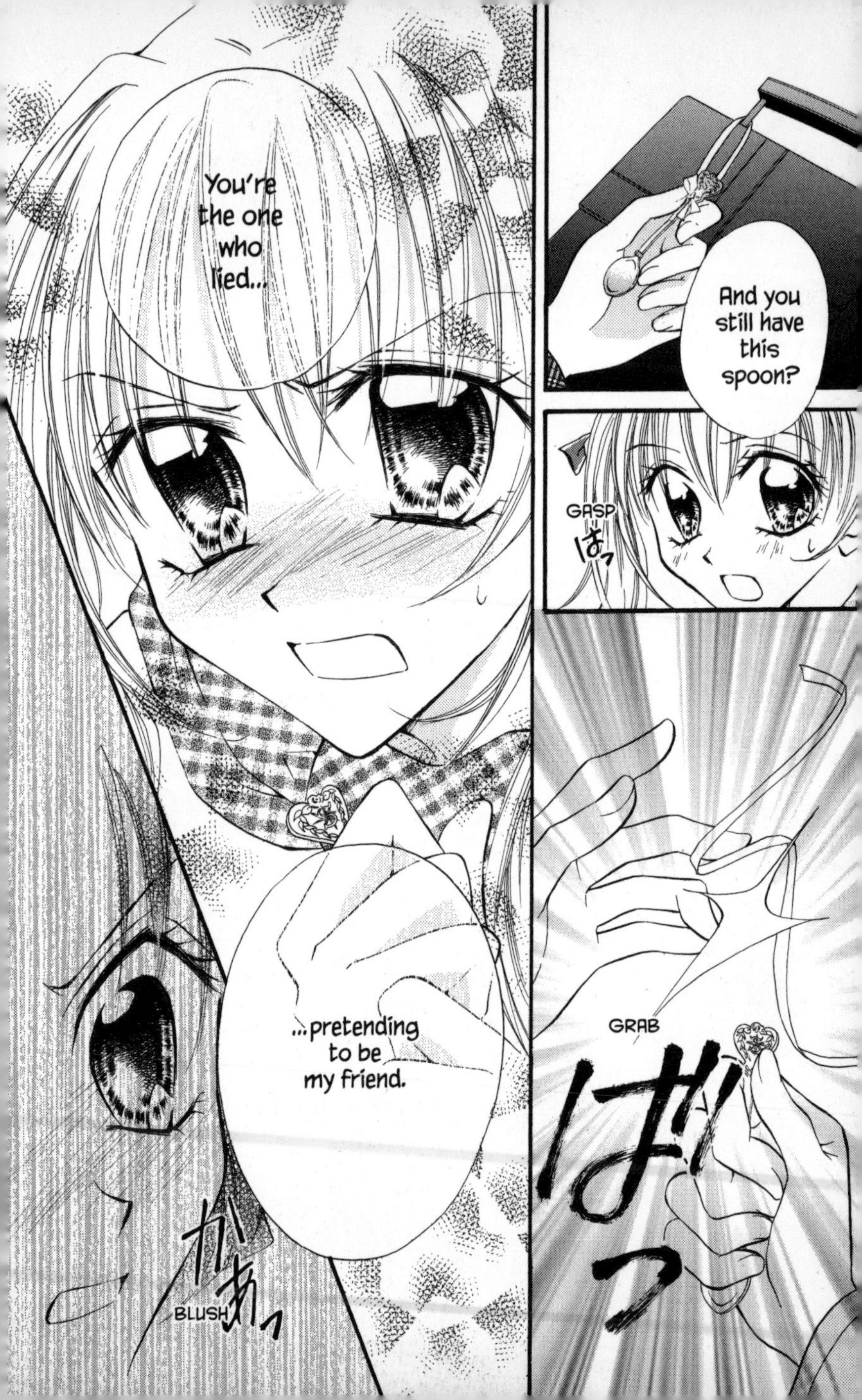
And you still have this spoon?
GASP
はっ
GRAB
ぱっ
You're the one who lied...
...pretending to be my friend.
BLUSH
かあっ

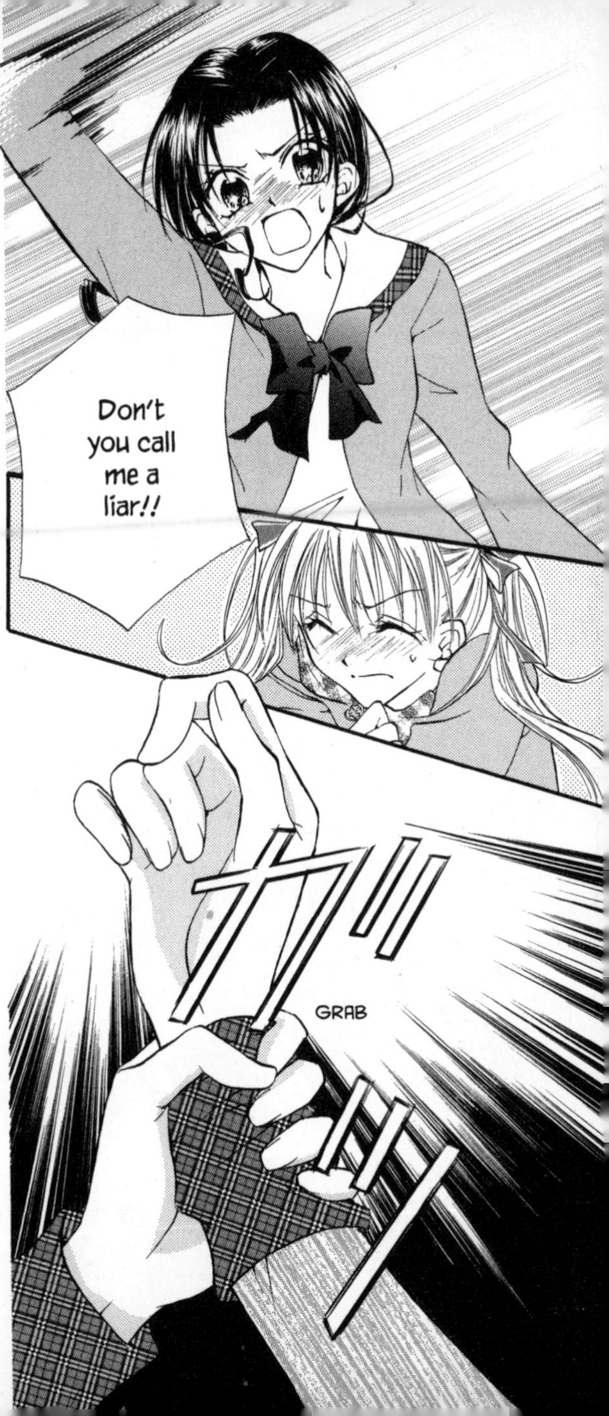
Don't you call me a liar!!
GRAB

Hello

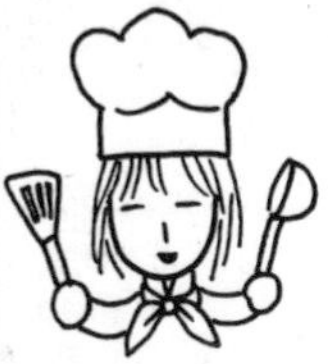

Hi there! This is Ando, who's been drawing a manga about cooking when she hardly cooks herself. Lately during work I've been sucking on "Milkies." I love these!! I can eat a whole bag in a day. ♥ I even go through withdrawal when I run out. ♥ There are seasonal flavors, too. Strawberry, chocolate, and banana. But I like the original kind. ♥

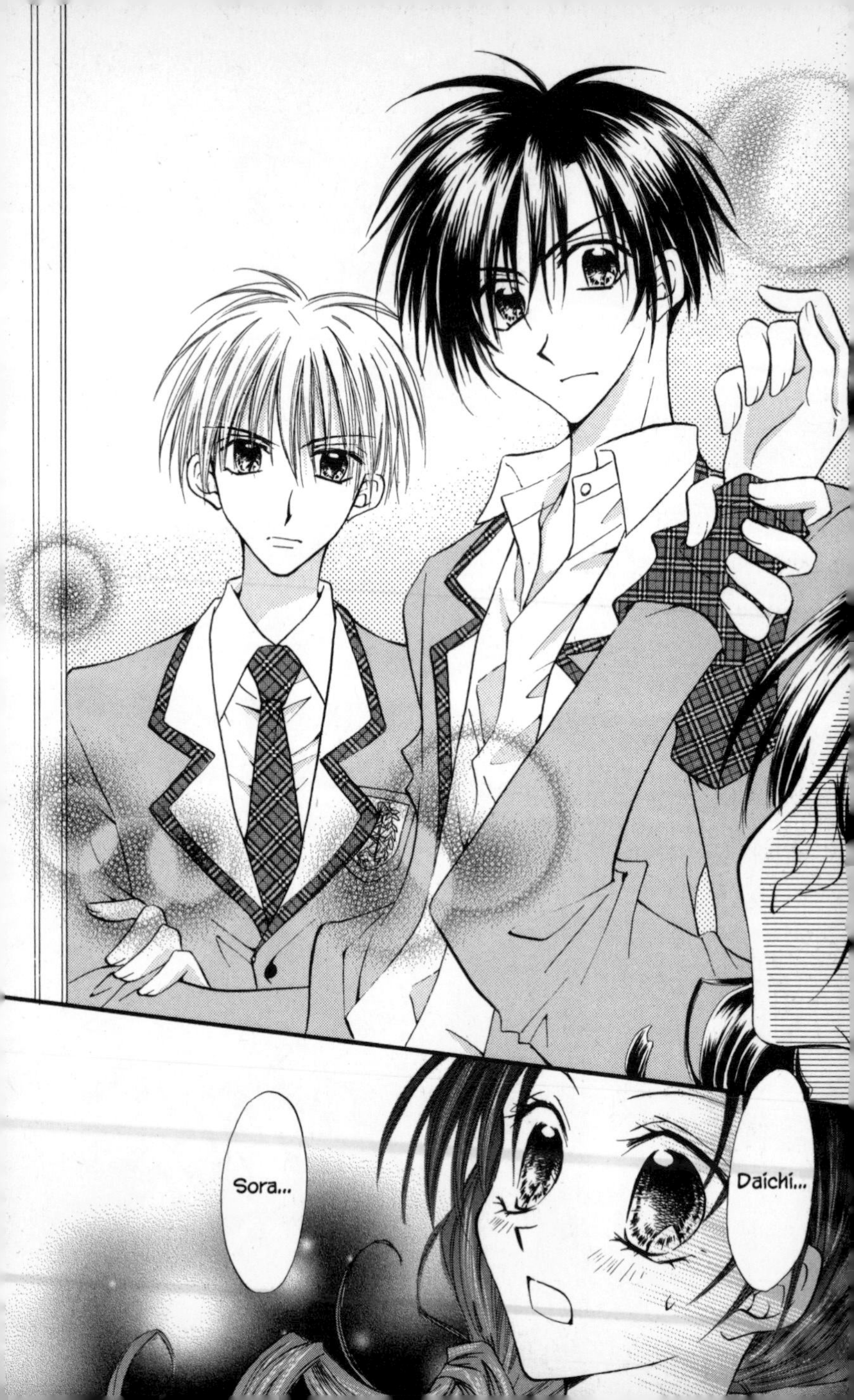
Daichi...
Sora...

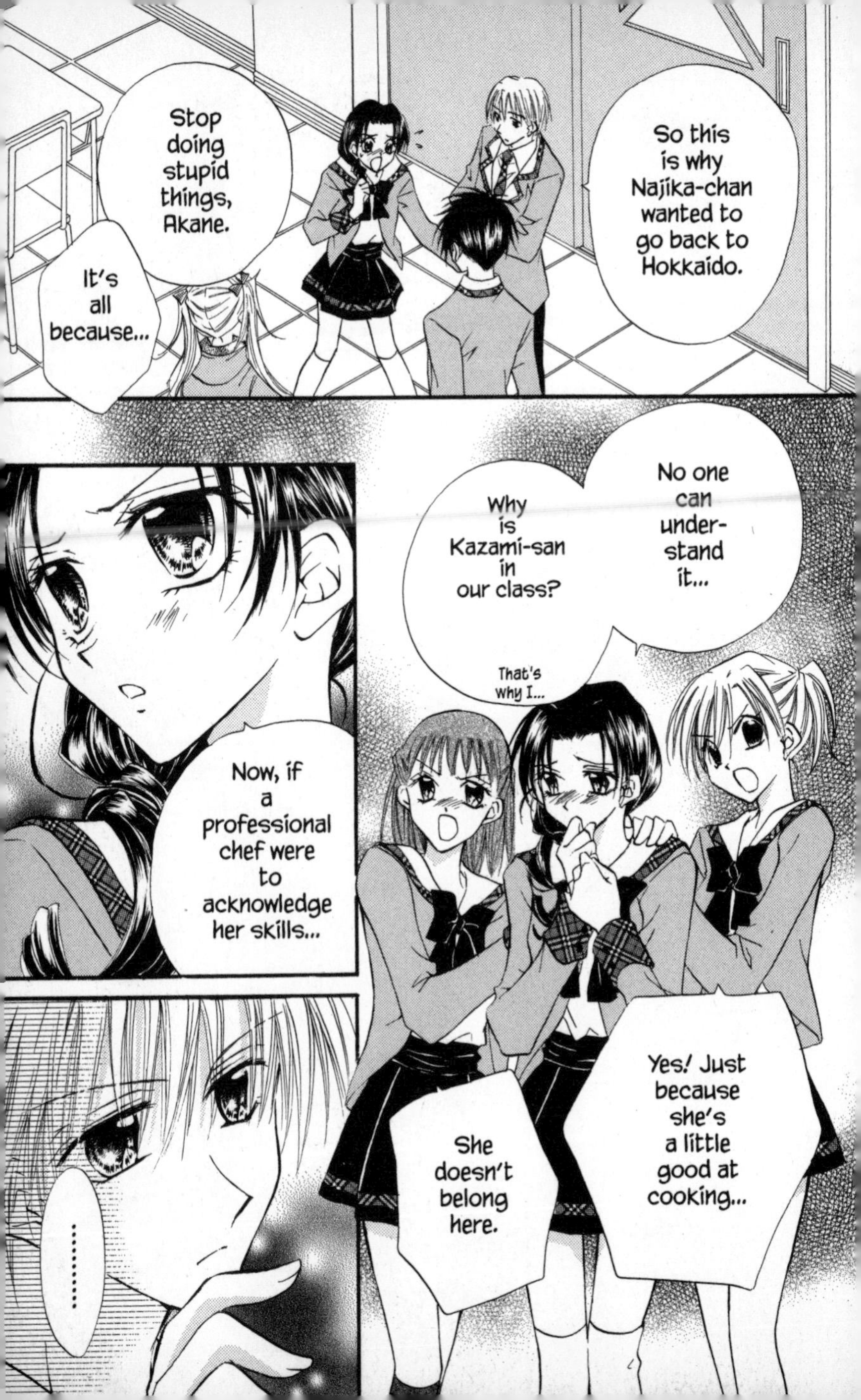
So this is why Najika-chan wanted to go back to Hokkaido.
Stop doing stupid things, Akane.
It's all because...
No one can understand it...
Why is Kazami-san in our class?
That's why I...
Yes! Just because she's a little good at cooking...
She doesn't belong here.
Now, if a professional chef were to acknowledge her skills...
......

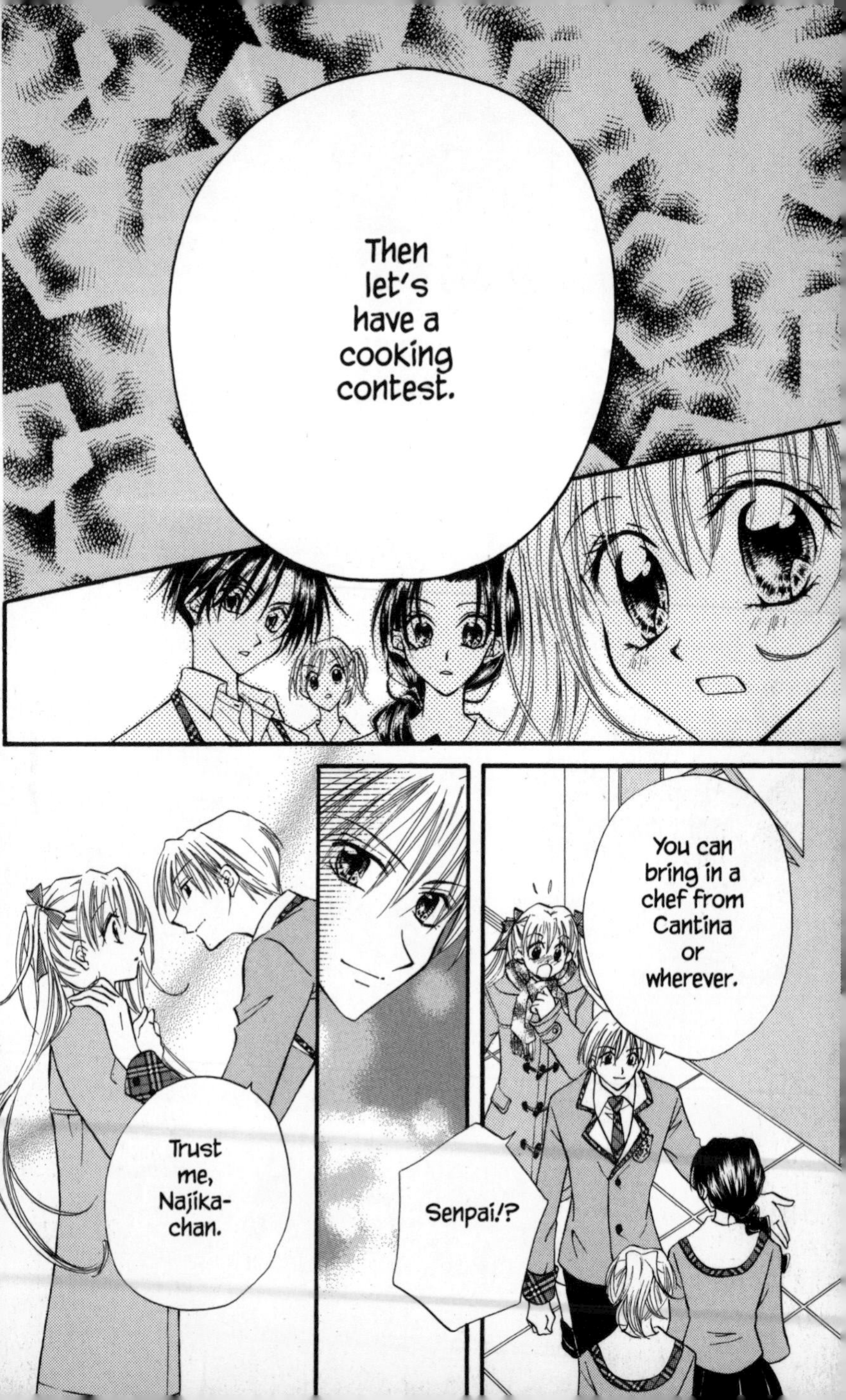
Then let's have a cooking contest.
You can bring in a chef from Cantina or wherever.
Senpai!?
Trust me, Najika-chan.

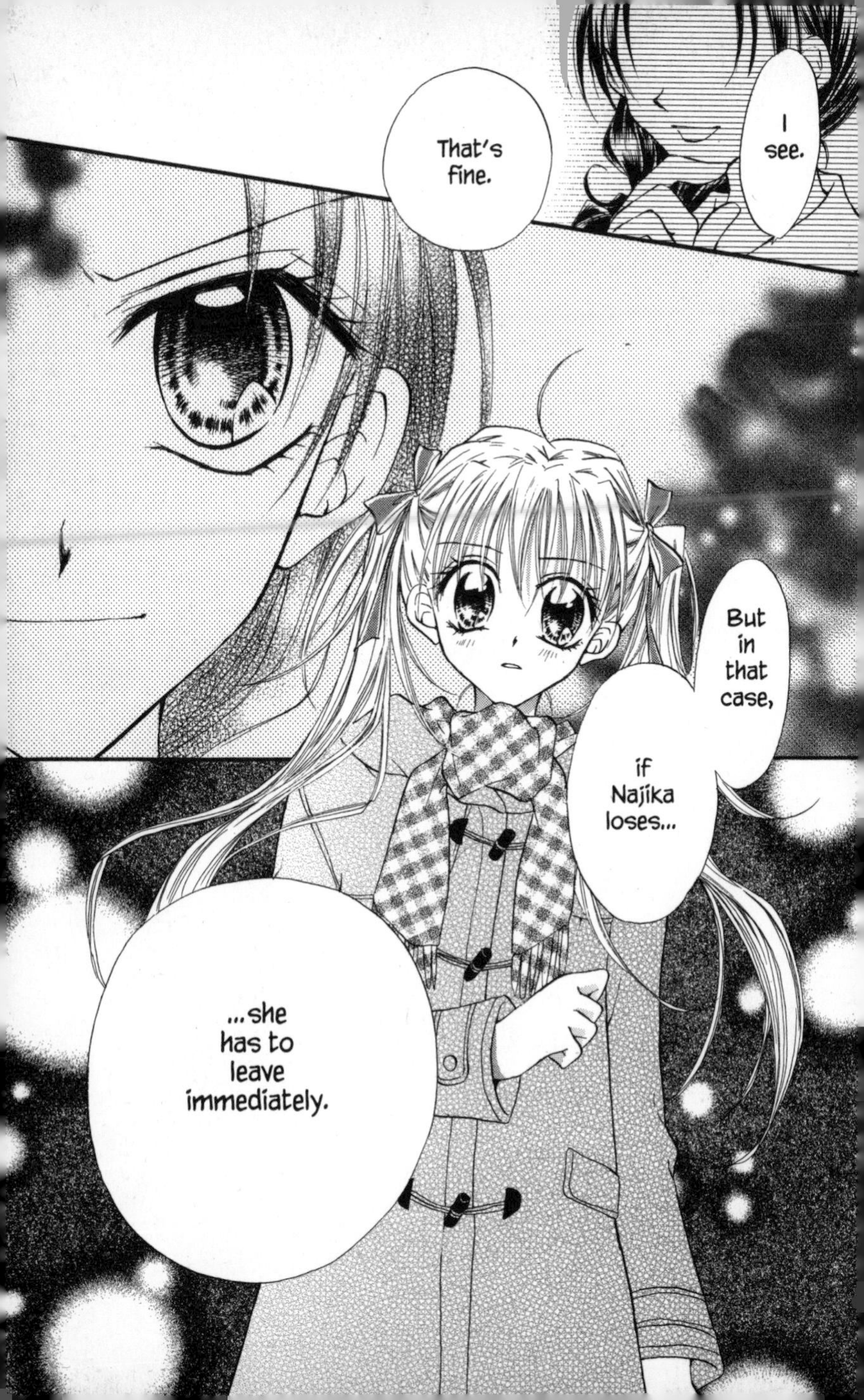
I see.
That's fine.
But in that case,
if Najika loses...
...she has to leave immediately.

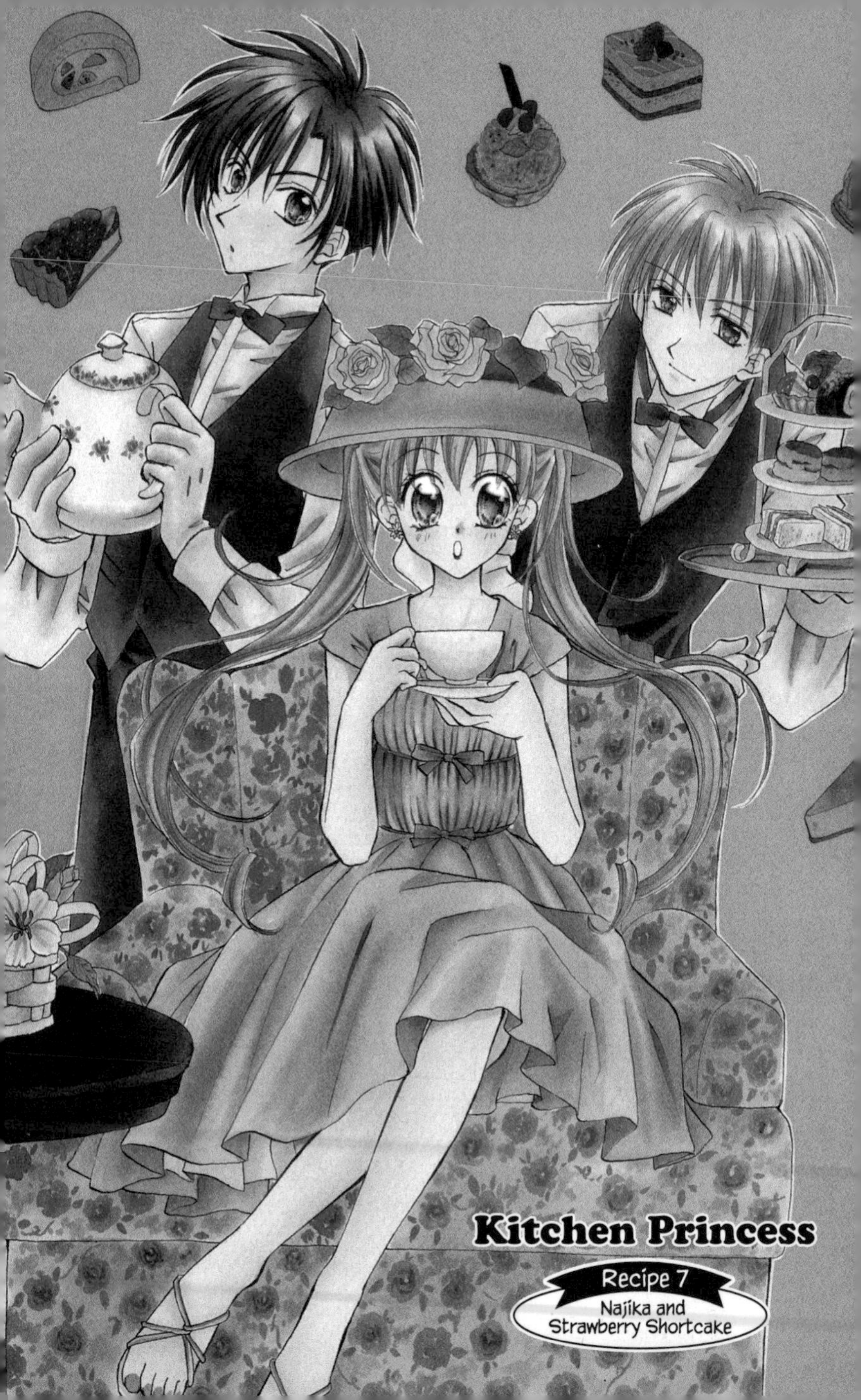
Kitchen Princess
Recipe 7
Najika and Strawberry Shortcake

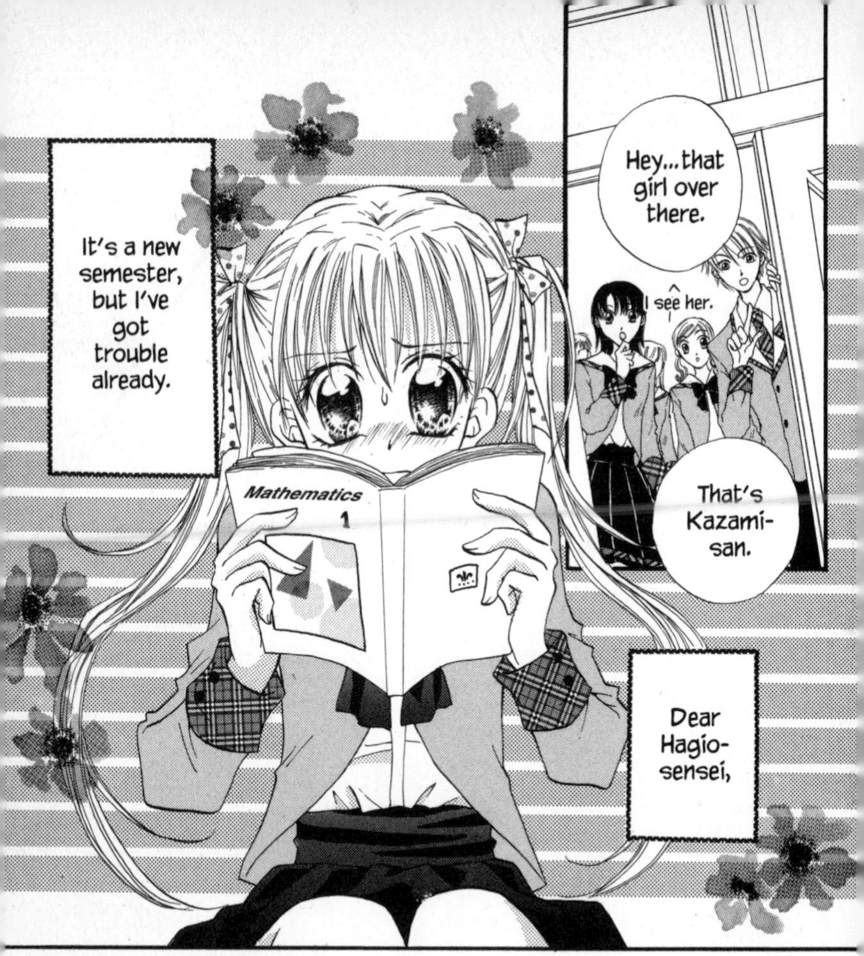
Hey...that girl over there.
I see her.
That's Kazami-san.
Dear Hagio-sensei,
It's a new semester, but I've got trouble already.
Mathematics 1

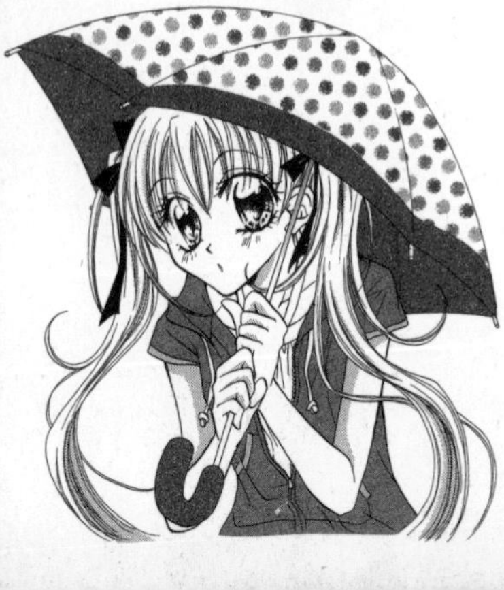

About Recipe 7's Splash Page

This is Najika chilling in a hotel lounge. The couch pattern was really difficult, and I regretted drawing it so many times while filling it in. Her clothes have a 1950s American feel.

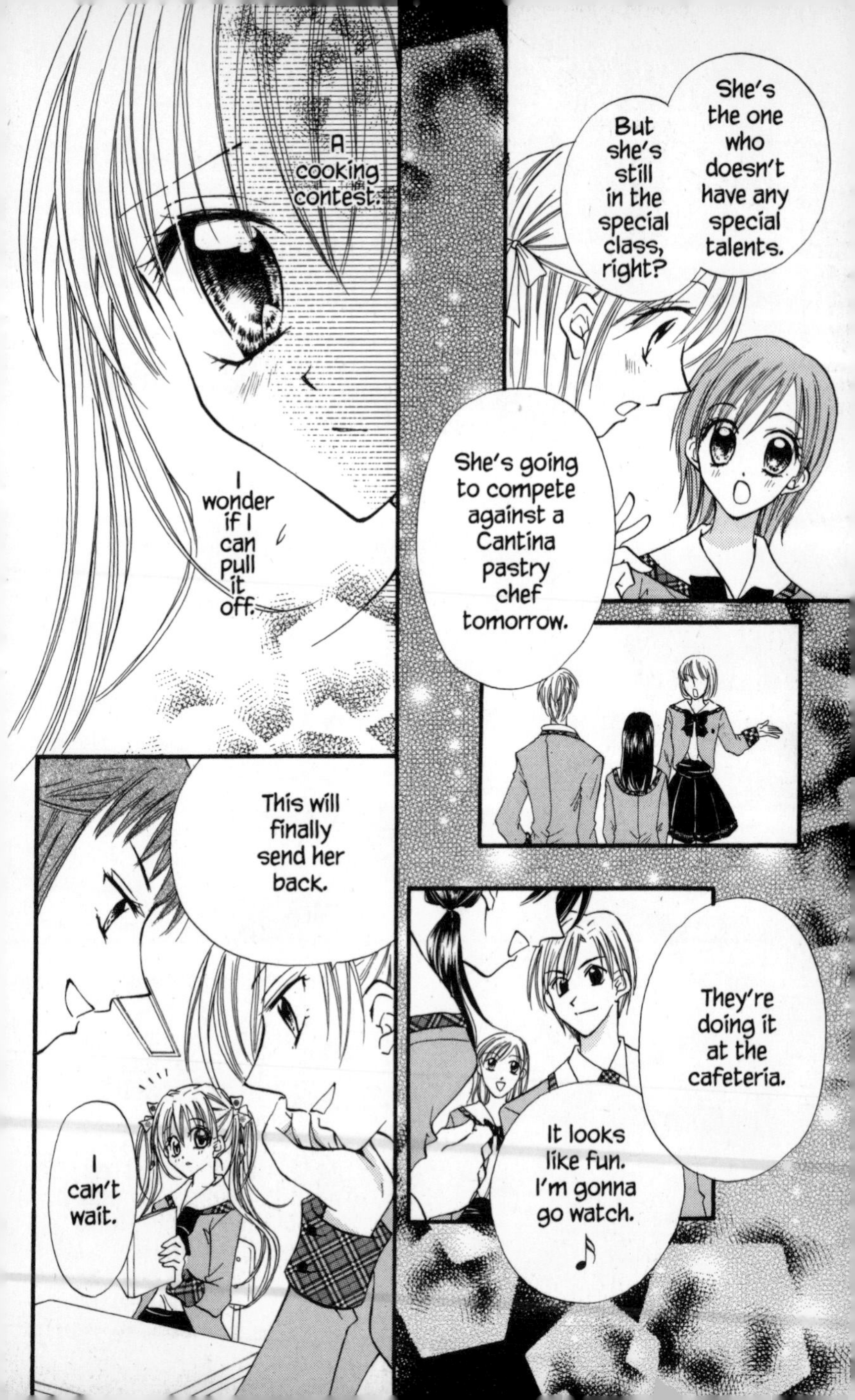
She's the one who doesn't have any special talents.
But she's still in the special class, right?
She's going to compete against a Cantina pastry chef tomorrow.
They're doing it at the cafeteria.
It looks like fun. I'm gonna go watch. ♪
A cooking contest.
I wonder if I can pull it off.
This will finally send her back.
I can't wait.

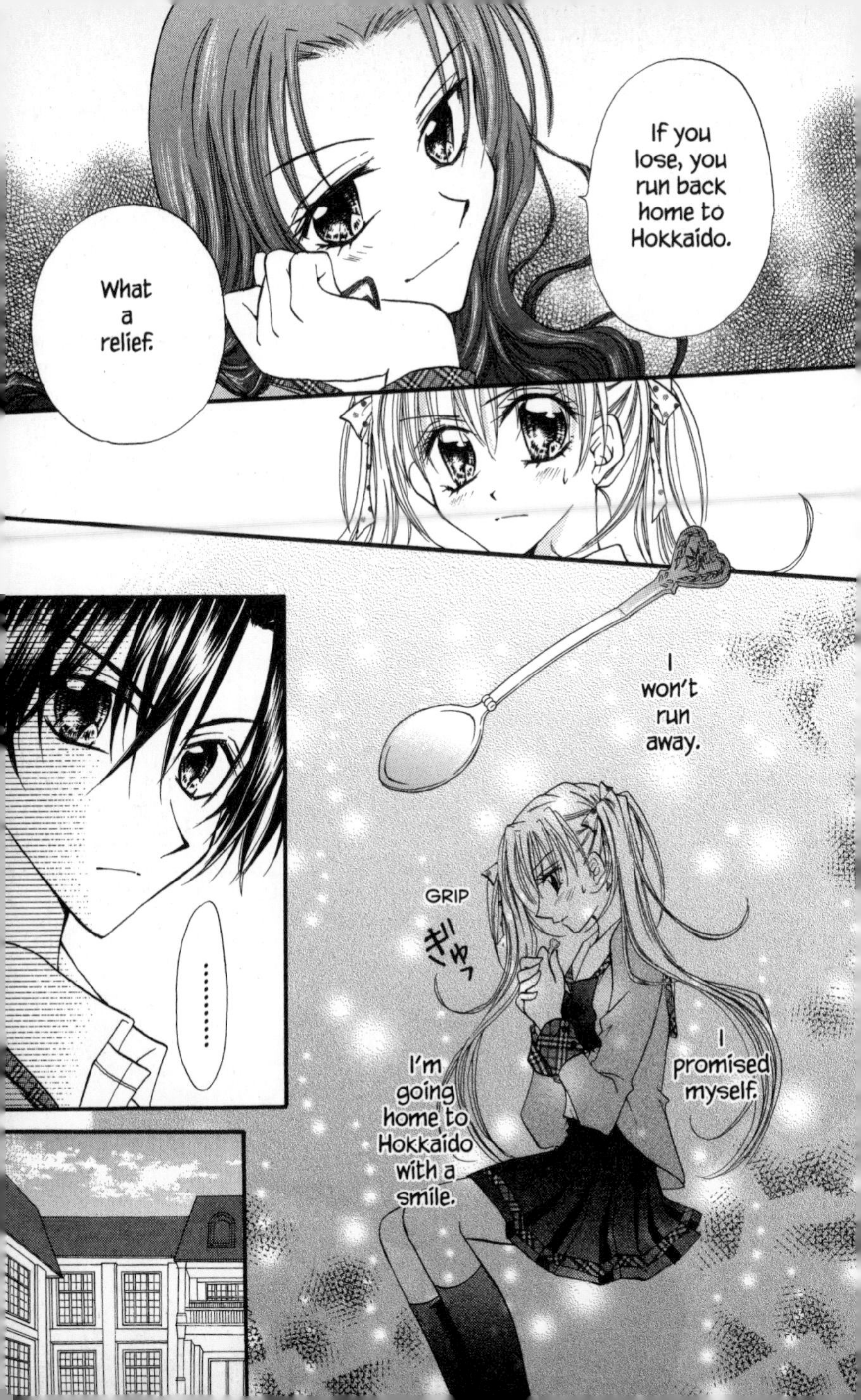
If you lose, you run back home to Hokkaido.
What a relief.
I won't run away.
GRIP
ぎゅっ
I promised myself.
I'm going home to Hokkaido with a smile.
....

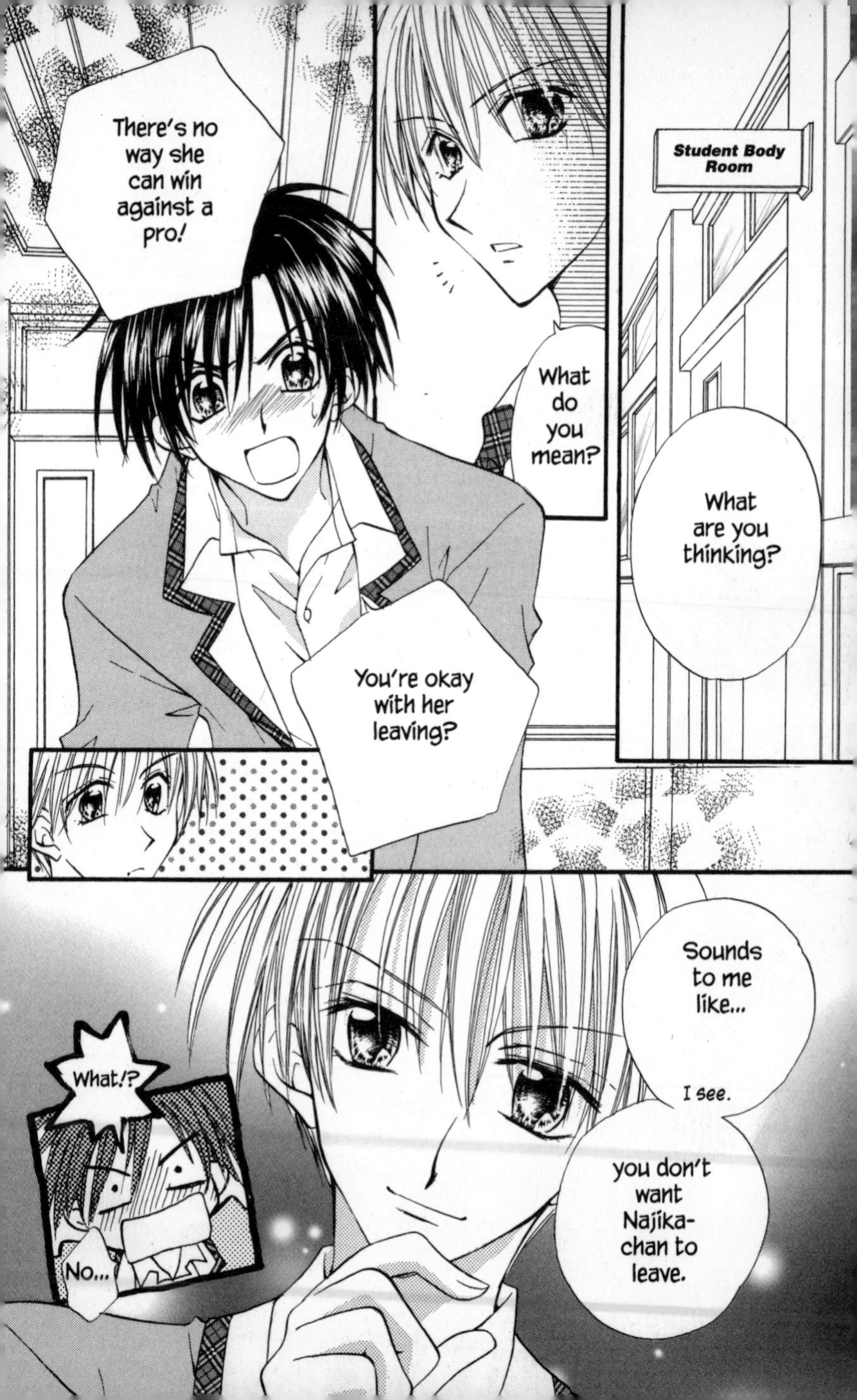
Student Body Room
What are you thinking?
What do you mean?
There's no way she can win against a pro!
You're okay with her leaving?
Sounds to me like...
I see.
you don't want Najika-chan to leave.
What!?
No...

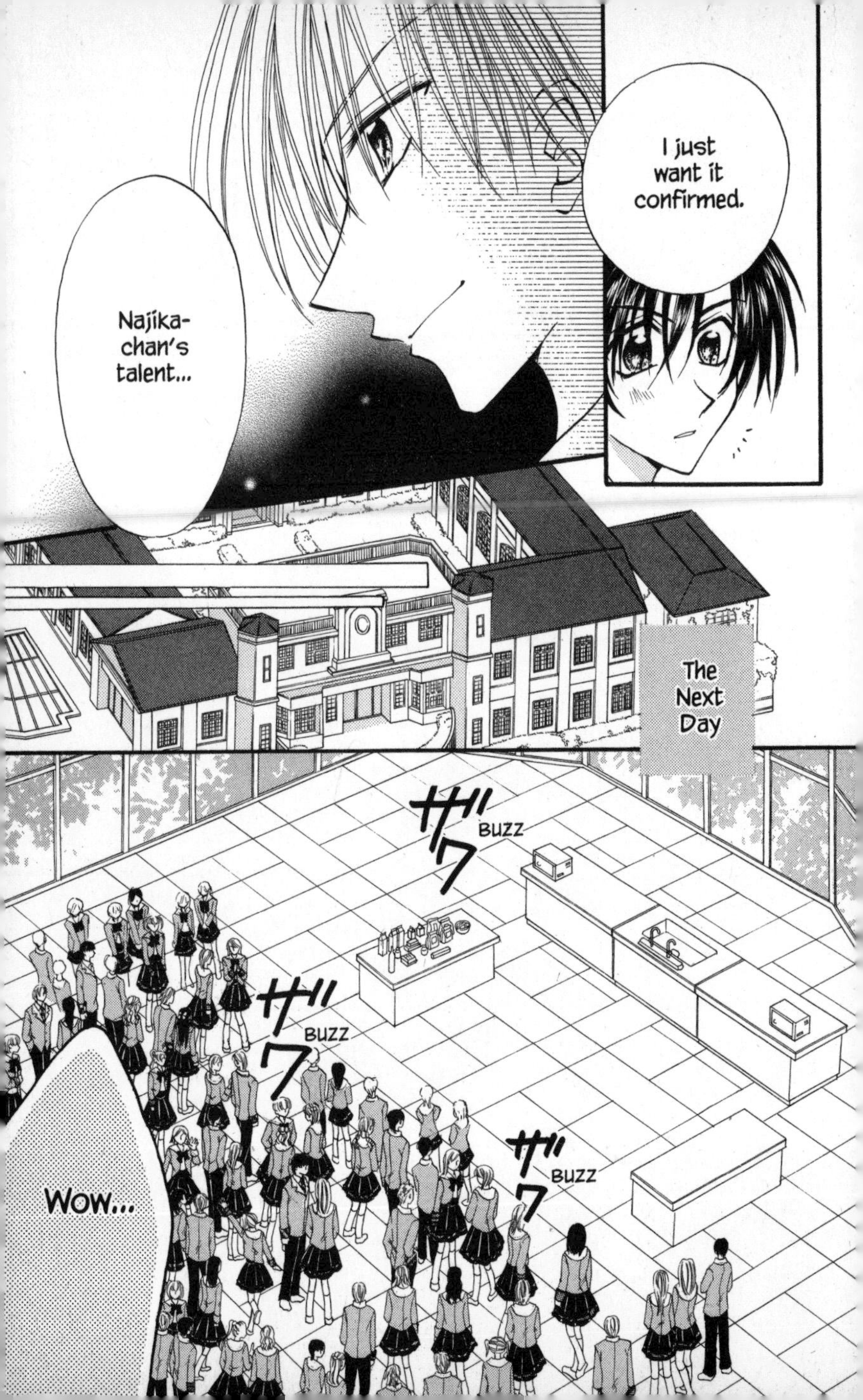
I just want it confirmed.
Najika-chan's talent...
The Next Day
ザワ BUZZ
ザワ BUZZ
ザワ BUZZ
Wow...

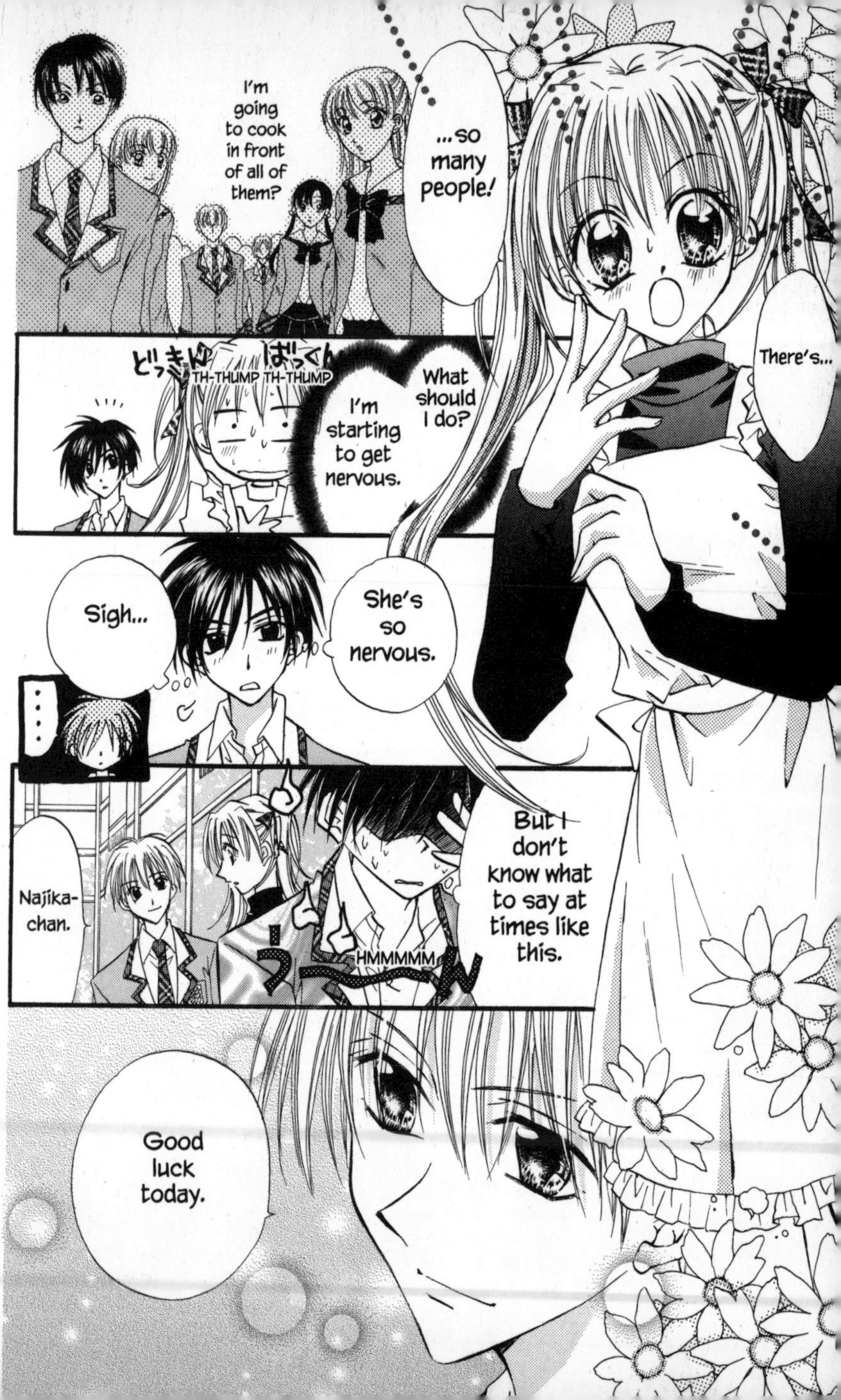
There's...
...so many people!
I'm going to cook in front of all of them?
What should I do?
I'm starting to get nervous.
どっきん ばっくん
TH-THUMP TH-THUMP
She's so nervous.
Sigh...
...
But I don't know what to say at times like this.
うーーん
HMMMMM
Najika-chan.
Good luck today.

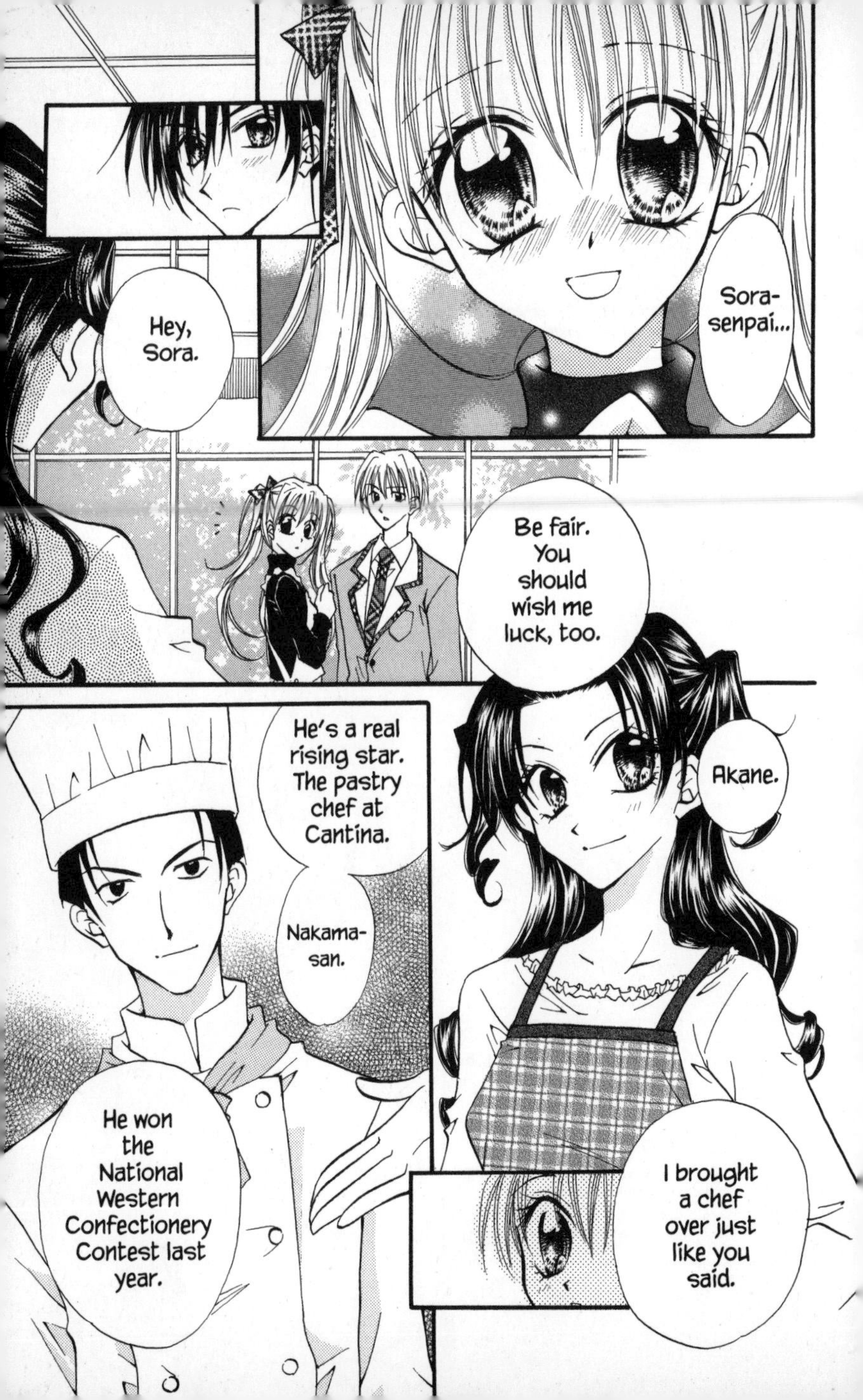
Sora-senpai...
Hey, Sora.
Be fair. You should wish me luck, too.
Akane.
I brought a chef over just like you said.
He's a real rising star. The pastry chef at Cantina.
Nakama-san.
He won the National Western Confectionery Contest last year.

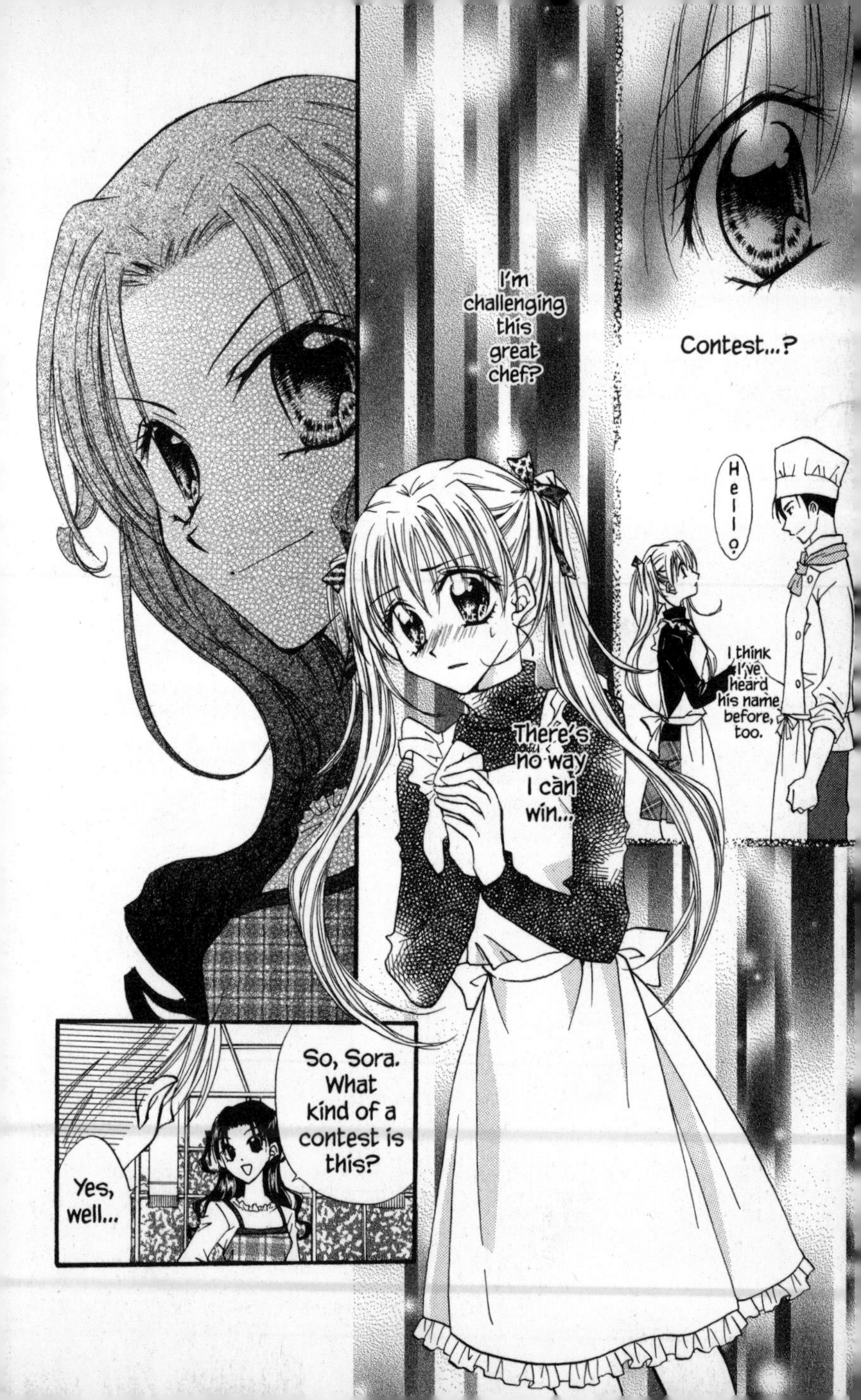
Contest...?
Hello.
I think I've heard his name before, too.
I'm challenging this great chef?
There's no way I can win...
So, Sora. What kind of a contest is this?
Yes, well...

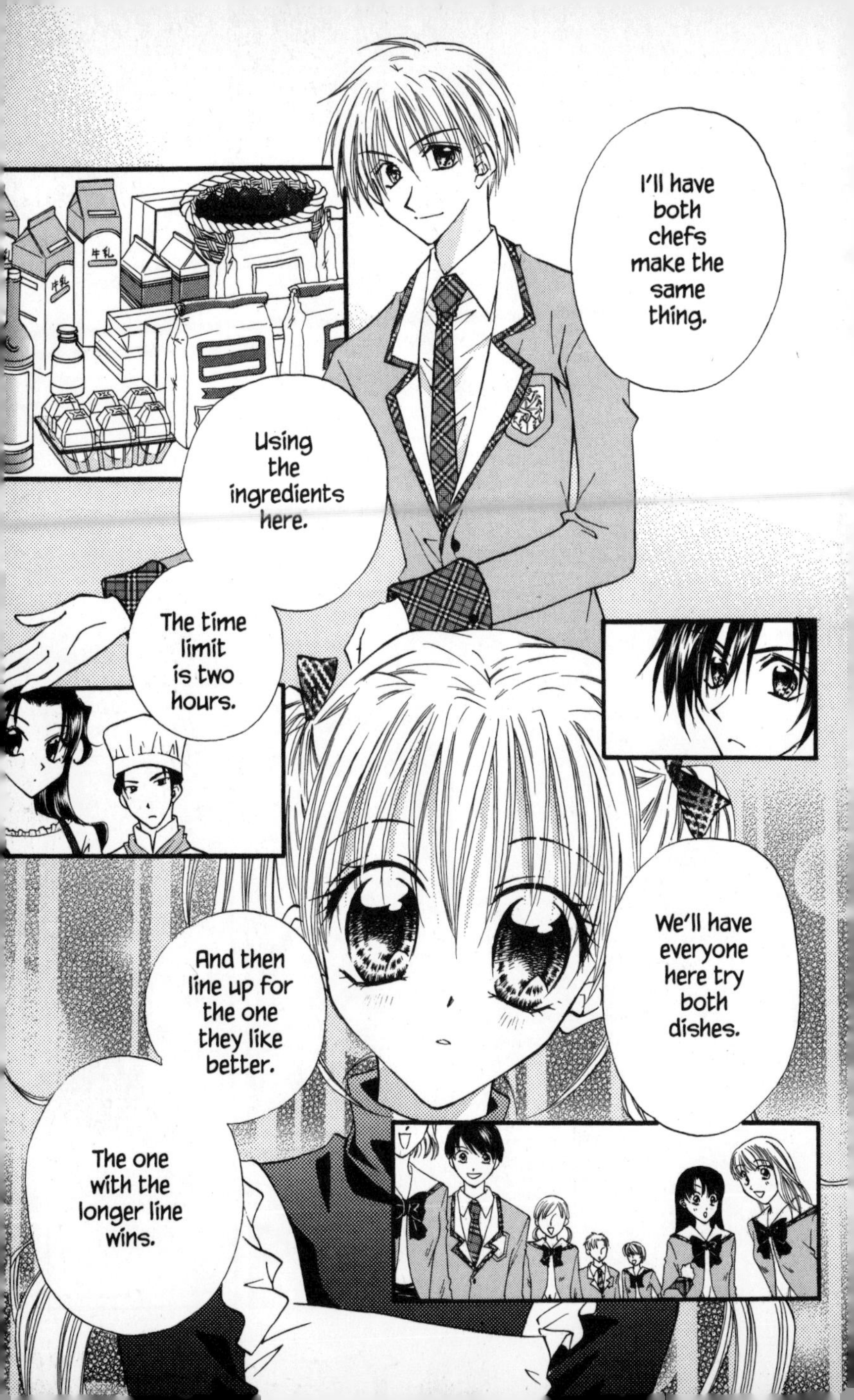
I'll have both chefs make the same thing.
Using the ingredients here.
The time limit is two hours.
We'll have everyone here try both dishes.
And then line up for the one they like better.
The one with the longer line wins.

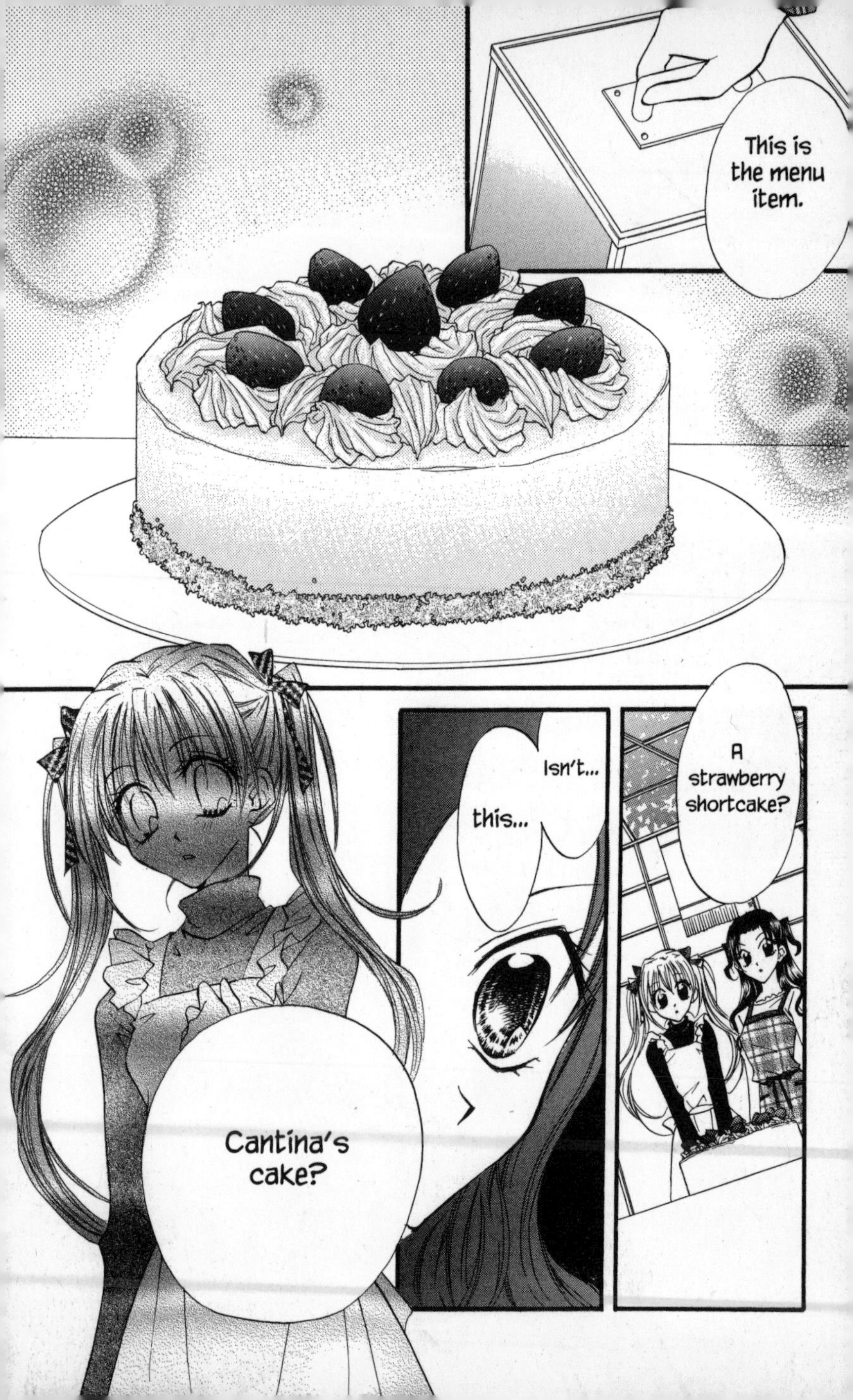
This is the menu item.
A strawberry shortcake?
Isn't... this...
Cantina's cake?

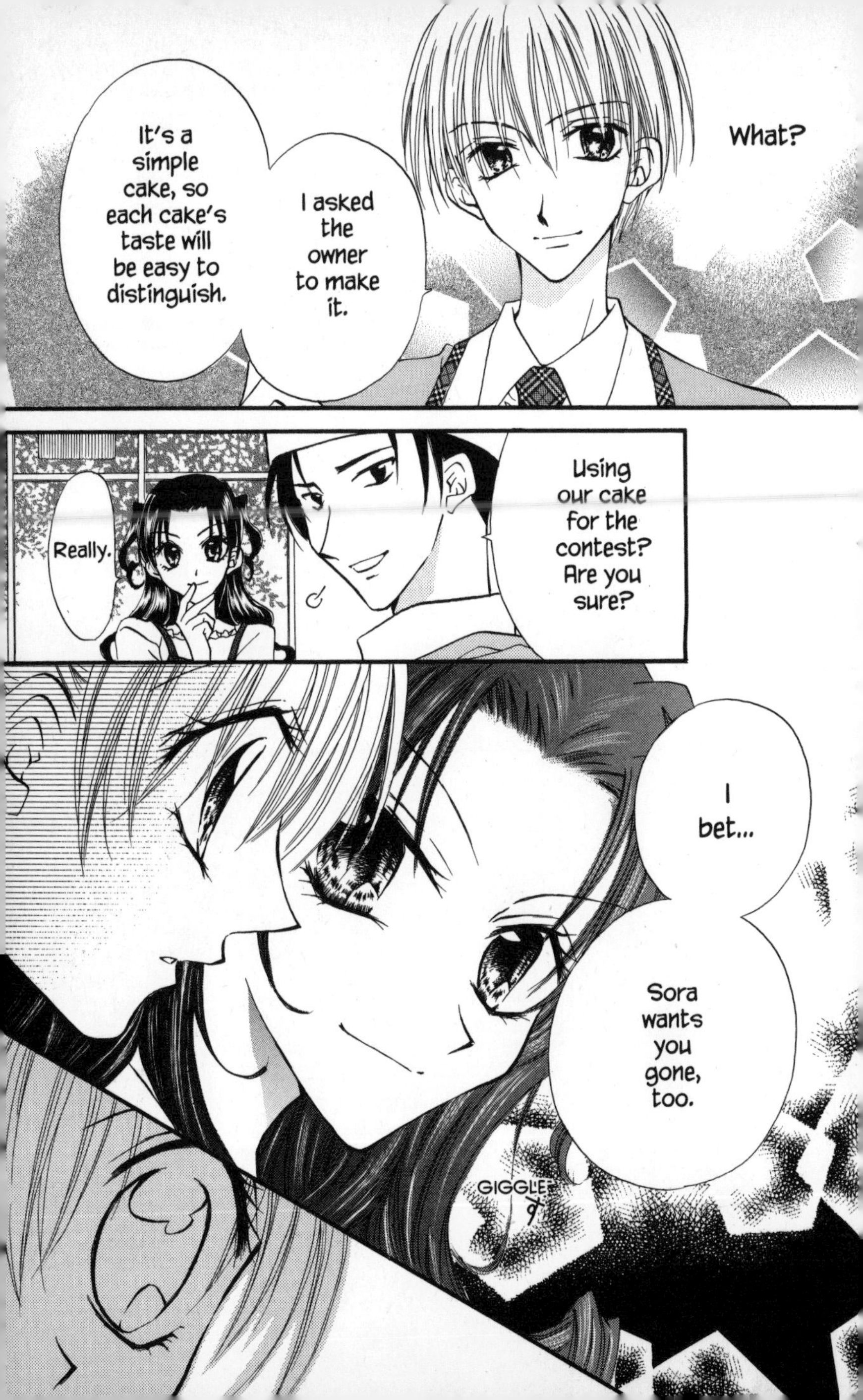
What?
I asked the owner to make it.
It's a simple cake, so each cake's taste will be easy to distinguish.
Using our cake for the contest? Are you sure?
Really.
I bet...
Sora wants you gone, too.
GIGGLE

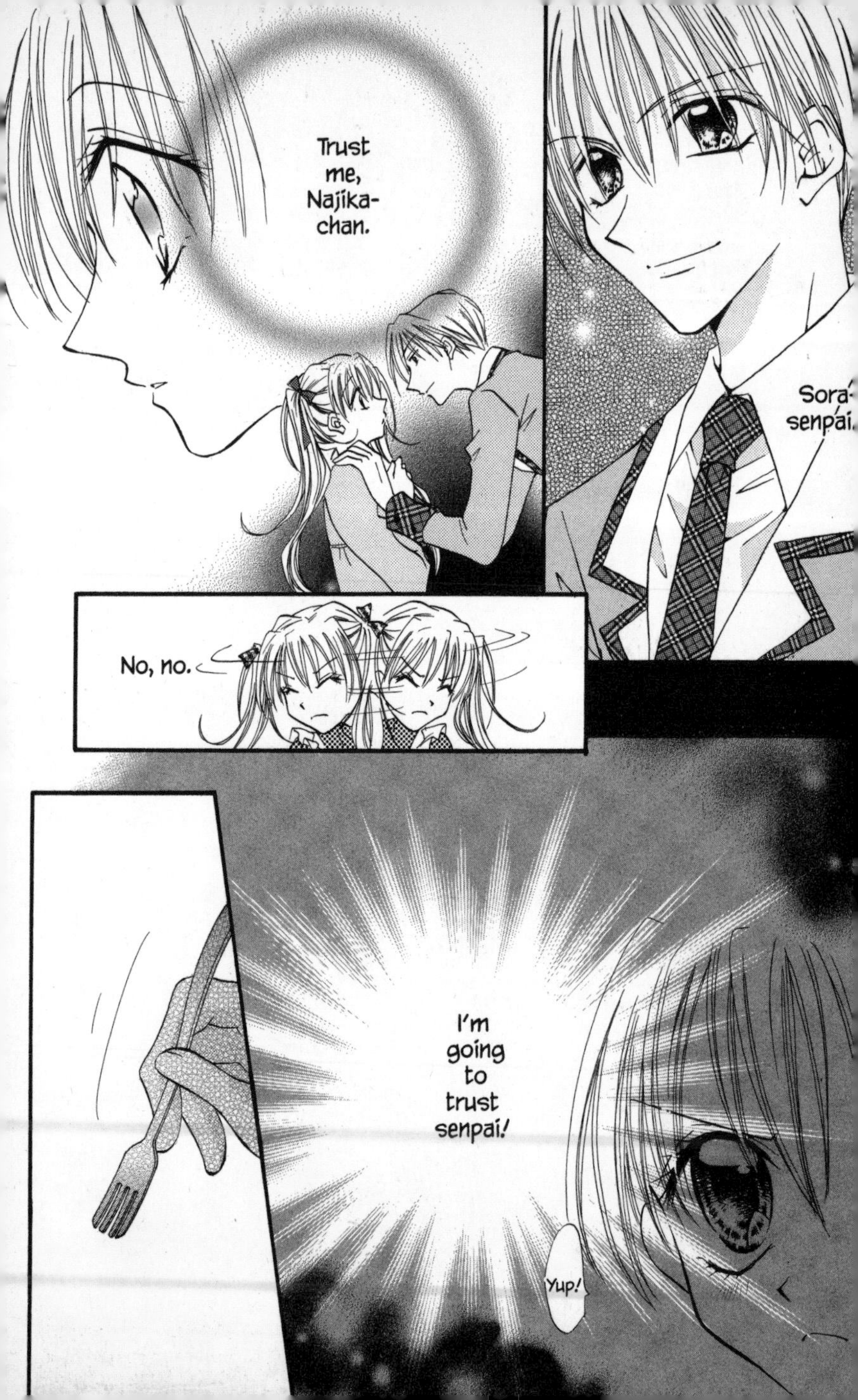
Sora-senpai.
Trust me, Najika-chan.
No, no.
I'm going to trust senpai!
Yup!

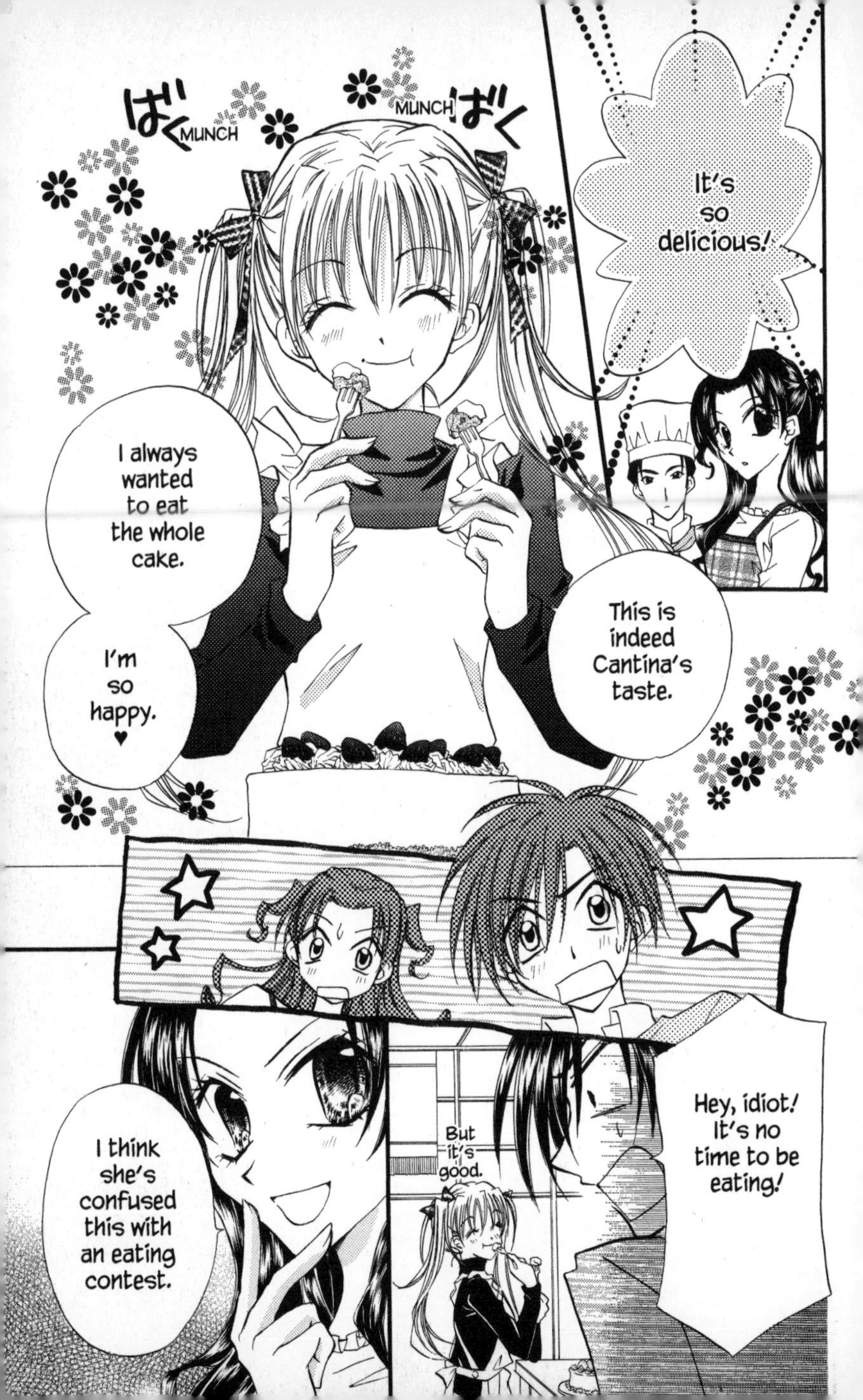

It's so delicious!
MUNCH ばく
ばく MUNCH
I always wanted to eat the whole cake.
I'm so happy. ♥
This is indeed Cantina's taste.
Hey, idiot! It's no time to be eating!
But it's good.
I think she's confused this with an eating contest.

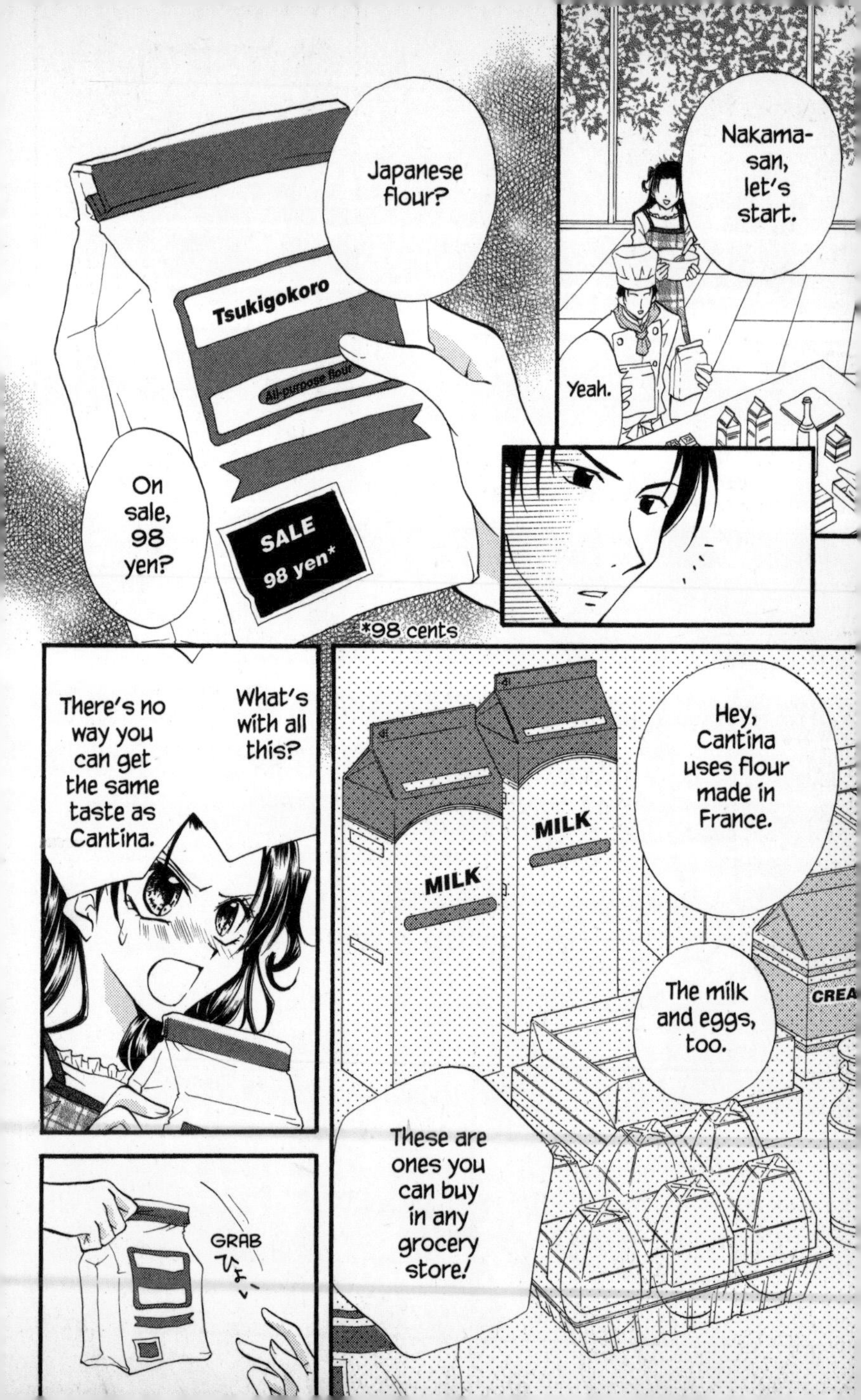
Nakama-san, let's start.
Yeah.
Japanese flour?
Tsukigokoro
All-purpose flour
SALE 98 yen*
On sale, 98 yen?
*98 cents
Hey, Cantina uses flour made in France.
MILK
MILK
CREA
The milk and eggs, too.
These are ones you can buy in any grocery store!
What's with all this?
There's no way you can get the same taste as Cantina.
GRAB
ひょい

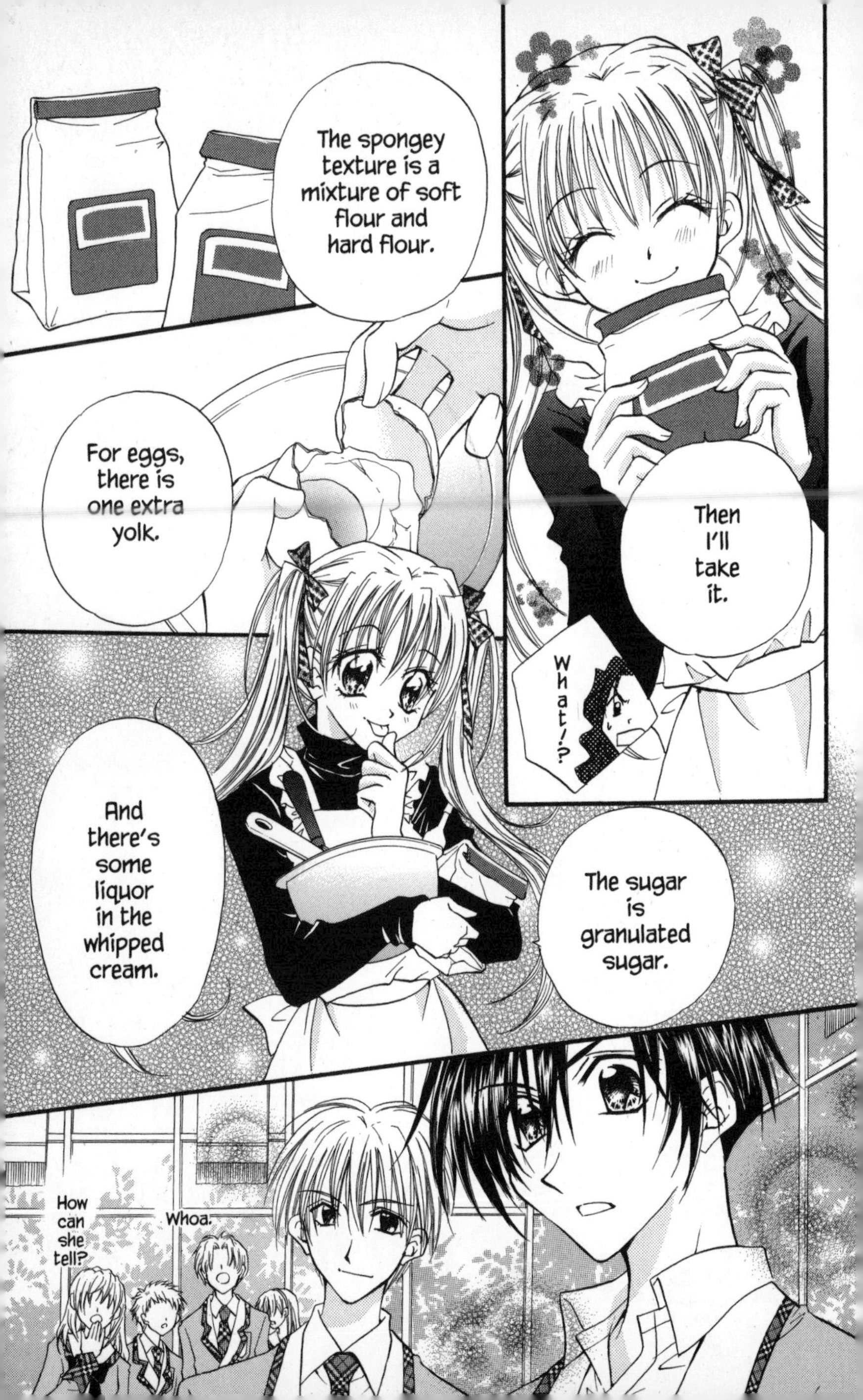
Then I'll take it.
What!?
The spongey texture is a mixture of soft flour and hard flour.
For eggs, there is one extra yolk.
The sugar is granulated sugar.
And there's some liquor in the whipped cream.
Whoa.
How can she tell?

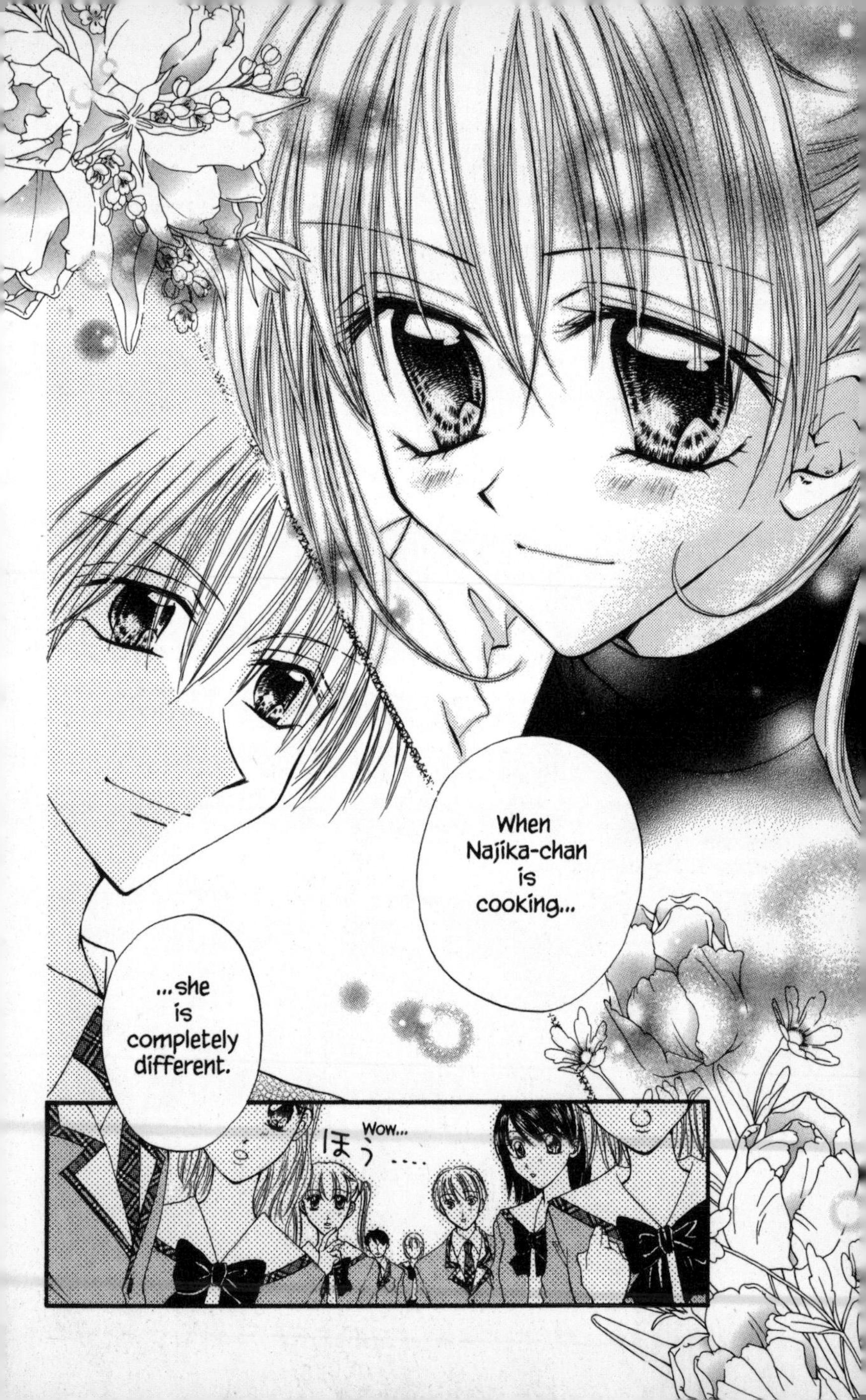
When Najika-chan is cooking...
...she is completely different.
ほう....
Wow...

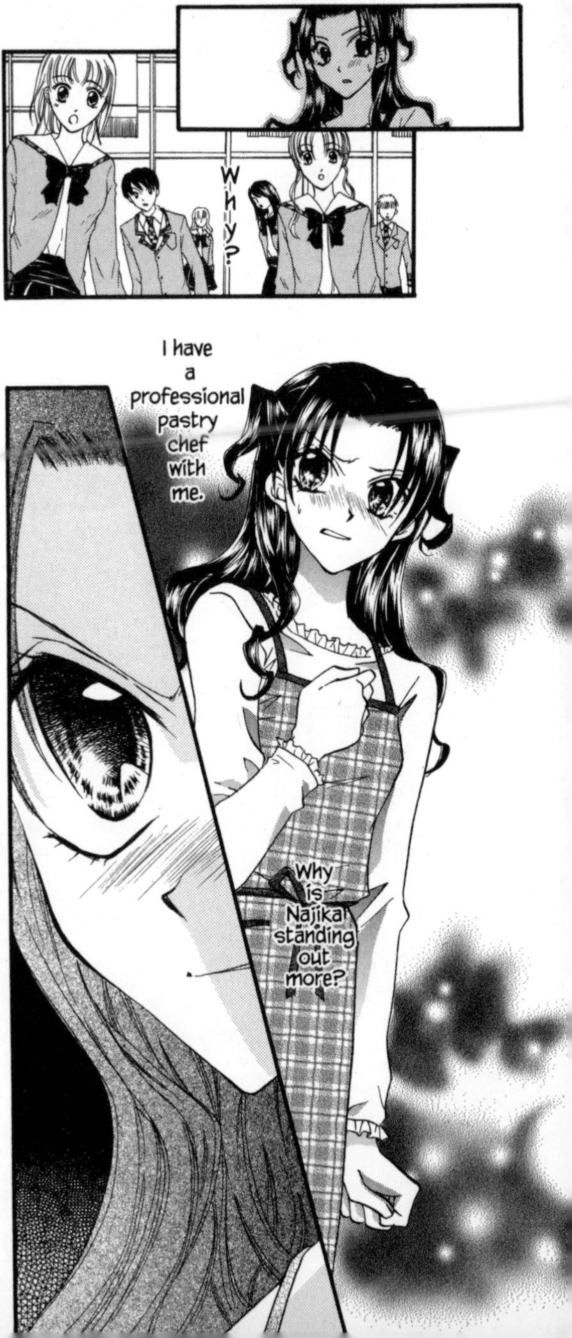
Why?
I have a professional pastry chef with me.
Why is Najika standing out more?

This is a first for me. I would like to talk about memories from each chapter. There may be spoilers, so please read it after you read the story. ♡

Recipe 6

In this chapter, Najika makes the chocolate macaroons. Miyuki-sensei actually sent some, so I got to eat them. Since they were so good, I decided to make them. But it was impossible. Why? Because I don't have an oven...

Recipe 7

When I was younger, I remember making something where I had to whisk the eggs really hard. And I imagined how I would feel if someone dropped it, so I let Akane do that to Najika (laugh). A store that has good strawberry shortcake has good everything else, don't you think? ♥

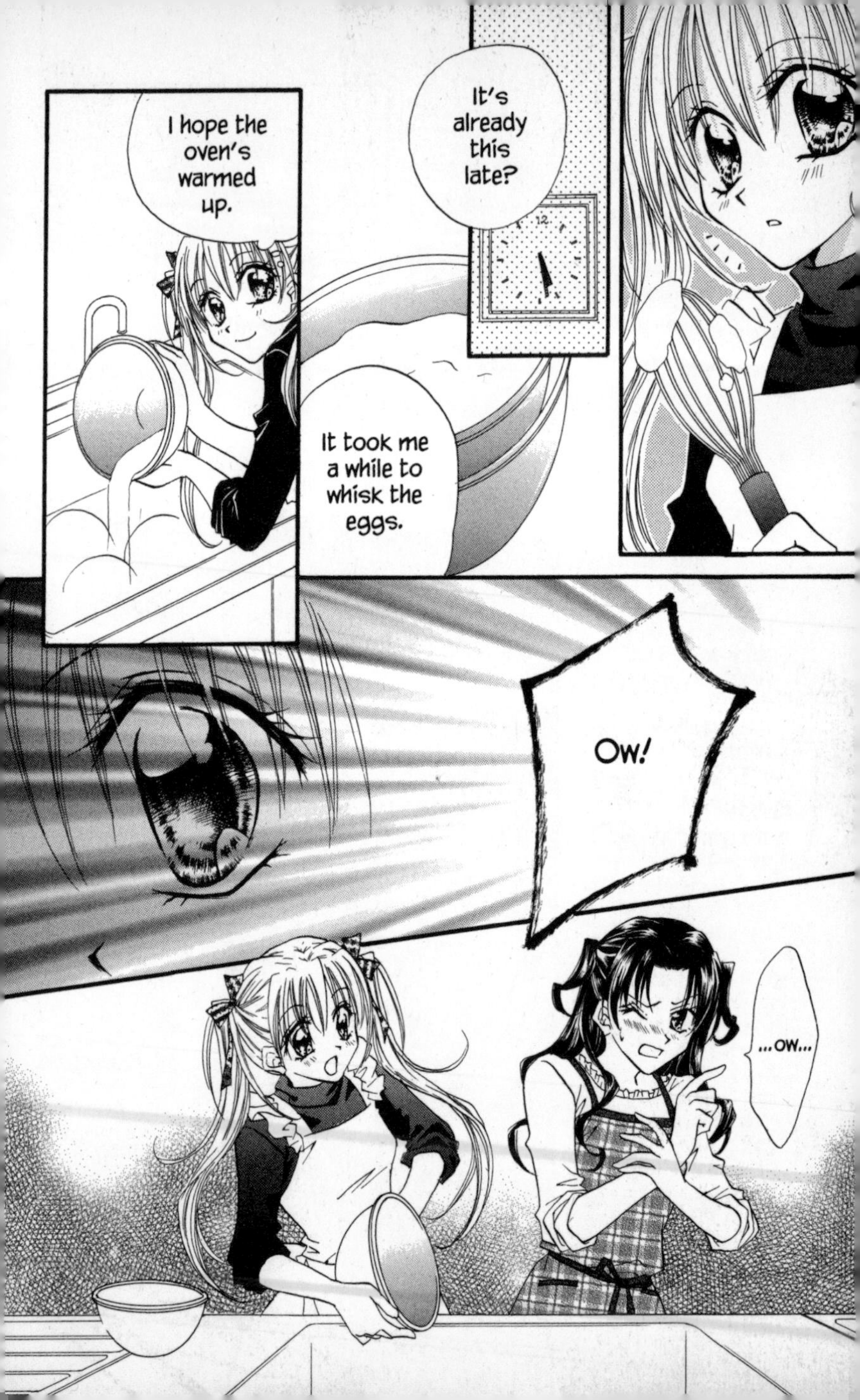
It's already this late?
It took me a while to whisk the eggs.
I hope the oven's warmed up.
Ow!
...ow...

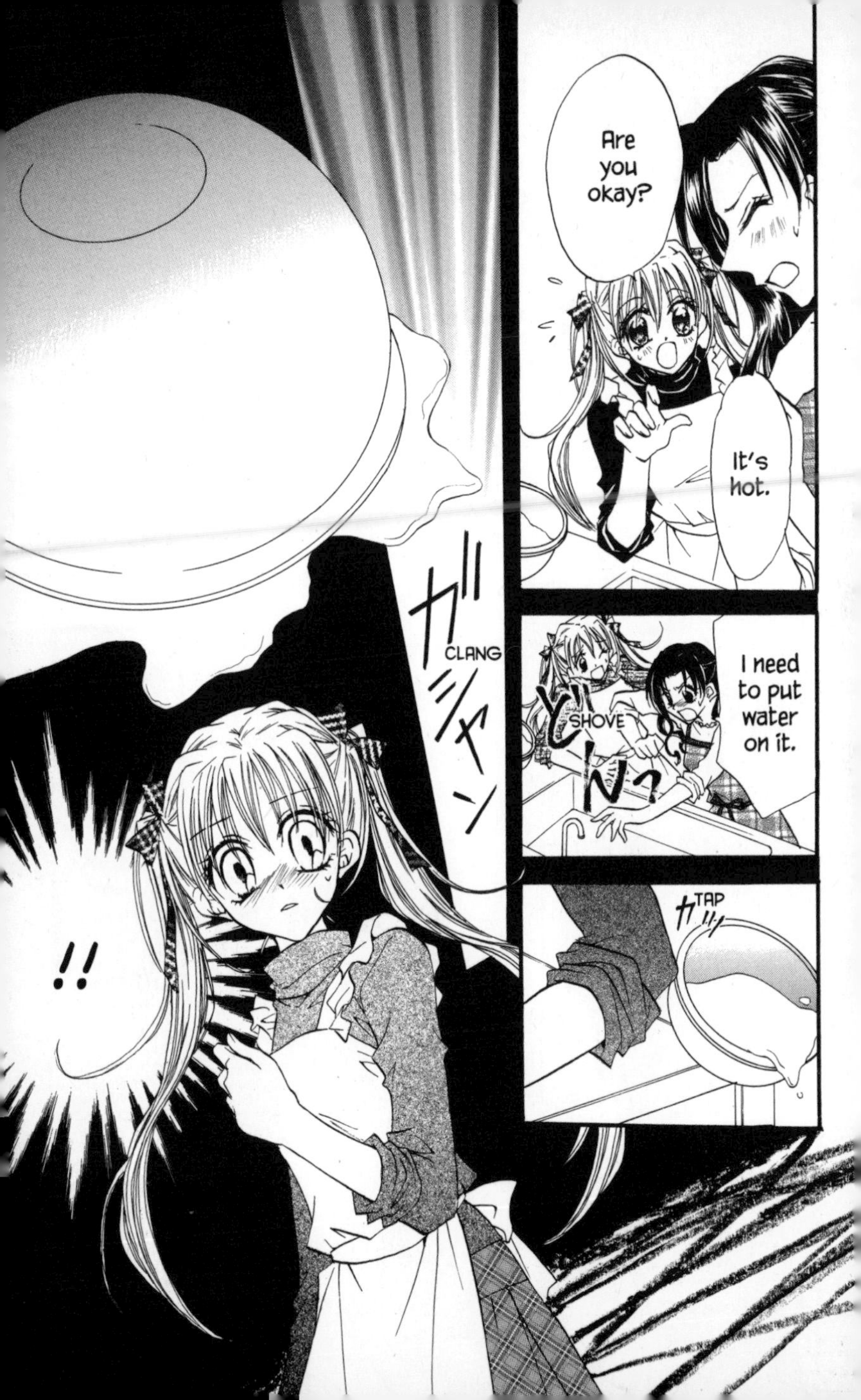
Are you okay?
It's hot.
I need to put water on it.
SHOVE
N?
TAP
CLANG
!!

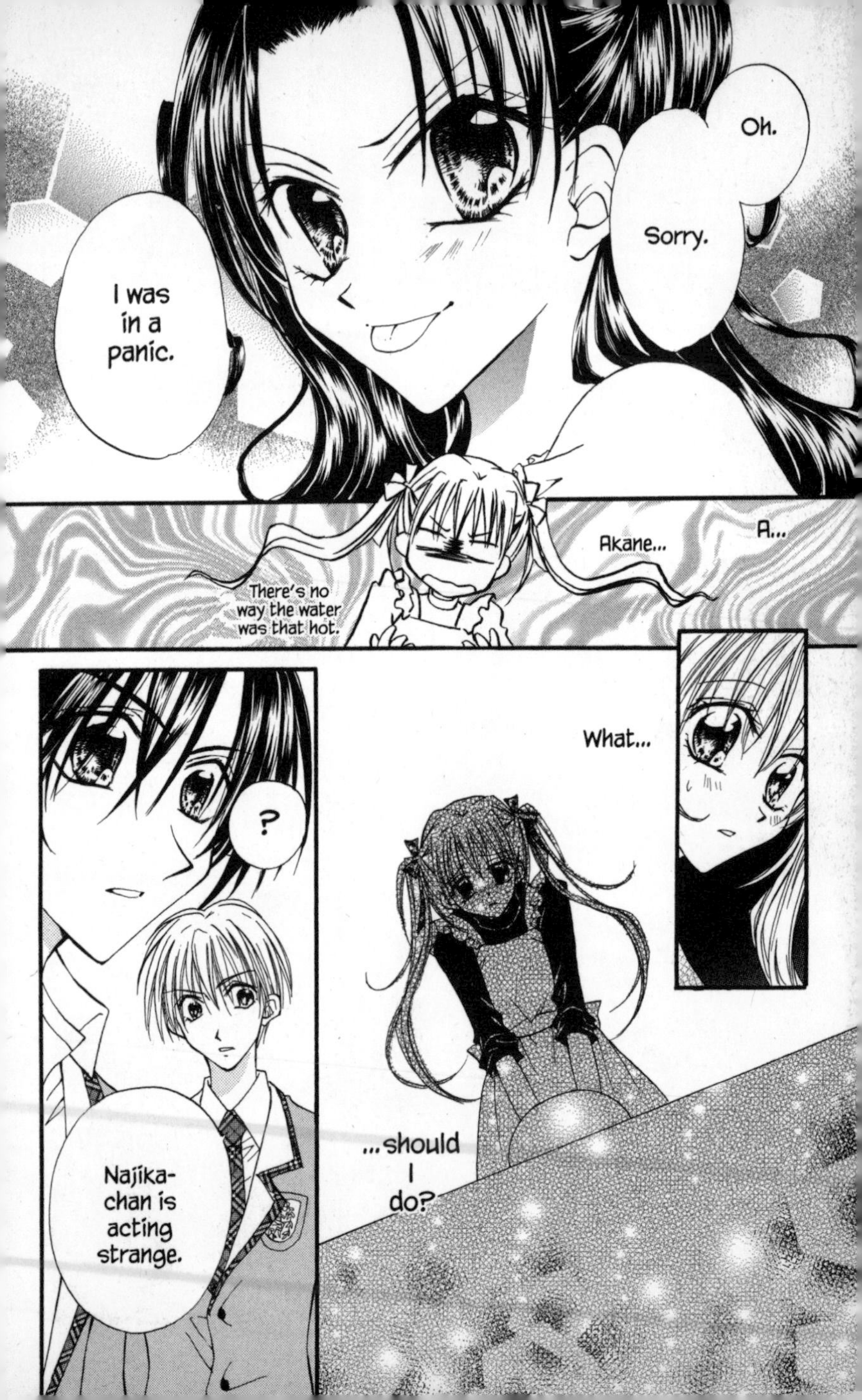
Oh.
Sorry.
I was in a panic.
A...
Akane...
There's no way the water was that hot.
What...
...should I do?
?
Najika-chan is acting strange.

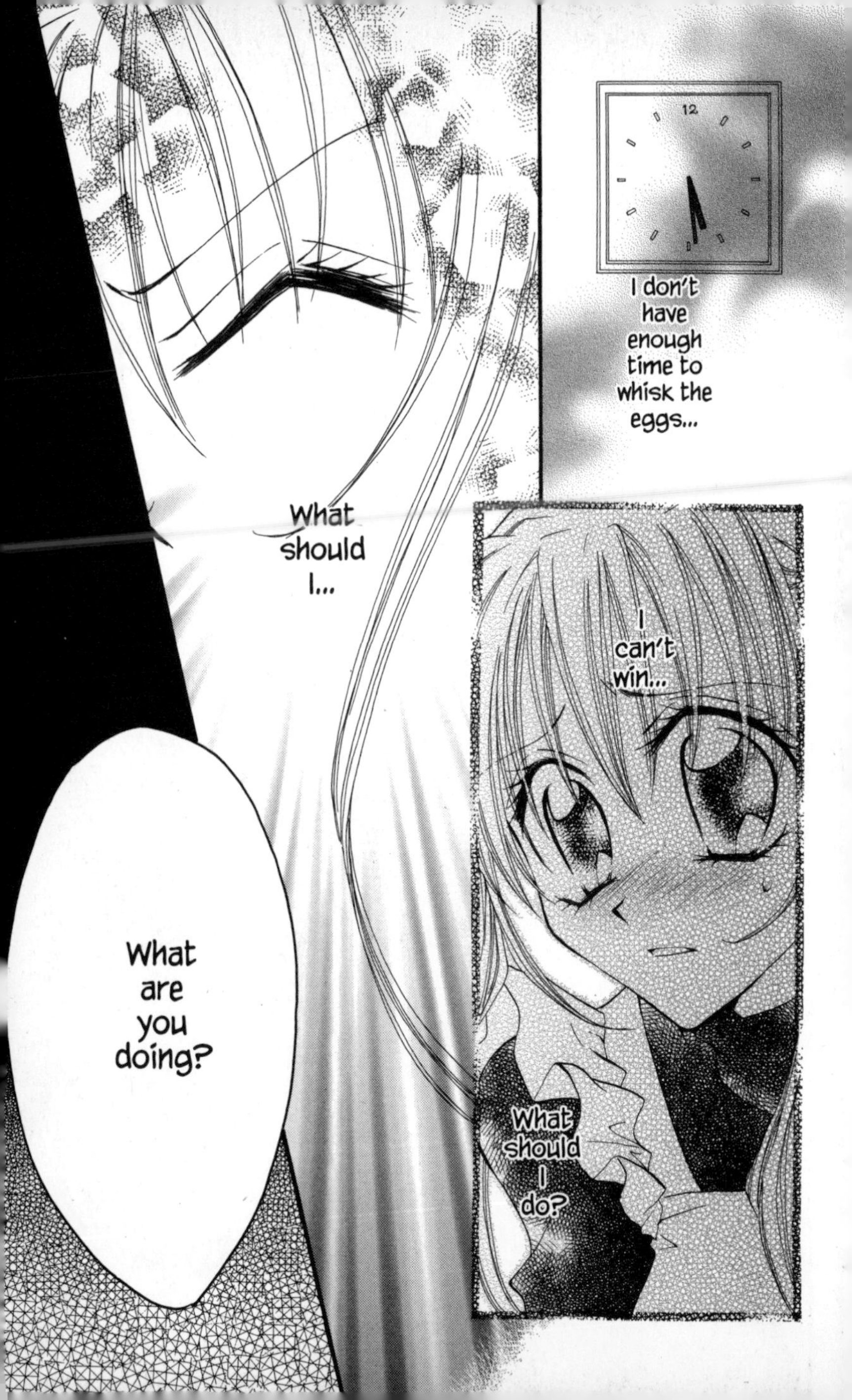
I don't have enough time to whisk the eggs...
I can't win...
What should I do?
What should I...
What are you doing?

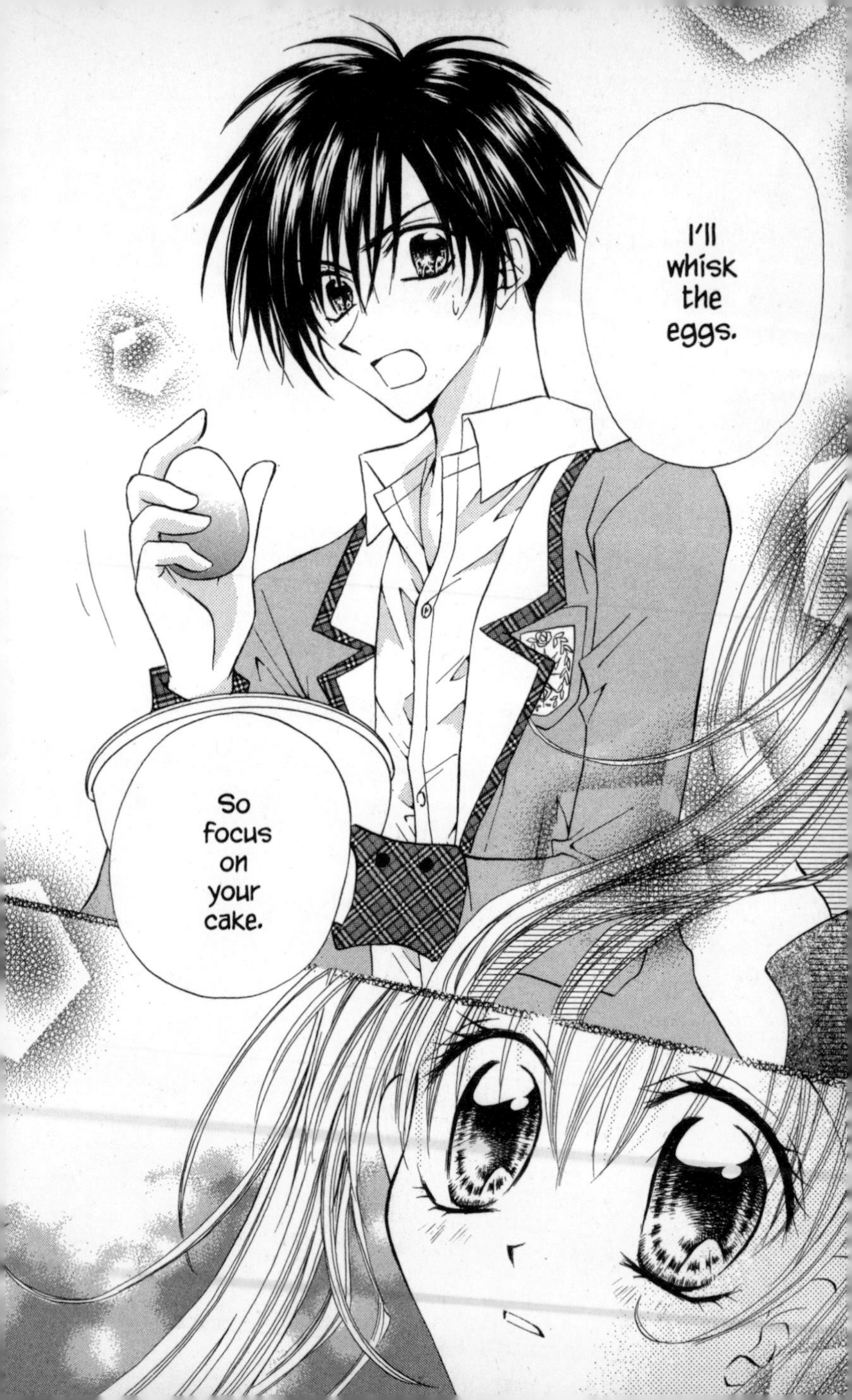
I'll whisk the eggs.
So focus on your cake.

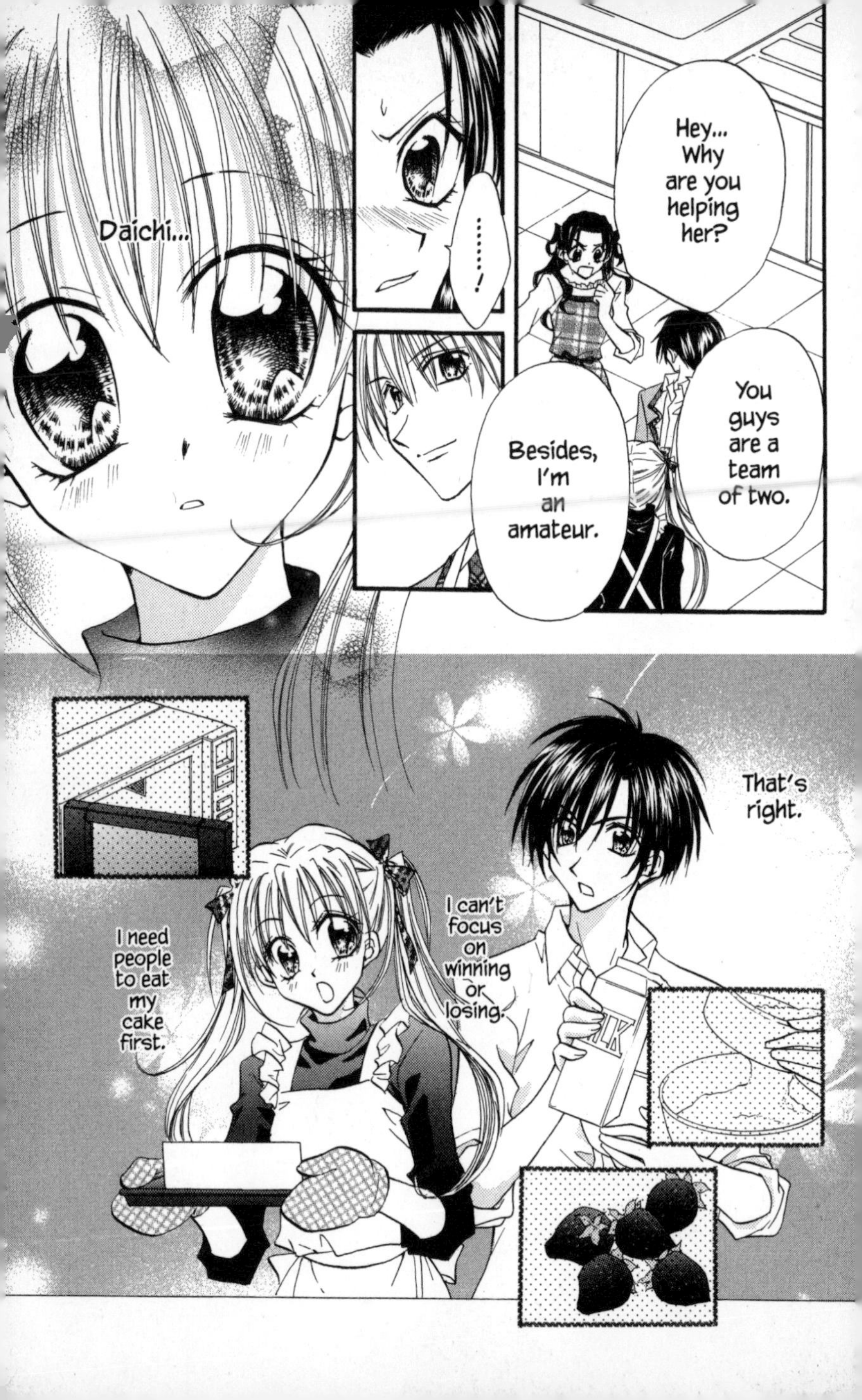
Hey... Why are you helping her?
You guys are a team of two.
......!
Besides, I'm an amateur.
Daichi...
That's right.
I can't focus on winning or losing.
I need people to eat my cake first.
MILK

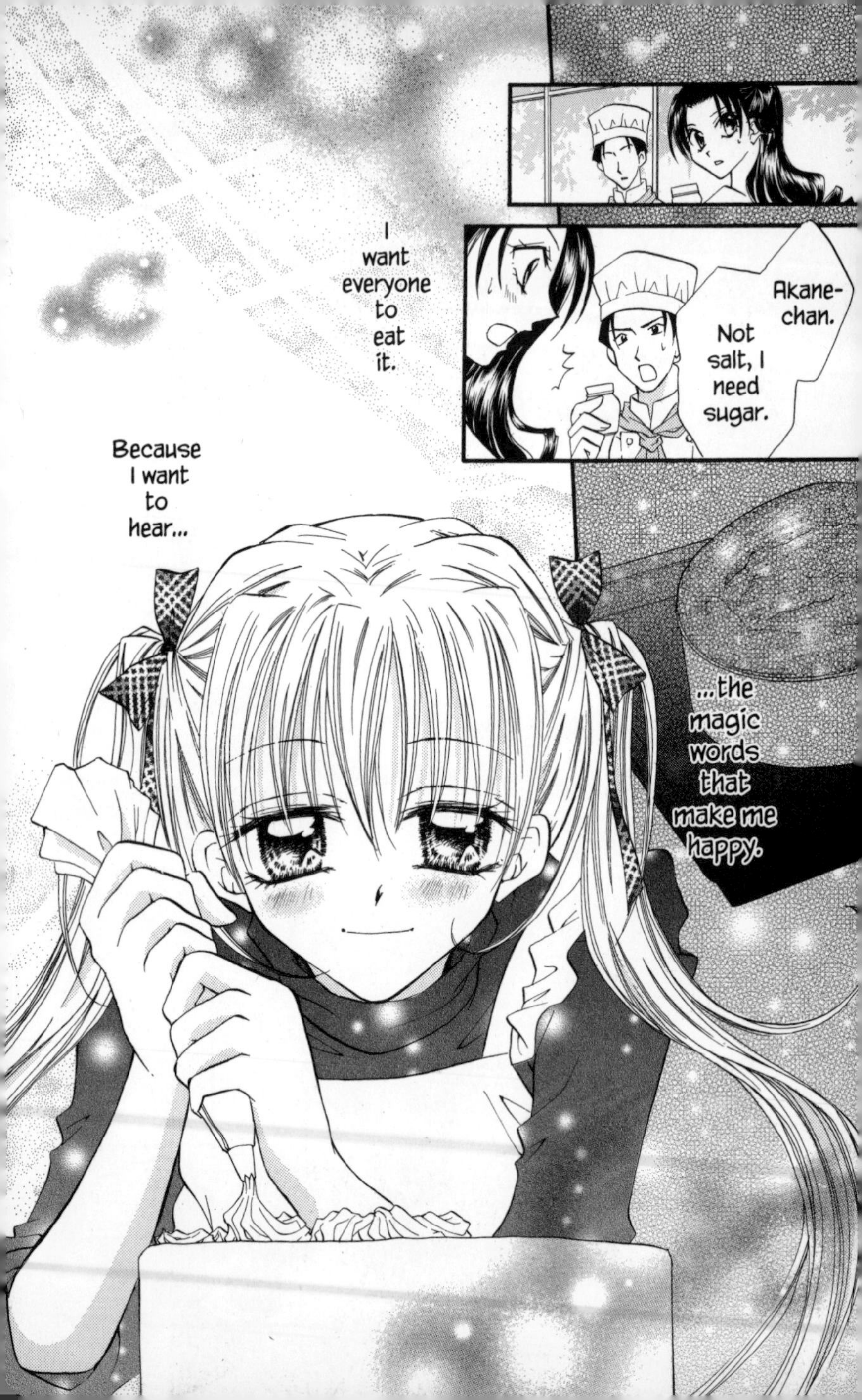
Akane-chan.
Not salt, I need sugar.
I want everyone to eat it.
Because I want to hear...
...the magic words that make me happy.

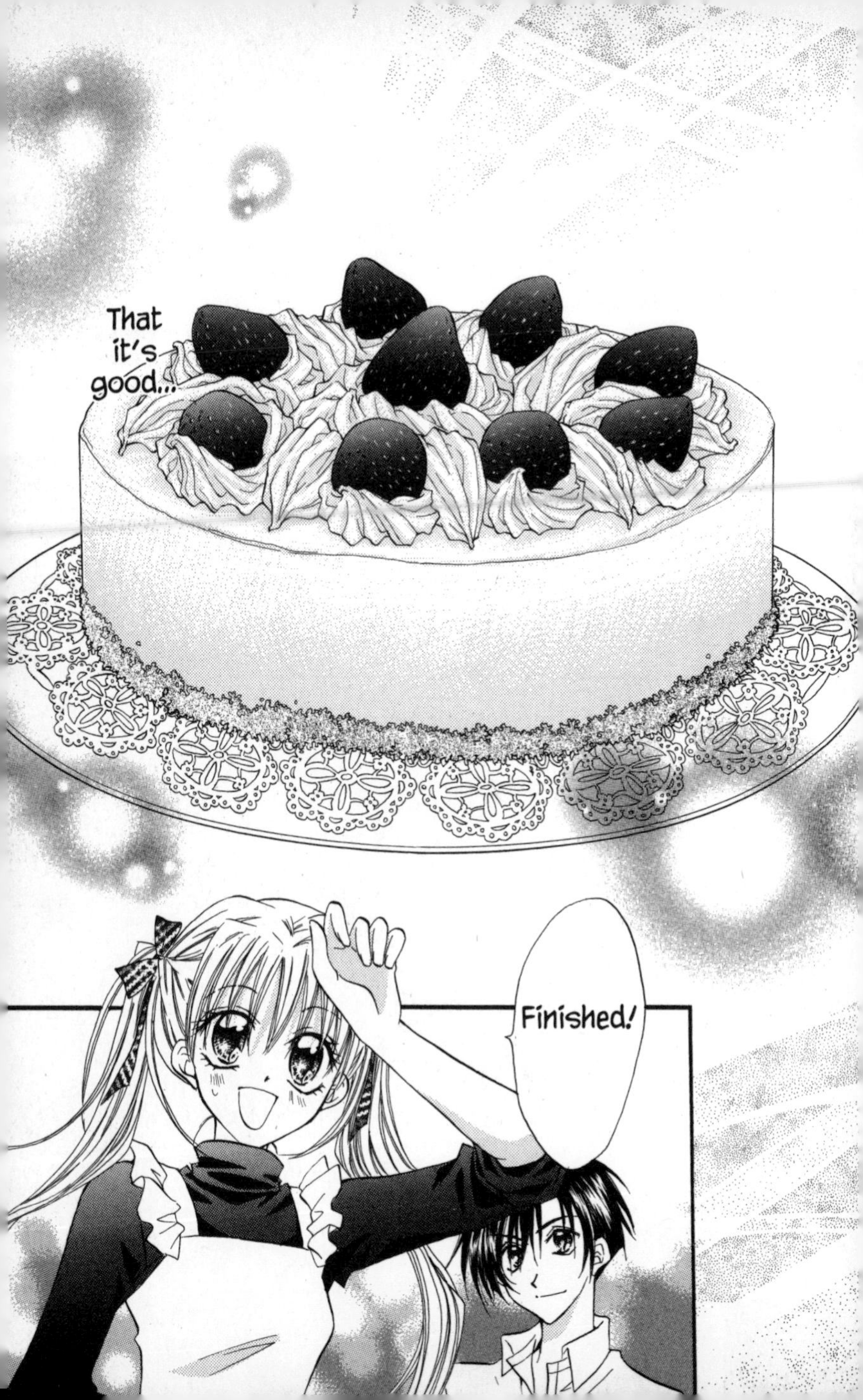
That it's good...
Finished!

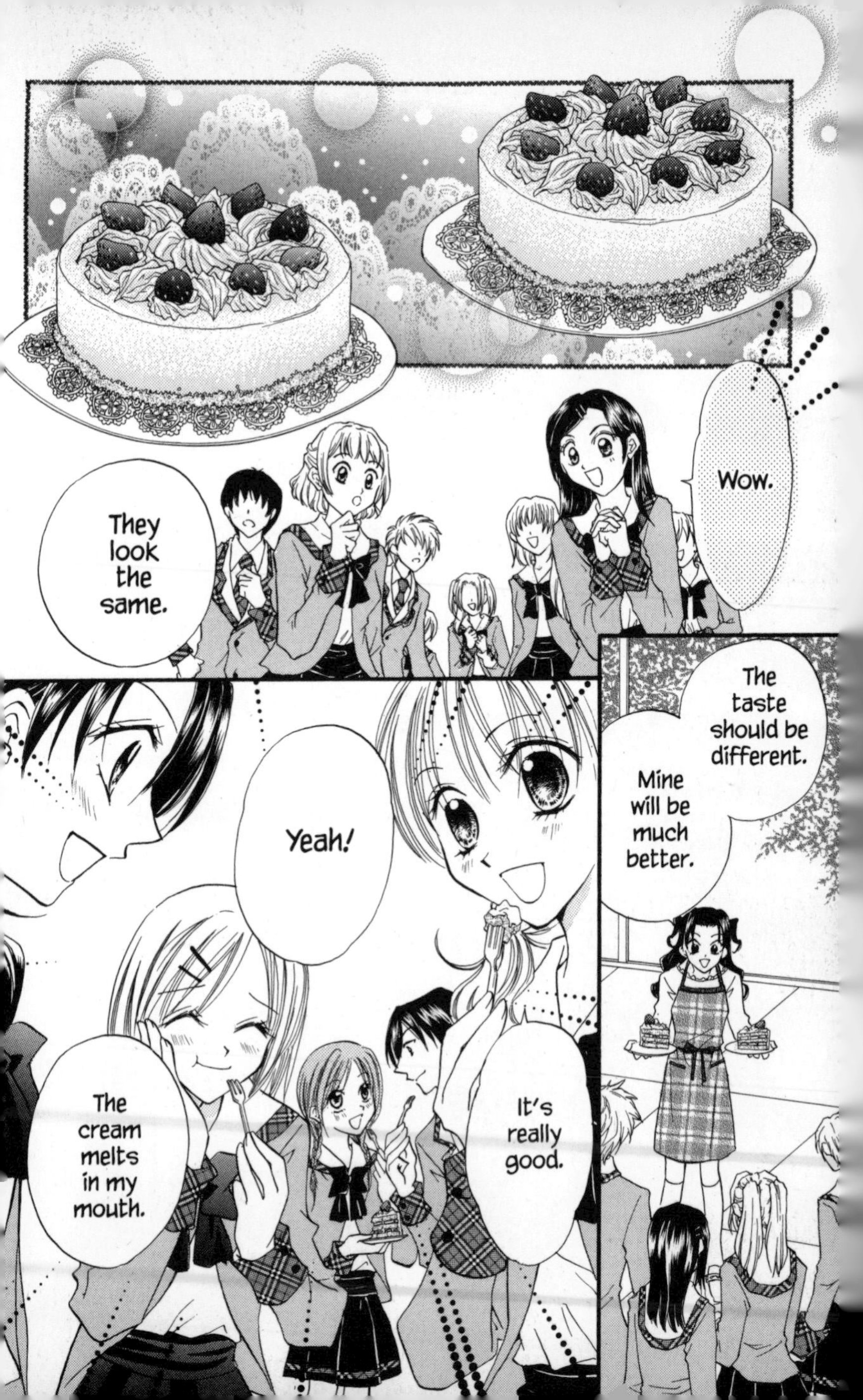
Wow.
They look the same.
The taste should be different.
Mine will be much better.
Yeah!
It's really good.
The cream melts in my mouth.

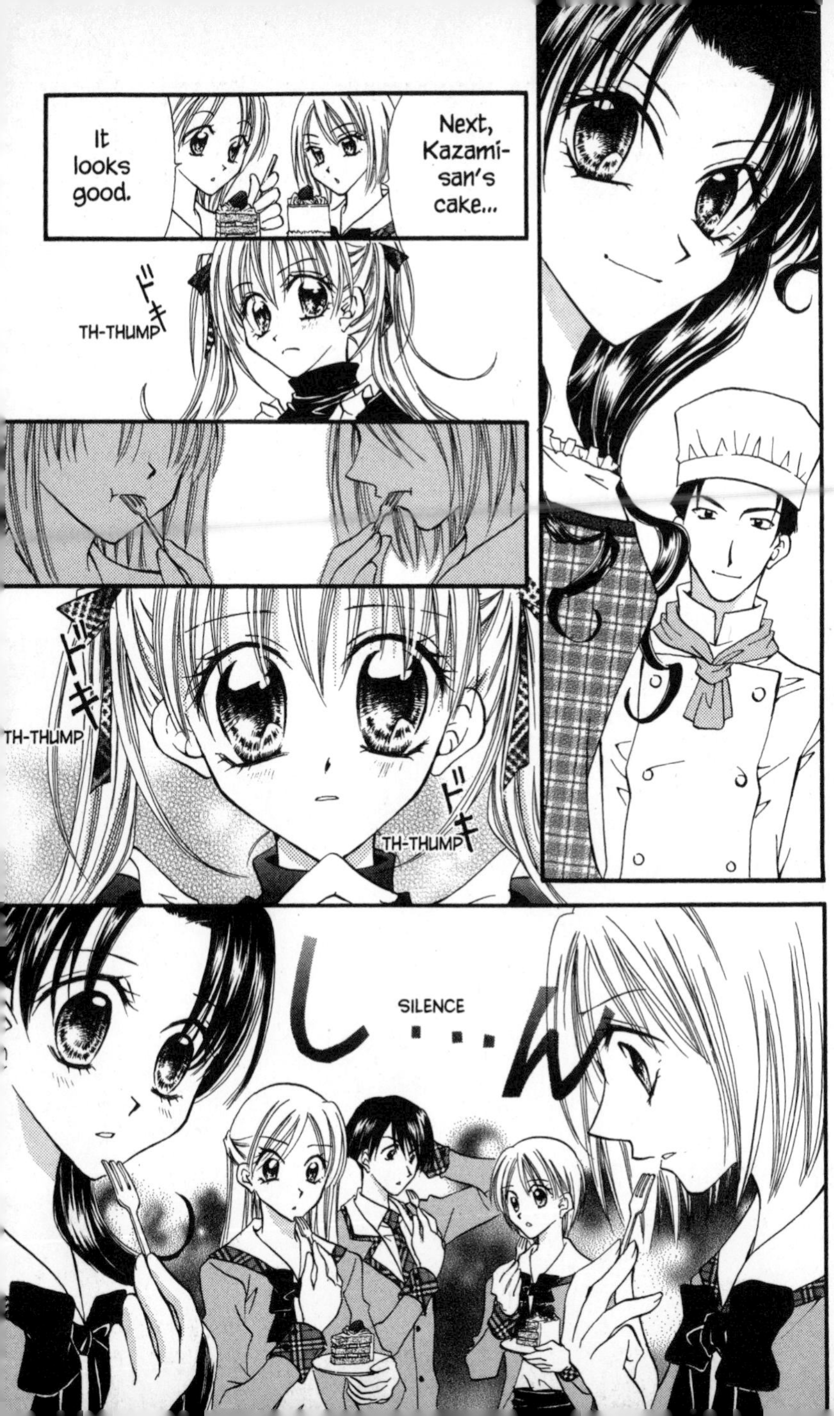
Next, Kazami-san's cake...
It looks good.
ドキ
TH-THUMP
ドキ
TH-THUMP
ドキ
TH-THUMP
し…ん
SILENCE

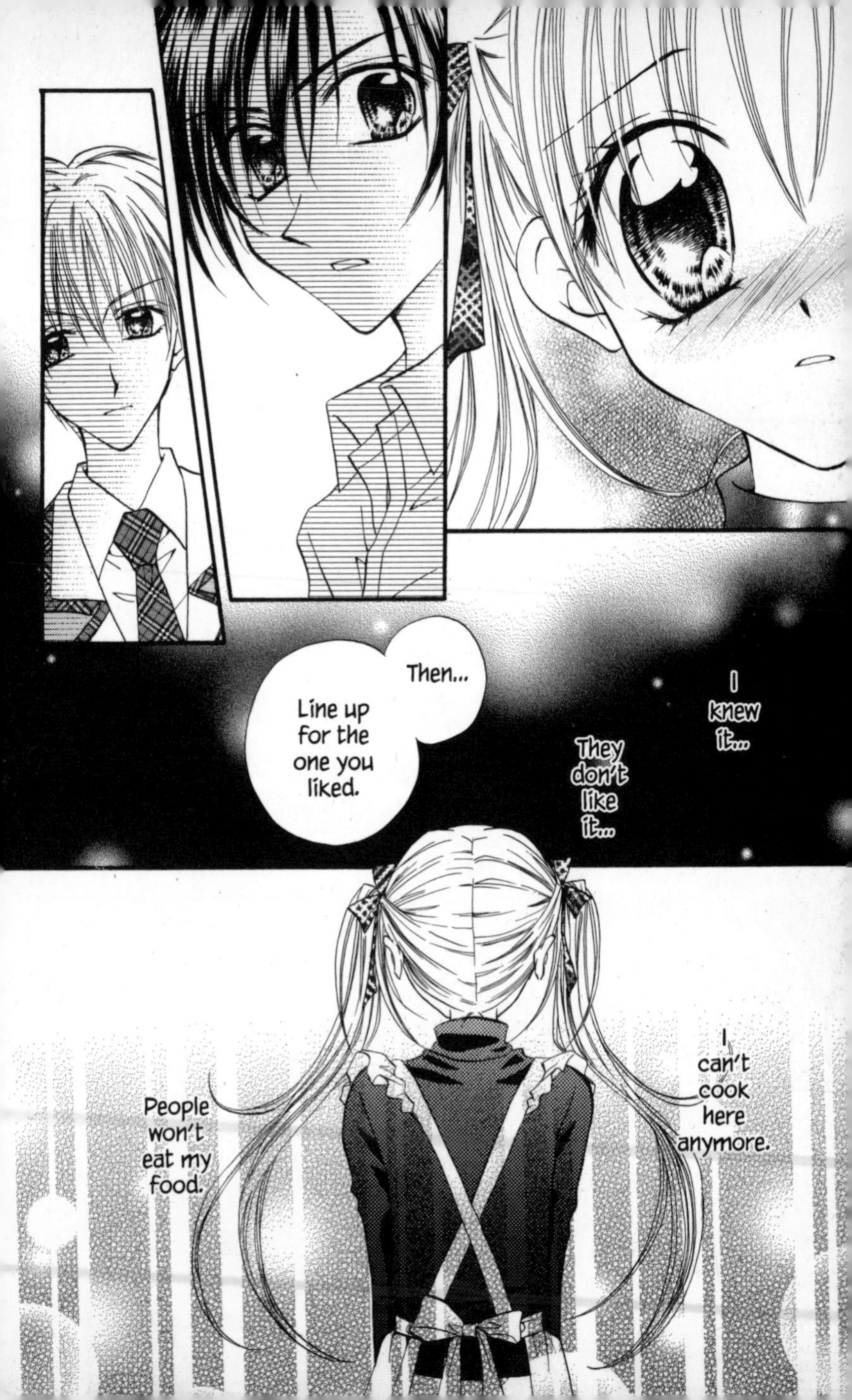
I knew it...
They don't like it...
Then... Line up for the one you liked.
I can't cook here anymore.
People won't eat my food.

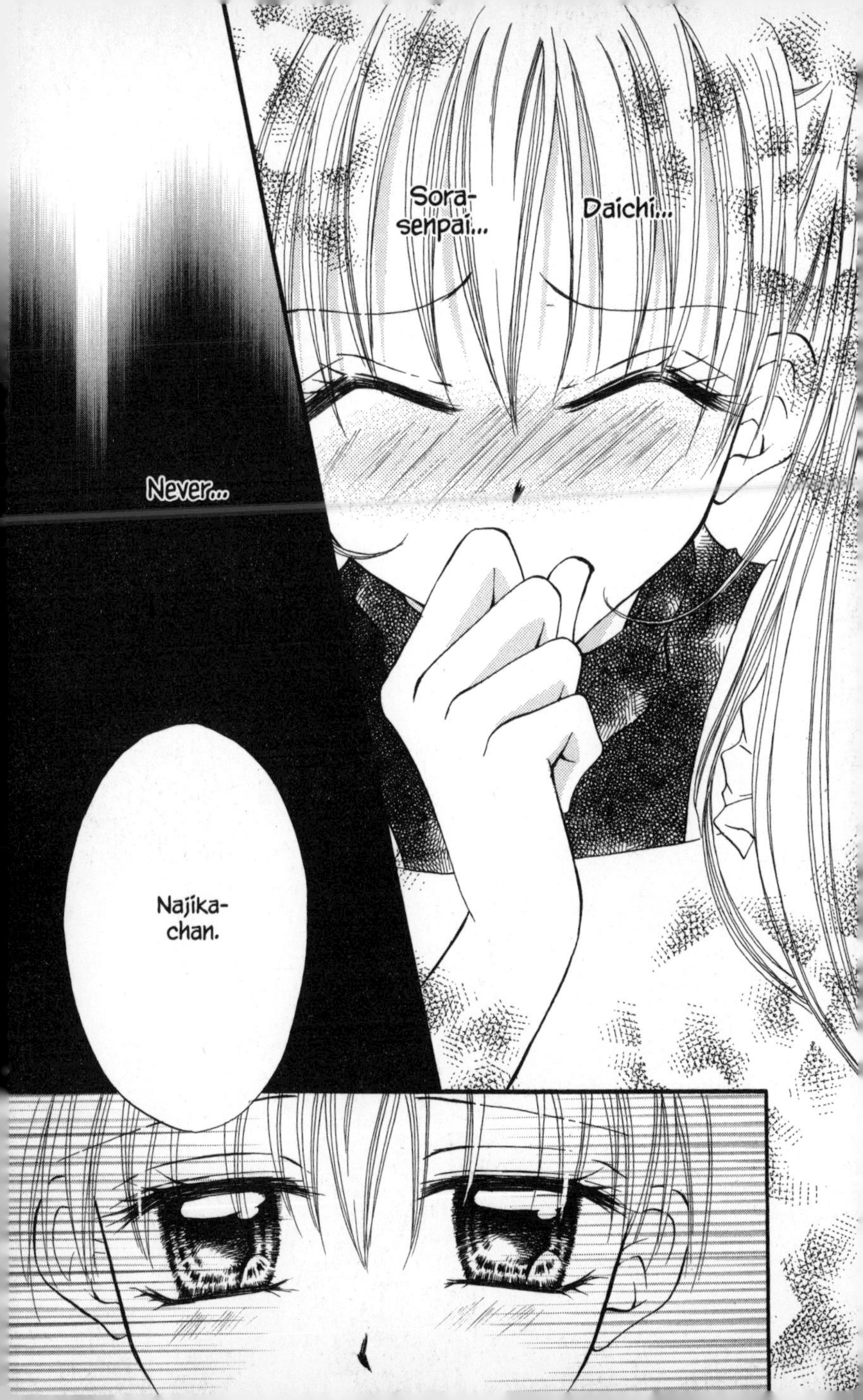
Daichi...
Sora-senpai...
Never...
Najika-chan.

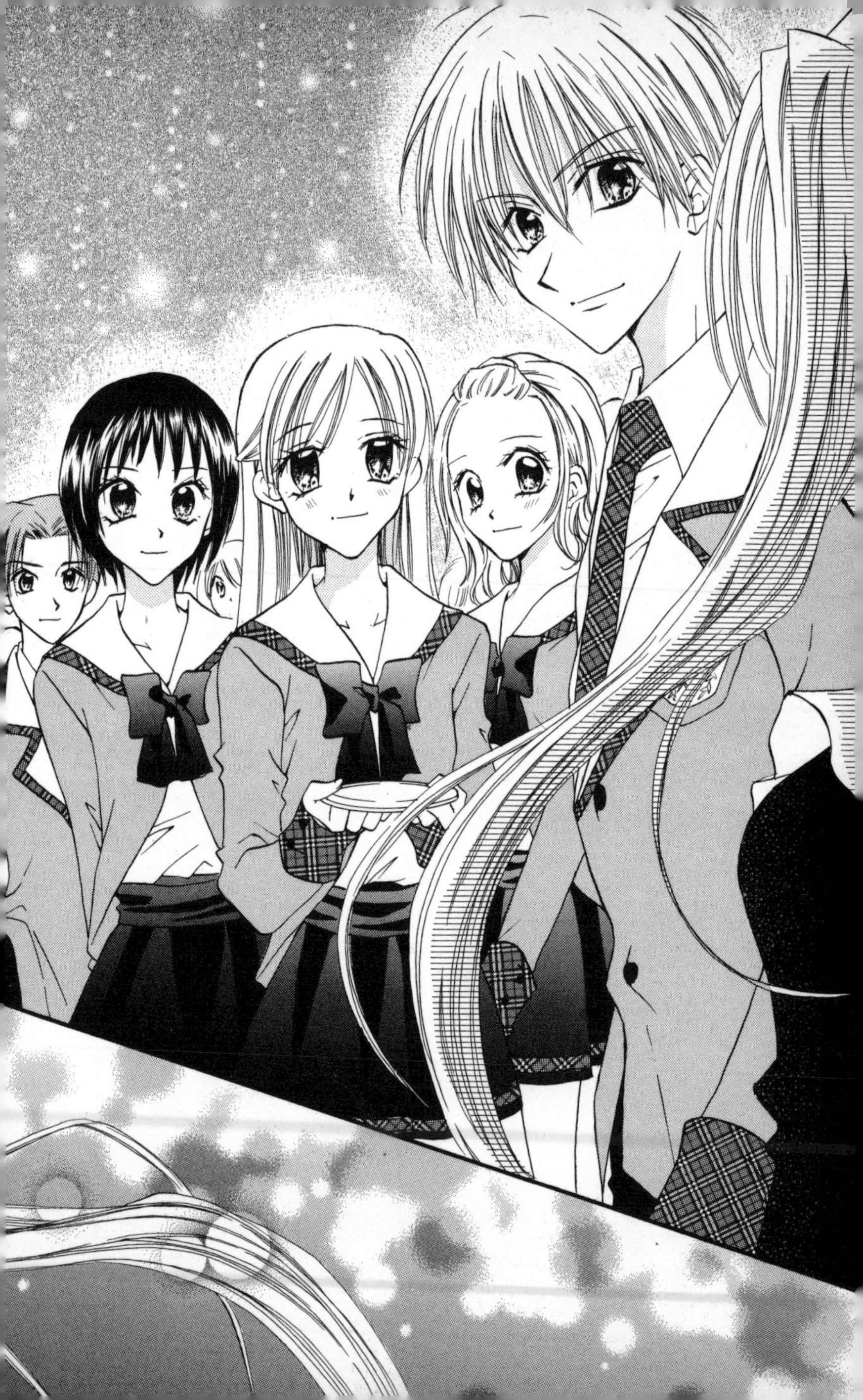

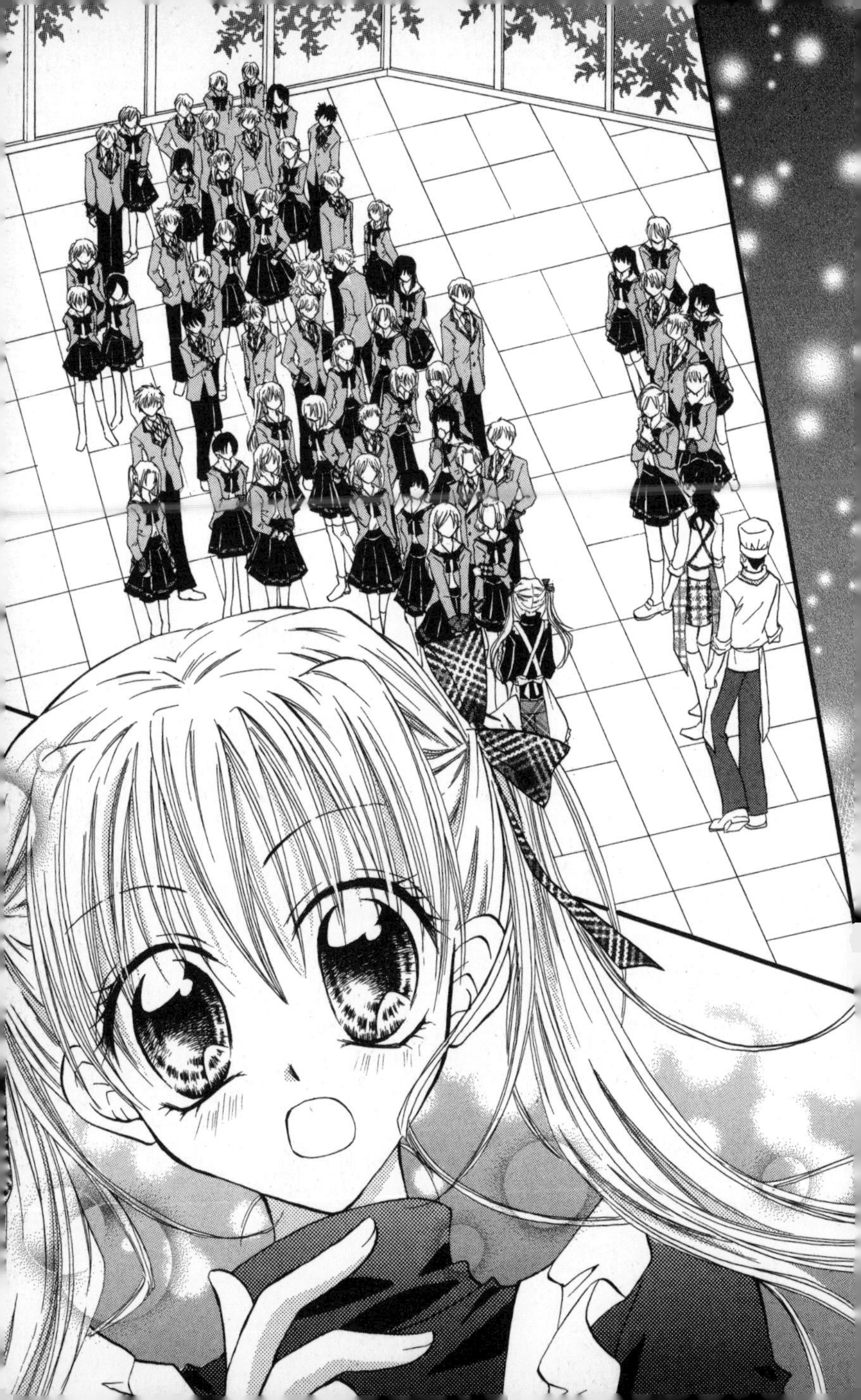

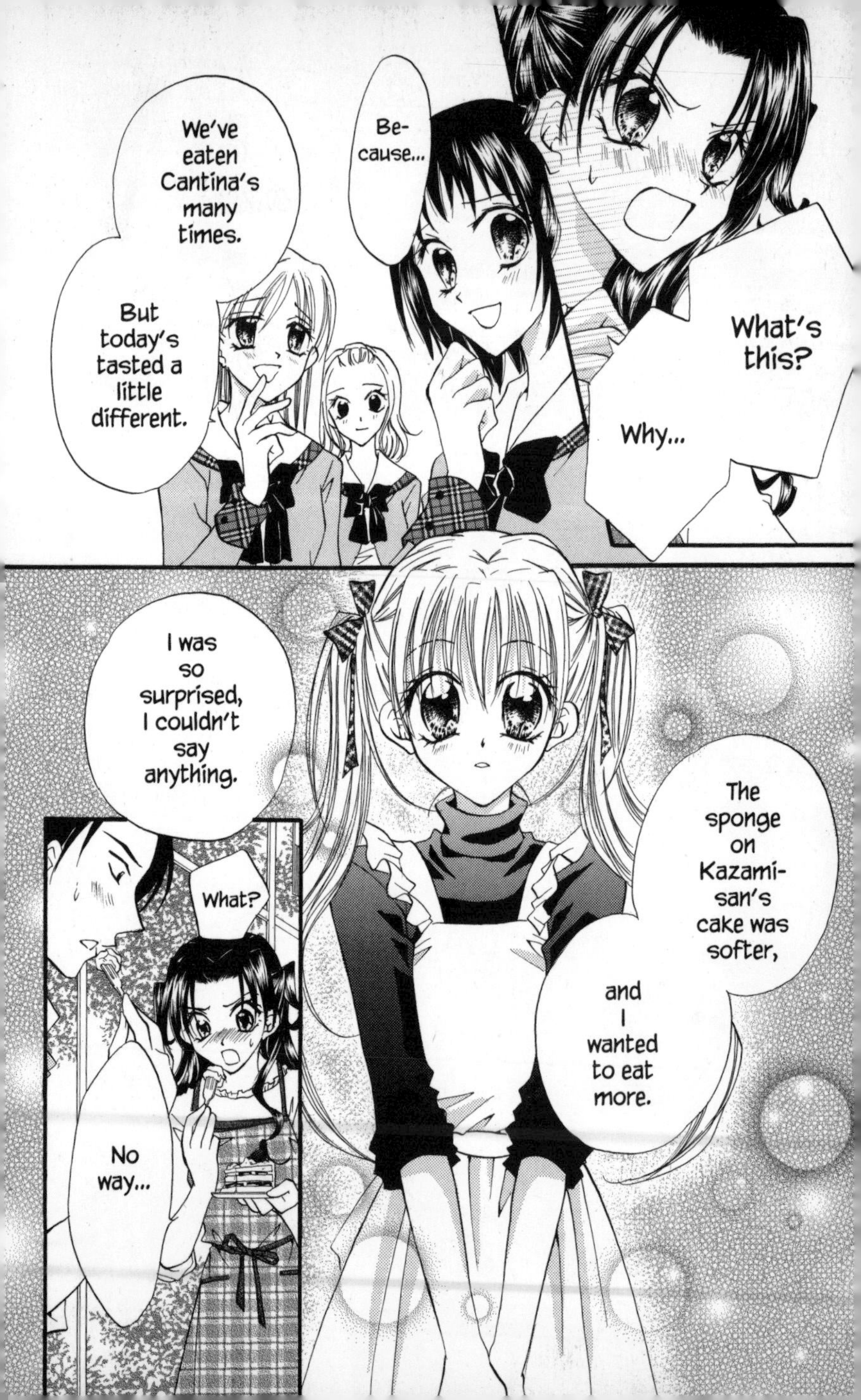
What's this?
Why...
Be- cause...
We've eaten Cantina's many times.
But today's tasted a little different.
I was so surprised, I couldn't say anything.
The sponge on Kazami-san's cake was softer,
and I wanted to eat more.
What?
No way...

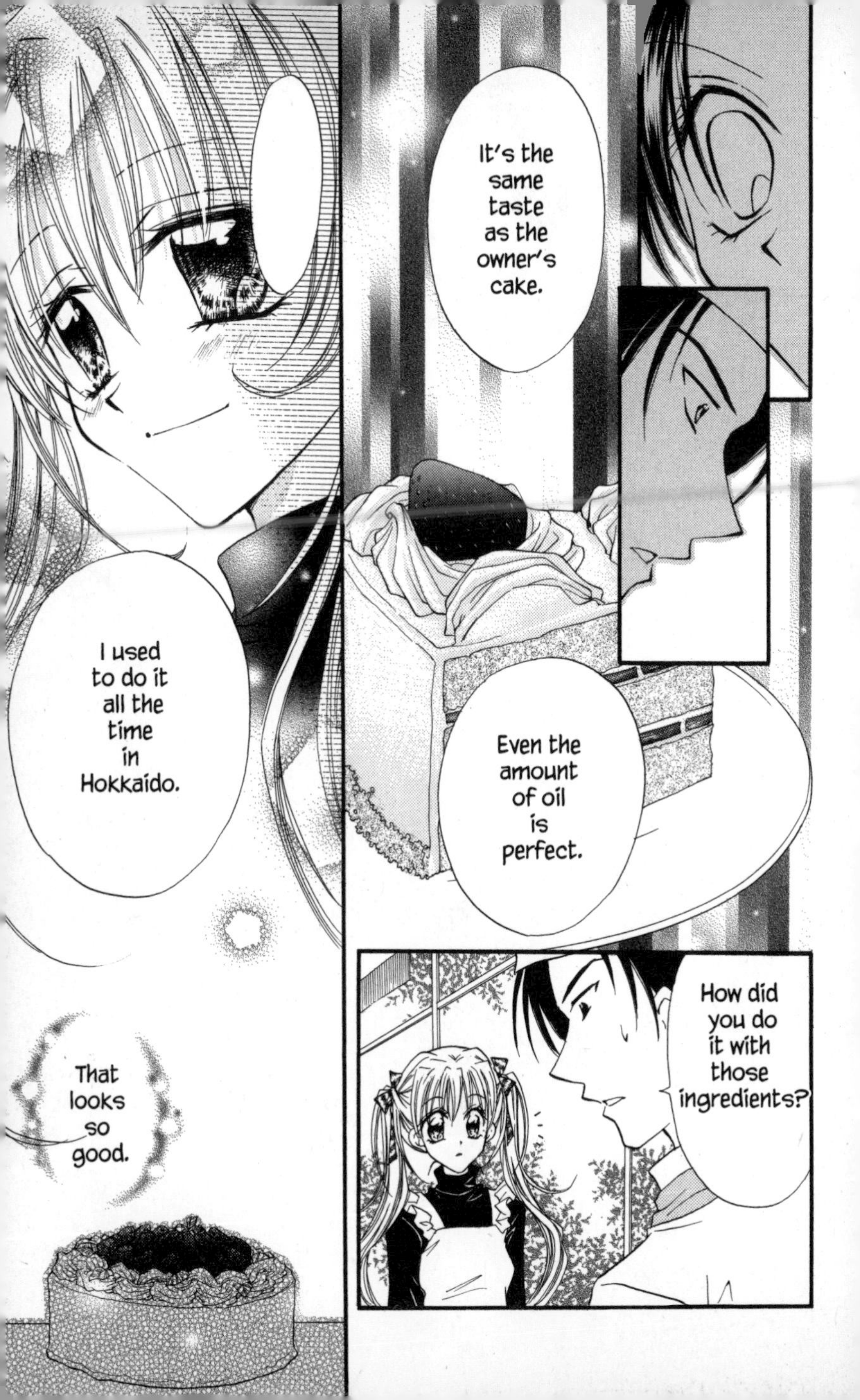
It's the same taste as the owner's cake.
Even the amount of oil is perfect.
How did you do it with those ingredients?
I used to do it all the time in Hokkaido.
That looks so good.

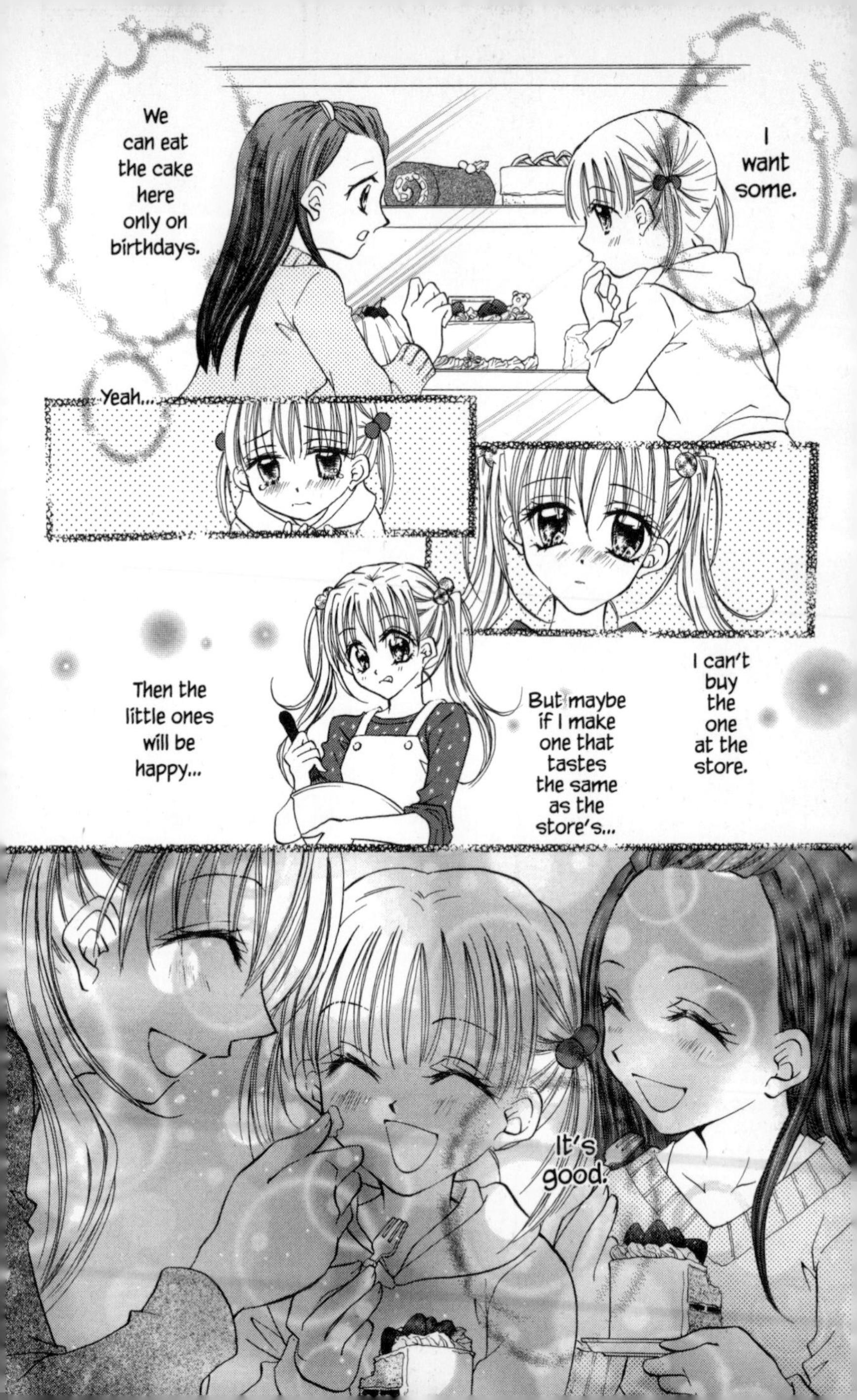
I want some.
We can eat the cake here only on birthdays.
Yeah...
I can't buy the one at the store.
But maybe if I make one that tastes the same as the store's...
Then the little ones will be happy...
It's good.

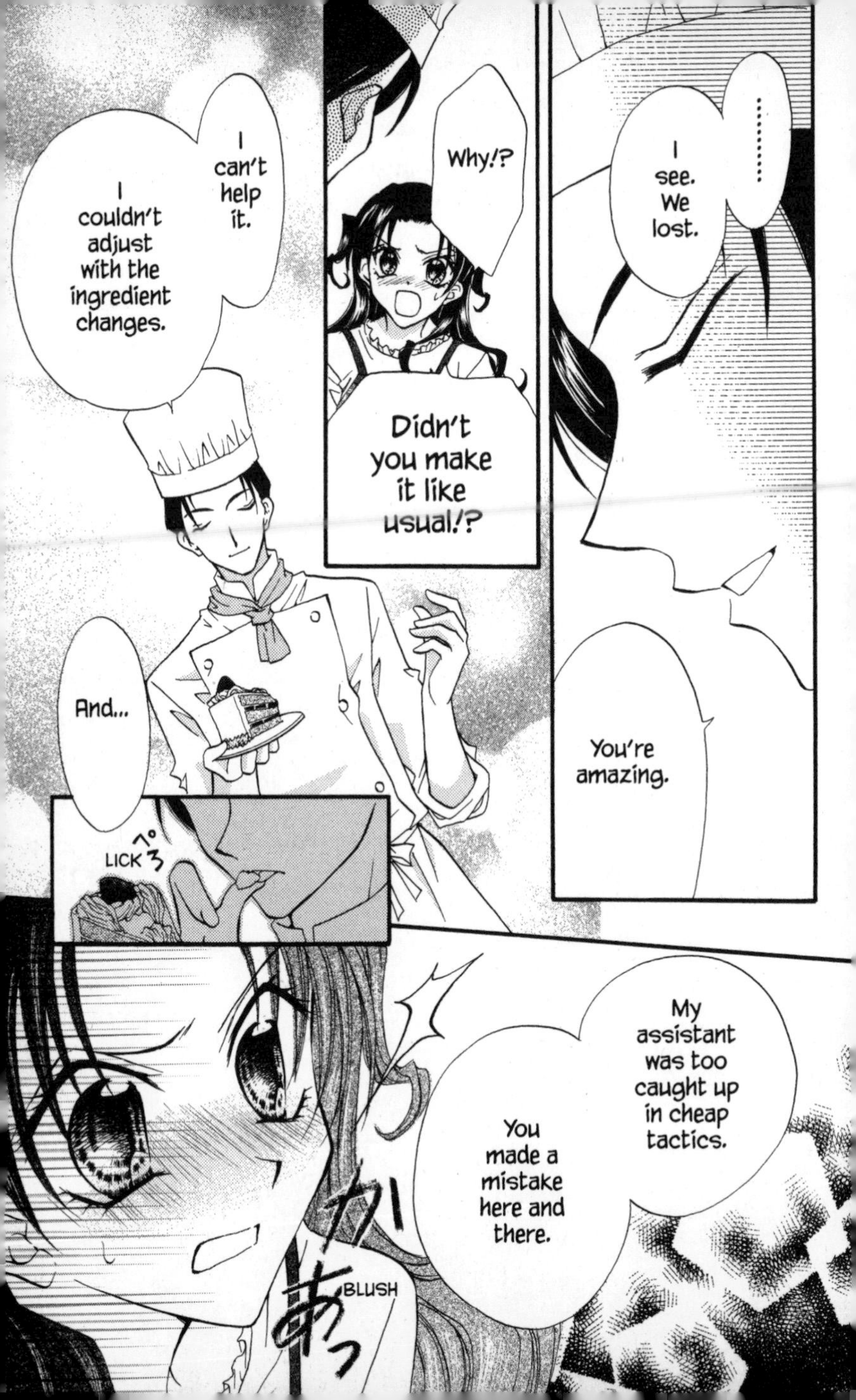
......
I see. We lost.
You're amazing.
Why!?
Didn't you make it like usual!?
I can't help it.
I couldn't adjust with the ingredient changes.
And...
LICK
My assistant was too caught up in cheap tactics.
You made a mistake here and there.
BLUSH

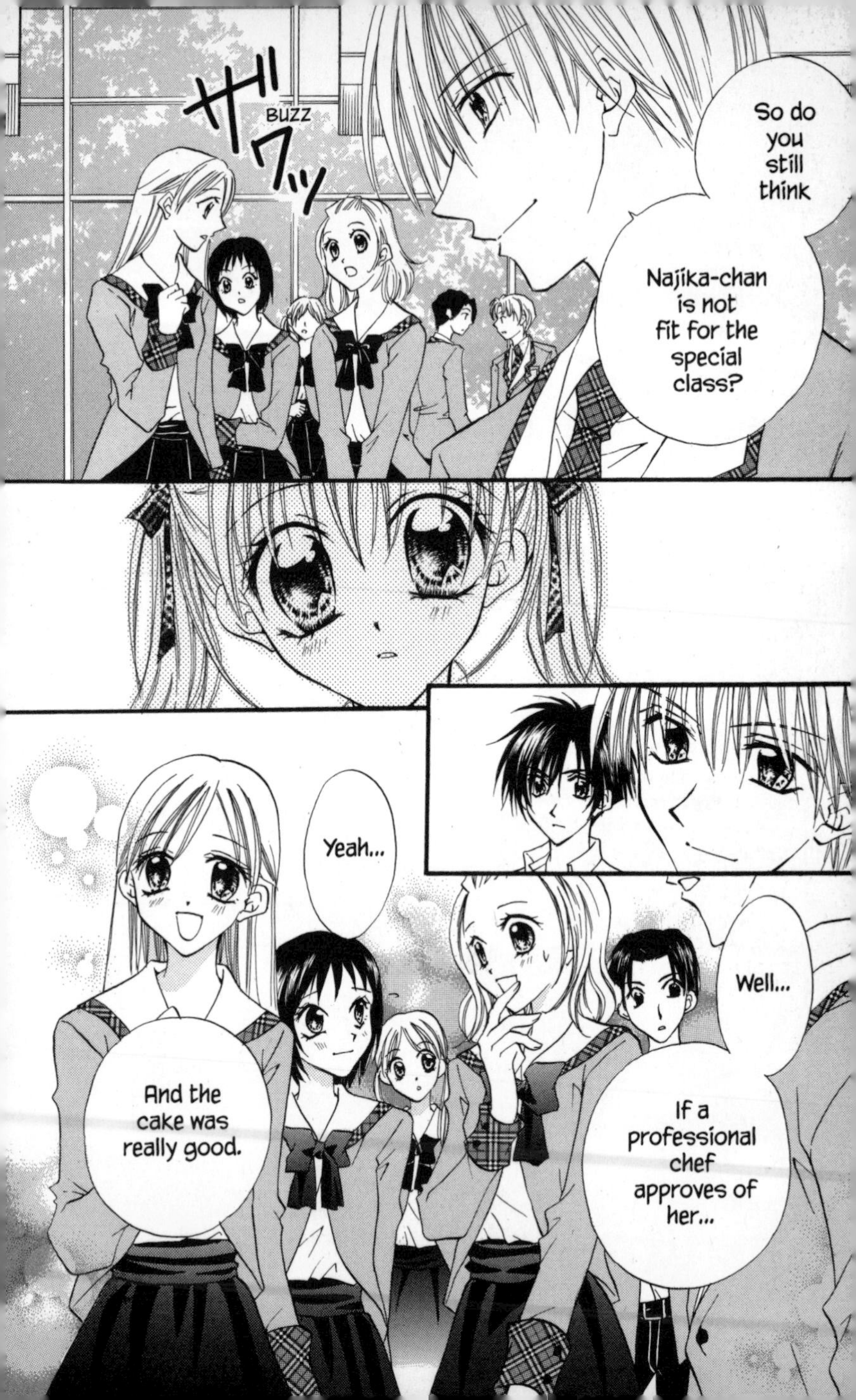
So do you still think
Najika-chan is not fit for the special class?
ザワッ
BUZZ
Well...
If a professional chef approves of her...
Yeah...
And the cake was really good.

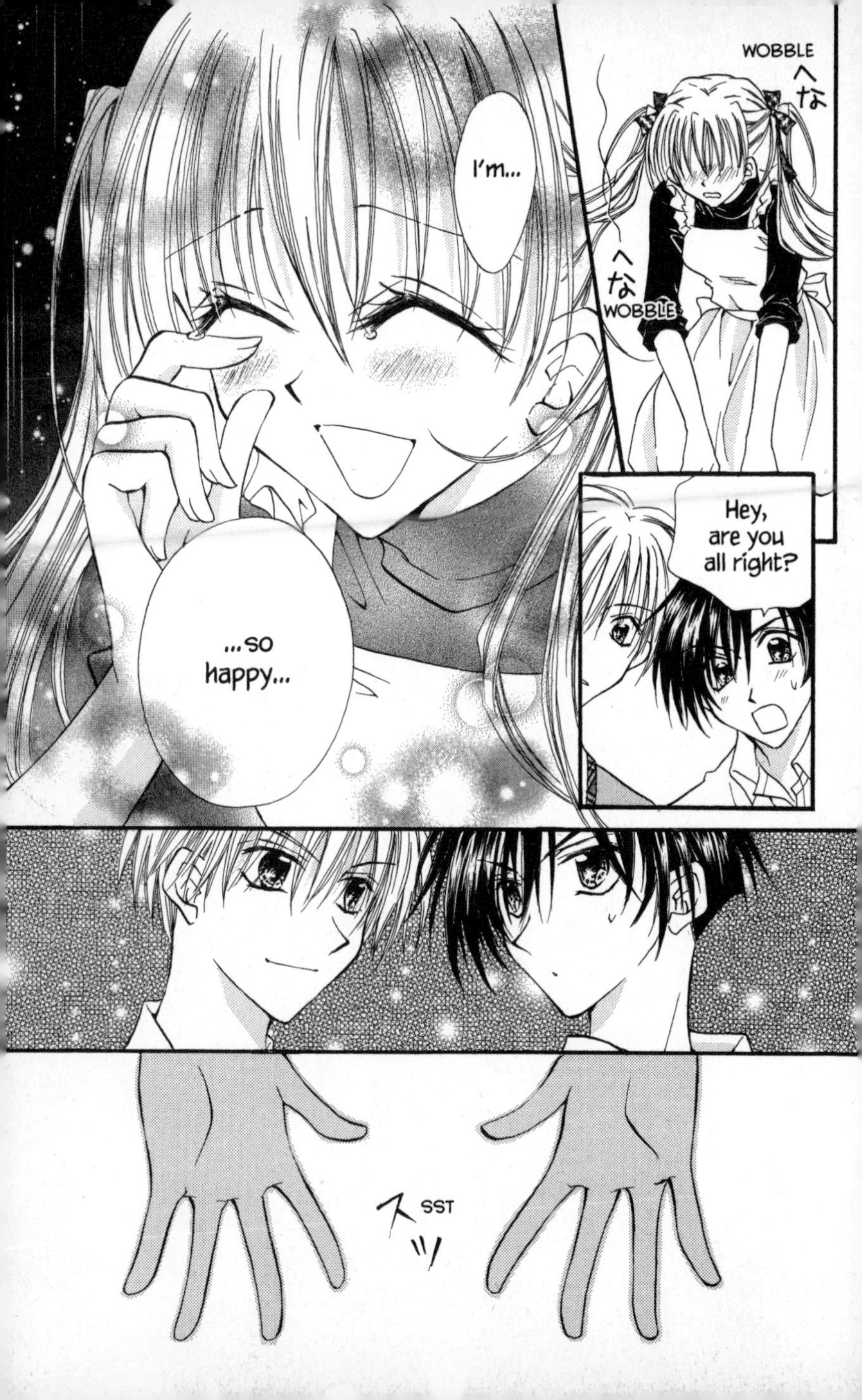
WOBBLE
へな
へな
WOBBLE
Hey, are you all right?
I'm...
...so happy...
スッ
SST

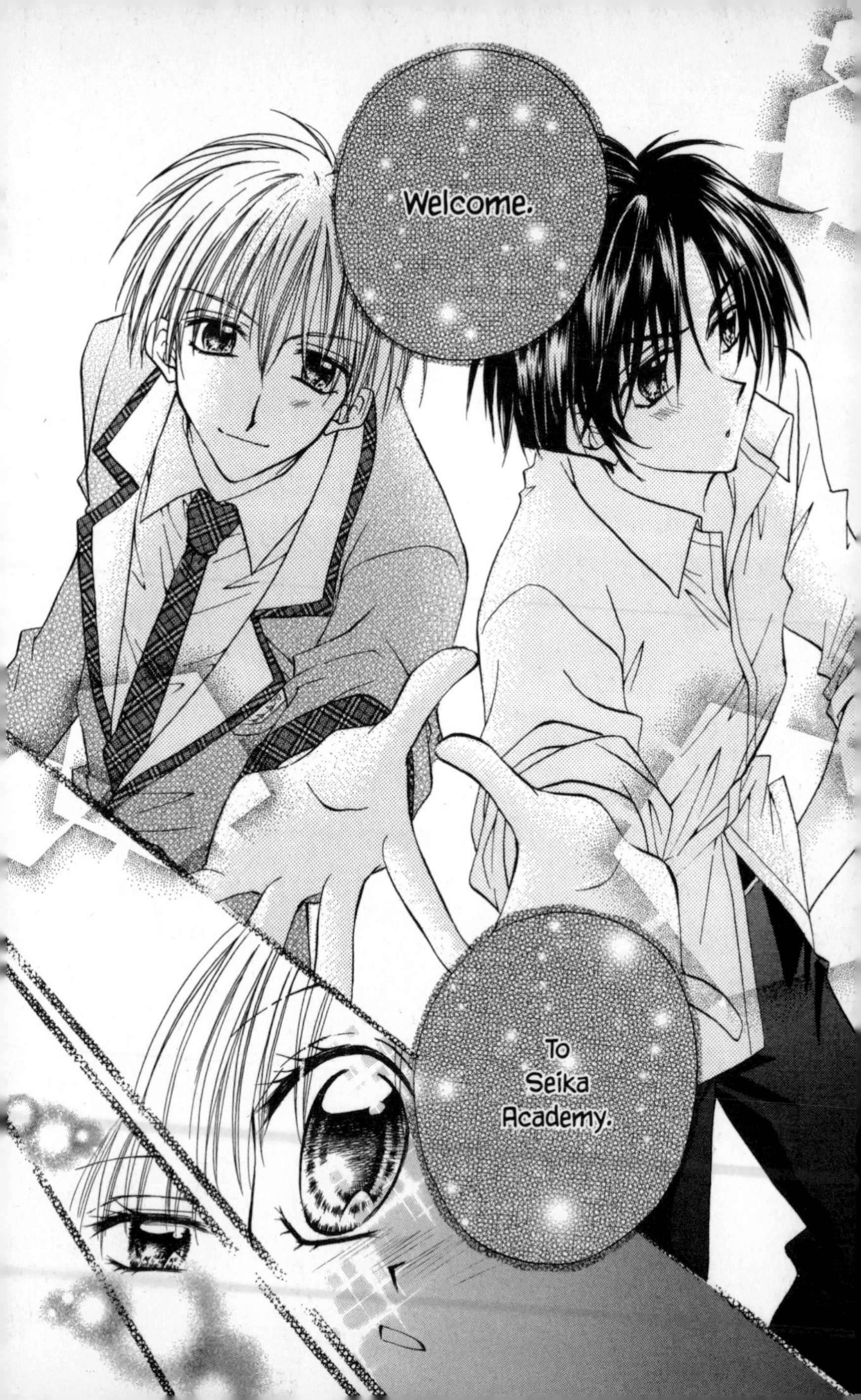
Welcome.
To Seika Academy.

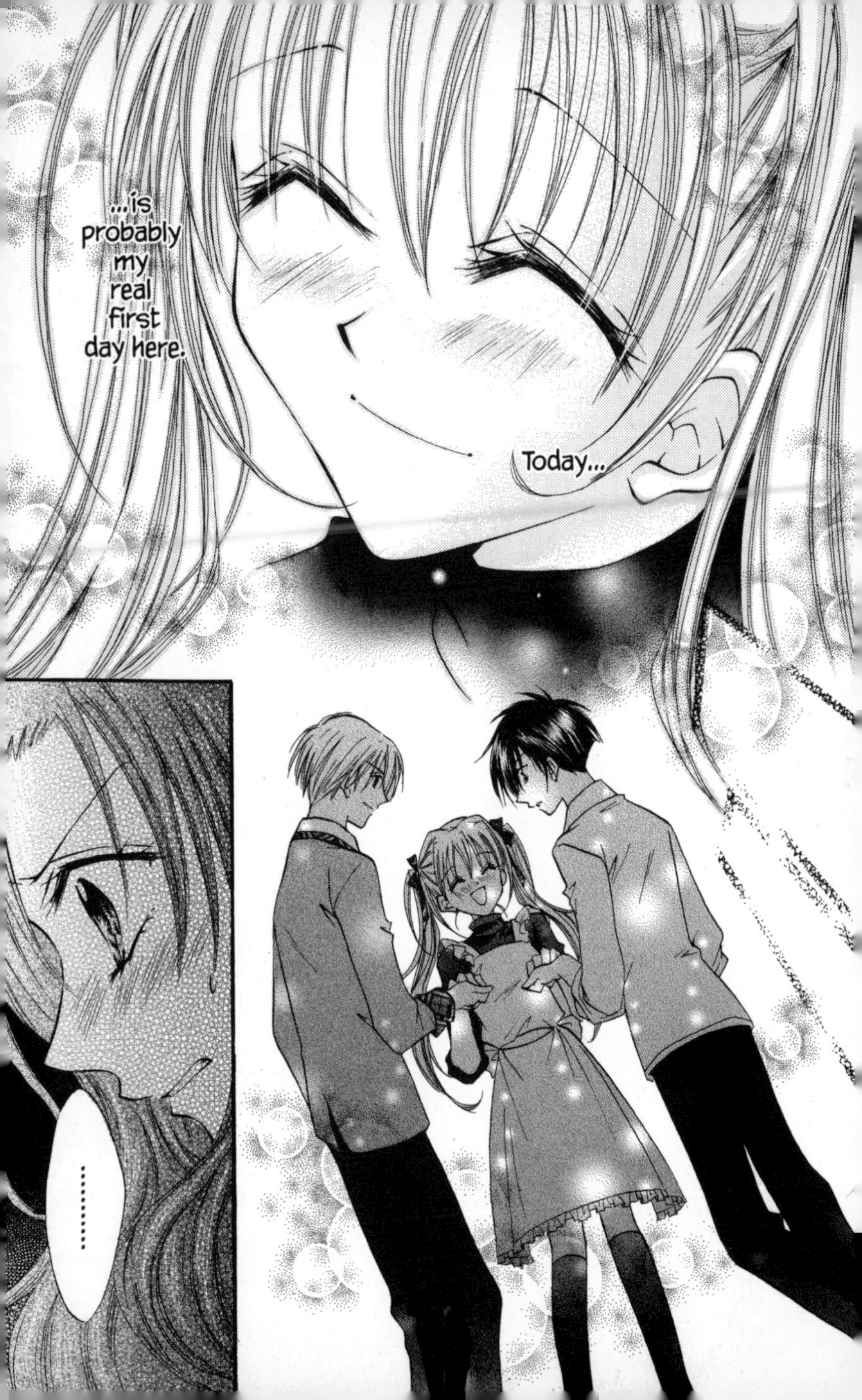
Today...
...is probably my real first day here.
....

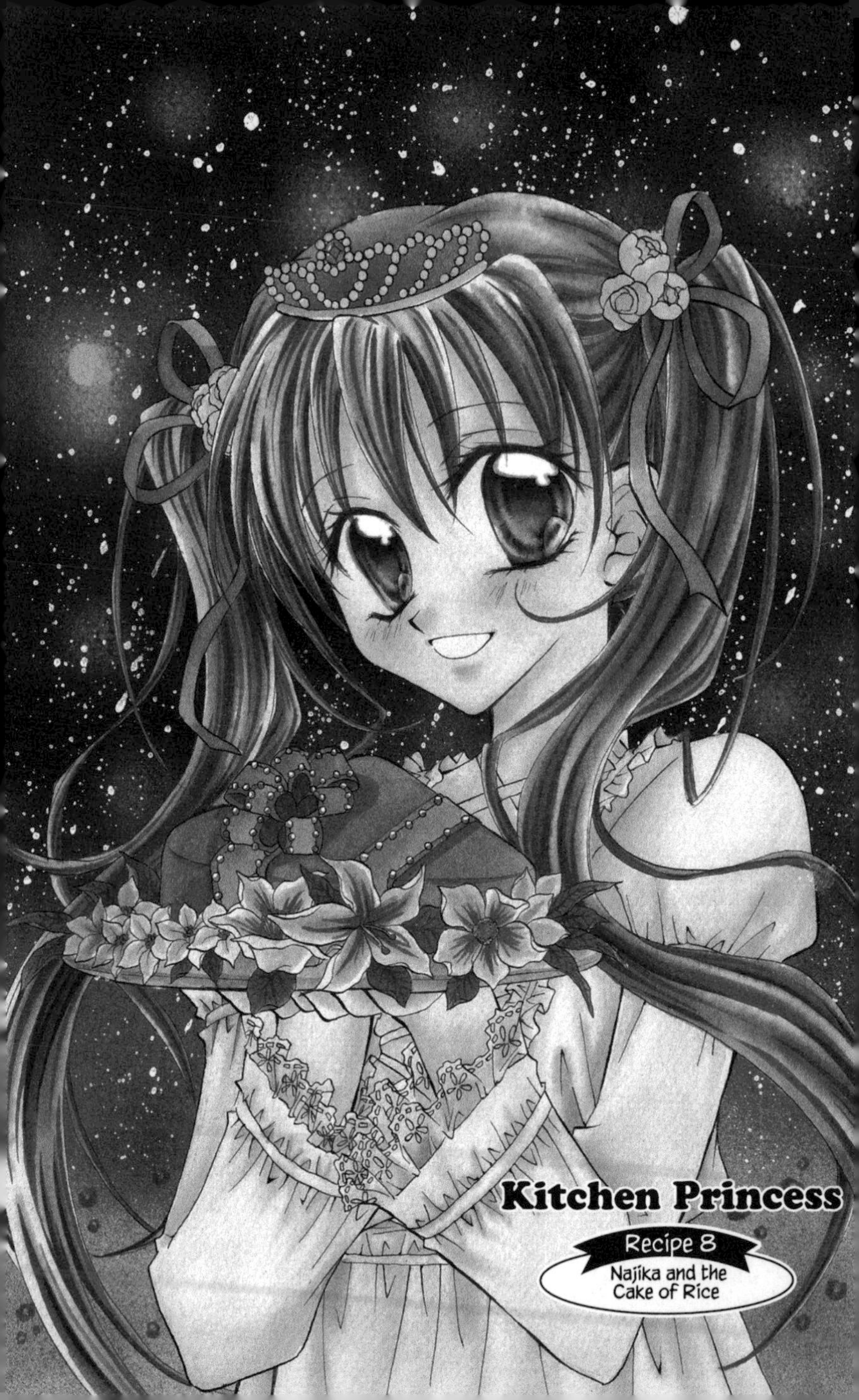
Kitchen Princess
Recipe 8
Najika and the Cake of Rice

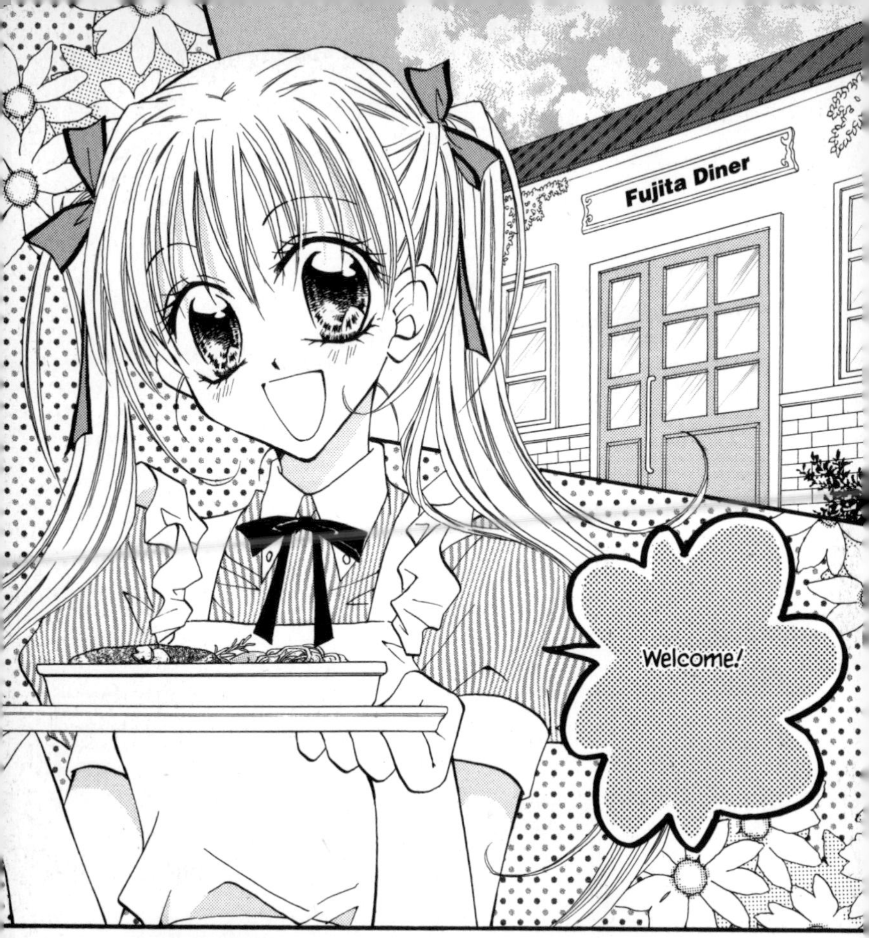
Fujita Diner
Welcome!

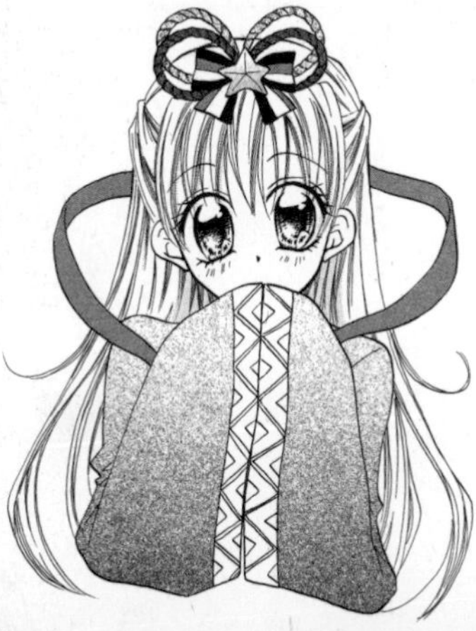

About Recipe 8's Splash Page

I had a really hard time getting the color right on the cake Najika is holding. And I didn't like the art as much until I put in the background. The background finished it off nicely. I think it was my first time drawing an expression like this, too...

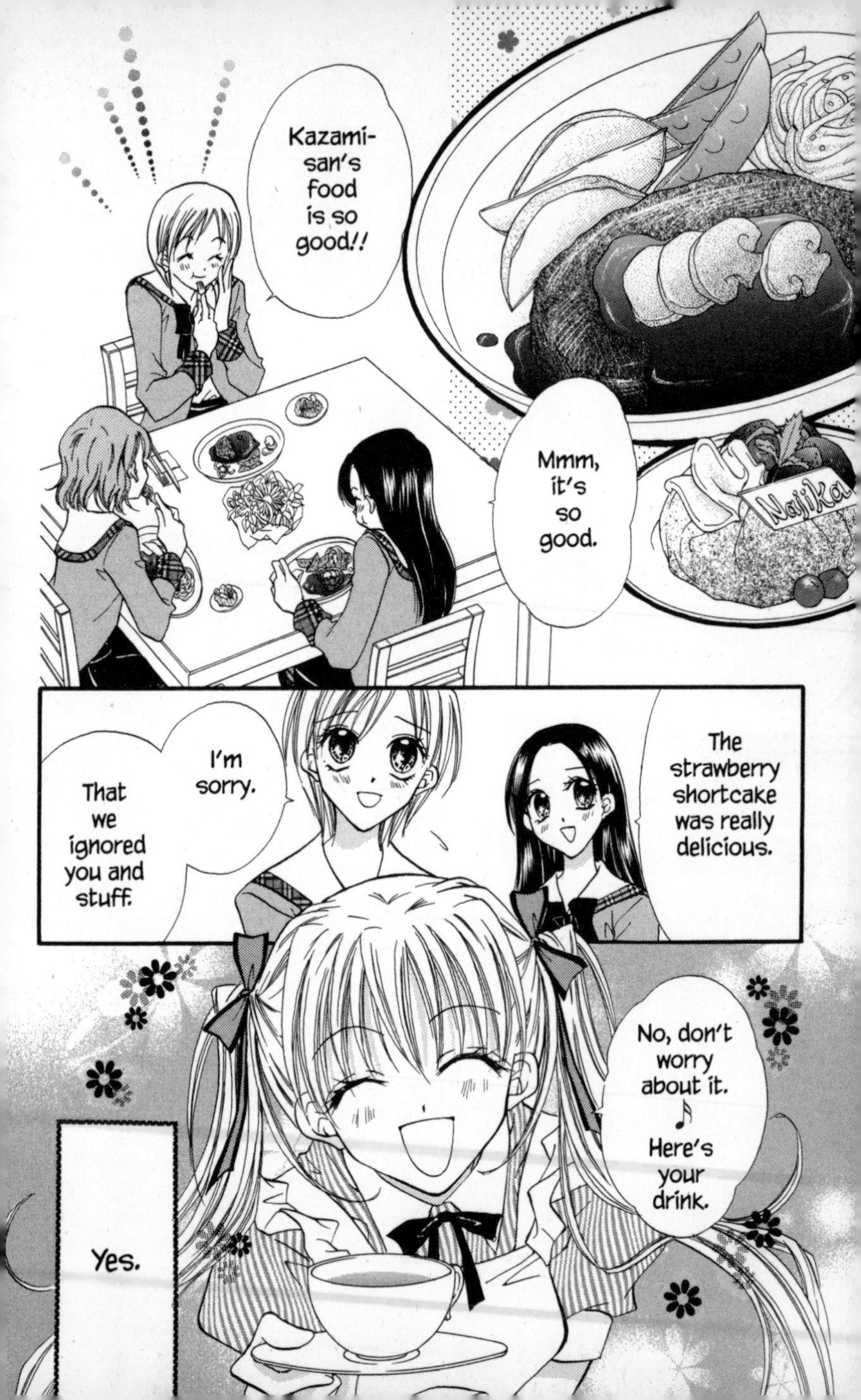
Kazami-san's food is so good!!
Mmm, it's so good.
Naiika
The strawberry shortcake was really delicious.
I'm sorry.
That we ignored you and stuff.
No, don't worry about it. ♪ Here's your drink.
Yes.

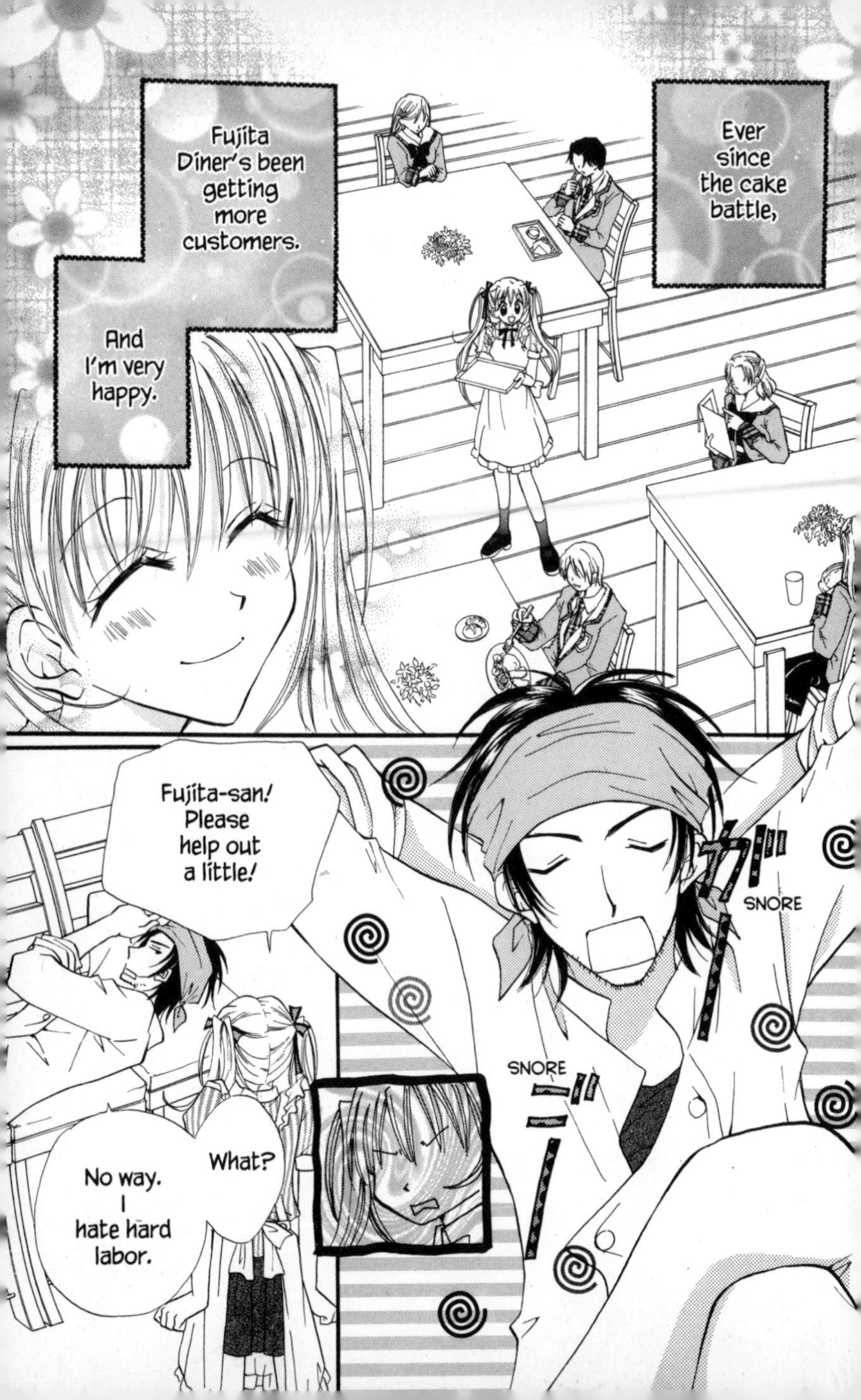
Ever since the cake battle,
Fujita Diner's been getting more customers.
And I'm very happy.
SNORE
Fujita-san! Please help out a little!
SNORE
What?
No way. I hate hard labor.

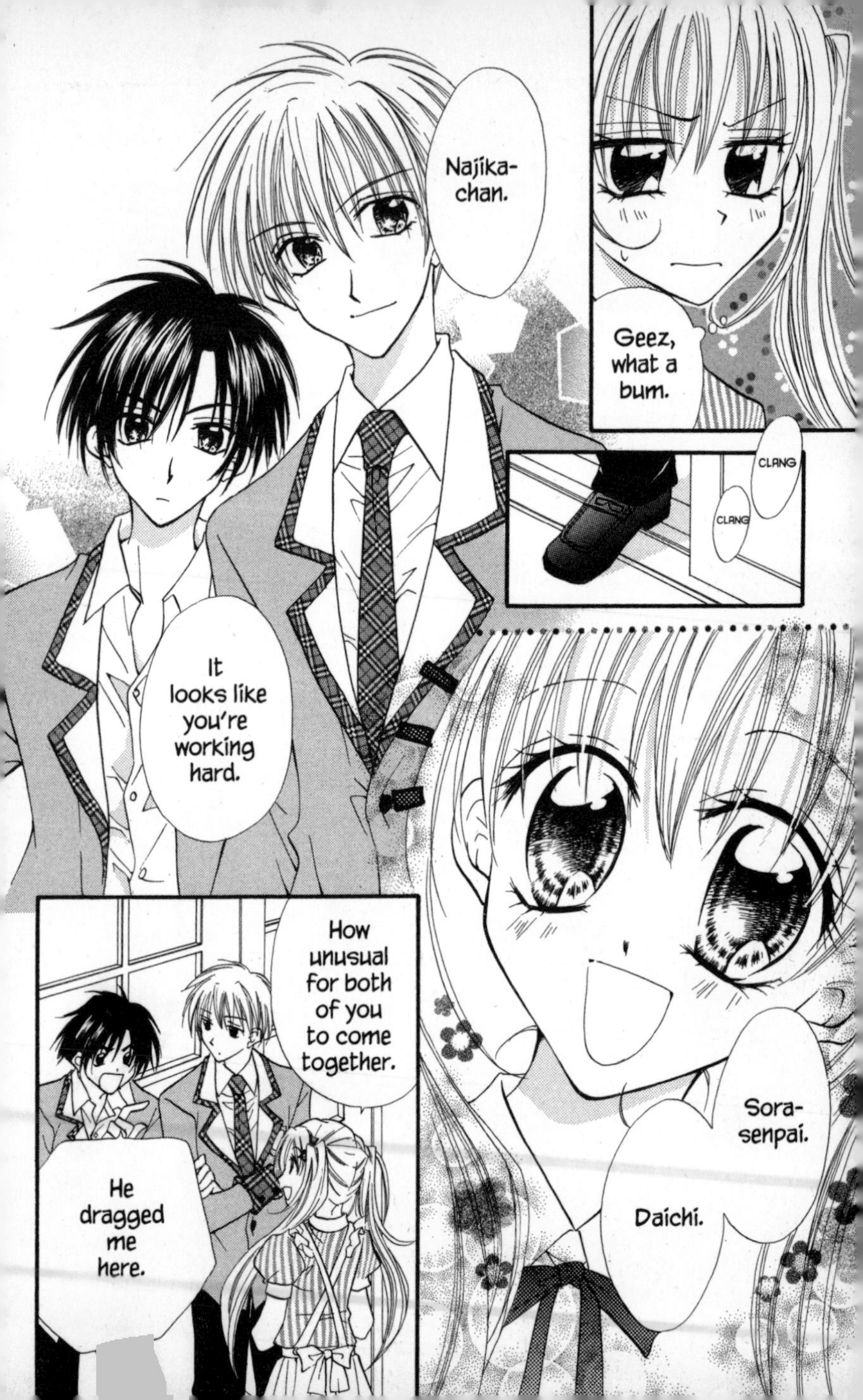

Geez, what a bum.
CLANG
CLANG
Sora-senpai.
Daichi.
Najika-chan.
It looks like you're working hard.
How unusual for both of you to come together.
He dragged me here.

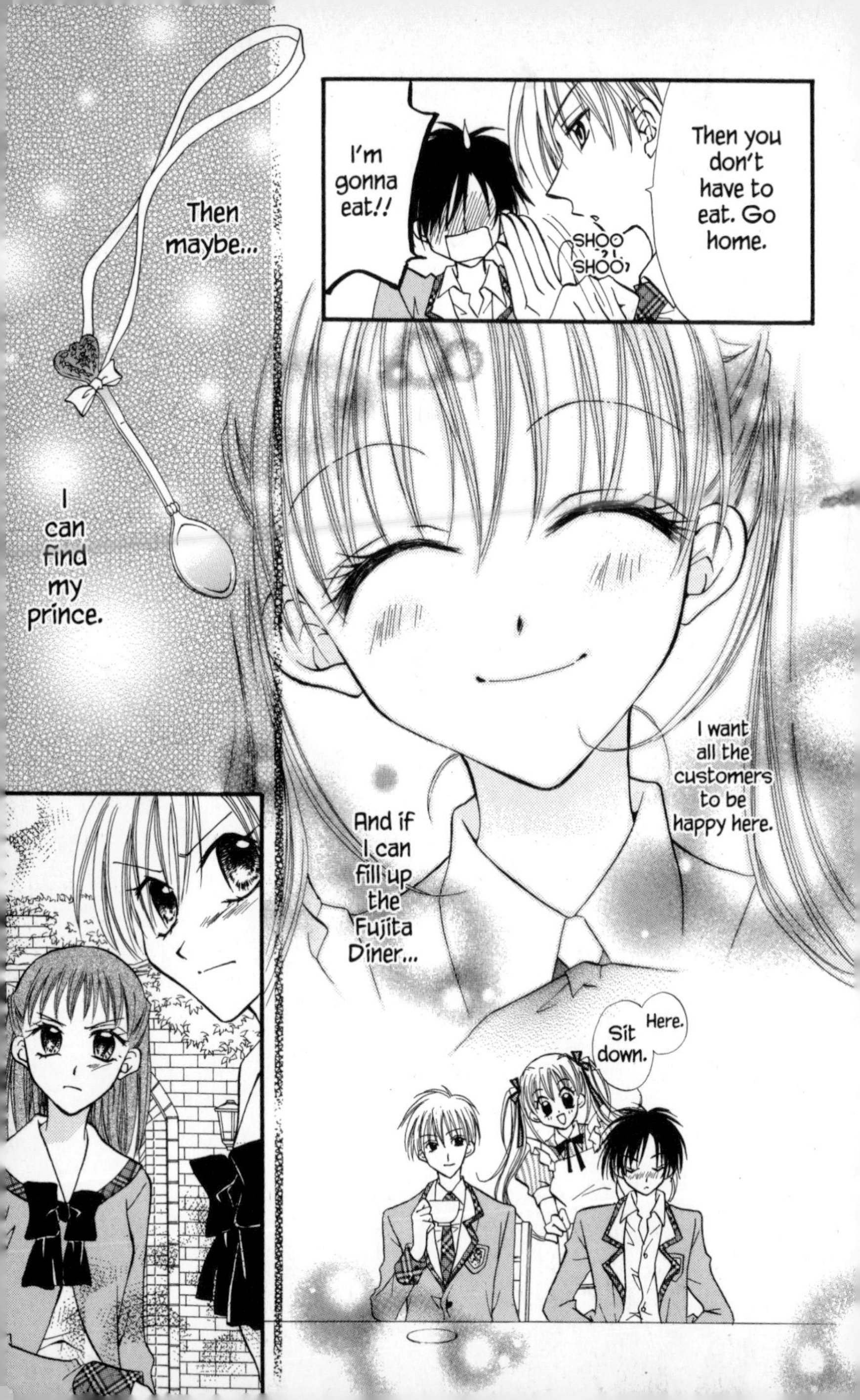
Then you don't have to eat. Go home.
SHOO SHOO
I'm gonna eat!!
I want all the customers to be happy here.
And if I can fill up the Fujita Diner...
Then maybe...
I can find my prince.
Here.
Sit down.

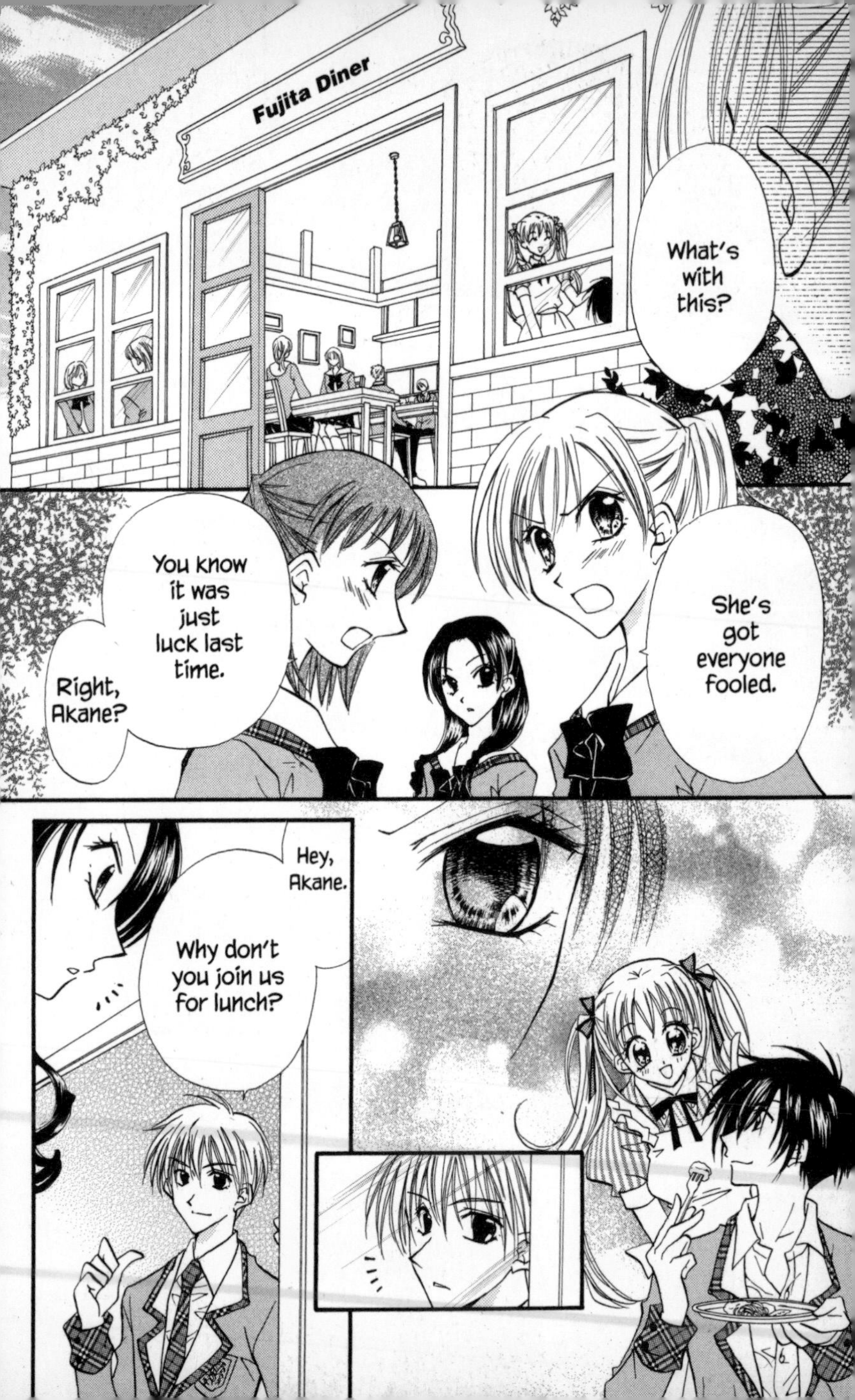
What's with this?
Fujita Diner
She's got everyone fooled.
You know it was just luck last time.
Right, Akane?
Hey, Akane.
Why don't you join us for lunch?

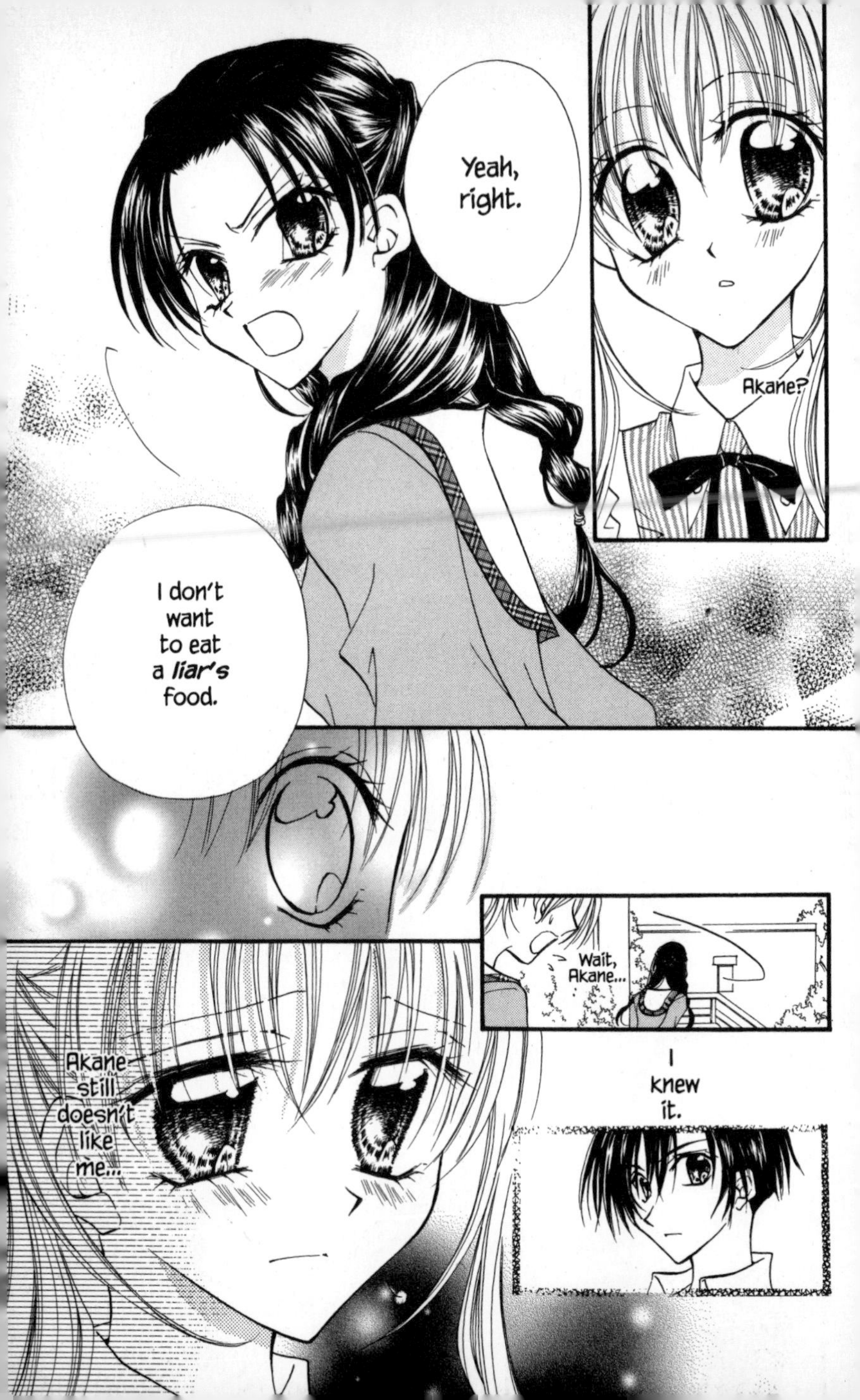
Akane?
Yeah, right.
I don't want to eat a *liar's* food.
Wait, Akane...
I knew it.
Akane still doesn't like me...

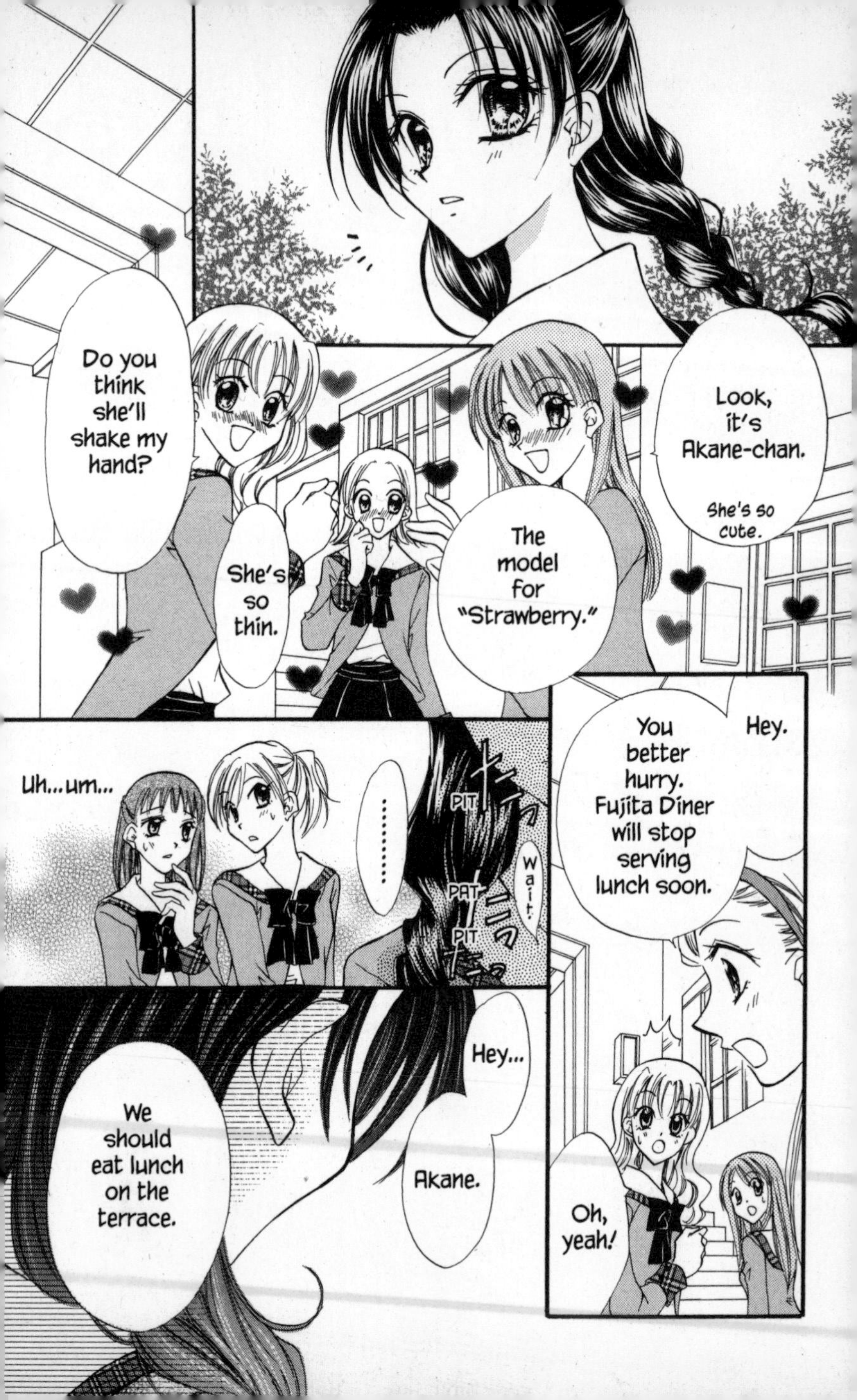
Look, it's Akane-chan.
She's so cute.
The model for "Strawberry."
She's so thin.
Do you think she'll shake my hand?
Hey.
You better hurry. Fujita Diner will stop serving lunch soon.
Oh, yeah!
Wait.
PIT
PAT
PIT
....
Uh...um...
Hey...
Akane.
We should eat lunch on the terrace.

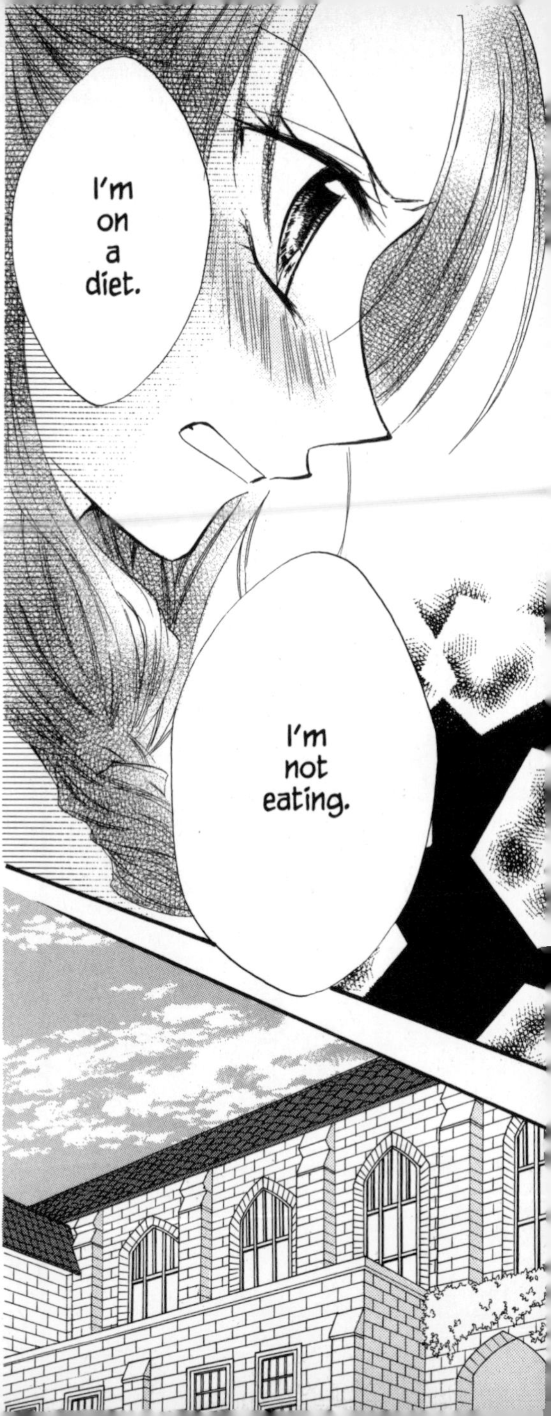
I'm on a diet.
I'm not eating.

***Recipe* 8**

For this chapter, I got to observe the *Nakayoshi* photo shoot for Nami Uehara. Sigh...She's so cute and has a great figure. I was very shocked.

***Recipe* 9**

For dieting, it's best to lose 2.5kg (about 5 1/2 lbs.) in a month...It's best to make your body burn more fat, but that's easier said than done...Anyway, I hear it's good to drink 2 liters (a little over a half gallon) of water every day!

***Recipe* 10**

I have to admit, I didn't know there was such a thing as a frozen pie sheet!! So I tried buying one. But as I mentioned before, I don't have an oven, so it's still sitting in my freezer...What should I do with it?

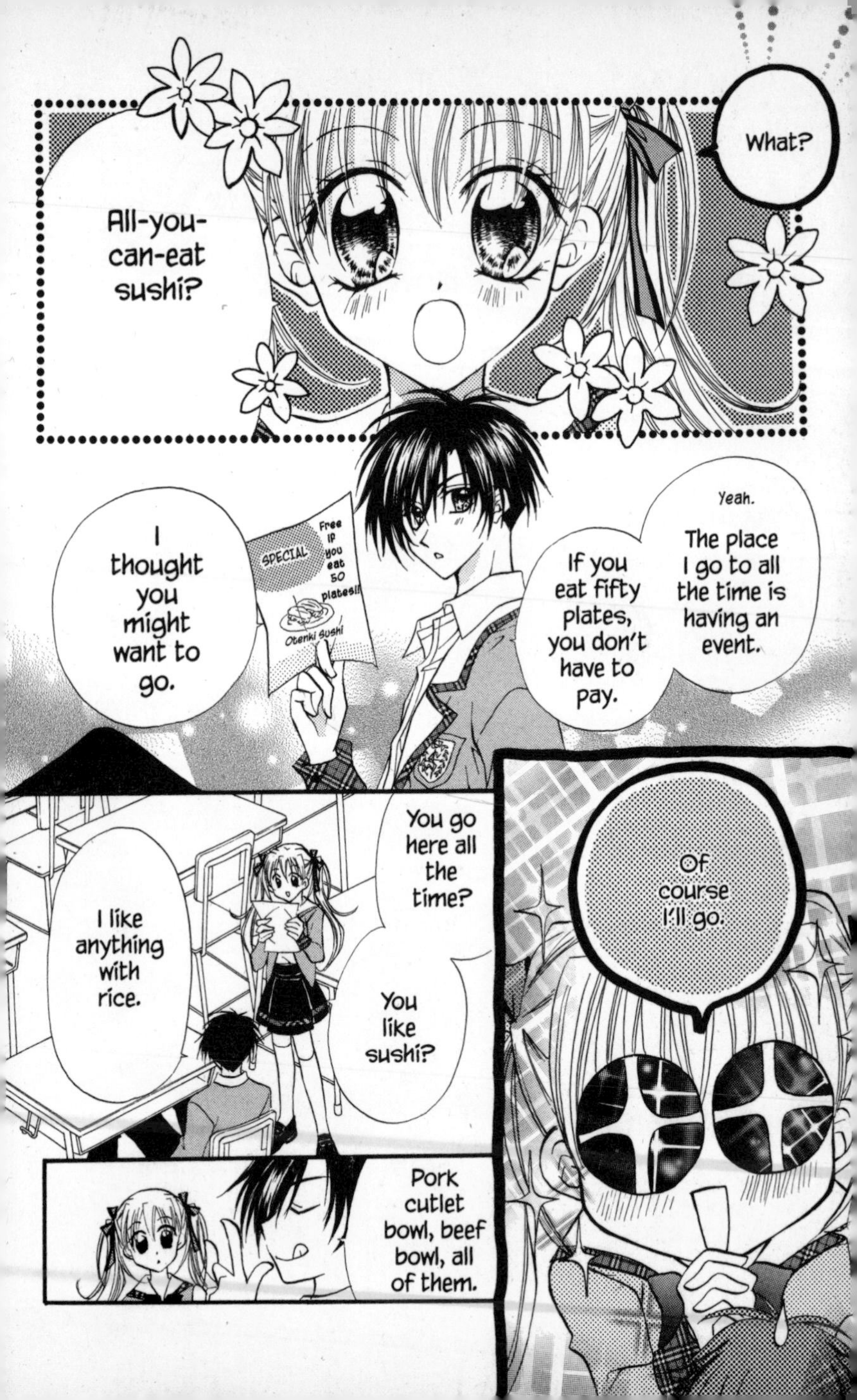
What?
All-you-can-eat sushi?
Yeah.
The place I go to all the time is having an event.
If you eat fifty plates, you don't have to pay.
SPECIAL
Free if you eat 50 plates!!
Otenki Sushi
I thought you might want to go.
Of course I'll go.
You go here all the time?
You like sushi?
I like anything with rice.
Pork cutlet bowl, beef bowl, all of them.

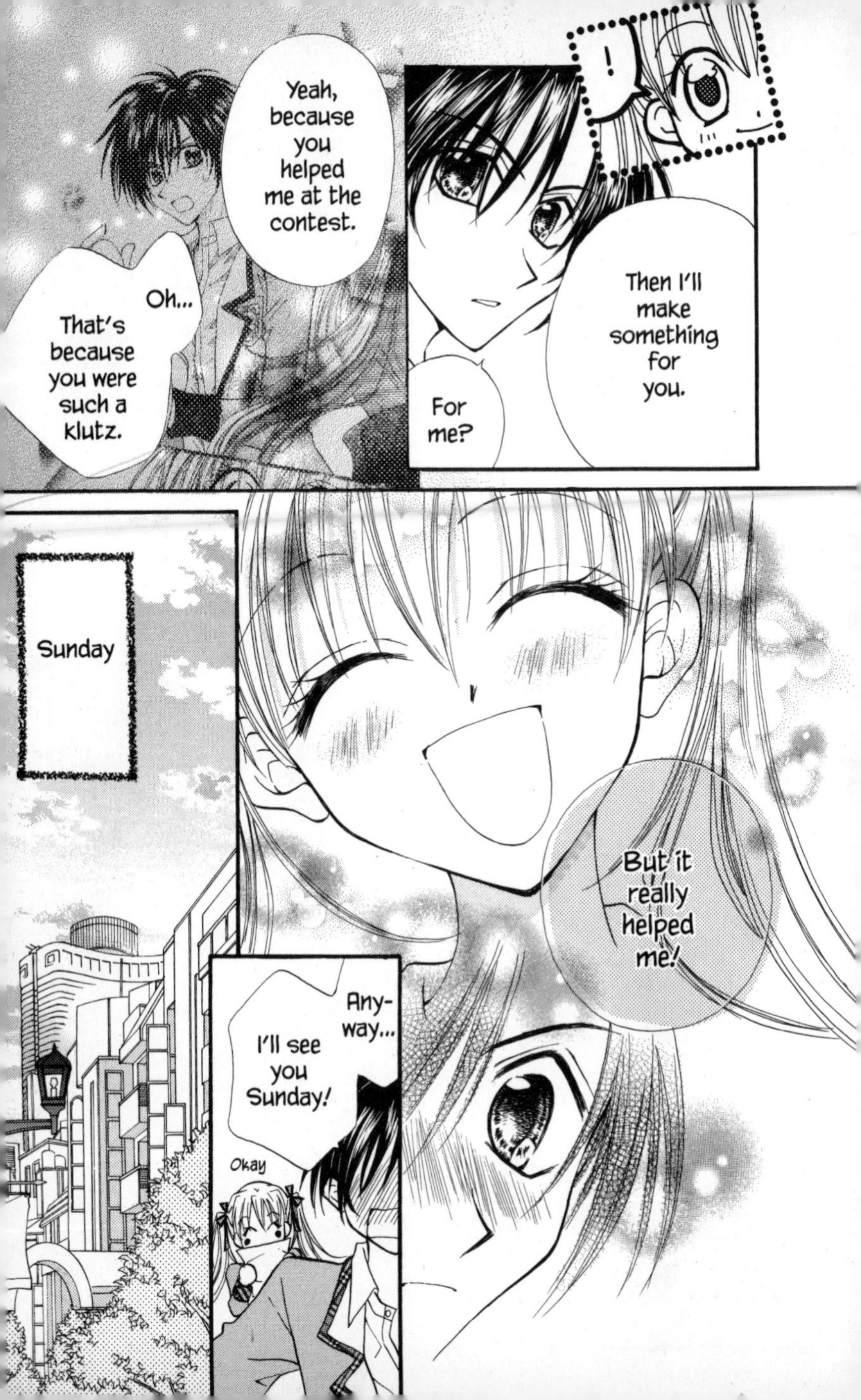
!
Then I'll make something for you.
For me?
Yeah, because you helped me at the contest.
Oh...
That's because you were such a klutz.
But it really helped me!
Any-way...
I'll see you Sunday!
Okay
Sunday

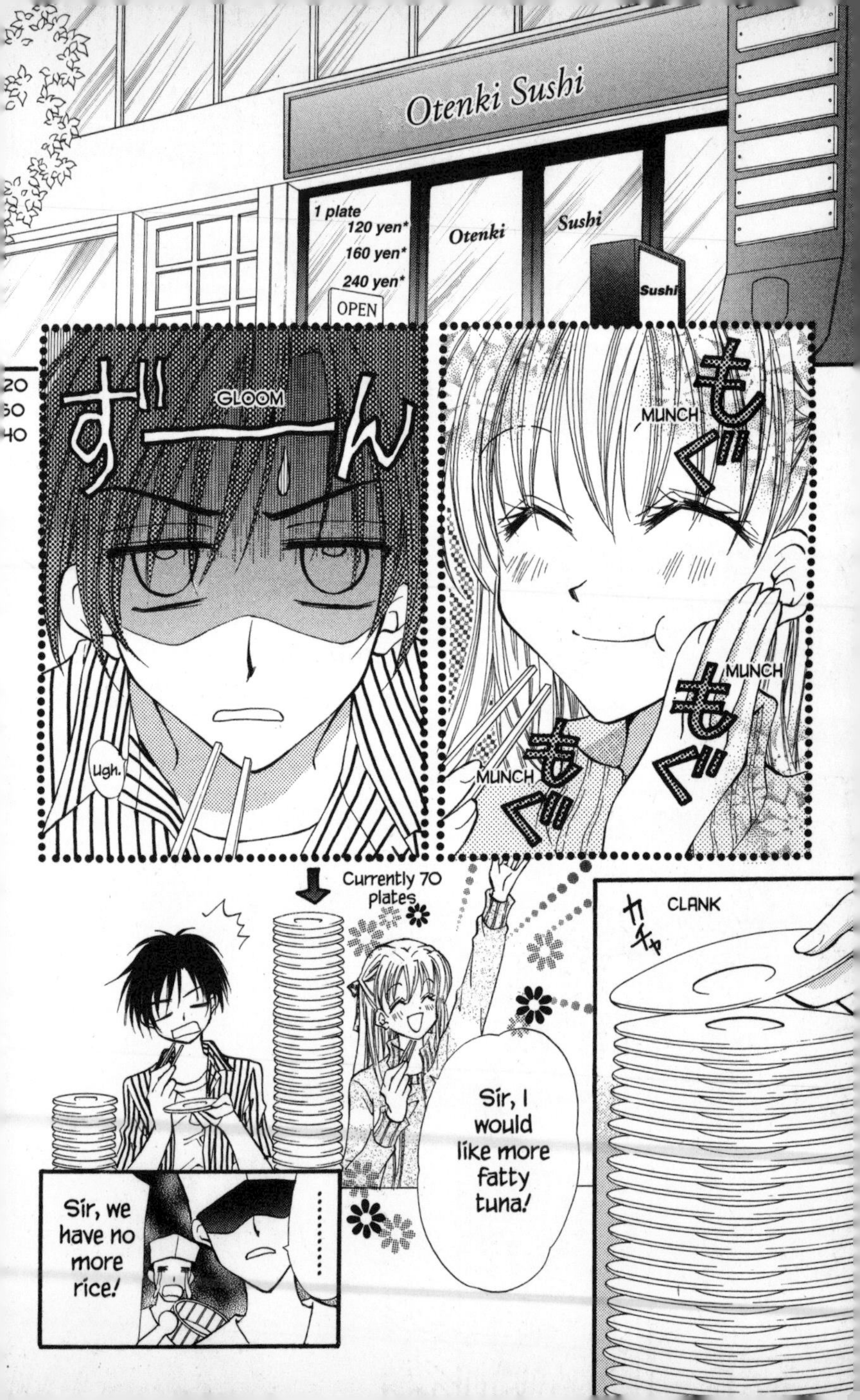

Otenki Sushi
1 plate
120 yen*
160 yen*
240 yen*
Otenki
Sushi
OPEN
Sushi
もぐ
MUNCH
もぐ
MUNCH
もぐ
MUNCH
すーん
GLOOM
Ugh.
カチャ
CLANK
Currently 70 plates
Sir, I would like more fatty tuna!
......
Sir, we have no more rice!

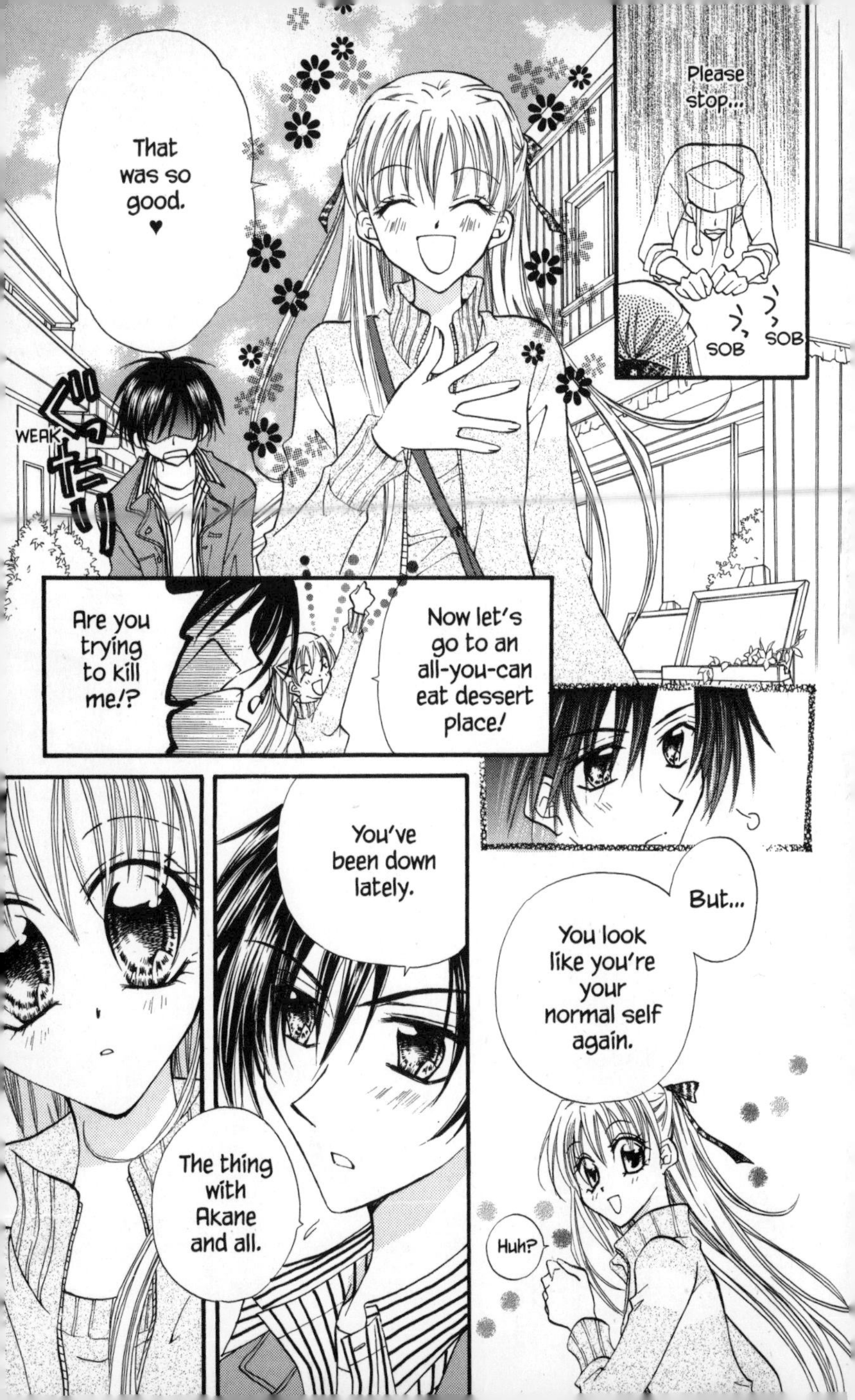
Please stop...
SOB SOB
That was so good. ♥
WEAK
Now let's go to an all-you-can eat dessert place!
Are you trying to kill me!?
But...
You look like you're your normal self again.
Huh?
You've been down lately.
The thing with Akane and all.

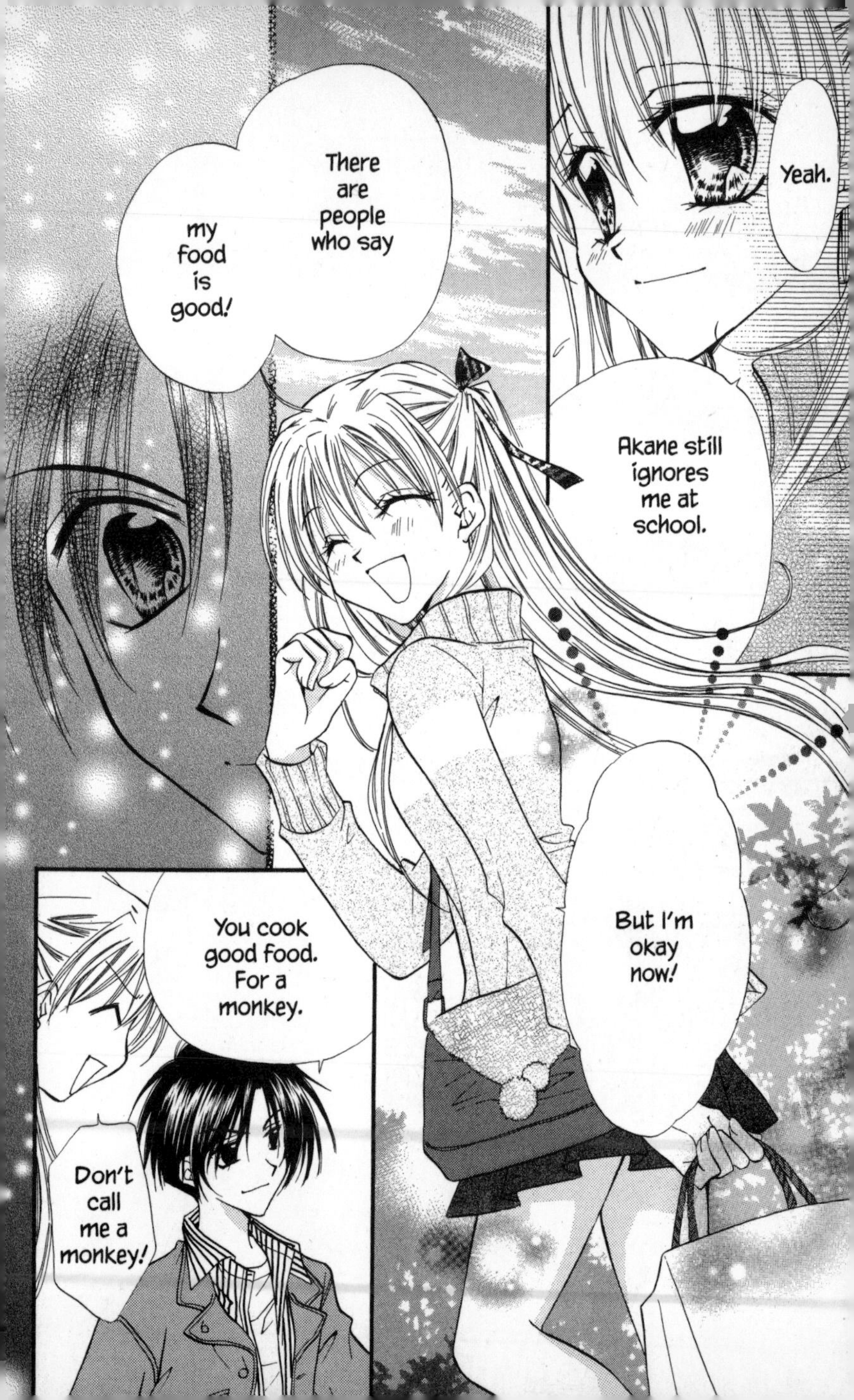
Yeah.
Akane still ignores me at school.
But I'm okay now!
There are people who say my food is good!
You cook good food. For a monkey.
Don't call me a monkey!

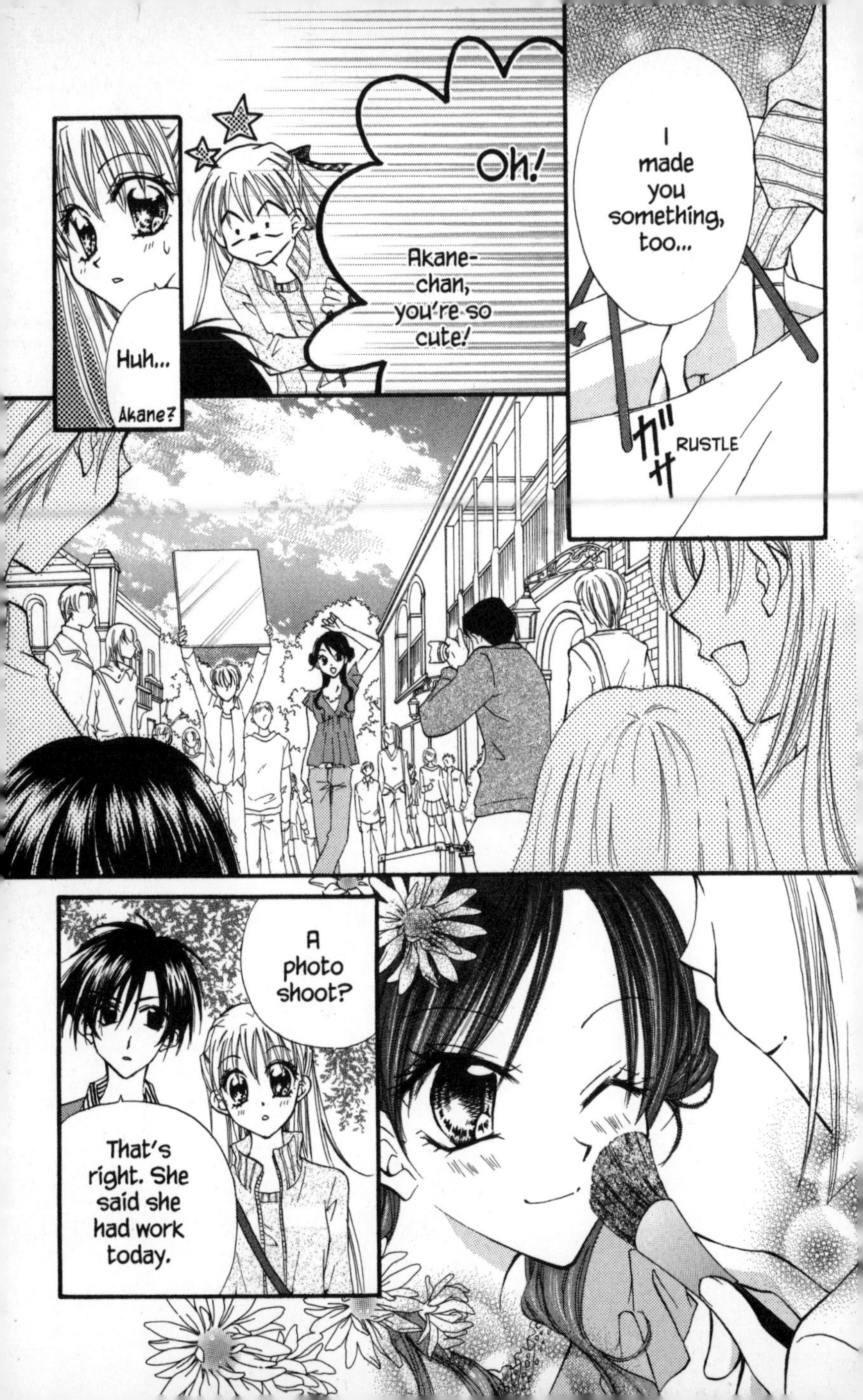

I made you something, too...
ガサ
RUSTLE
Oh!
Akane-chan, you're so cute!
Huh...
Akane?
A photo shoot?
That's right. She said she had work today.

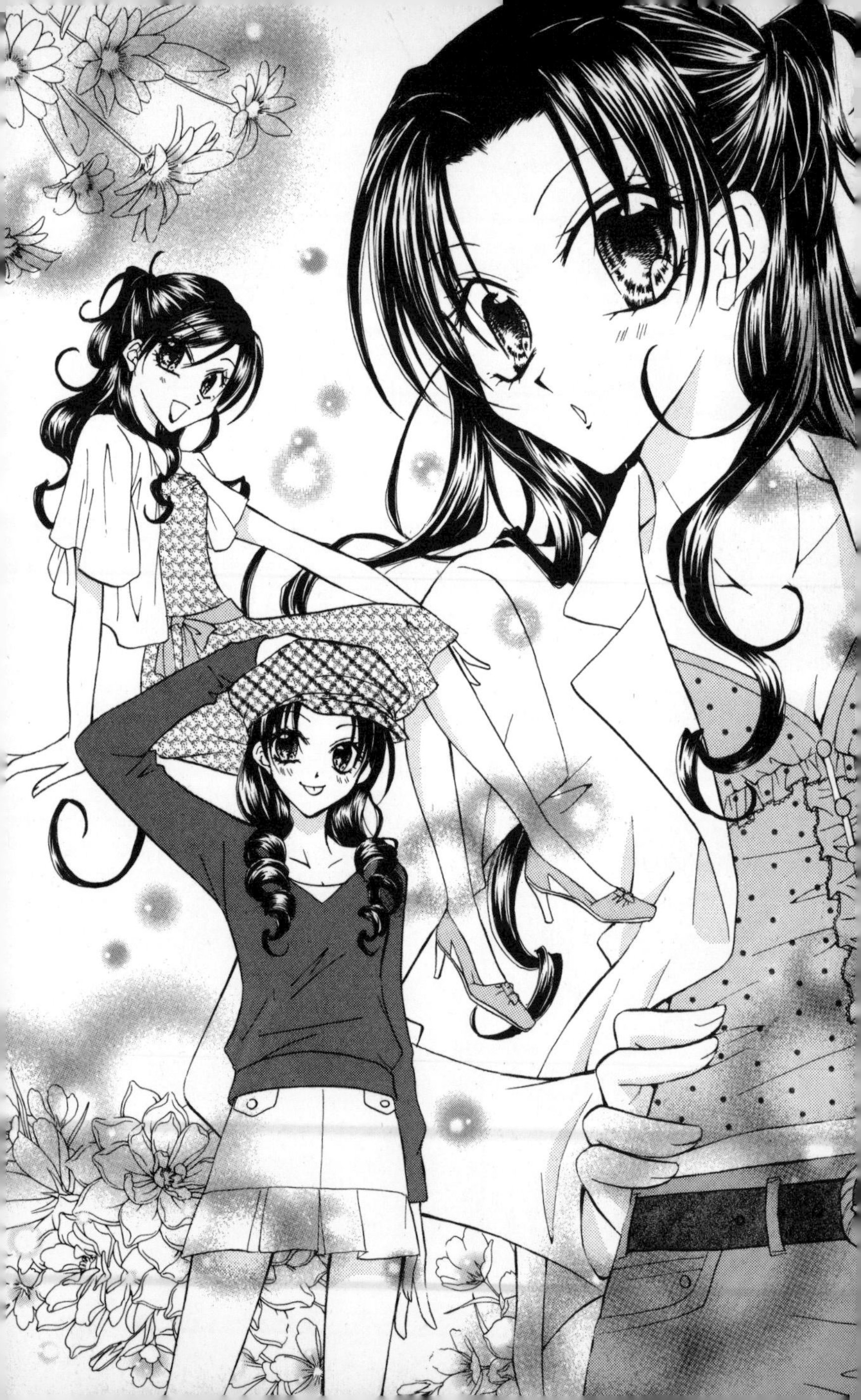

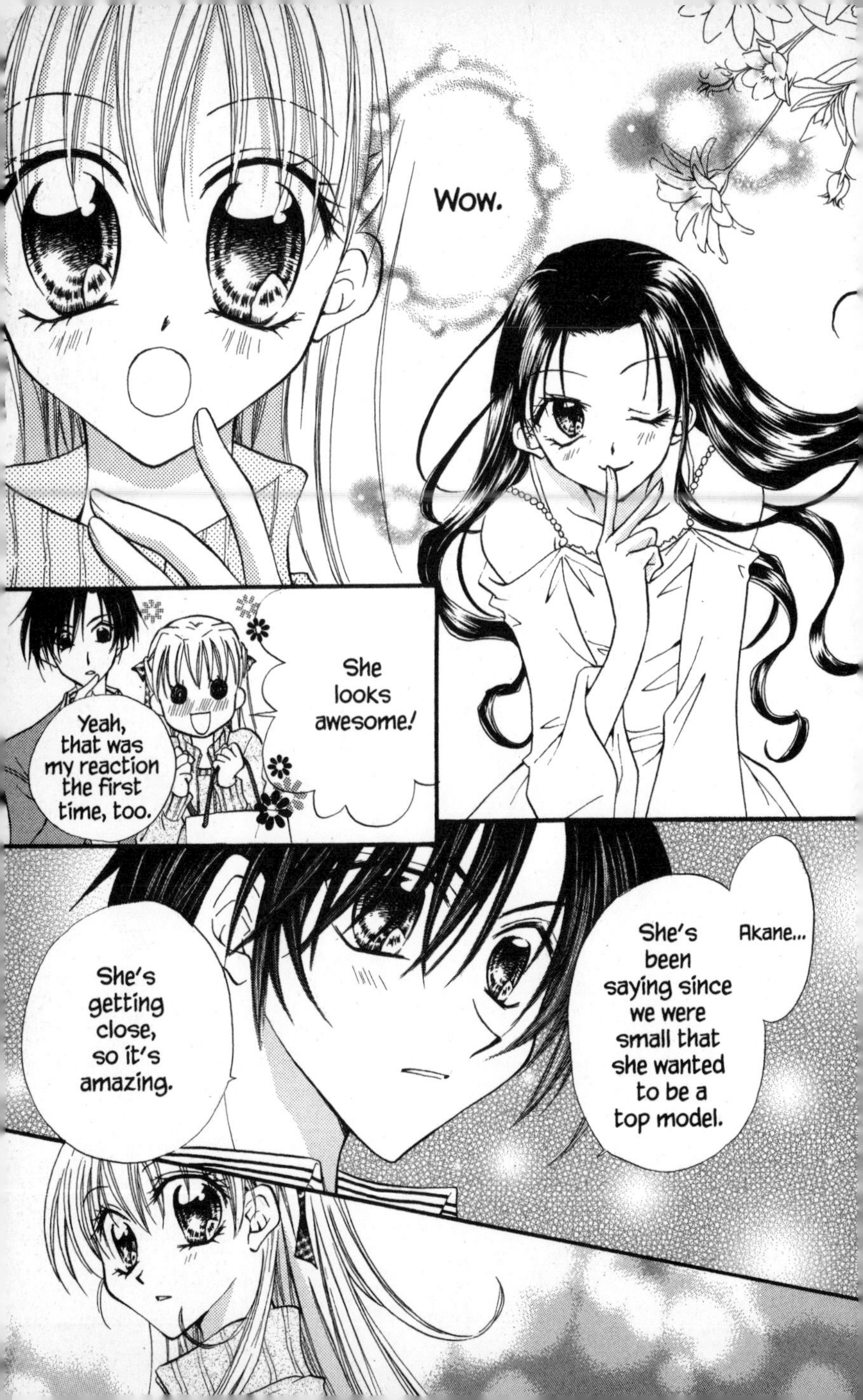
Wow.
She looks awesome!
Yeah, that was my reaction the first time, too.
Akane...
She's been saying since we were small that she wanted to be a top model.
She's getting close, so it's amazing.

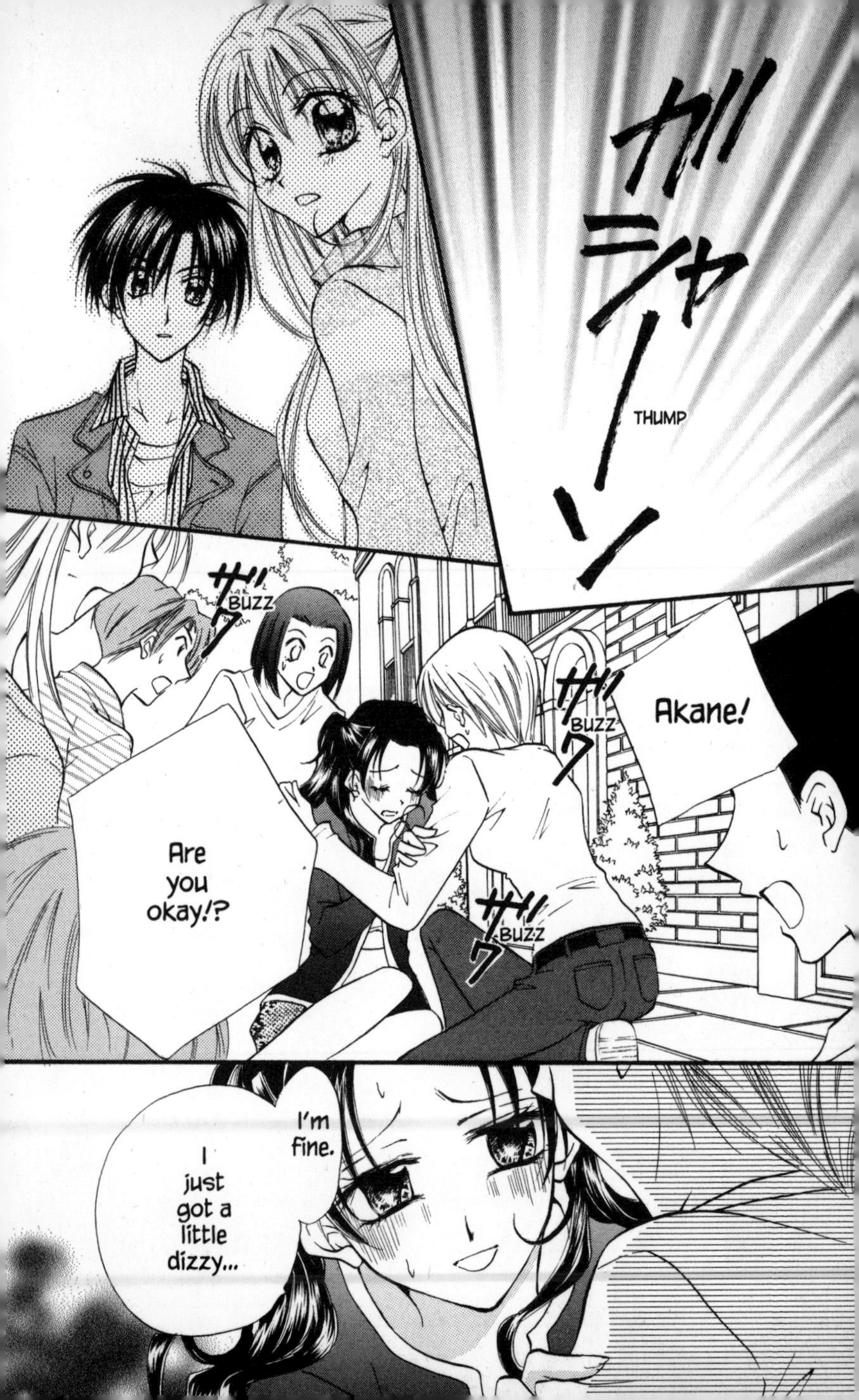
ガシャーン
THUMP
Akane!
ザワ
BUZZ
ザワ
BUZZ
ザワ
BUZZ
Are you okay!?
I'm fine.
I just got a little dizzy...

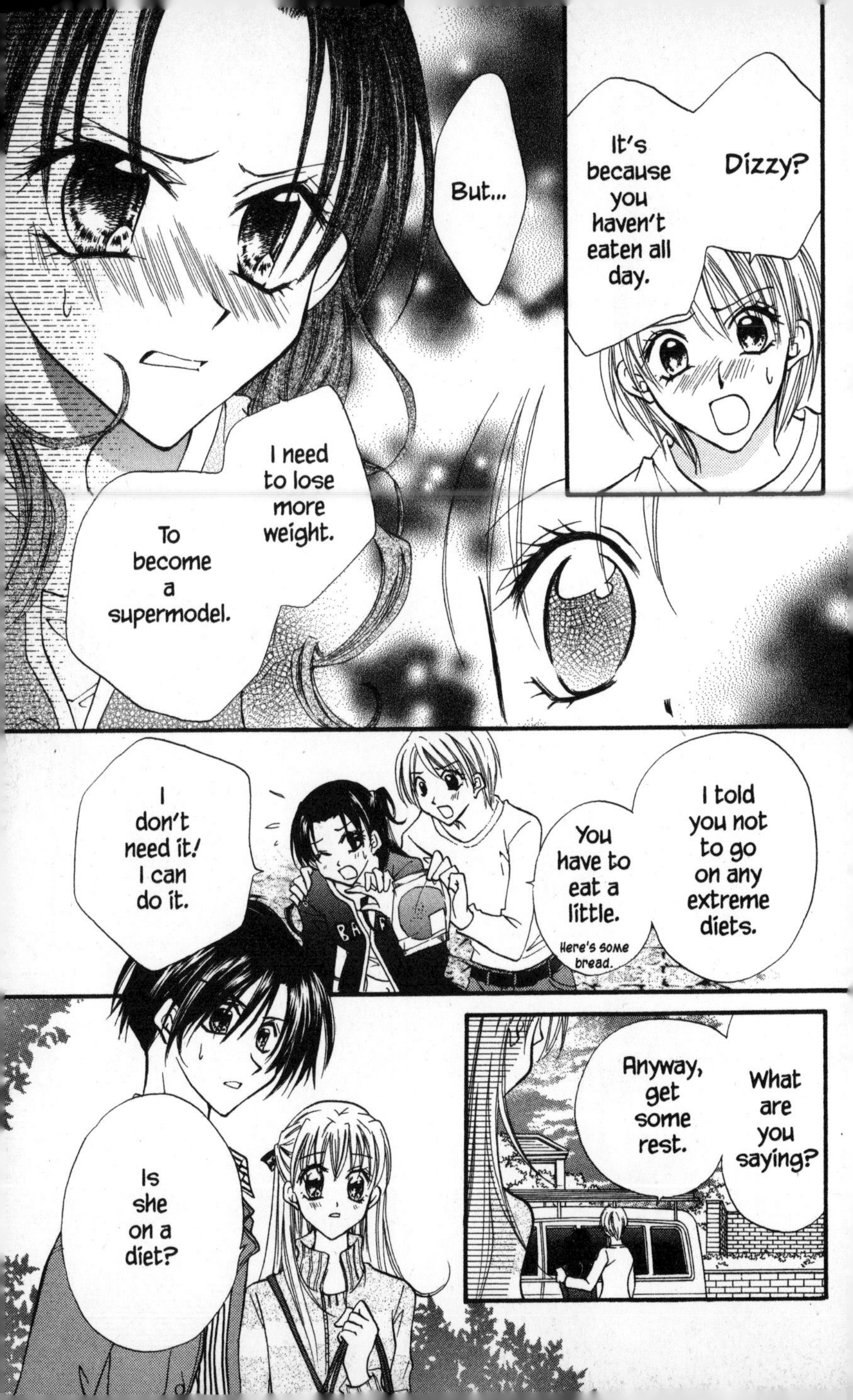
Dizzy?
It's because you haven't eaten all day.
But...
I need to lose more weight.
To become a supermodel.
I told you not to go on any extreme diets.
You have to eat a little.
Here's some bread.
I don't need it! I can do it.
What are you saying?
Anyway, get some rest.
Is she on a diet?

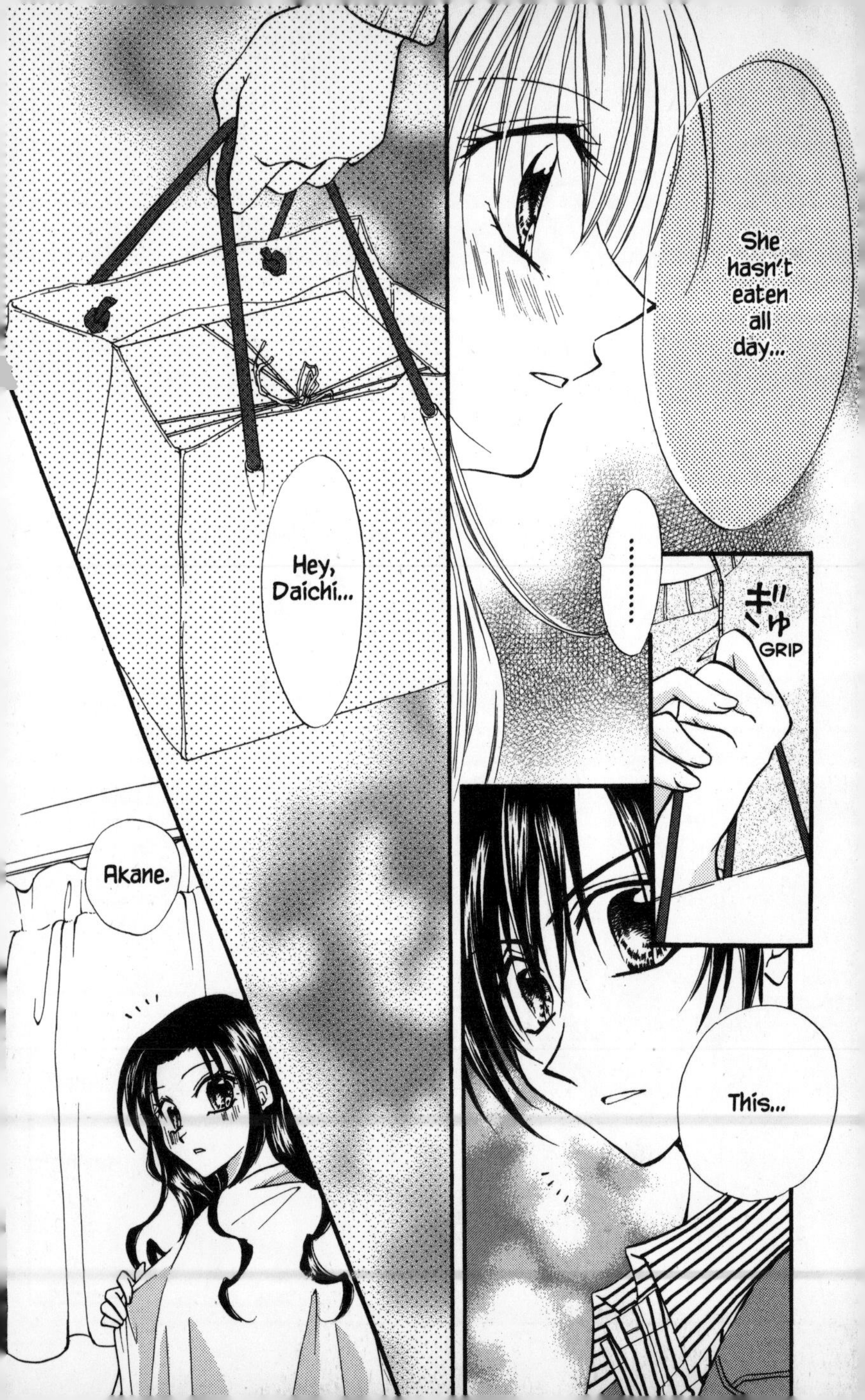
She hasn't eaten all day...
......
ぎゅ
GRIP
This...
Hey, Daichi...
Akane.

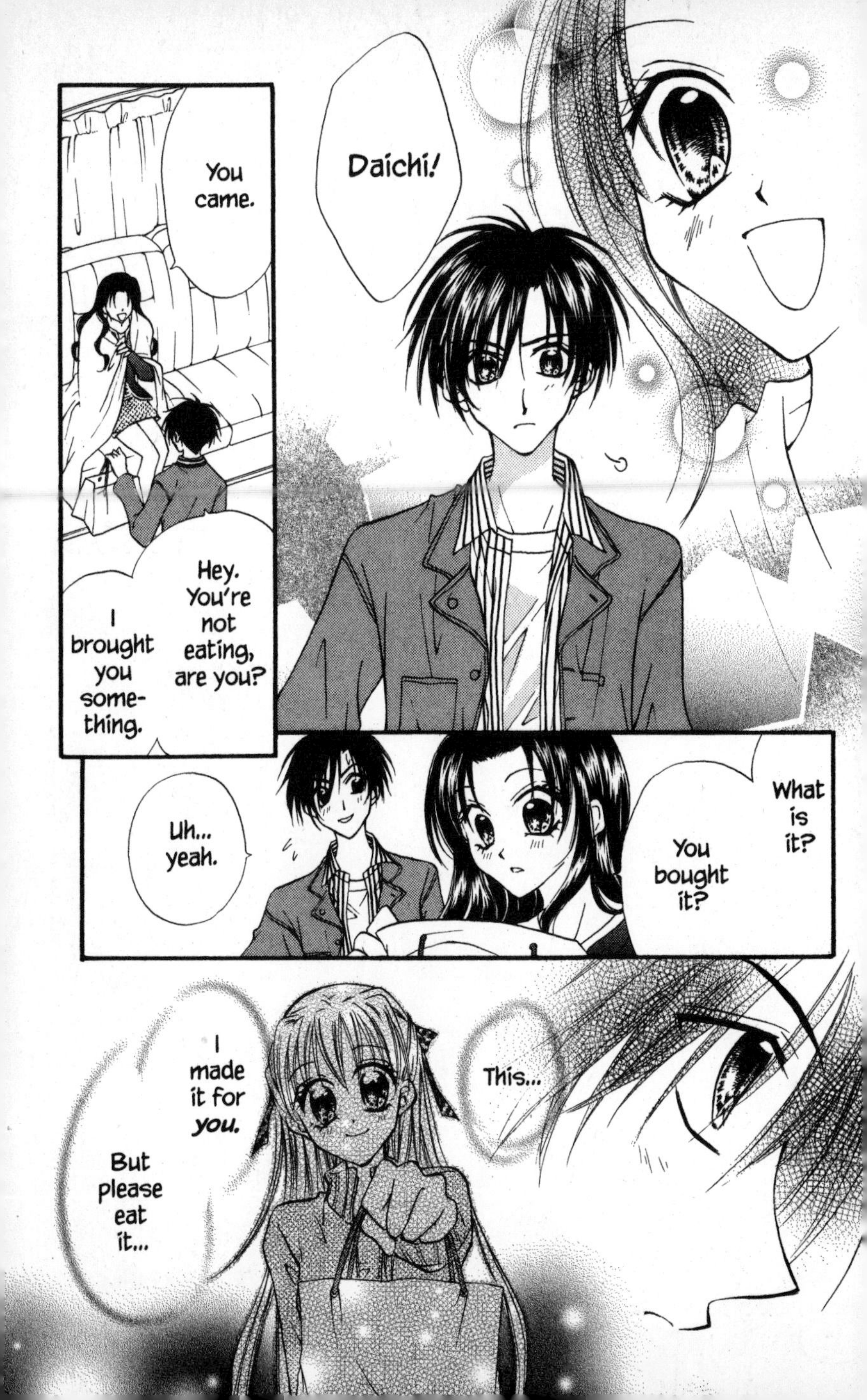
Daichi!
You came.
Hey. You're not eating, are you?
I brought you something.
What is it?
You bought it?
Uh... yeah.
This...
I made it for *you.*
But please eat it...

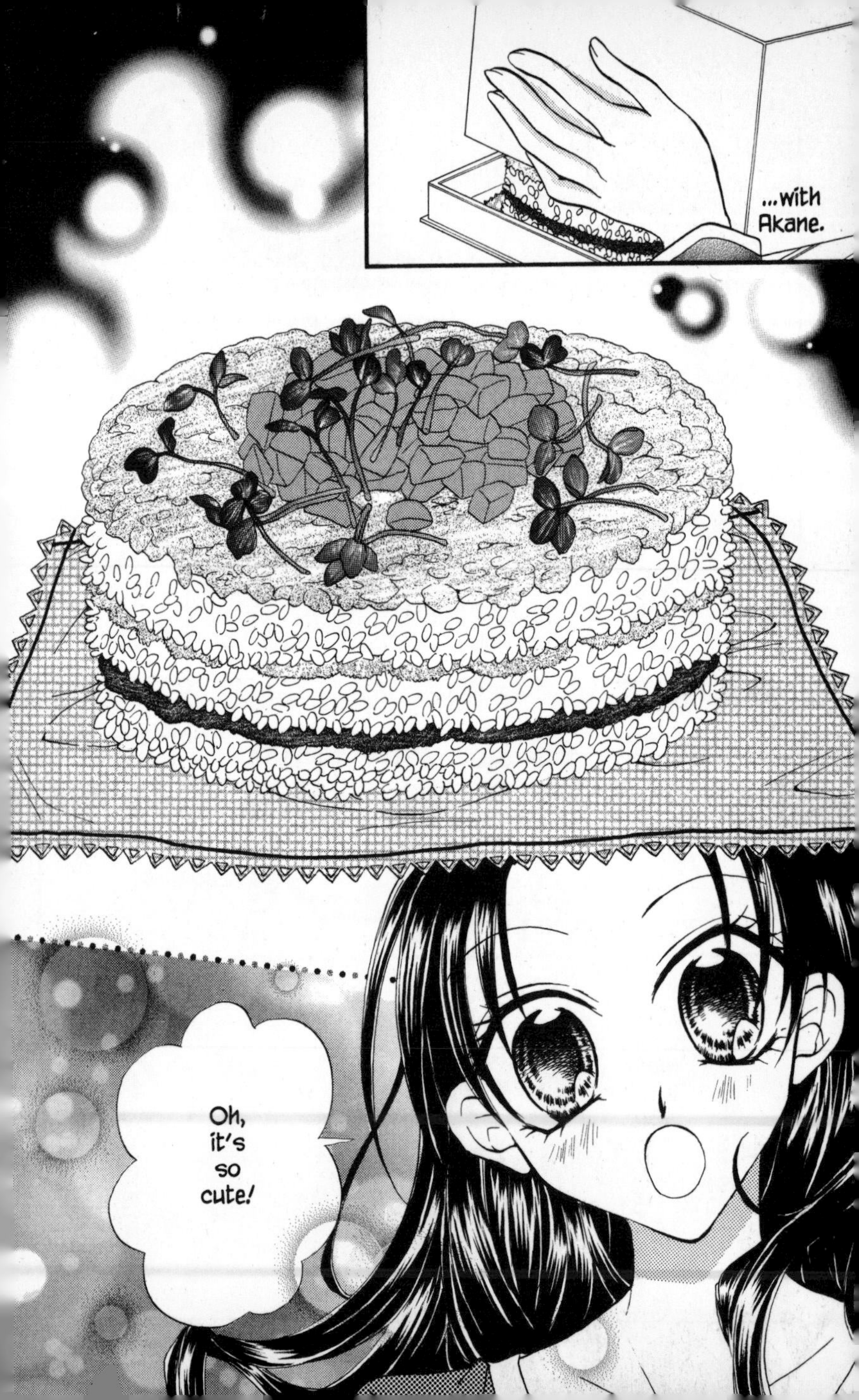
...with Akane.
Oh, it's so cute!

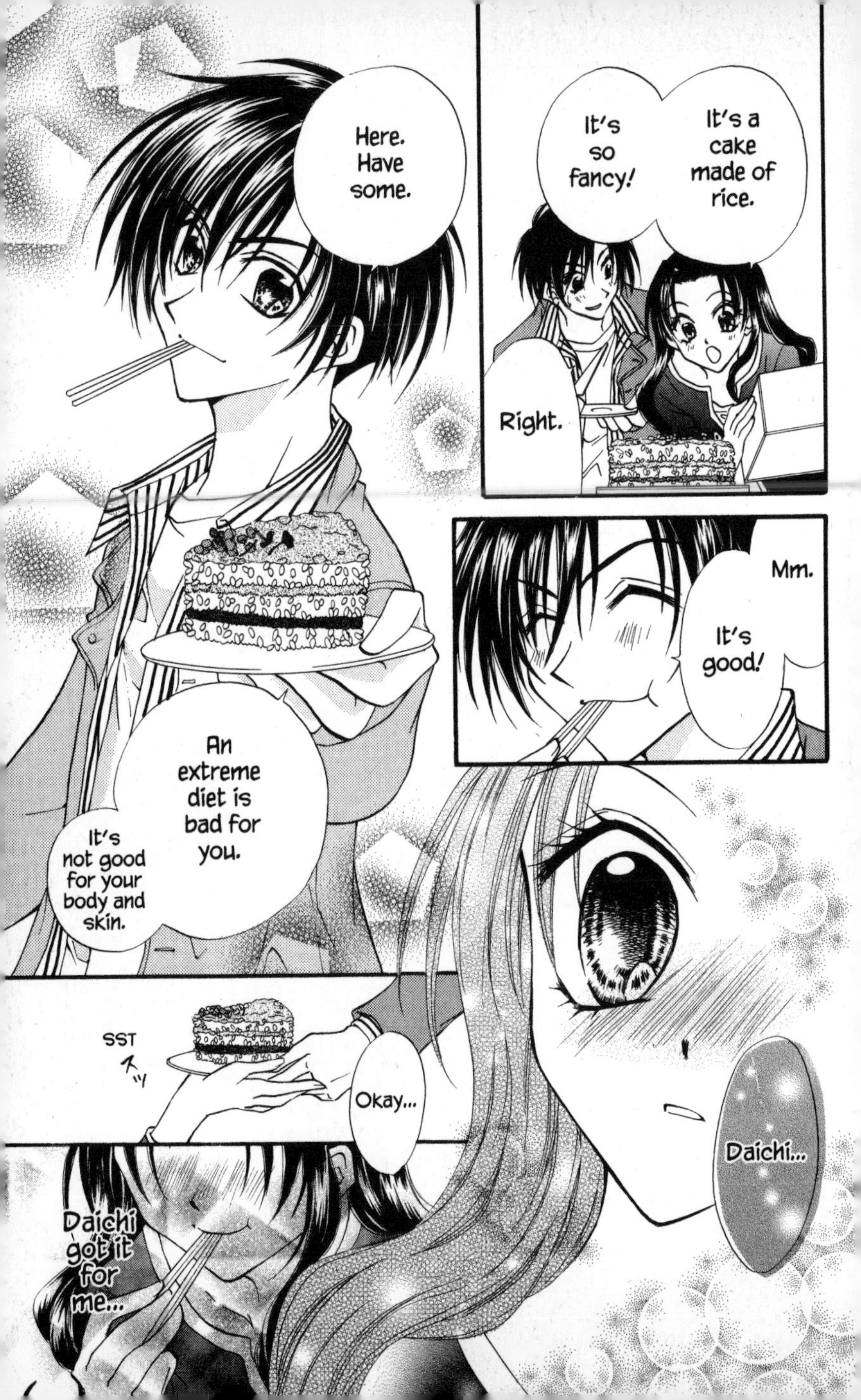
It's a cake made of rice.
It's so fancy!
Right.
Mm.
It's good!
Here. Have some.
An extreme diet is bad for you.
It's not good for your body and skin.
Daichi...
SST
スッ
Okay...
Daichi got it for me...

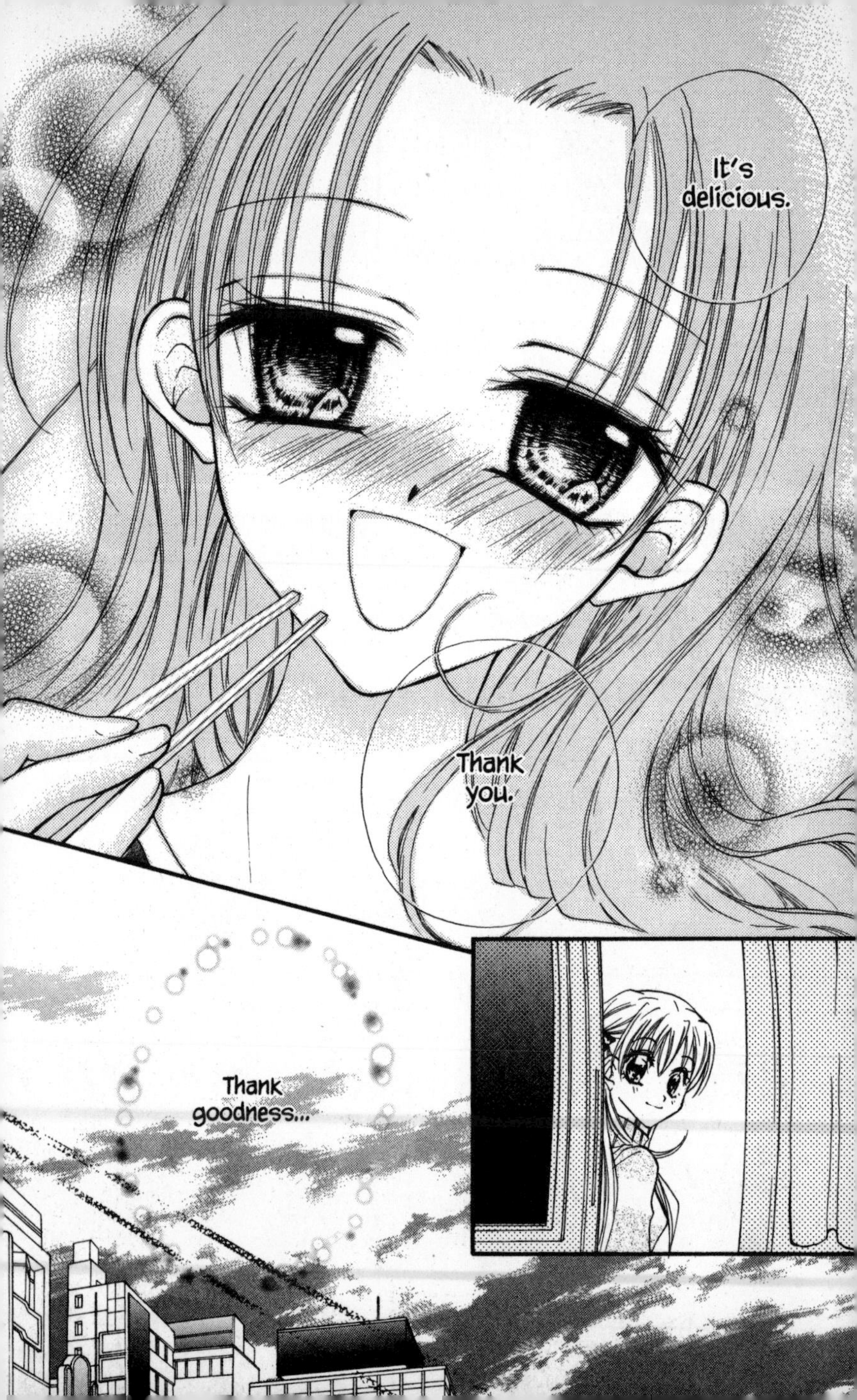
It's delicious.
Thank you.
Thank goodness...

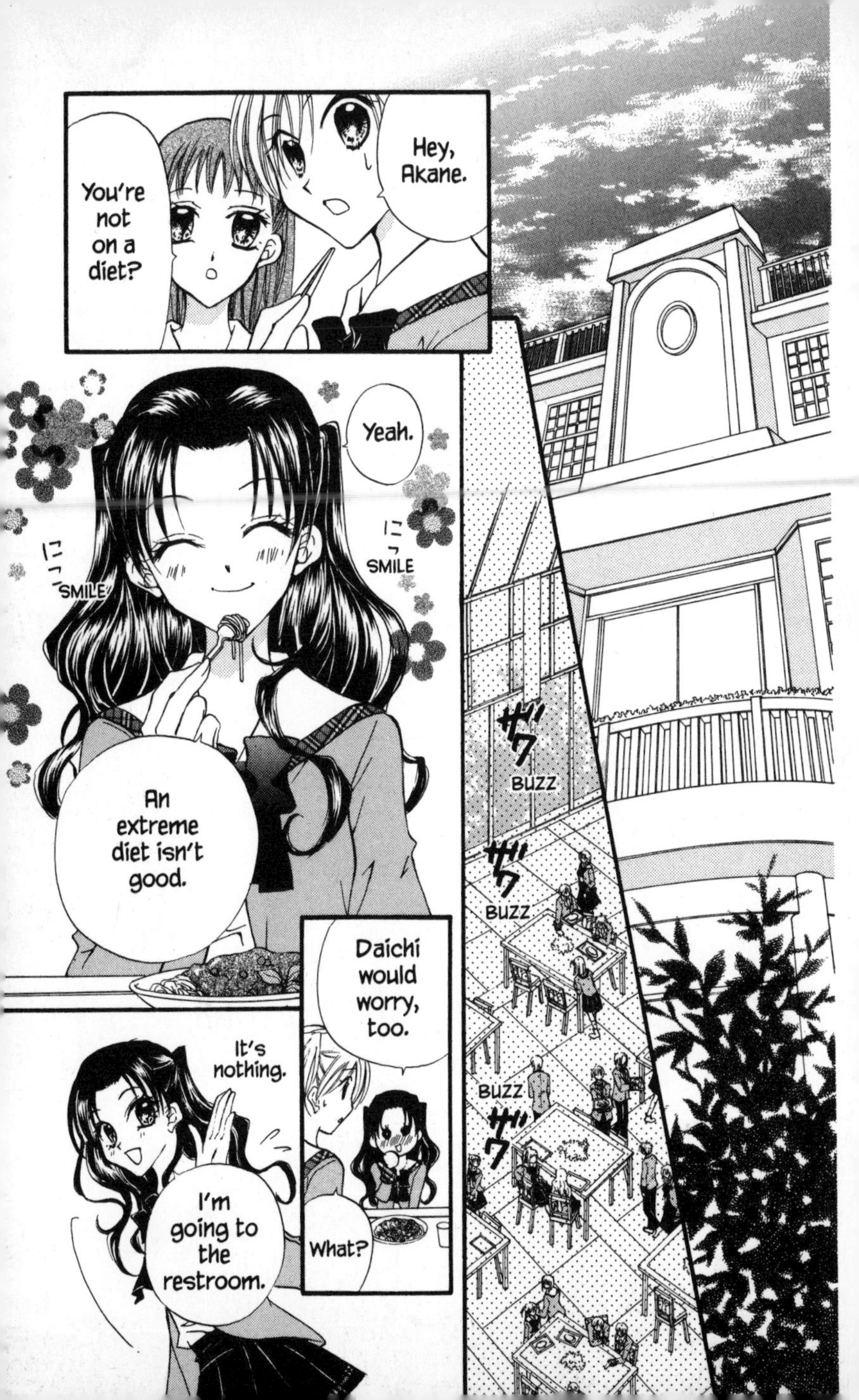
BUZZ
BUZZ
BUZZ
Hey, Akane.
You're not on a diet?
Yeah.
SMILE
SMILE
An extreme diet isn't good.
Daichi would worry, too.
What?
It's nothing.
I'm going to the restroom.

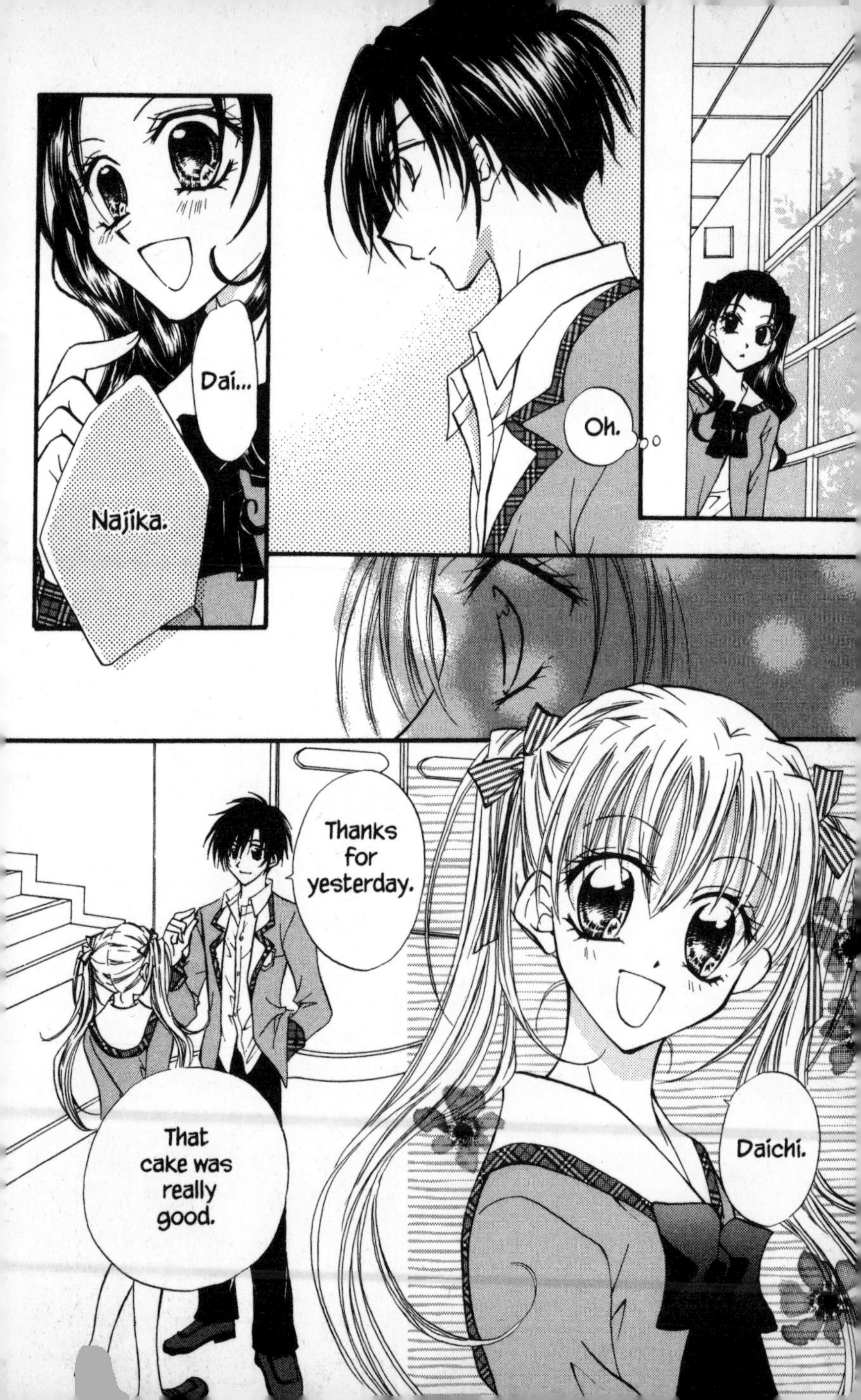
Oh.
Dai...
Najika.
Daichi.
Thanks for yesterday.
That cake was really good.

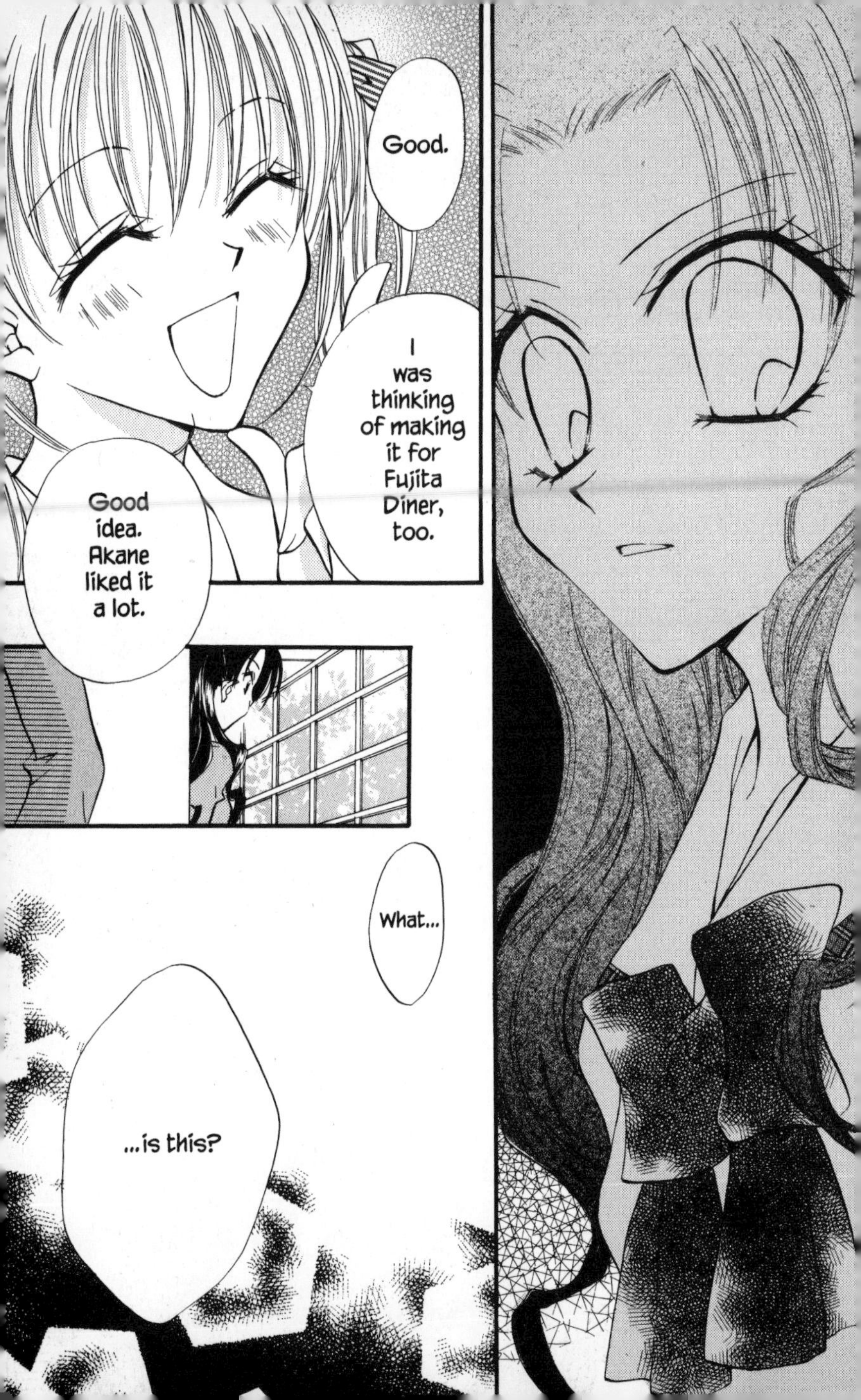
Good.
I was thinking of making it for Fujita Diner, too.
Good idea. Akane liked it a lot.
What...
...is this?

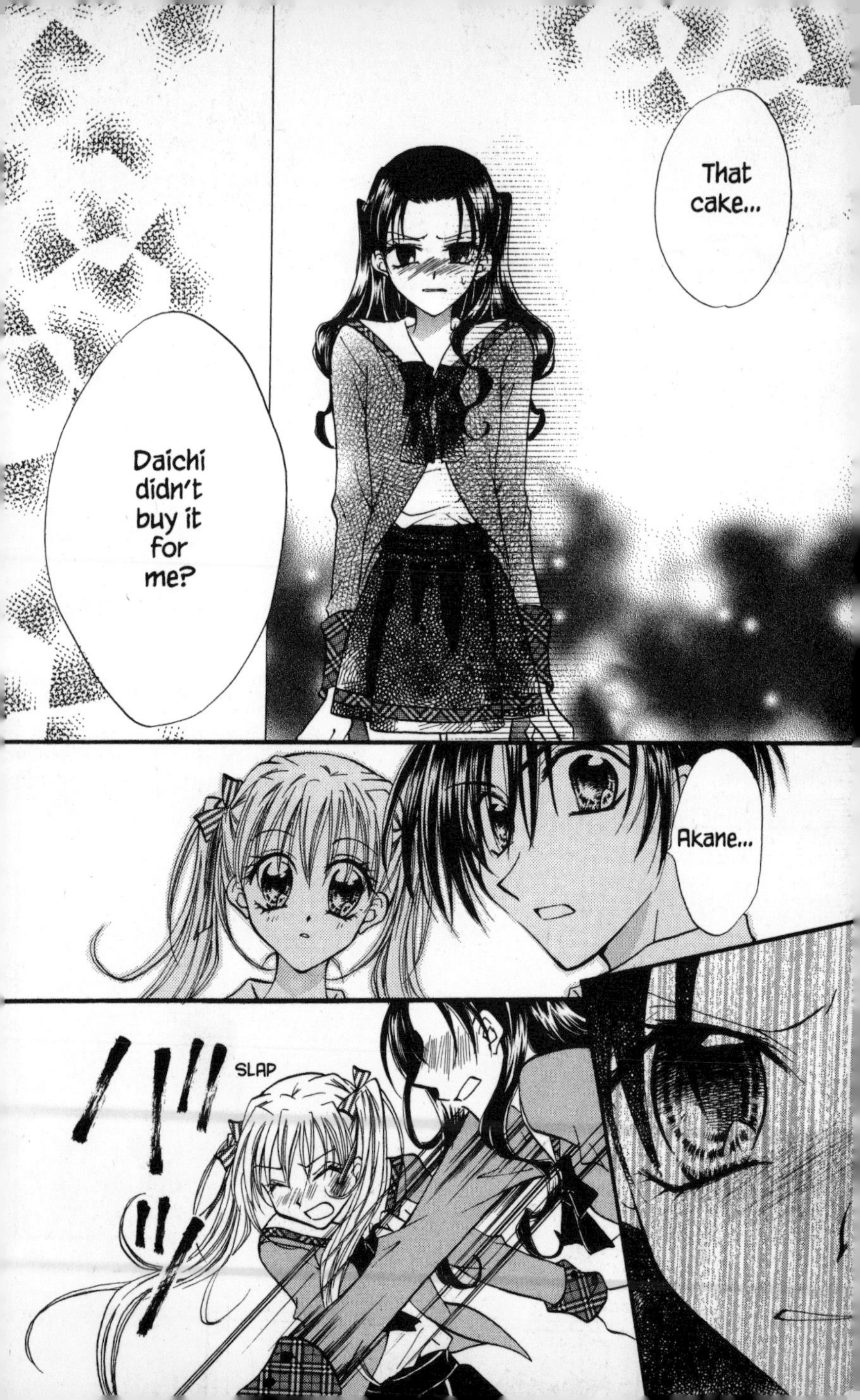
That cake...
Daichi didn't buy it for me?
Akane...
SLAP

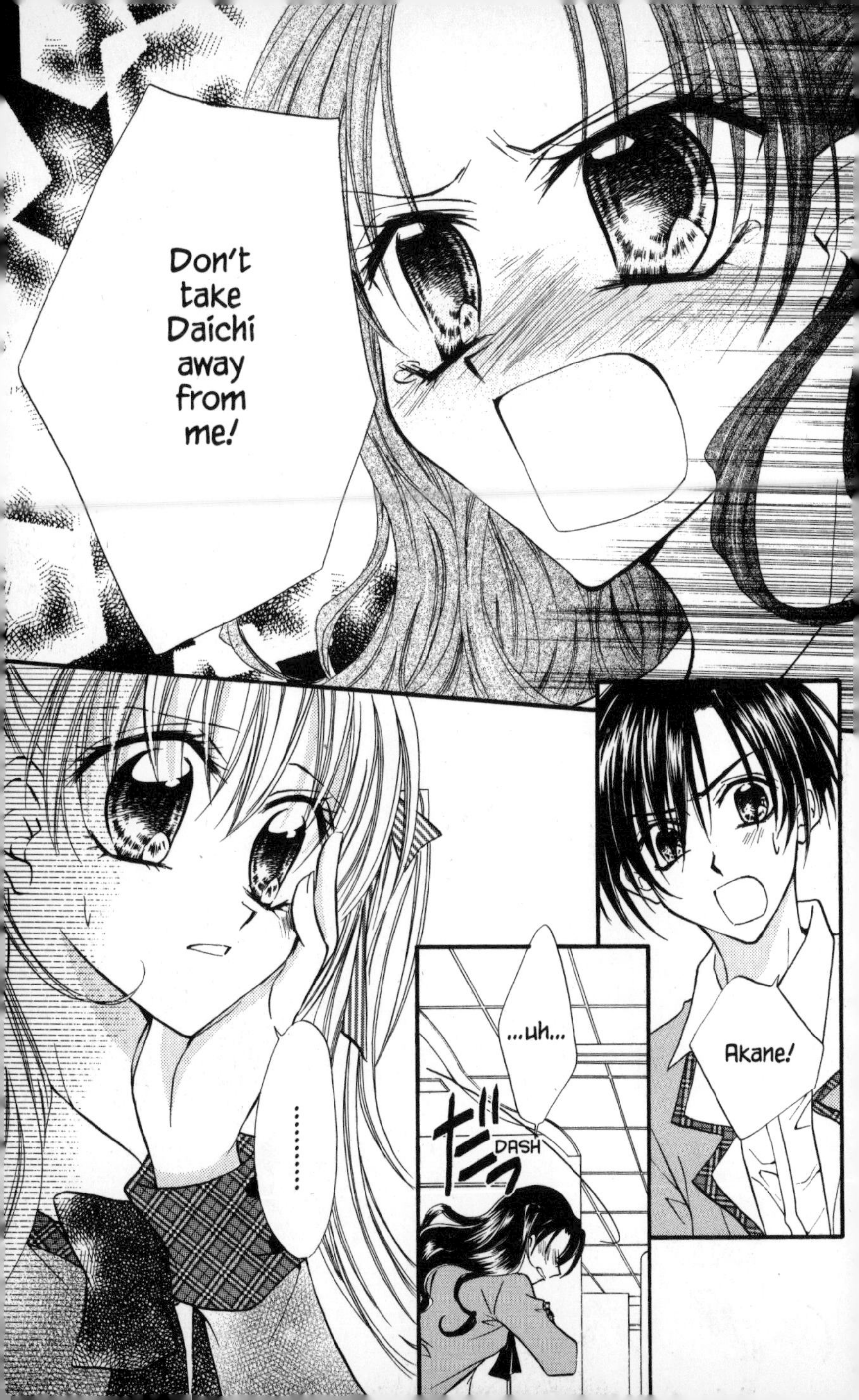
Don't take Daichi away from me!
Akane!
...uh...
DASH
....

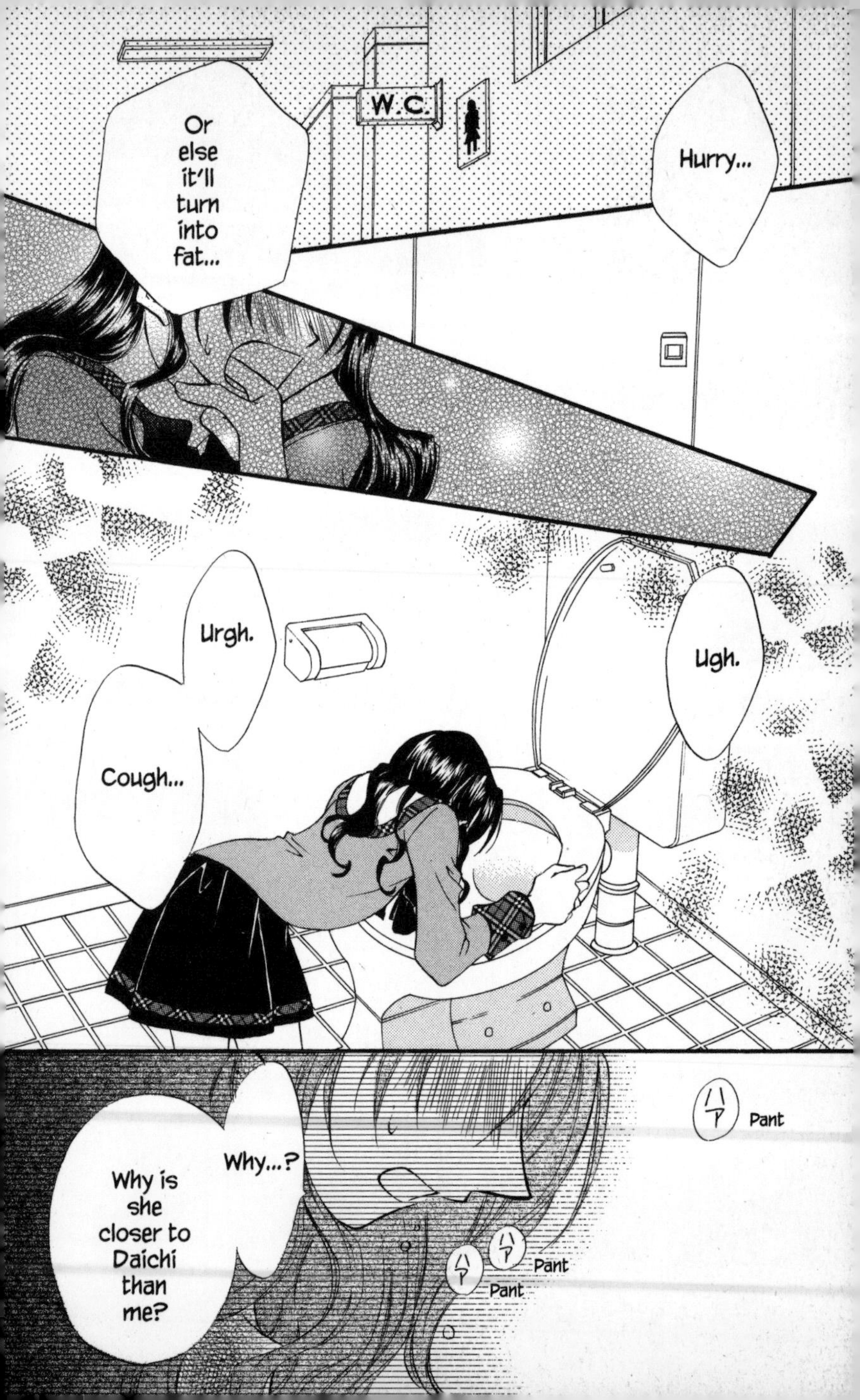
Hurry...
Or else it'll turn into fat...
W.C.
Ugh.
Urgh.
Cough...
ハァ Pant
ハァ Pant
ハァ Pant
Why...?
Why is she closer to Daichi than me?

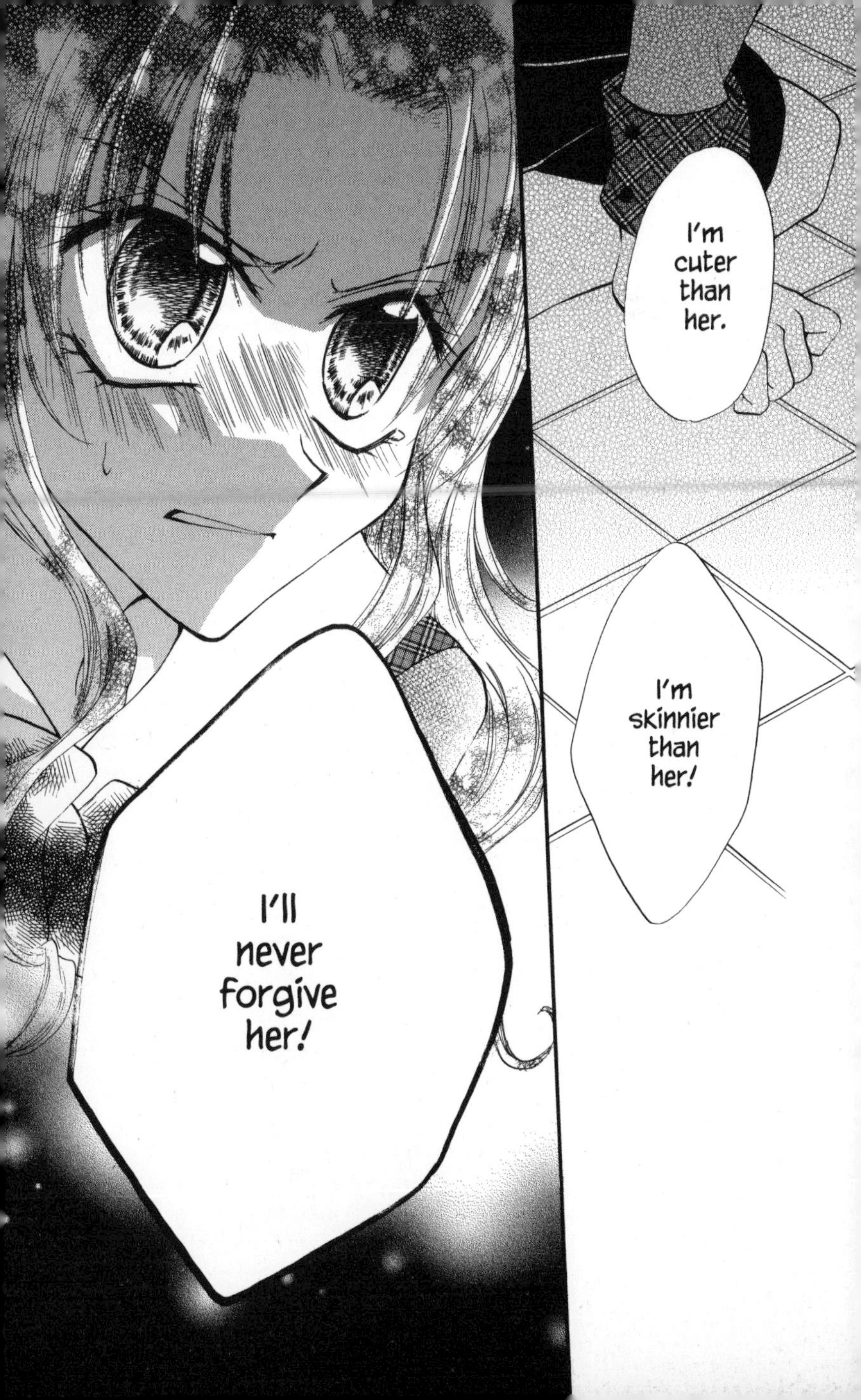
I'm cuter than her.
I'm skinnier than her!
I'll never forgive her!

A Map of Seika Academy (at least part of it)

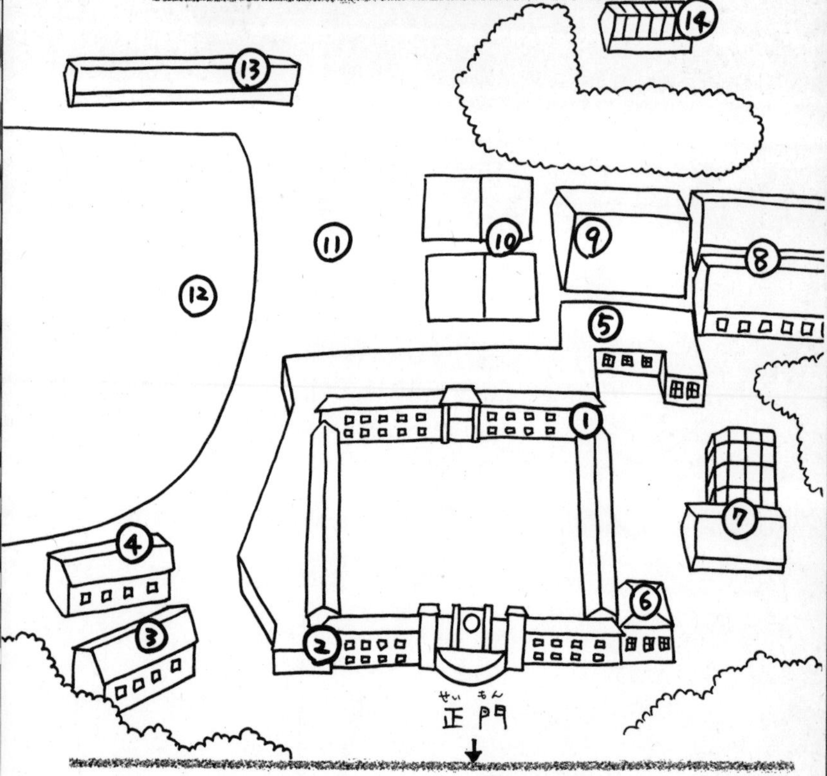
14
13
11
10
9
8
12
5
1
7
4
6
2
3
正門

1. The Junior High Section. Najika attends this.
2. High School Section
3. Girls' Dorm
4. Boys' Dorm
5. Building with Nurse's Office and Music Room
6. Hall where they had the Christmas presentation
7. Terrace and Cafeteria
8. Elementary School Section
9. Gym
10. Tennis Courts
11. Yard (big)
12. Field (really big)
13. Rooms for clubs
14. Fujita Diner

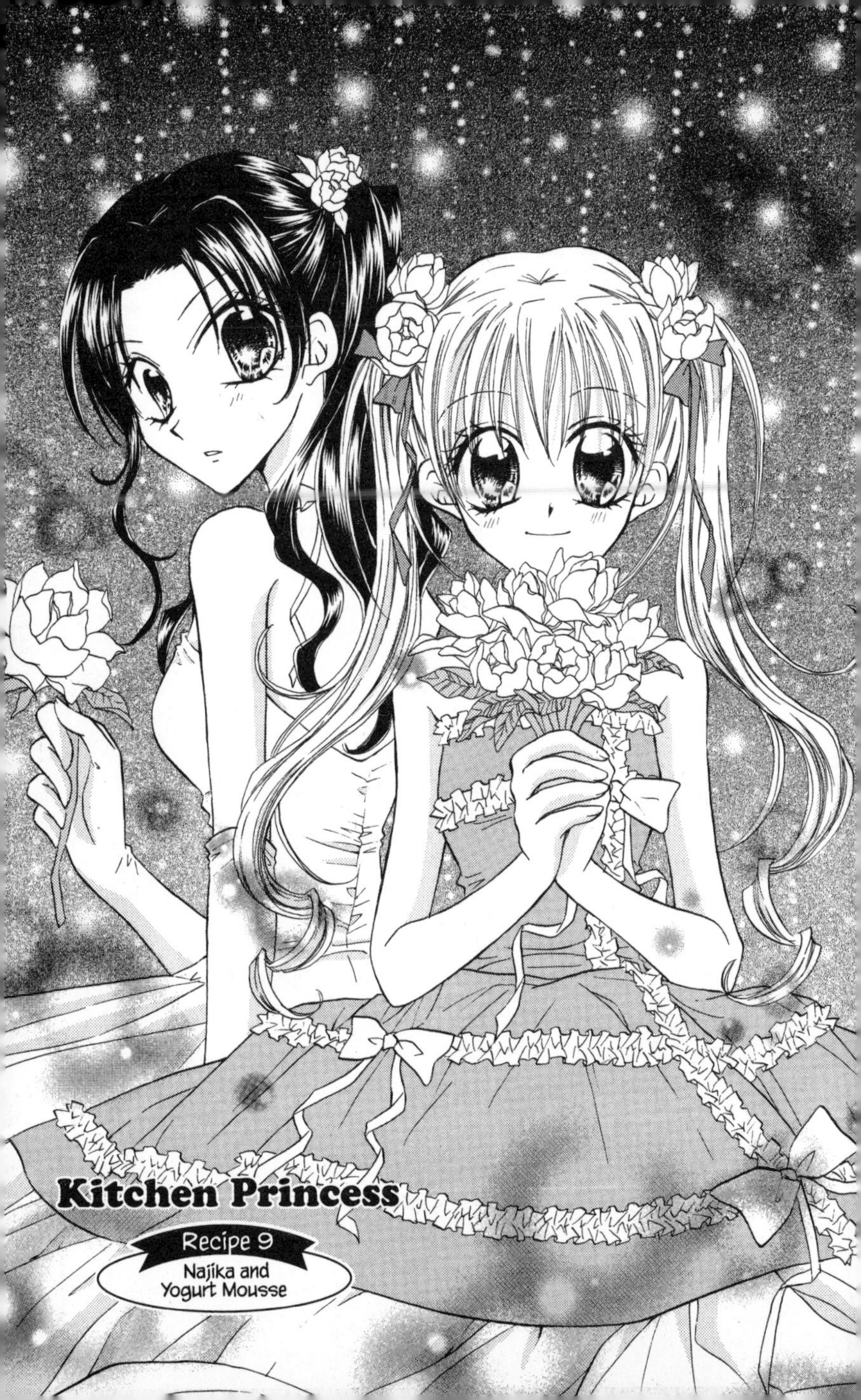
Kitchen Princess
Recipe 9
Najika and
Yogurt Mousse

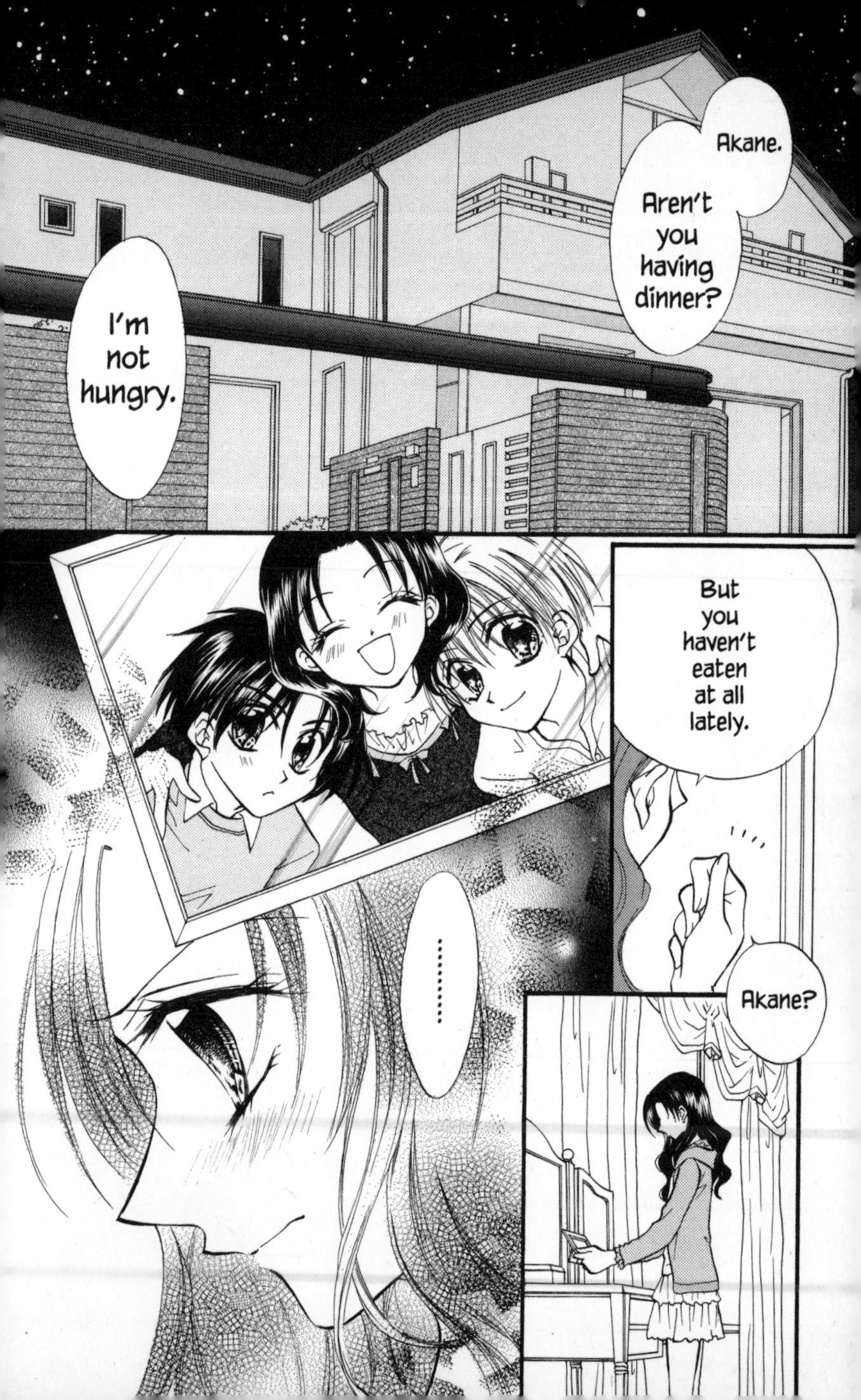

Akane.
Aren't you having dinner?
I'm not hungry.
But you haven't eaten at all lately.
Akane?
....

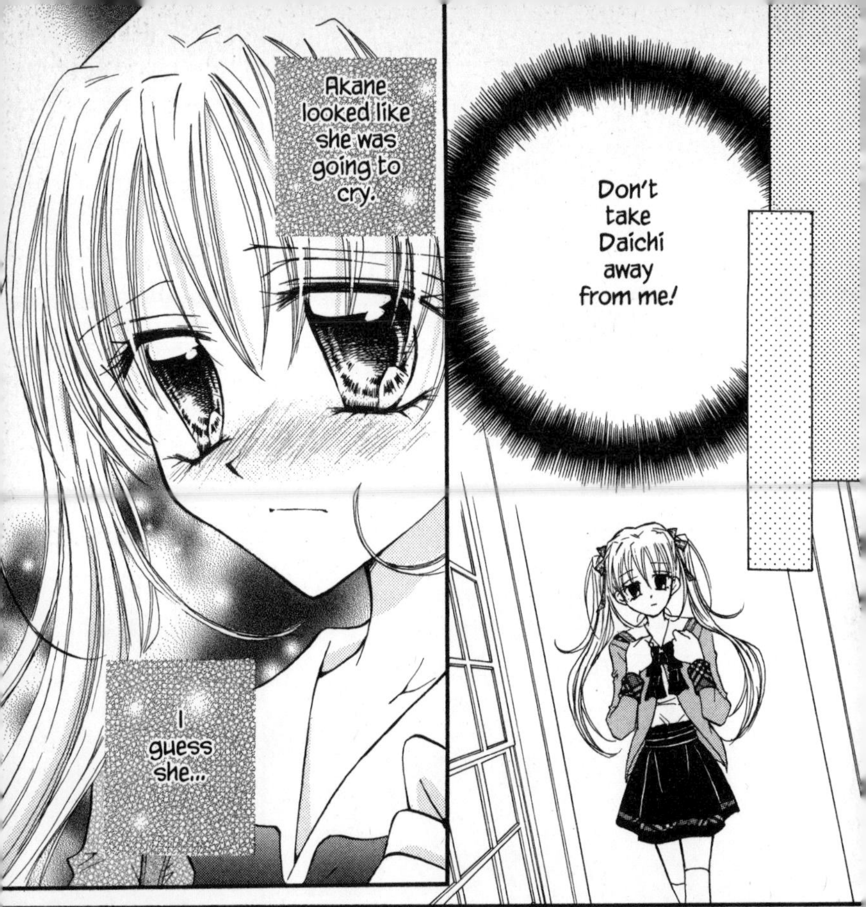
Don't take Daichi away from me!
Akane looked like she was going to cry.
I guess she...

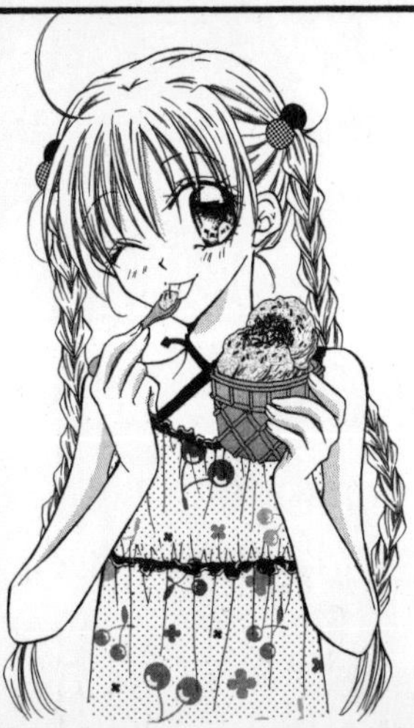

About Recipe 9's Splash Page

I always wanted to do a splash page with the two girls. And since the story was revolving around Akane, I decided to do it for this chapter. Akane's hair is fun to draw. ♪ Although coloring it in is hard work...

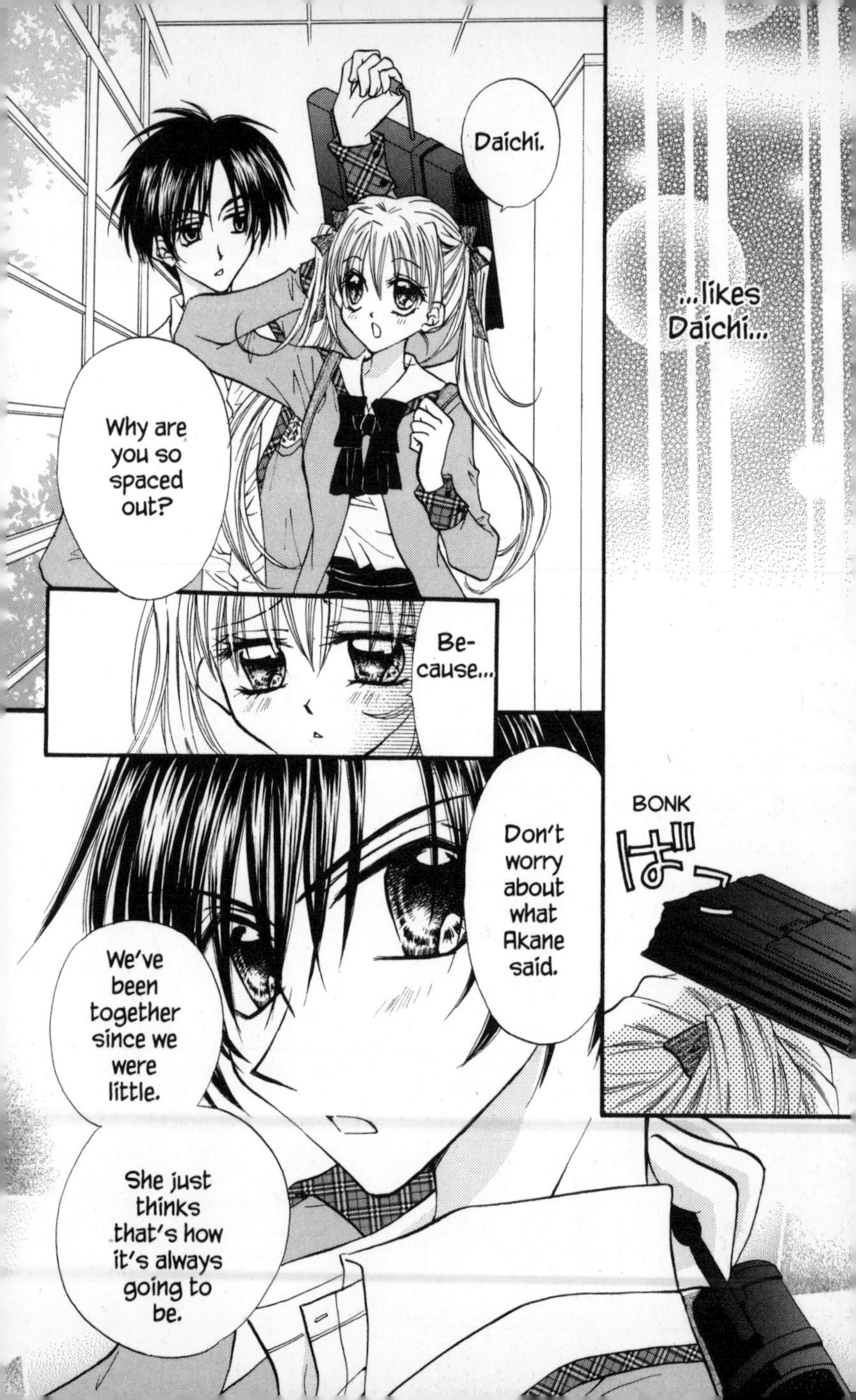

...likes Daichi...
Daichi.
Why are you so spaced out?
Be-cause...
BONK
Don't worry about what Akane said.
We've been together since we were little.
She just thinks that's how it's always going to be.

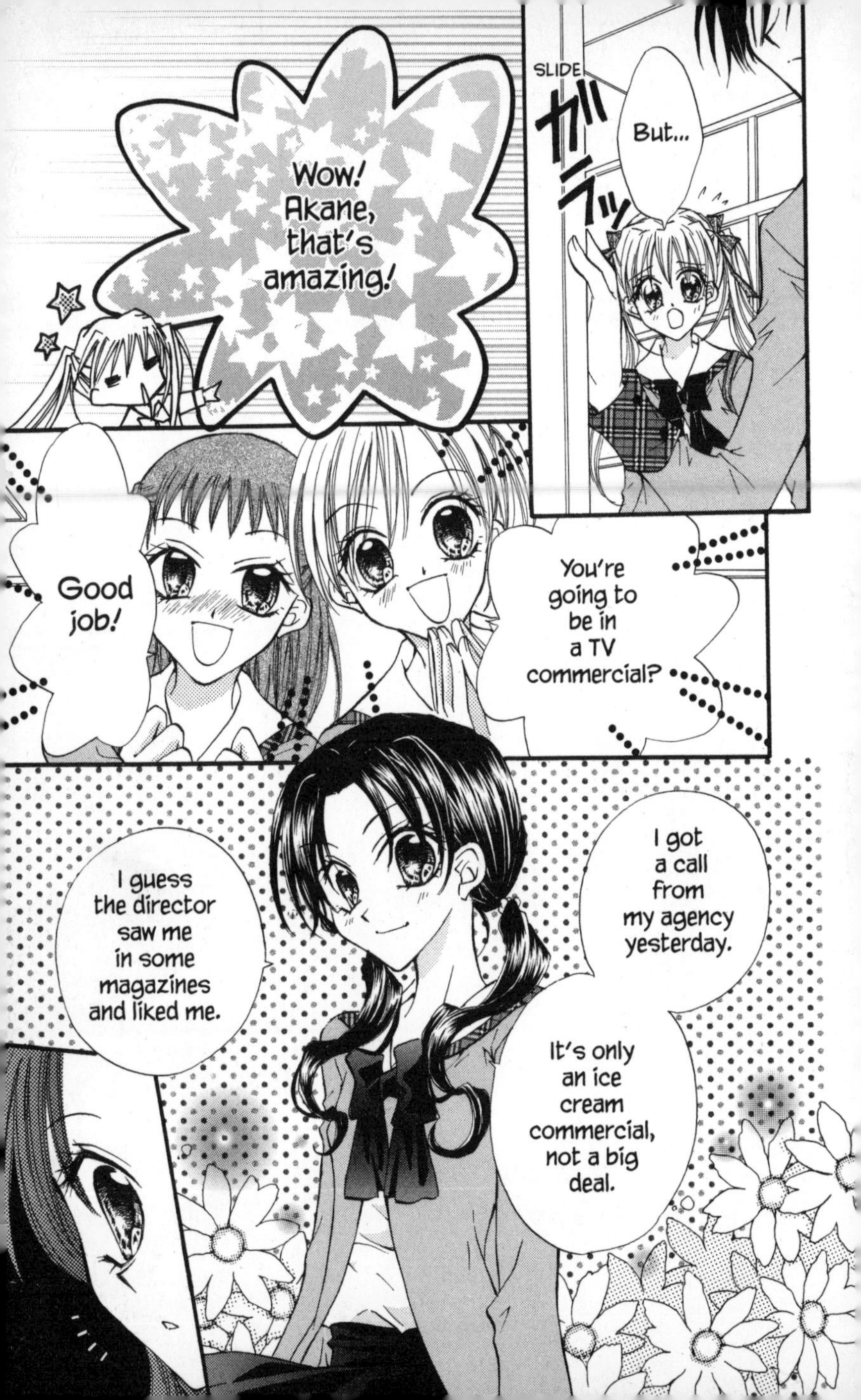
SLIDE
ガラッ
But...
Wow! Akane, that's amazing!
You're going to be in a TV commercial?
Good job!
I got a call from my agency yesterday.
I guess the director saw me in some magazines and liked me.
It's only an ice cream commercial, not a big deal.

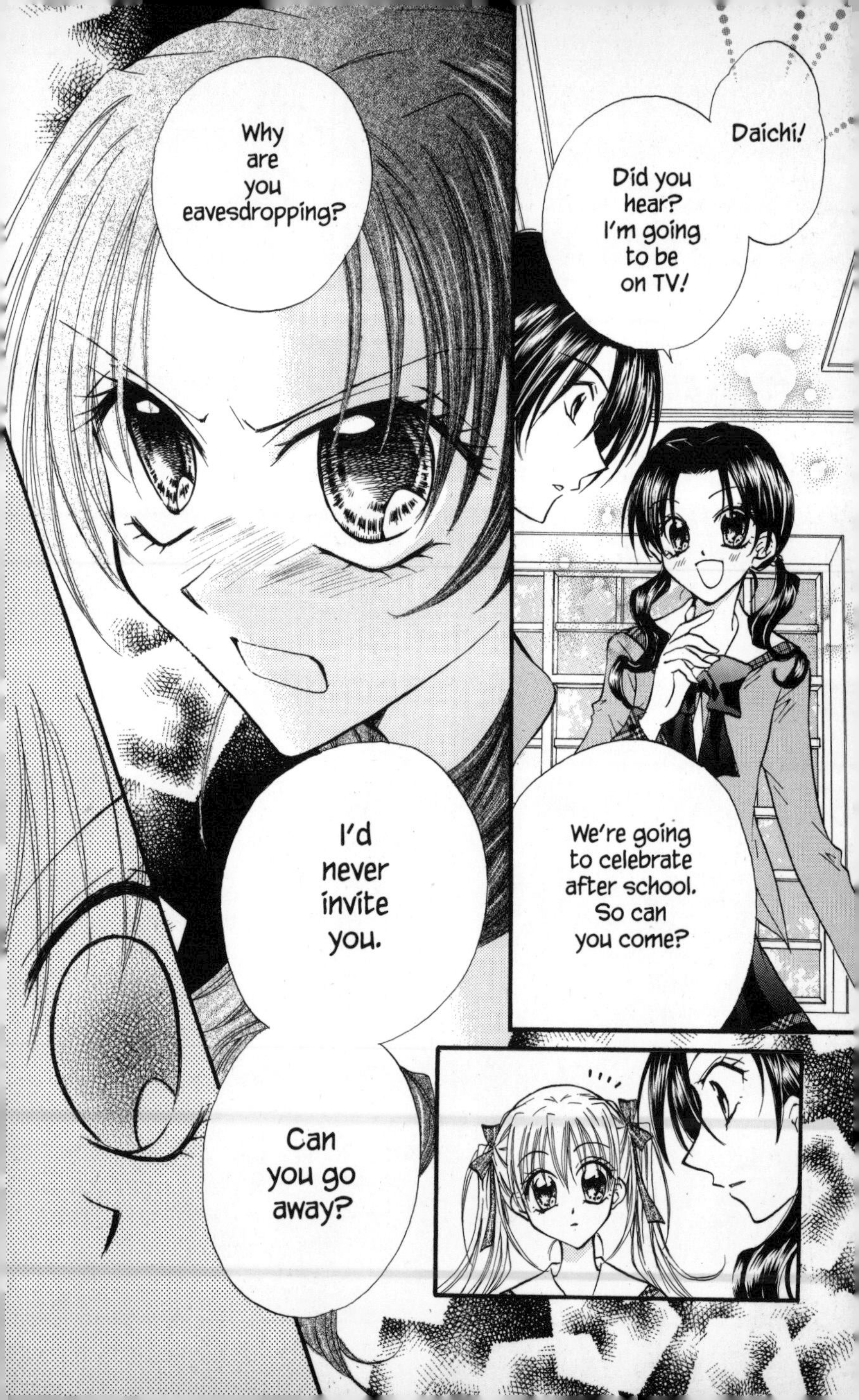
Daichi!
Did you hear? I'm going to be on TV!
We're going to celebrate after school. So can you come?
Why are you eavesdropping?
I'd never invite you.
Can you go away?

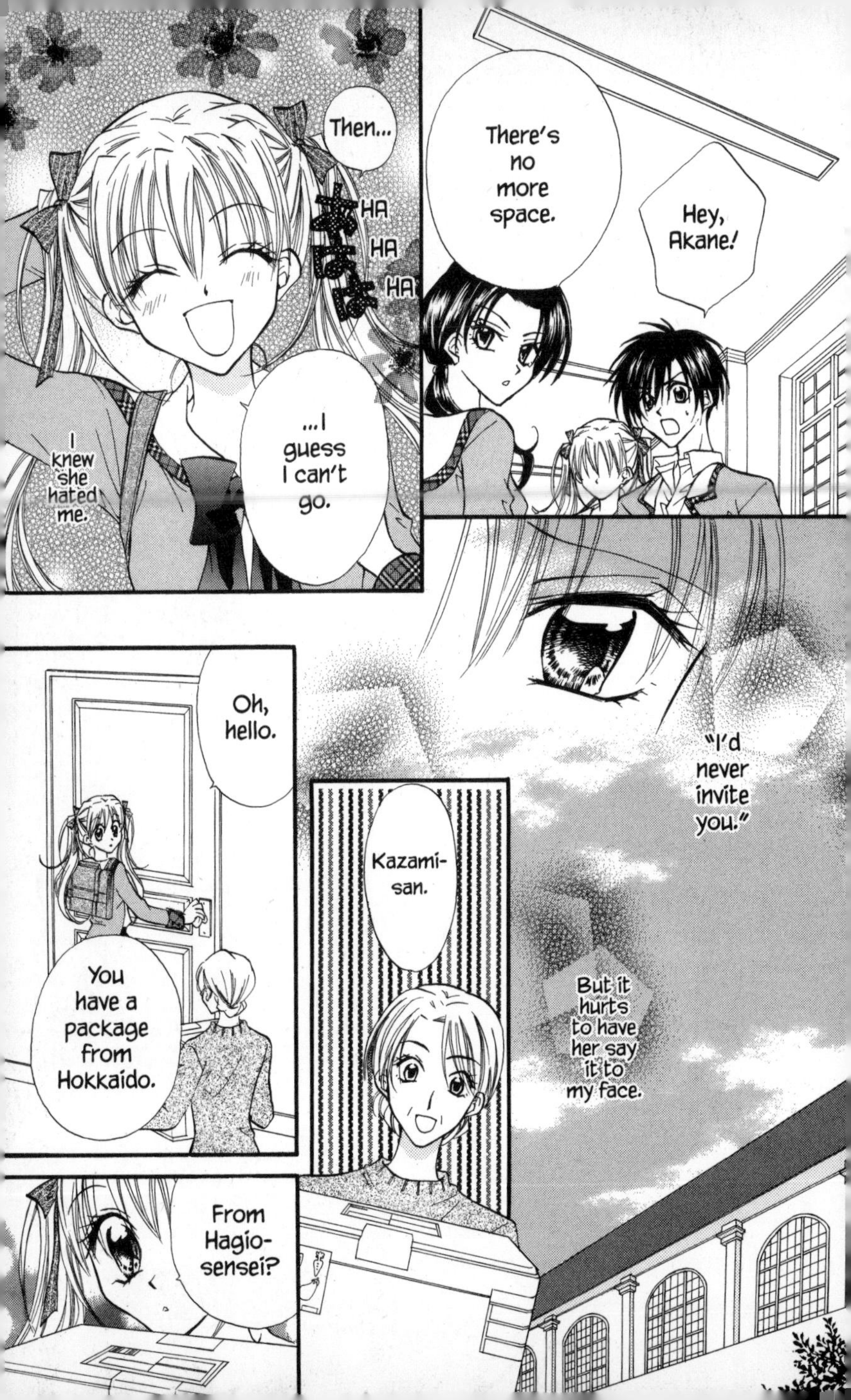
There's no more space.
Hey, Akane!
Then...
あはは
HA HA HA
...I guess I can't go.
I knew she hated me.
"I'd never invite you."
But it hurts to have her say it to my face.
Kazami-san.
Oh, hello.
You have a package from Hokkaido.
From Hagio-sensei?

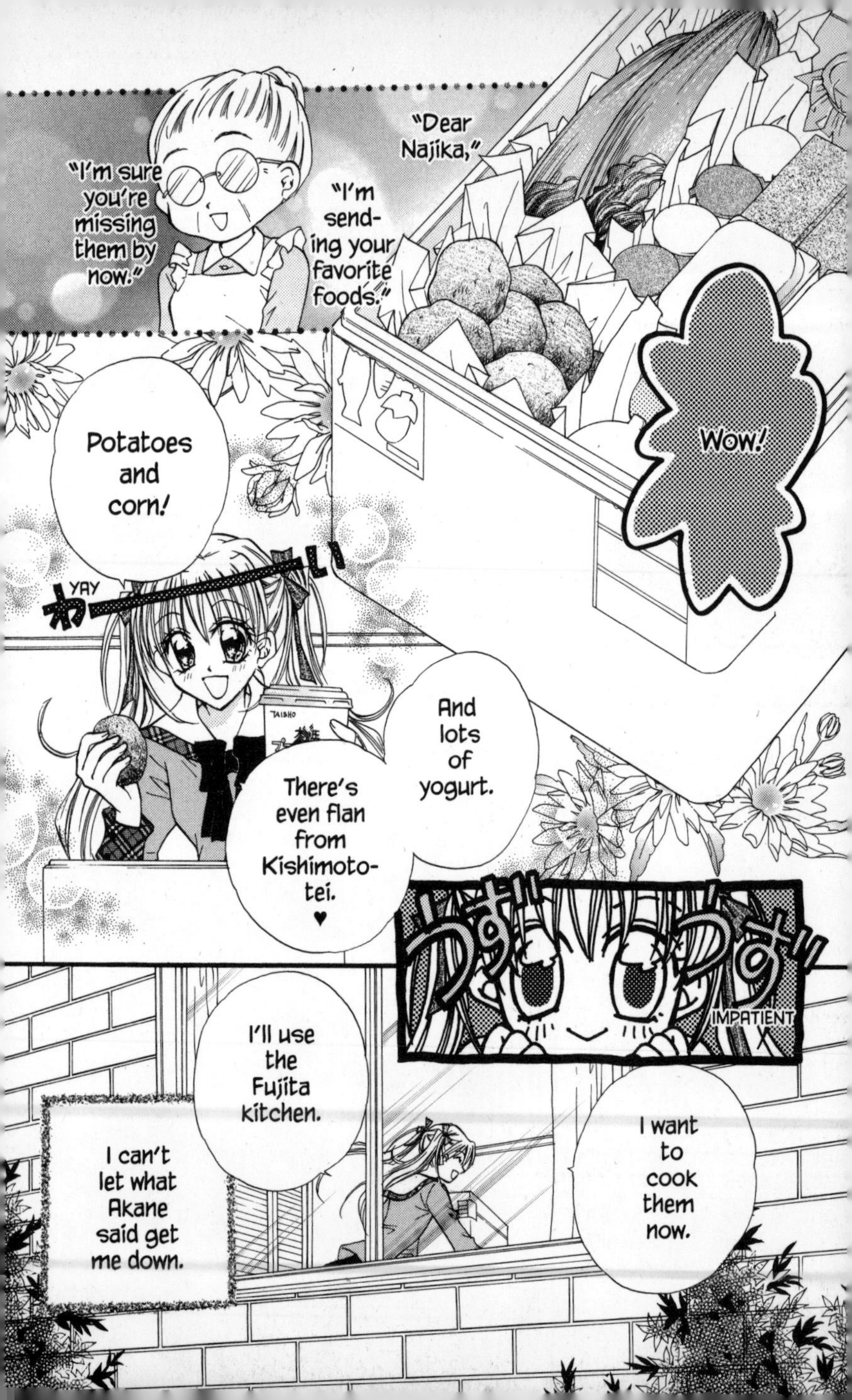
"Dear Najika,"
"I'm sending your favorite foods."
"I'm sure you're missing them by now."
Wow!
Potatoes and corn!
YAY
And lots of yogurt.
There's even flan from Kishimoto-tei. ♥
TAISHO
IMPATIENT
I want to cook them now.
I'll use the Fujita kitchen.
I can't let what Akane said get me down.

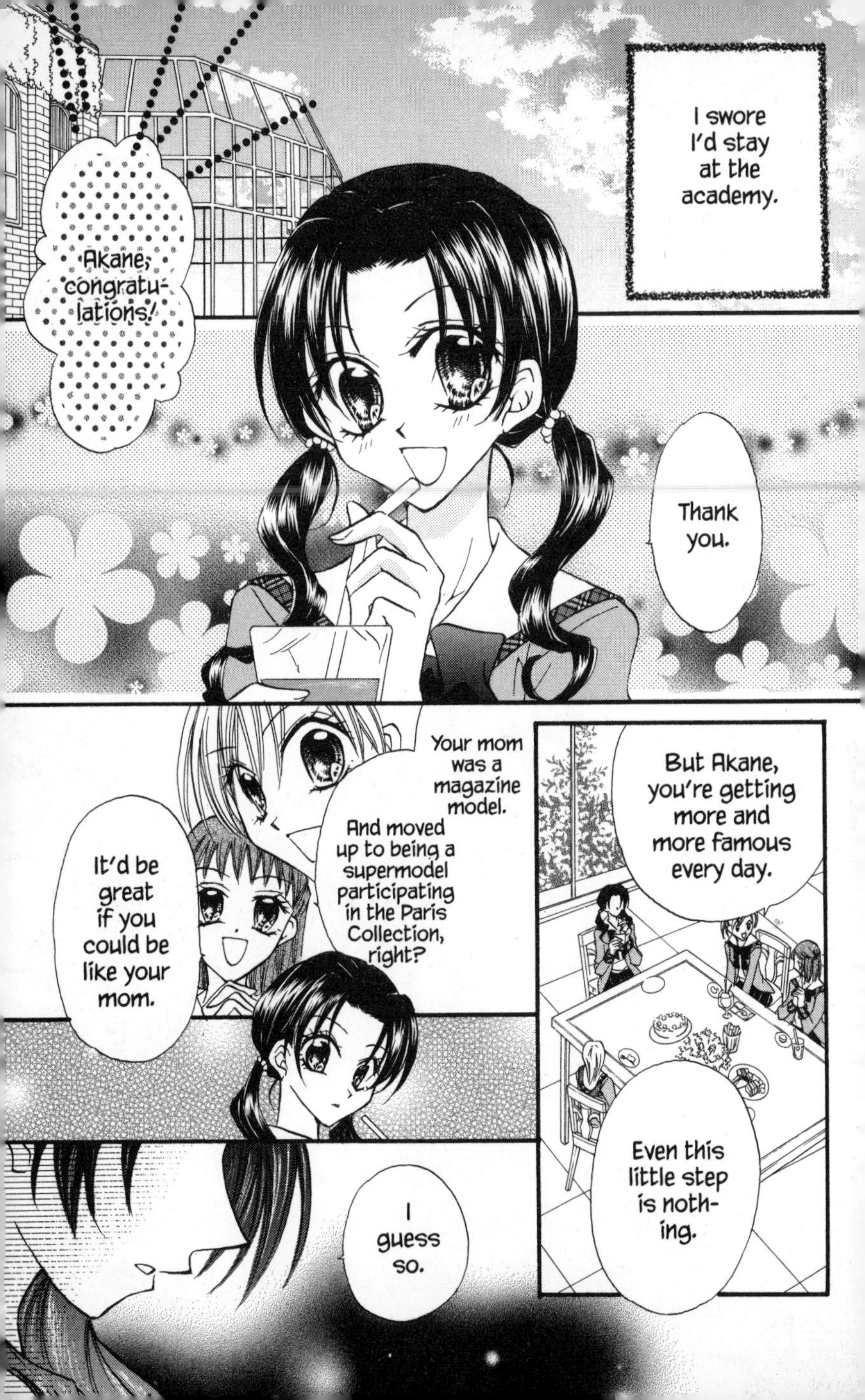

I swore I'd stay at the academy.
Akane, congratulations!
Thank you.
But Akane, you're getting more and more famous every day.
Even this little step is nothing.
Your mom was a magazine model.
And moved up to being a supermodel participating in the Paris Collection, right?
It'd be great if you could be like your mom.
I guess so.

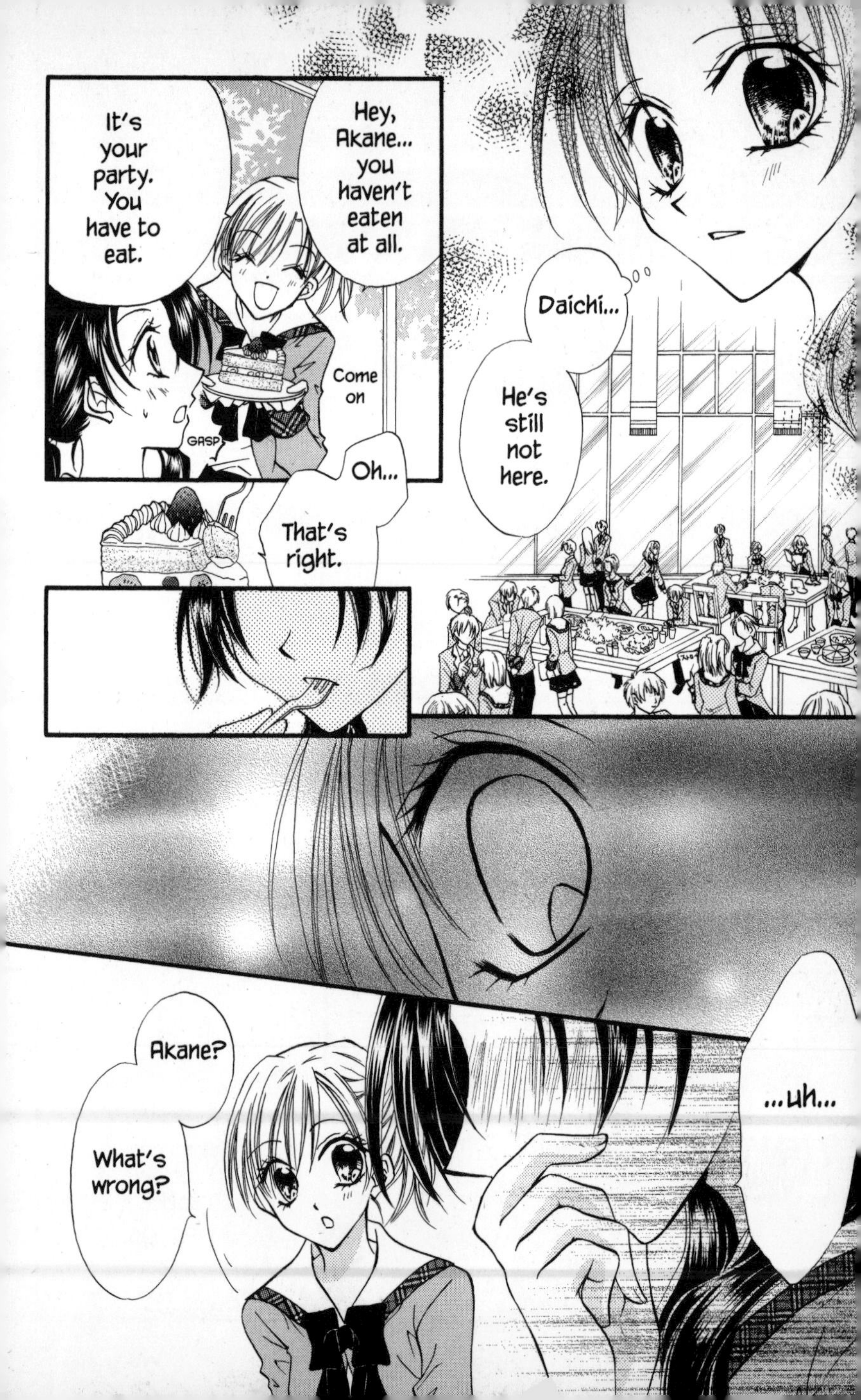
Daichi...
He's still not here.
Hey, Akane... you haven't eaten at all.
It's your party. You have to eat.
Come on
GASP
Oh...
That's right.
Akane?
What's wrong?
...uh...

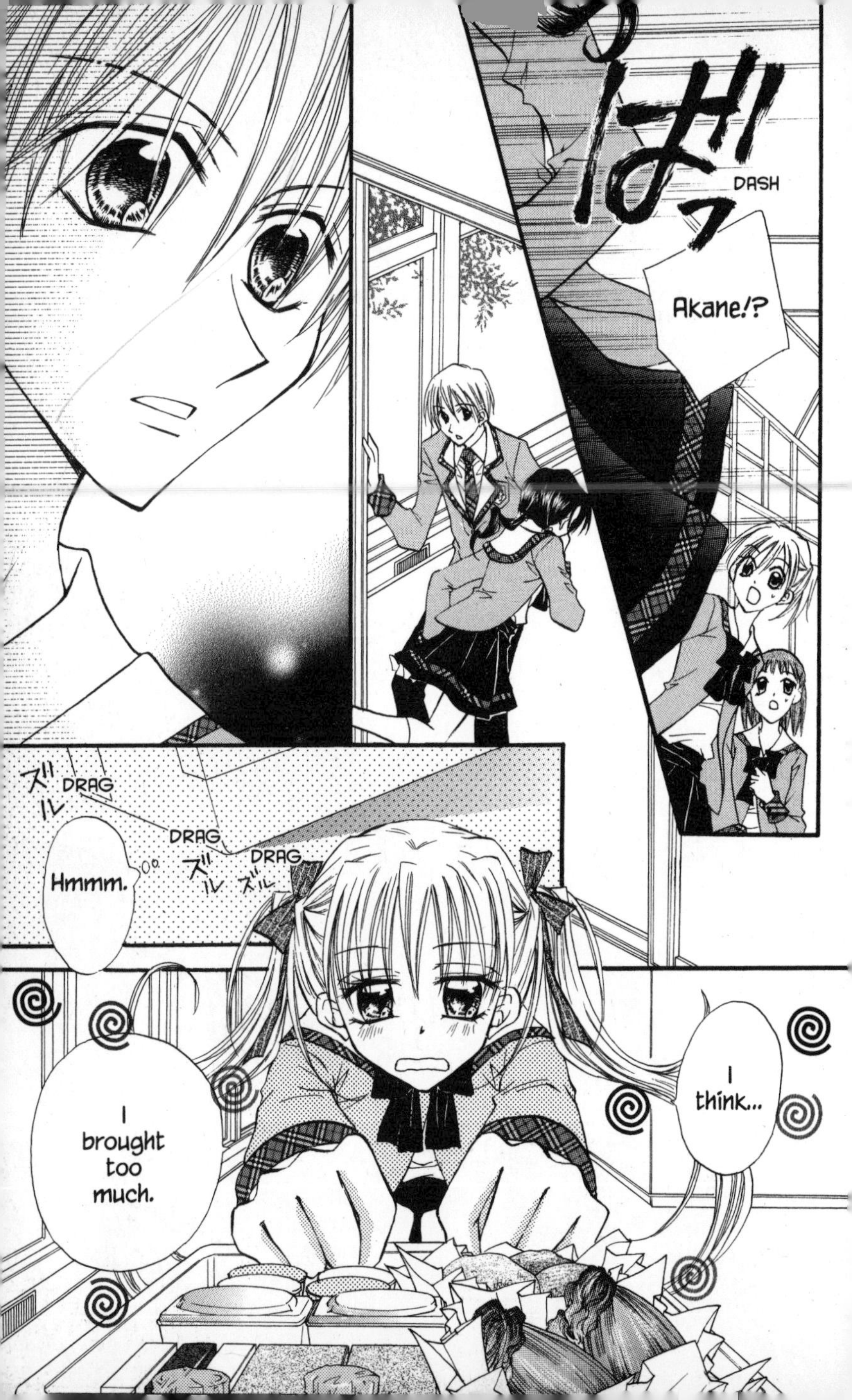
ぱっ
DASH
Akane!?
ズル DRAG
DRAG ズル
DRAG ズル
Hmmm.
I think...
I brought too much.

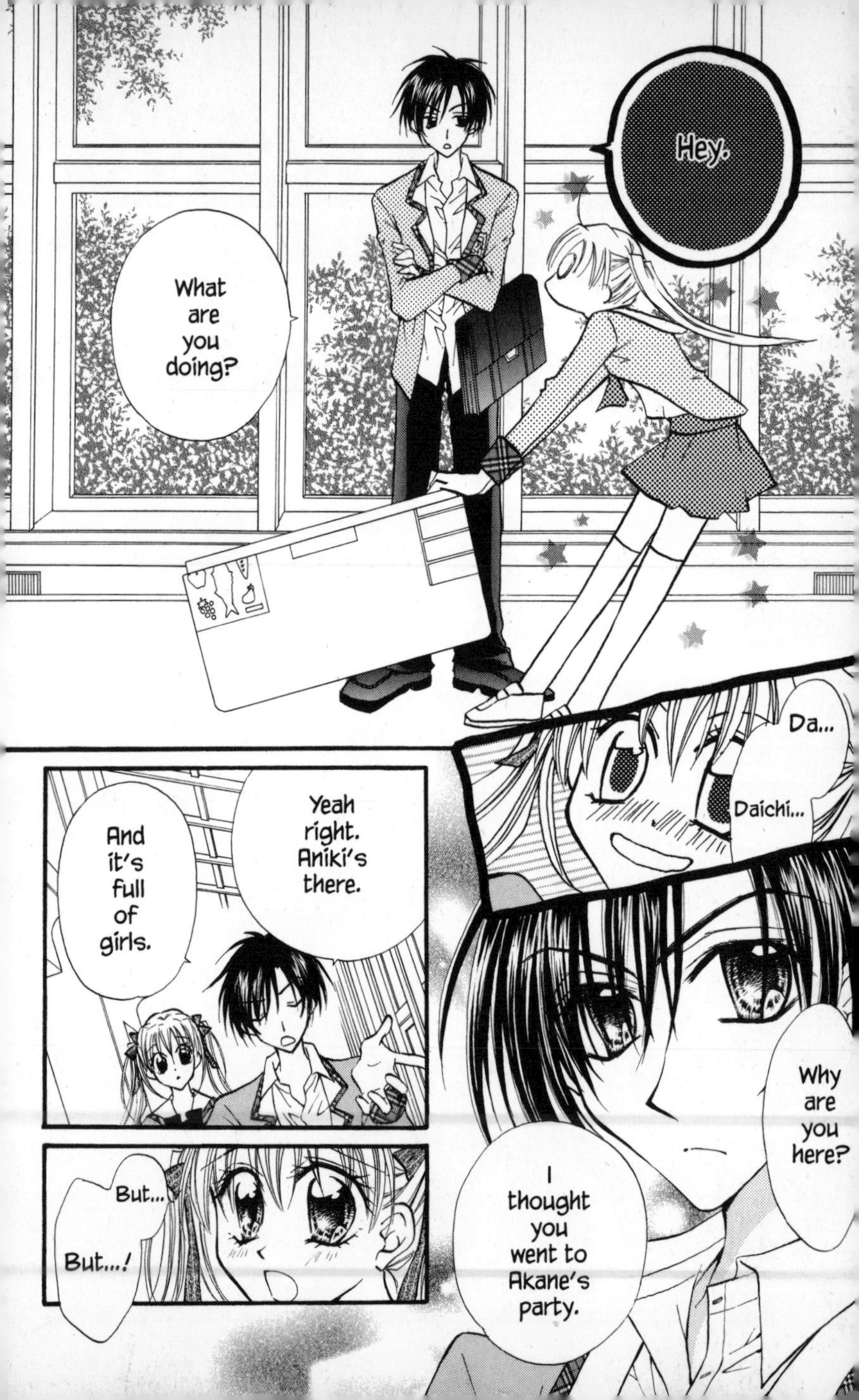
Hey.
What are you doing?
Da...
Daichi...
Why are you here?
I thought you went to Akane's party.
Yeah right. Aniki's there.
And it's full of girls.
But...
But...!

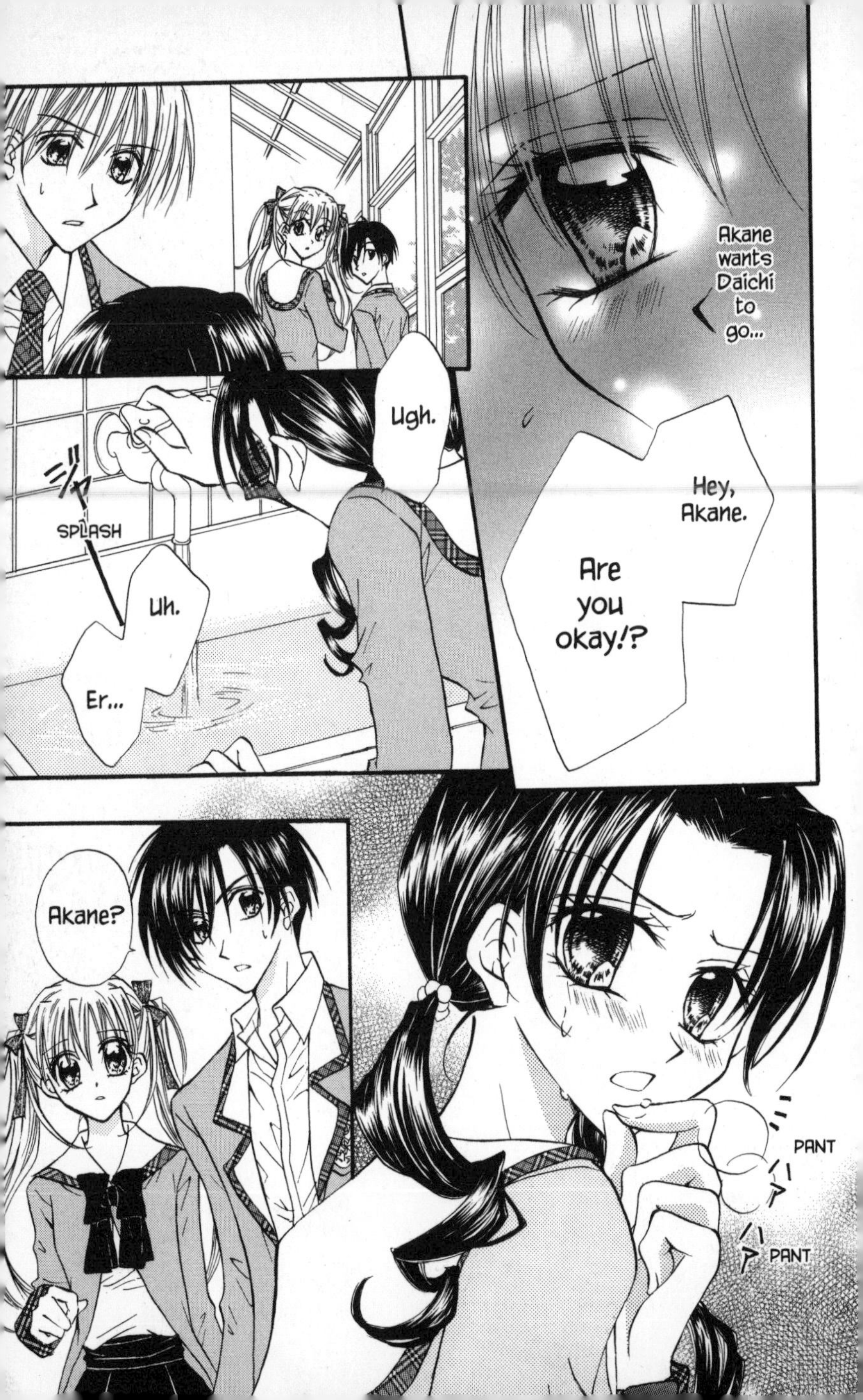
Akane wants Daichi to go...
Hey, Akane.
Are you okay!?
Ugh.
ジャ
SPLASH
Uh.
Er...
PANT
PANT
Akane?

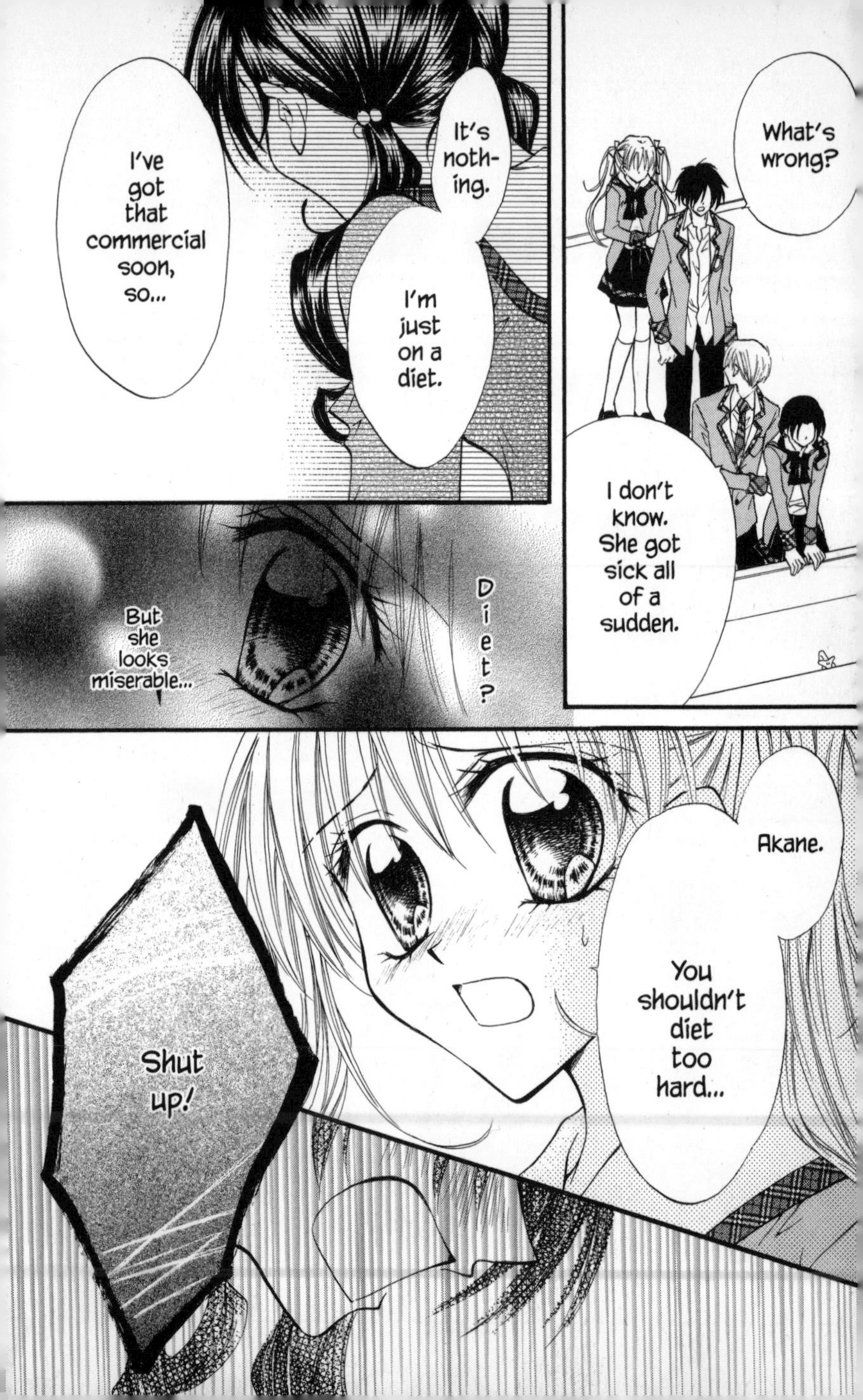
What's wrong?
I don't know. She got sick all of a sudden.
It's nothing.
I'm just on a diet.
I've got that commercial soon, so...
Diet?
But she looks miserable...
Akane.
You shouldn't diet too hard...
Shut up!

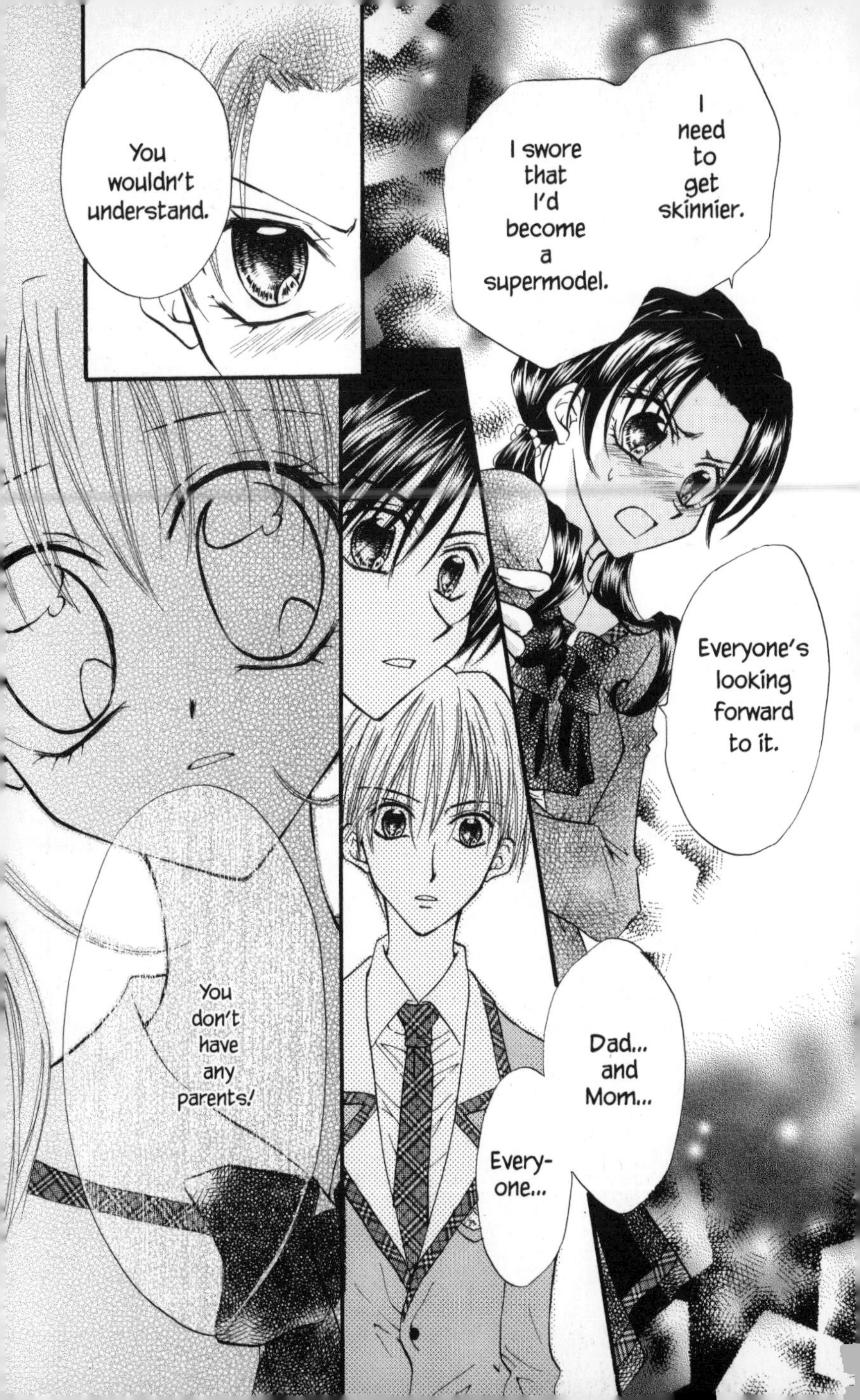
I need to get skinnier.
I swore that I'd become a supermodel.
You wouldn't understand.
Everyone's looking forward to it.
Dad... and Mom...
Every-one...
You don't have any parents!

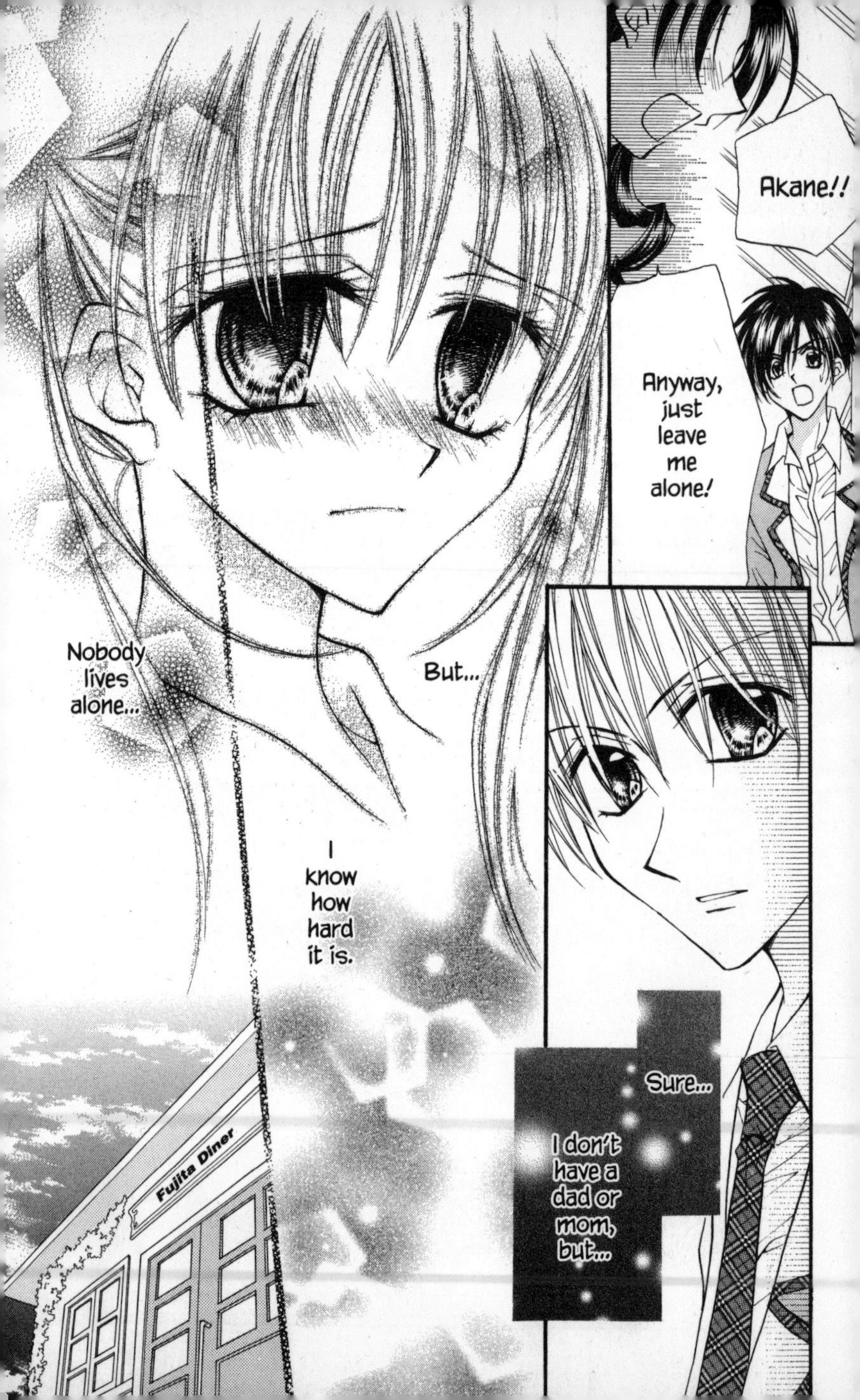
Akane!!
Anyway, just leave me alone!
Sure...
I don't have a dad or mom, but...
Nobody lives alone...
But...
I know how hard it is.
Fujita Diner

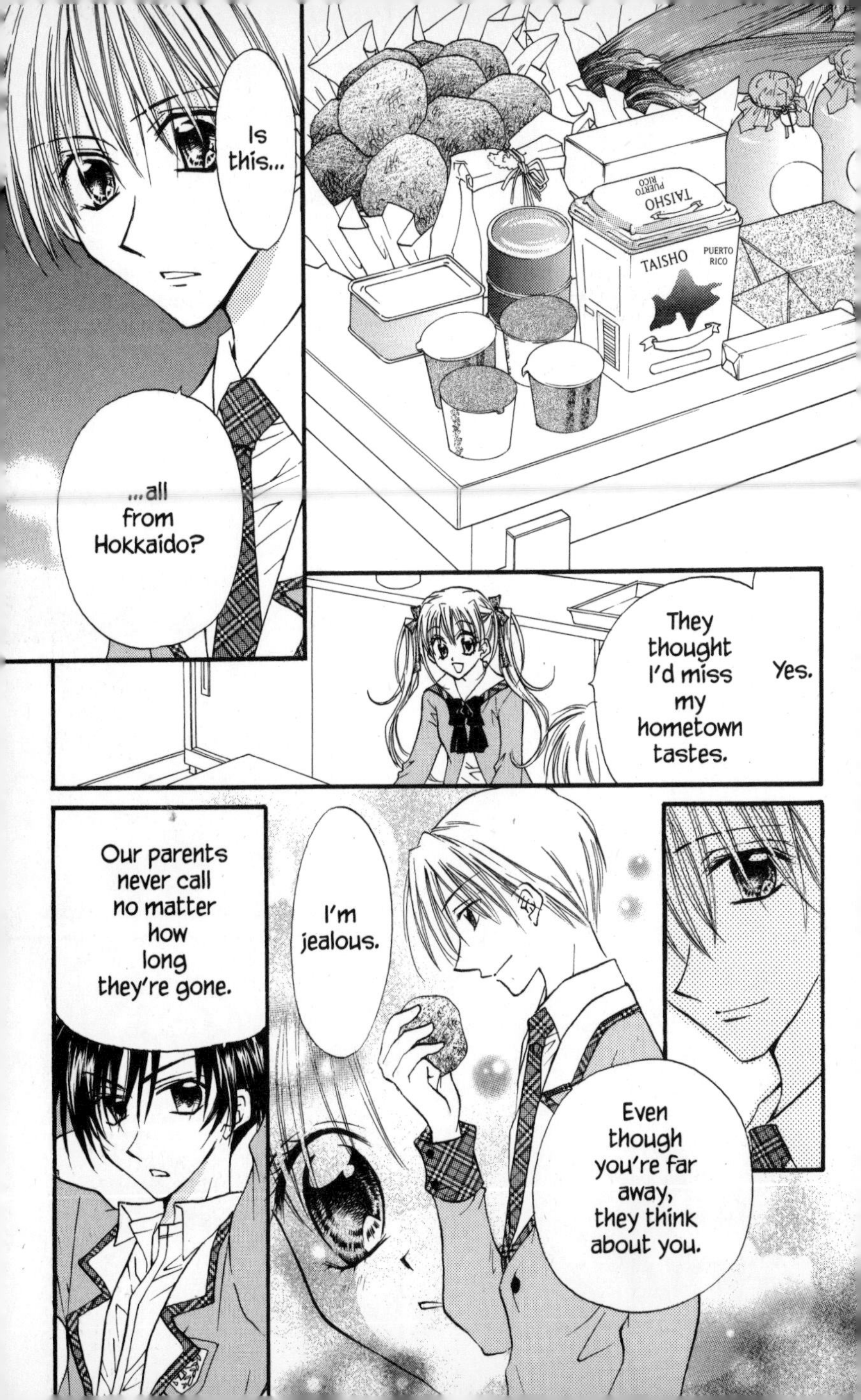

TAISHO PUERTO RICO
Is this...
...all from Hokkaido?
Yes.
They thought I'd miss my hometown tastes.
Even though you're far away, they think about you.
I'm jealous.
Our parents never call no matter how long they're gone.

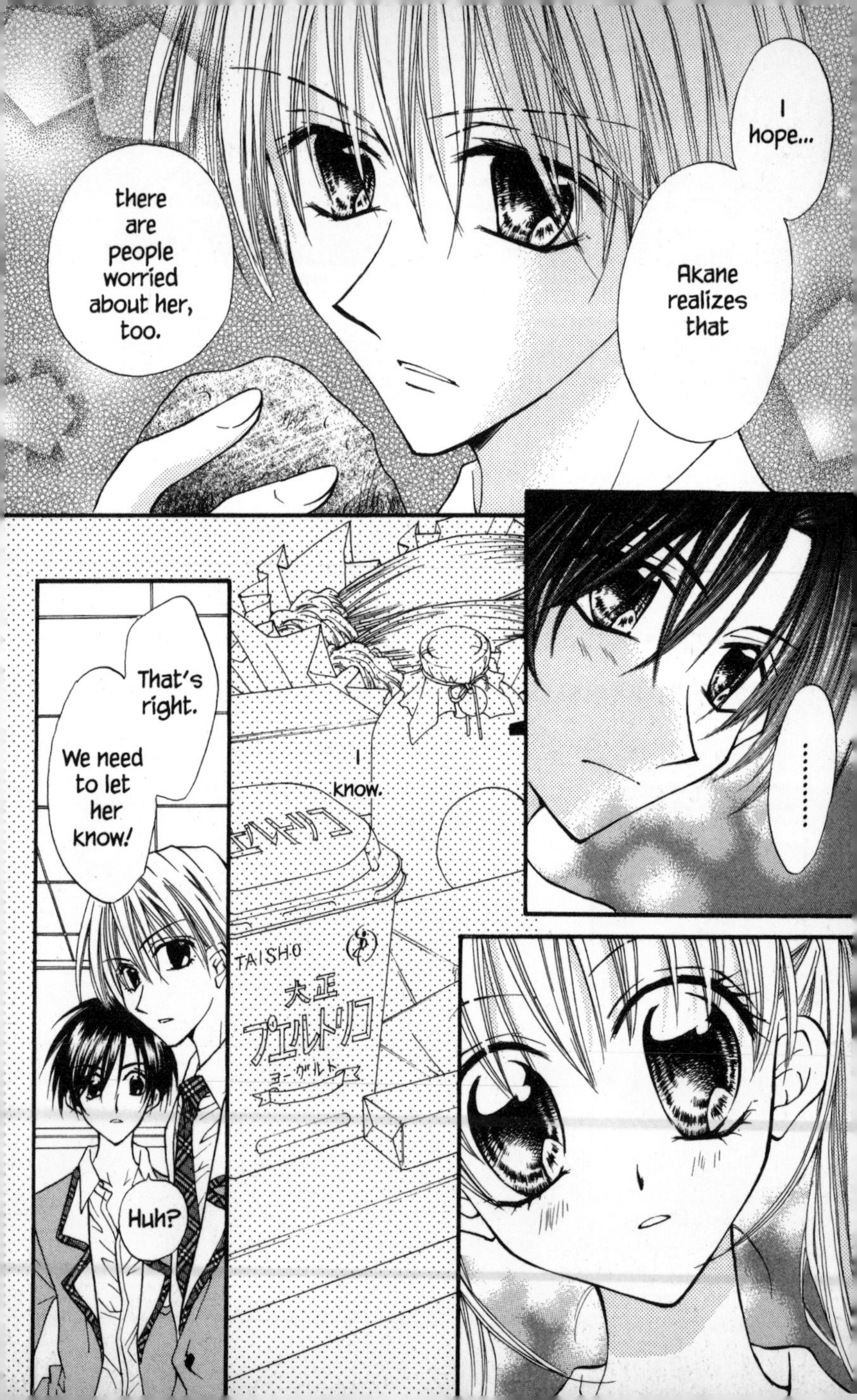
I hope...
Akane realizes that
there are people worried about her, too.
......
I know.
That's right.
We need to let her know!
Huh?
TAISHO
大正
プエルトリコ

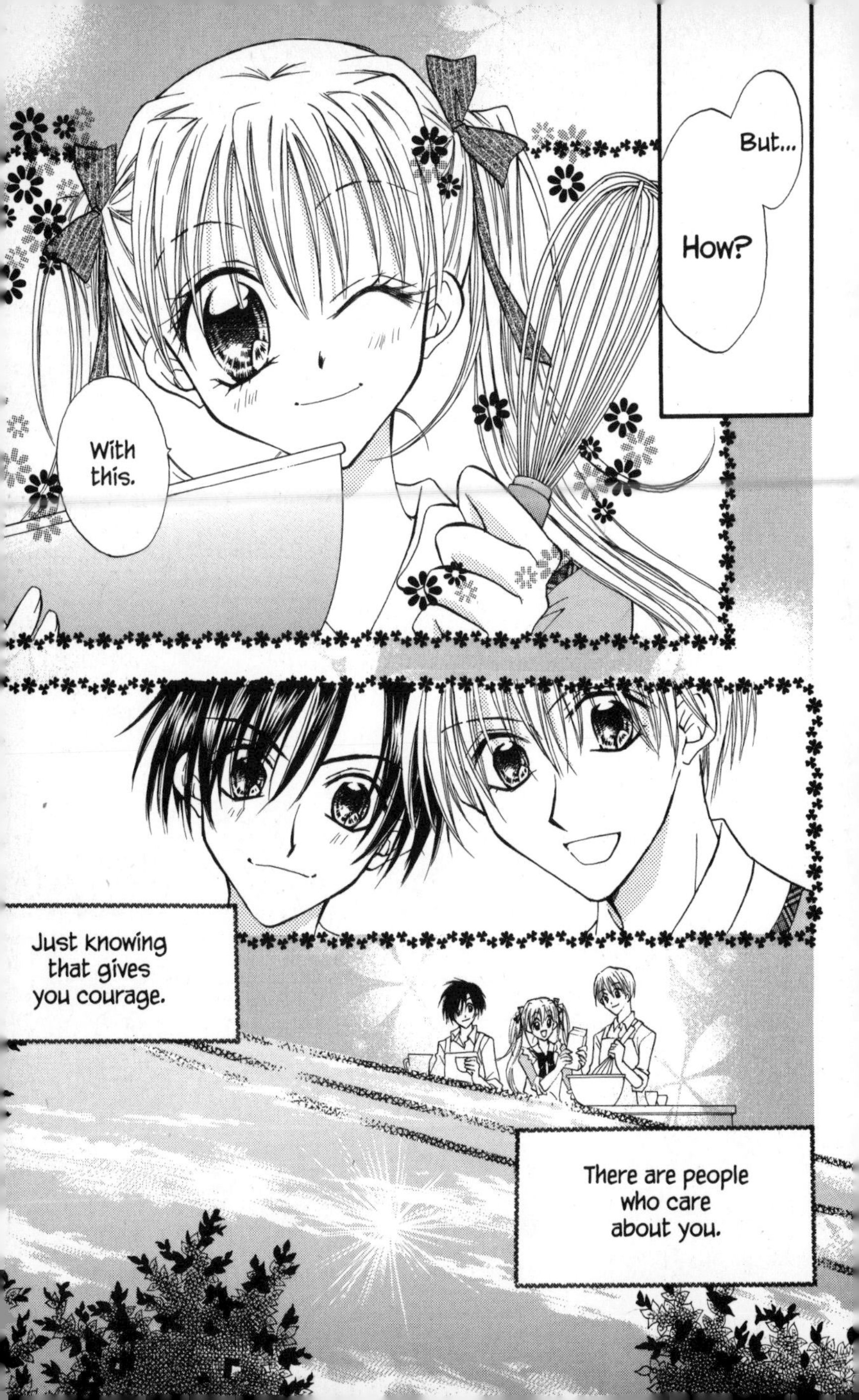
But...
How?
With this.
There are people who care about you.
Just knowing that gives you courage.

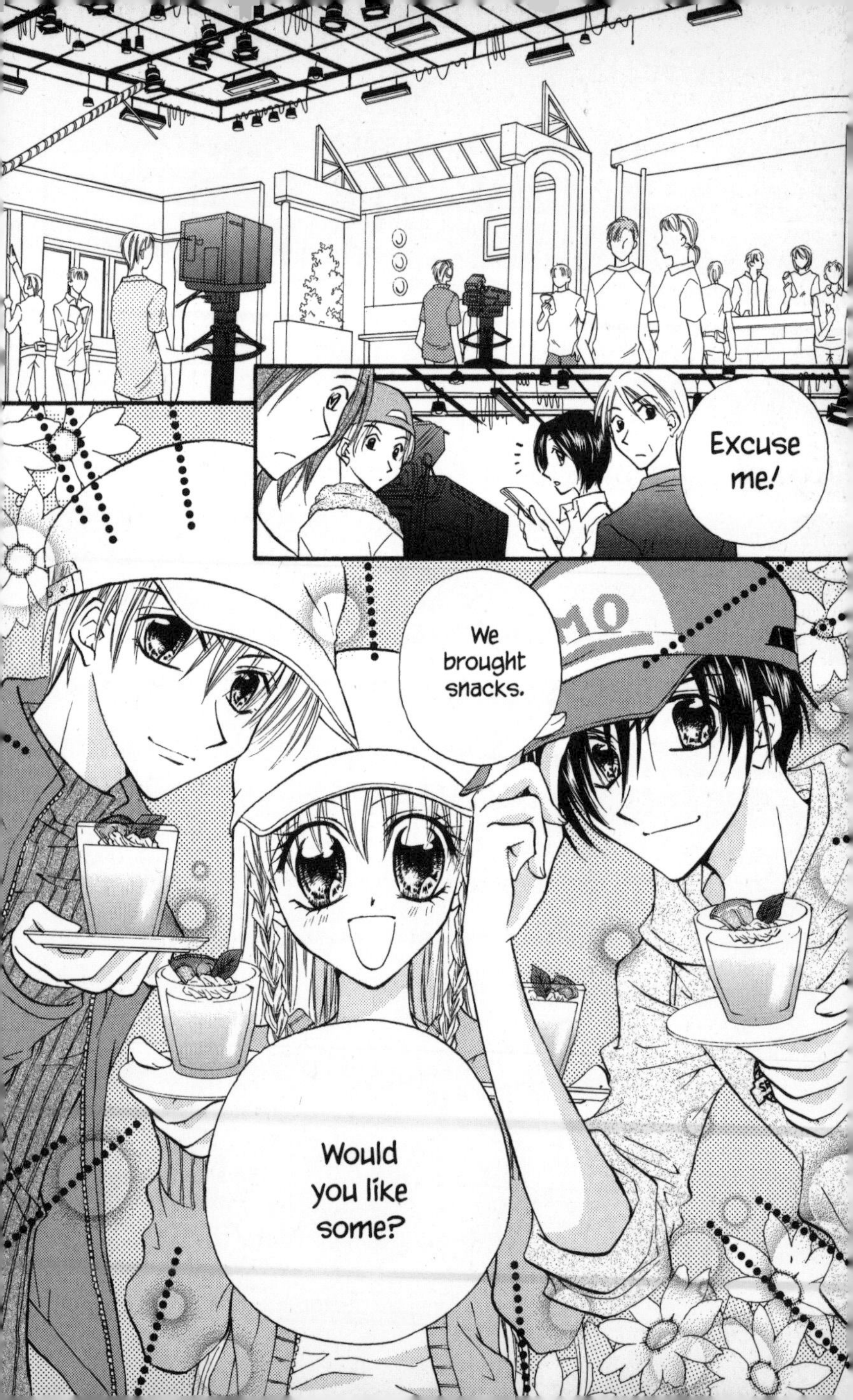
Excuse me!
We brought snacks.
Would you like some?

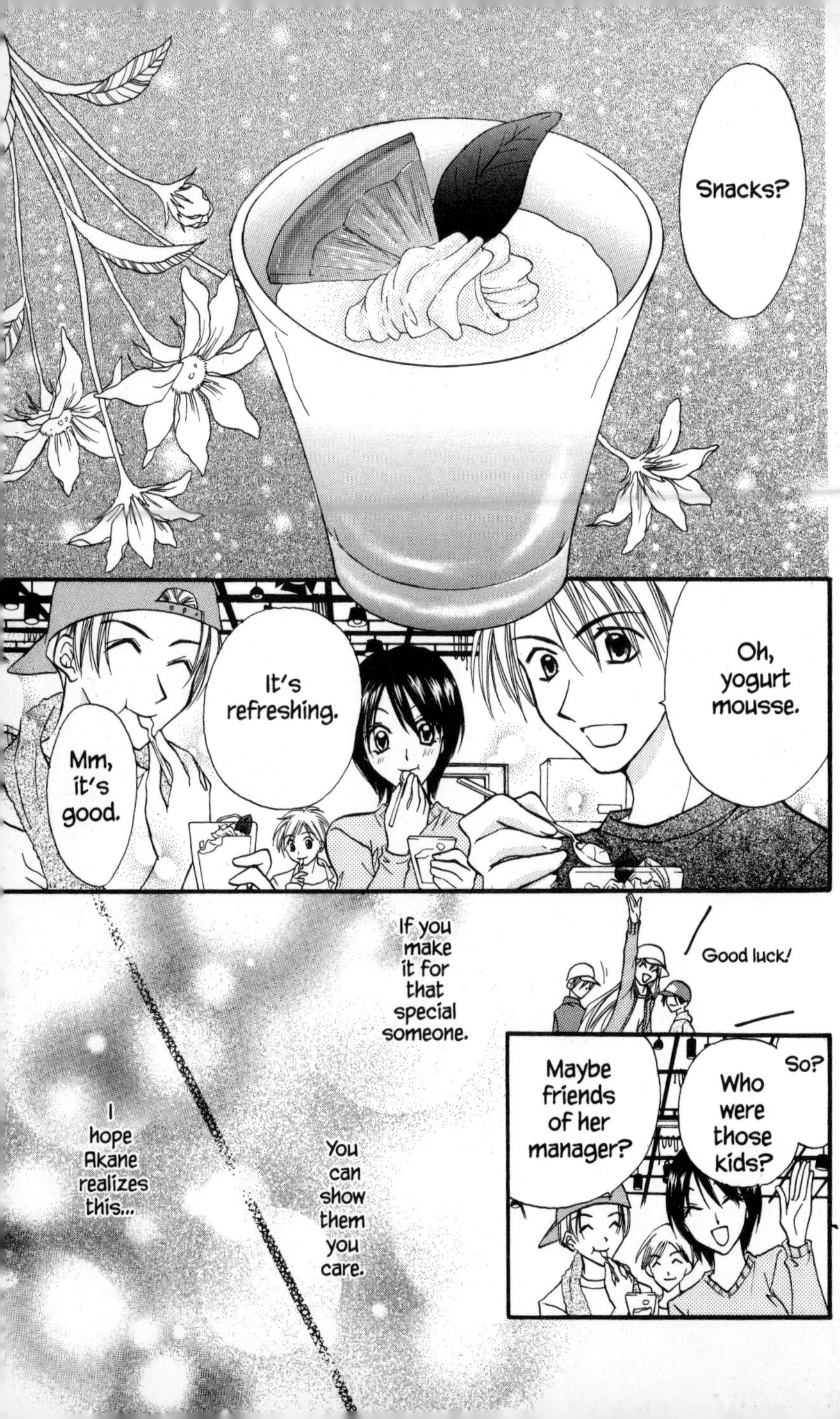
Snacks?
Oh, yogurt mousse.
It's refreshing.
Mm, it's good.
Good luck!
So?
Who were those kids?
Maybe friends of her manager?
If you make it for that special someone.
You can show them you care.
I hope Akane realizes this...

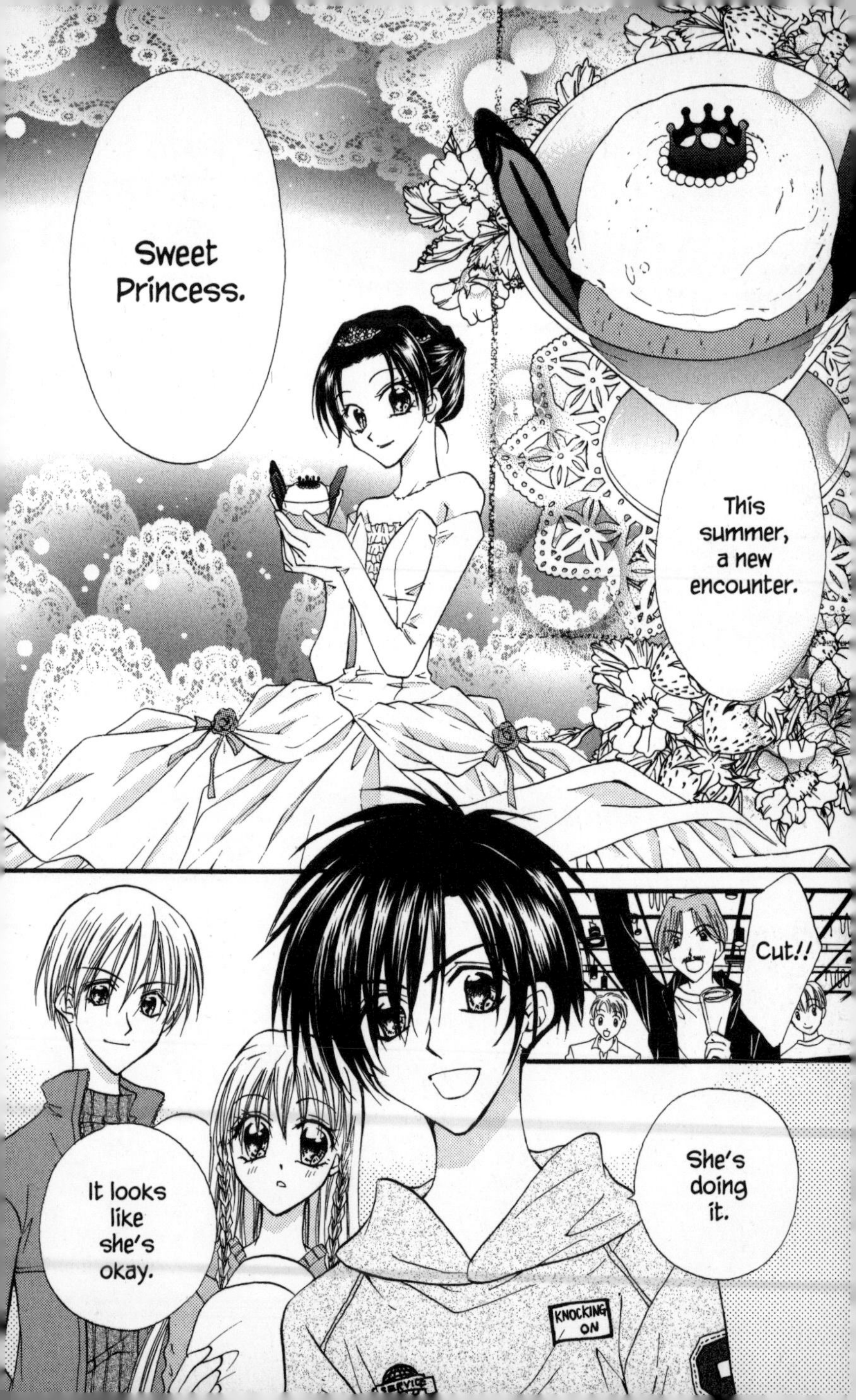
This summer, a new encounter.
Sweet Princess.
Cut!!
She's doing it.
It looks like she's okay.
KNOCKING ON

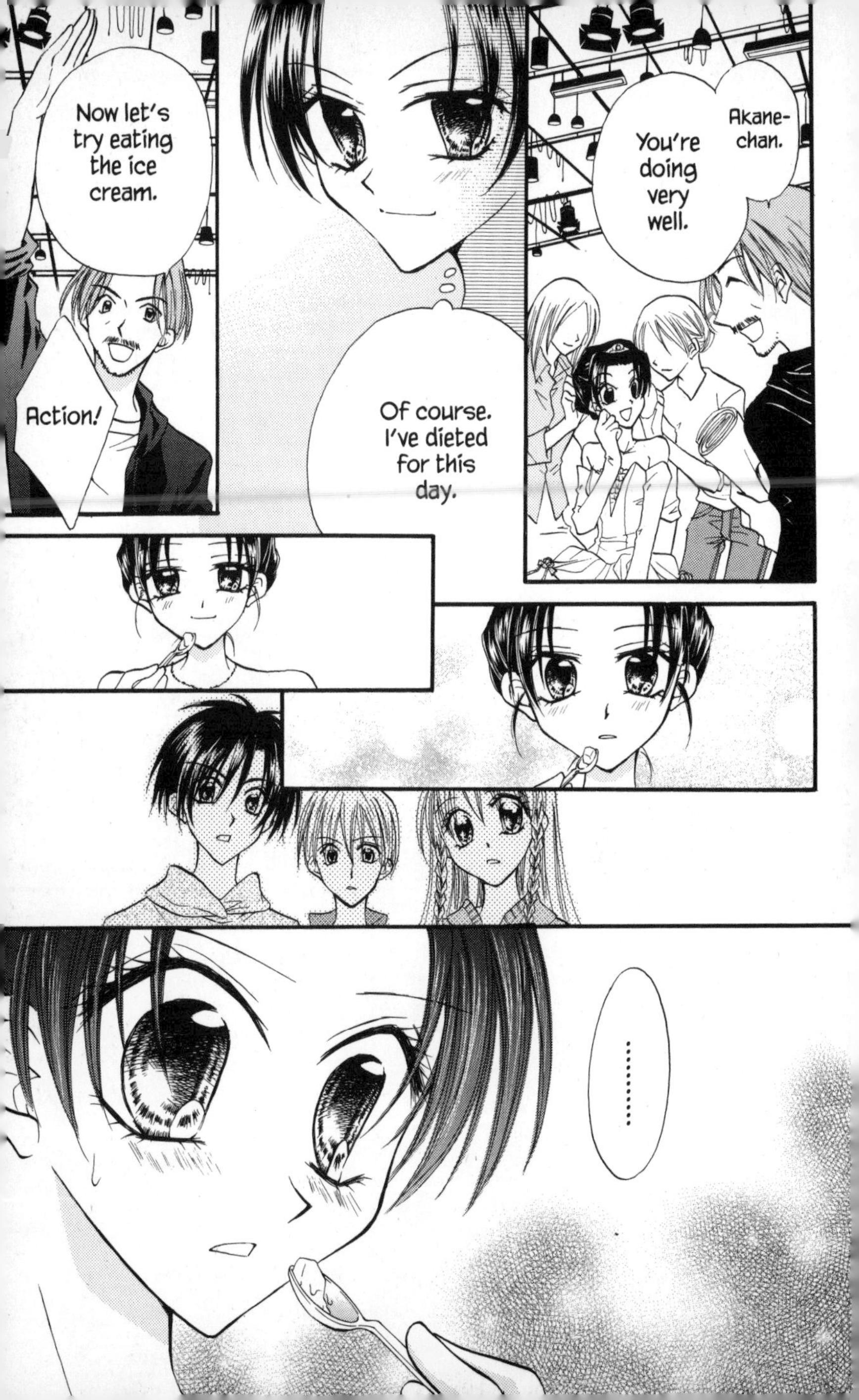
Akane-chan. You're doing very well.
Of course. I've dieted for this day.
Now let's try eating the ice cream.
Action!
……

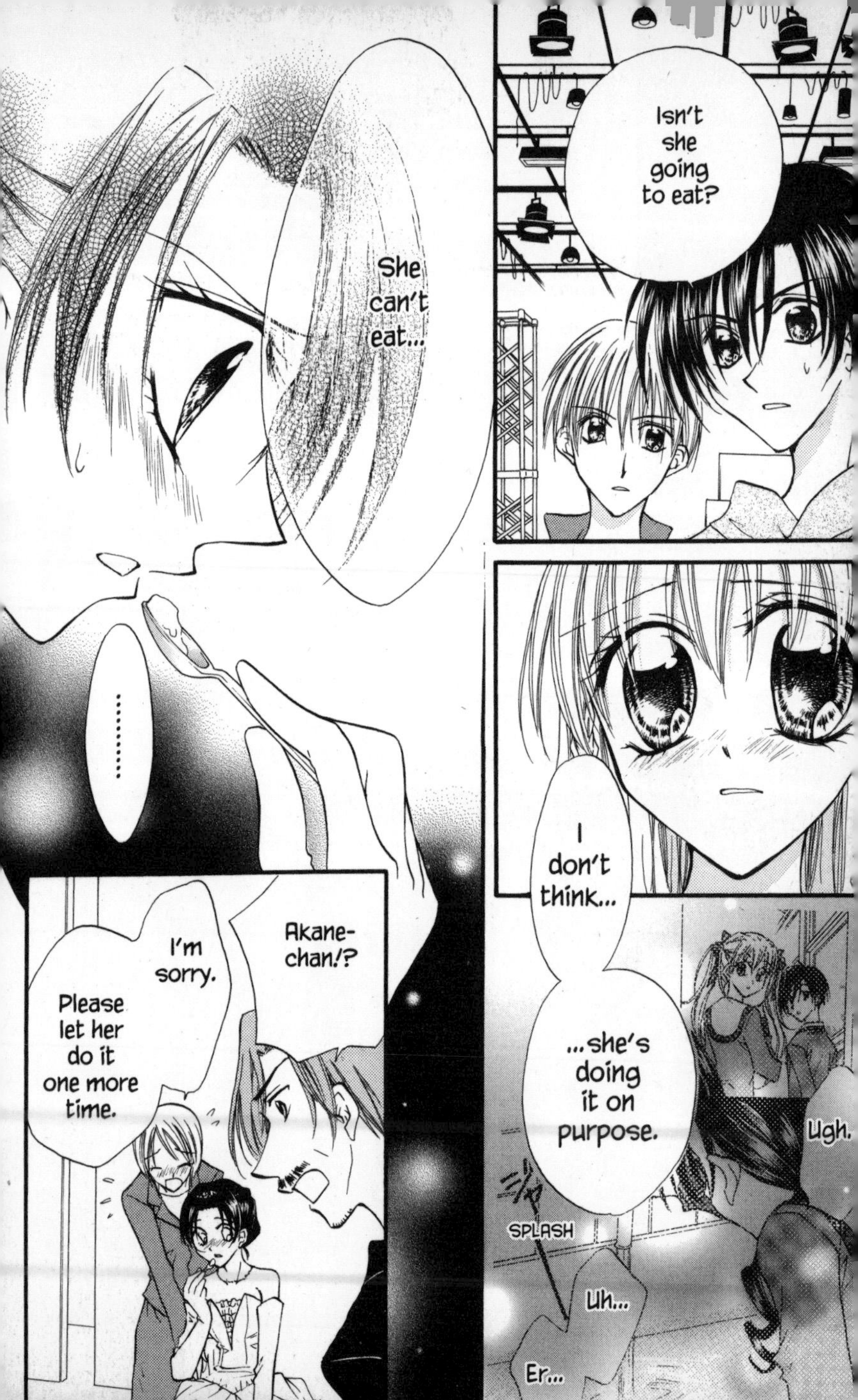
Isn't she going to eat?
I don't think...
...she's doing it on purpose.
Ugh.
SPLASH
Uh...
Er...
She can't eat...
....
Akane-chan!?
I'm sorry.
Please let her do it one more time.

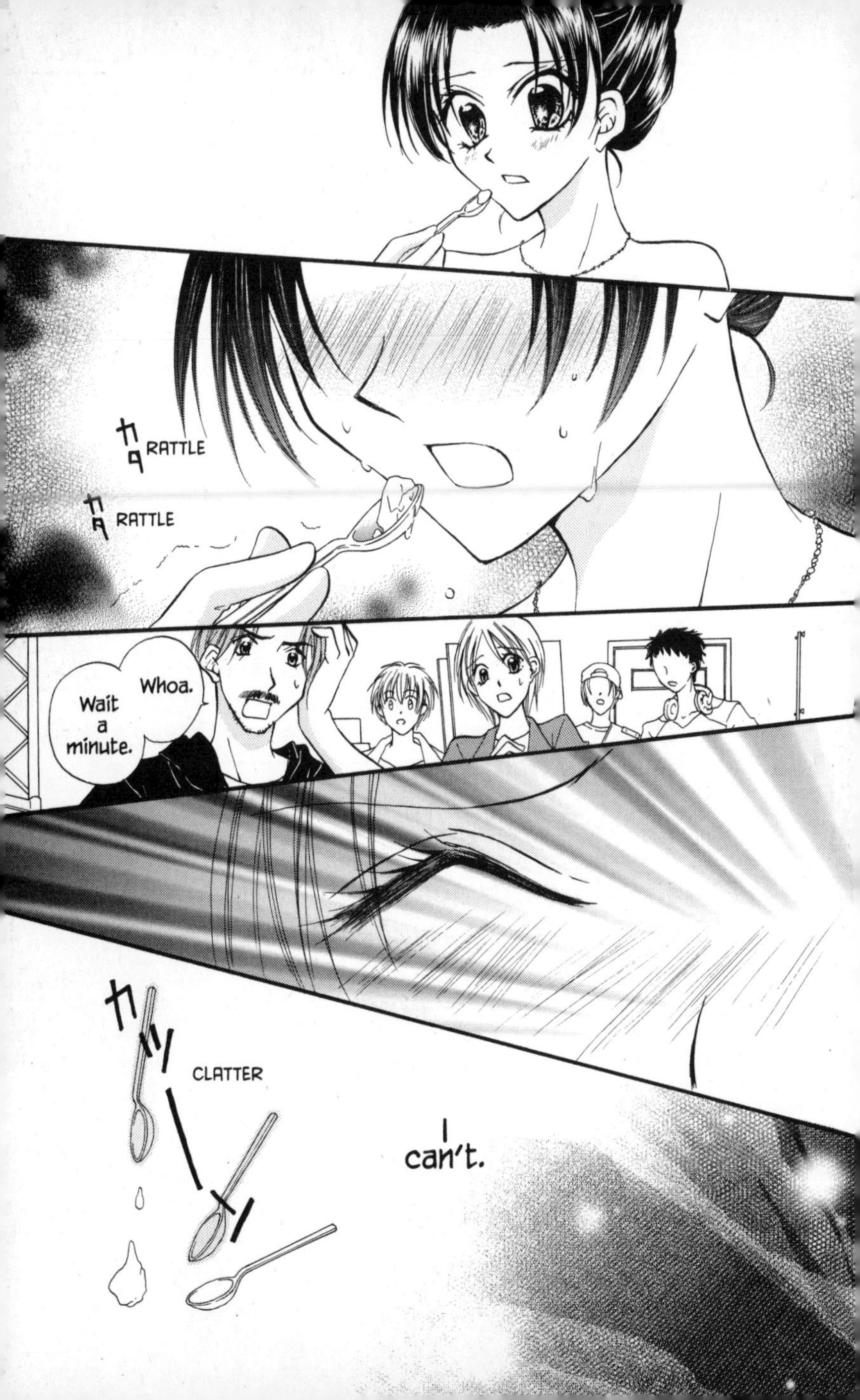
カタ RATTLE
カタ RATTLE
Whoa.
Wait a minute.
CLATTER
I can't.

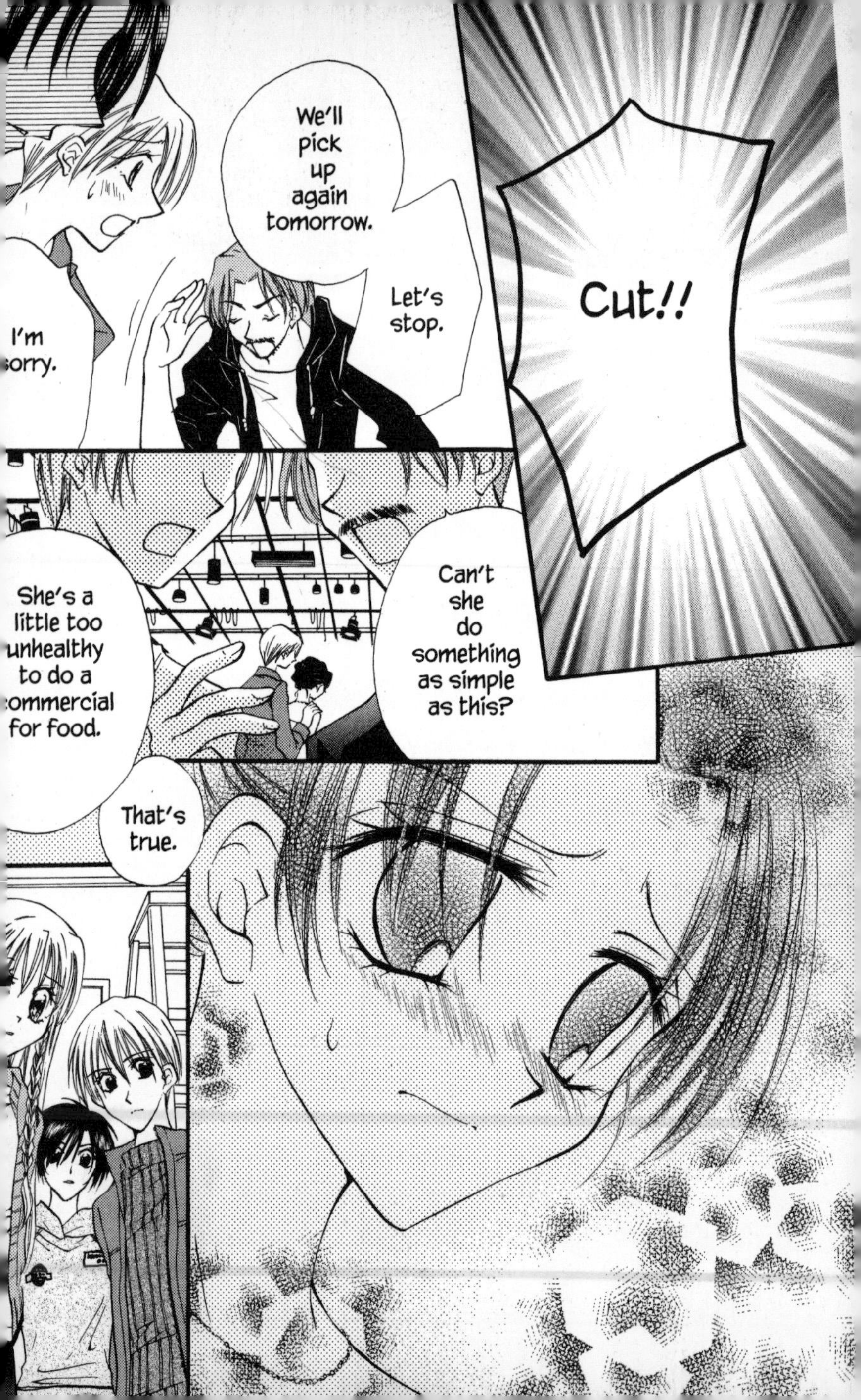
Cut!!
Let's stop.
We'll pick up again tomorrow.
I'm orry.
Can't she do something as simple as this?
She's a little too unhealthy to do a ommercial for food.
That's true.

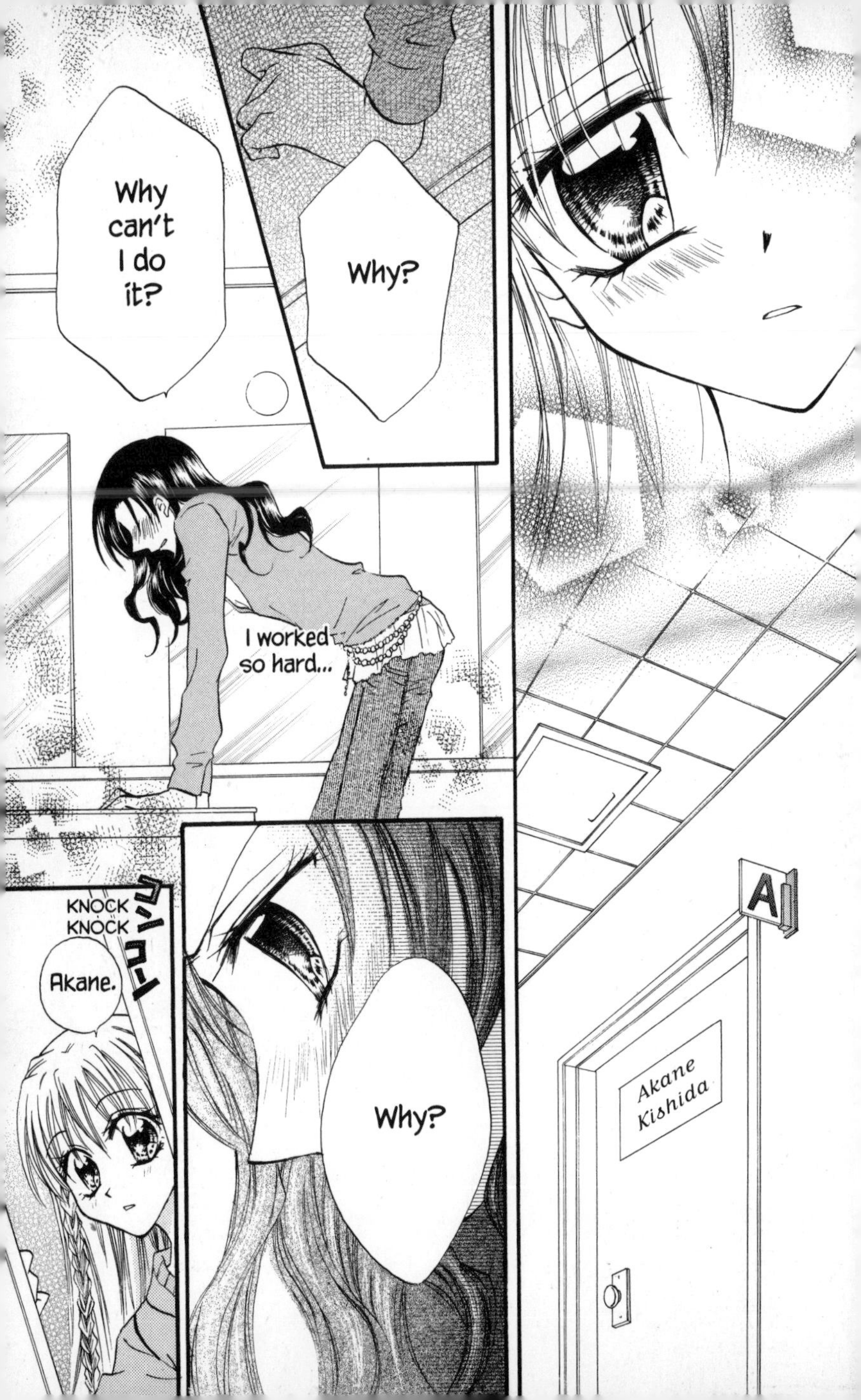

A
Akane Kishida
Why?
Why can't I do it?
I worked so hard...
Why?
KNOCK KNOCK
Akane.

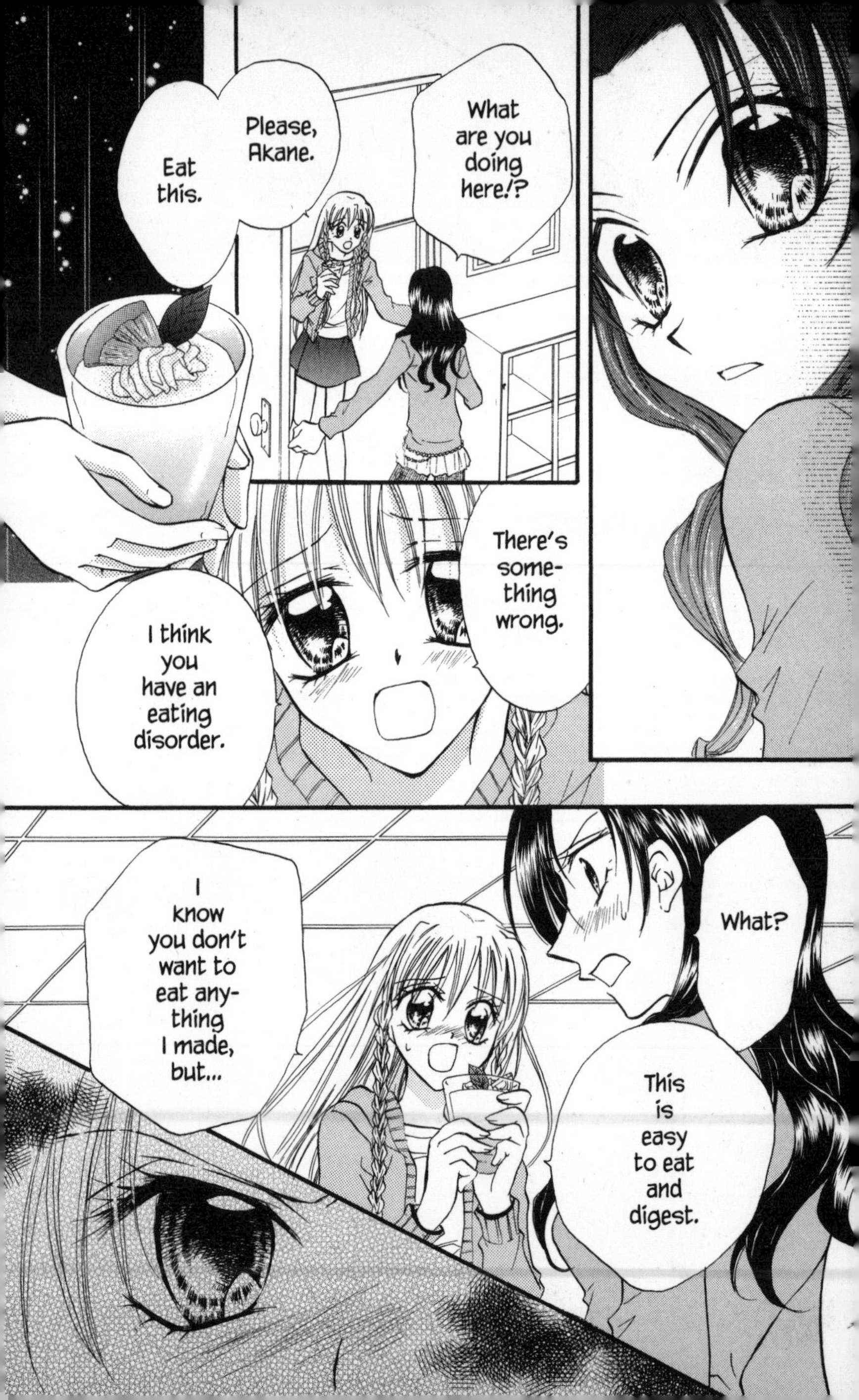
What are you doing here!?
Please, Akane.
Eat this.
There's some-thing wrong.
I think you have an eating disorder.
What?
I know you don't want to eat any-thing I made, but...
This is easy to eat and digest.

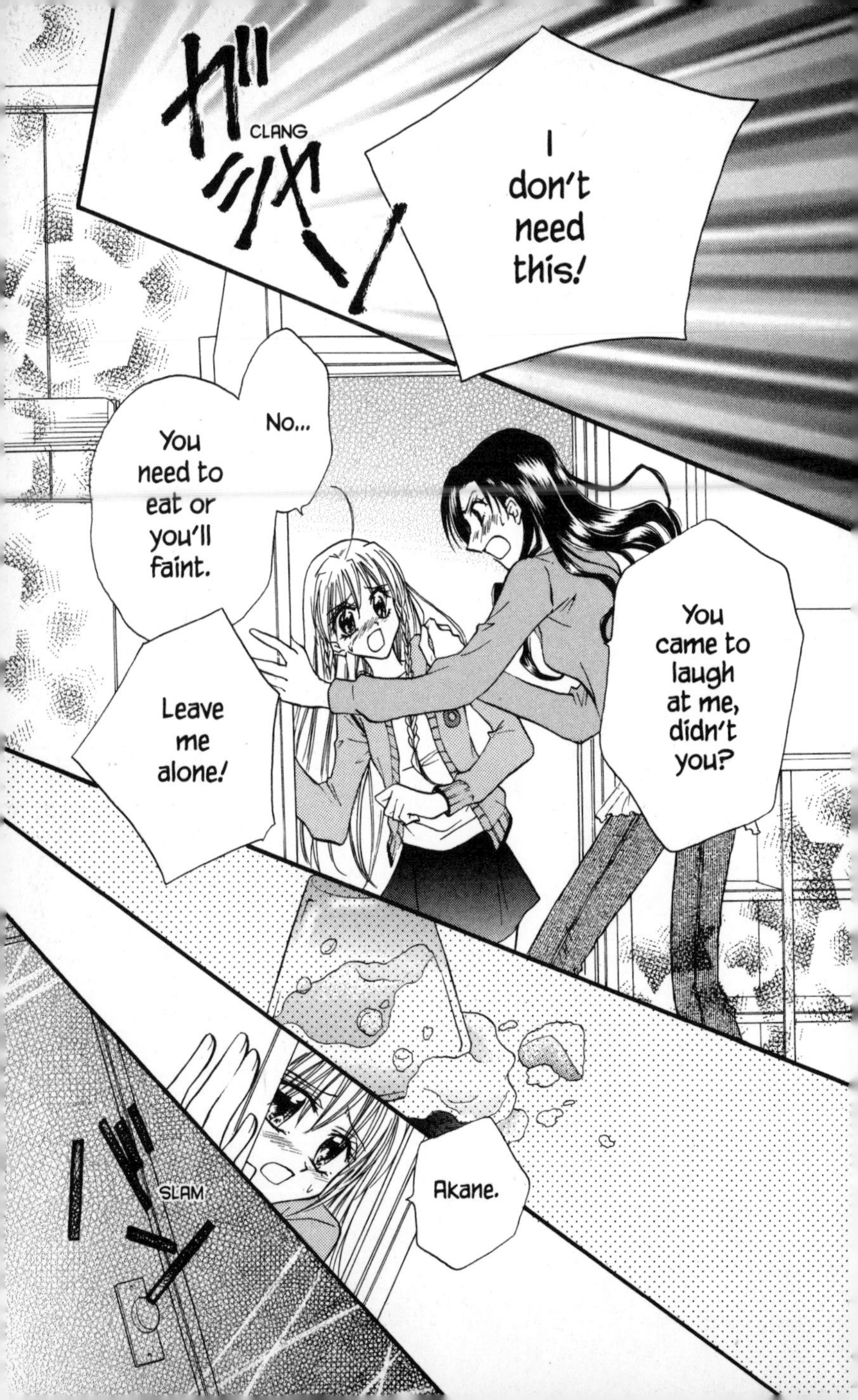
I don't need this!
CLANG
You came to laugh at me, didn't you?
No...
You need to eat or you'll faint.
Leave me alone!
Akane.
SLAM

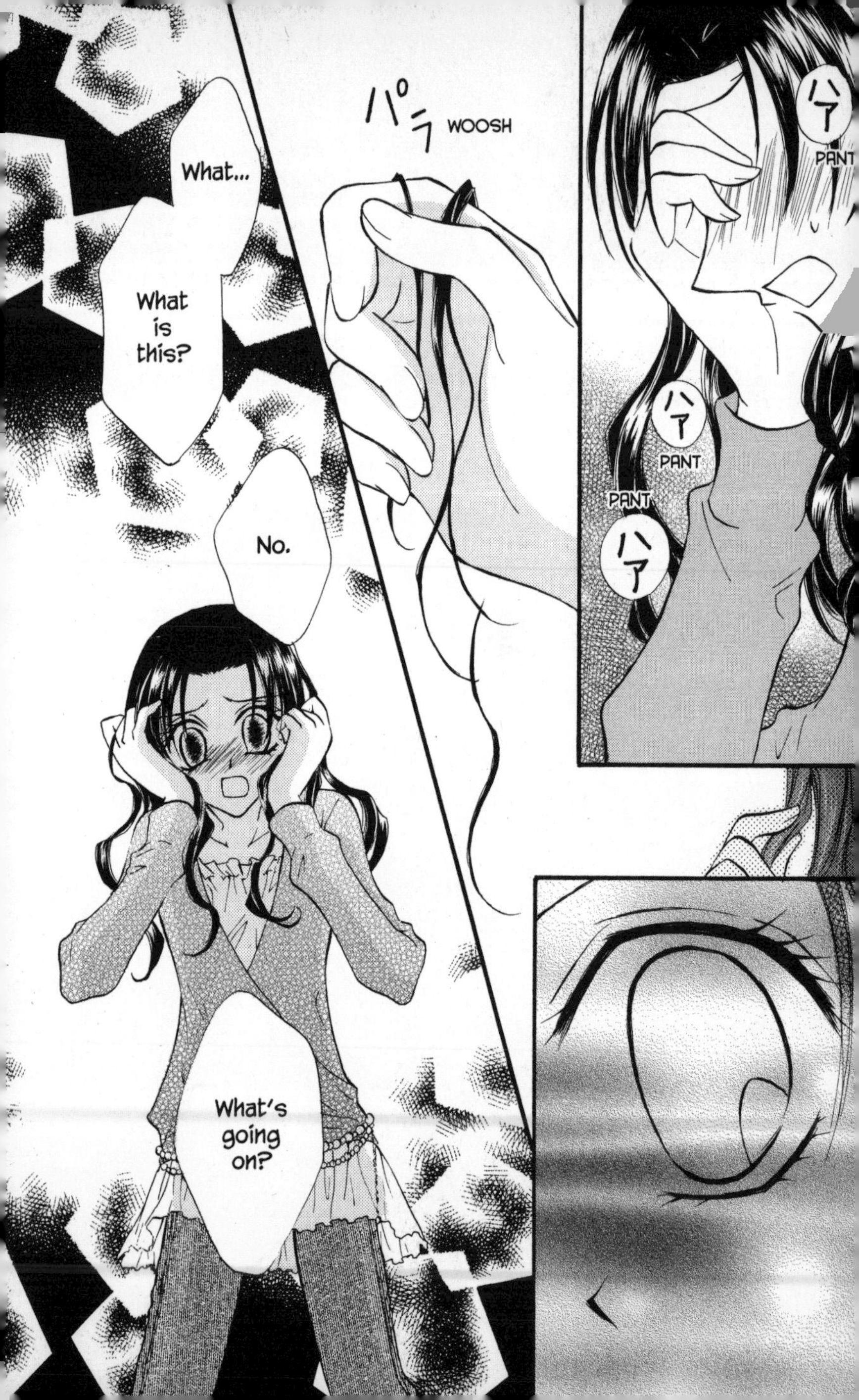

ハァ
PANT
ハァ
PANT
PANT
ハァ
パラ
WOOSH
What...
What is this?
No.
What's going on?

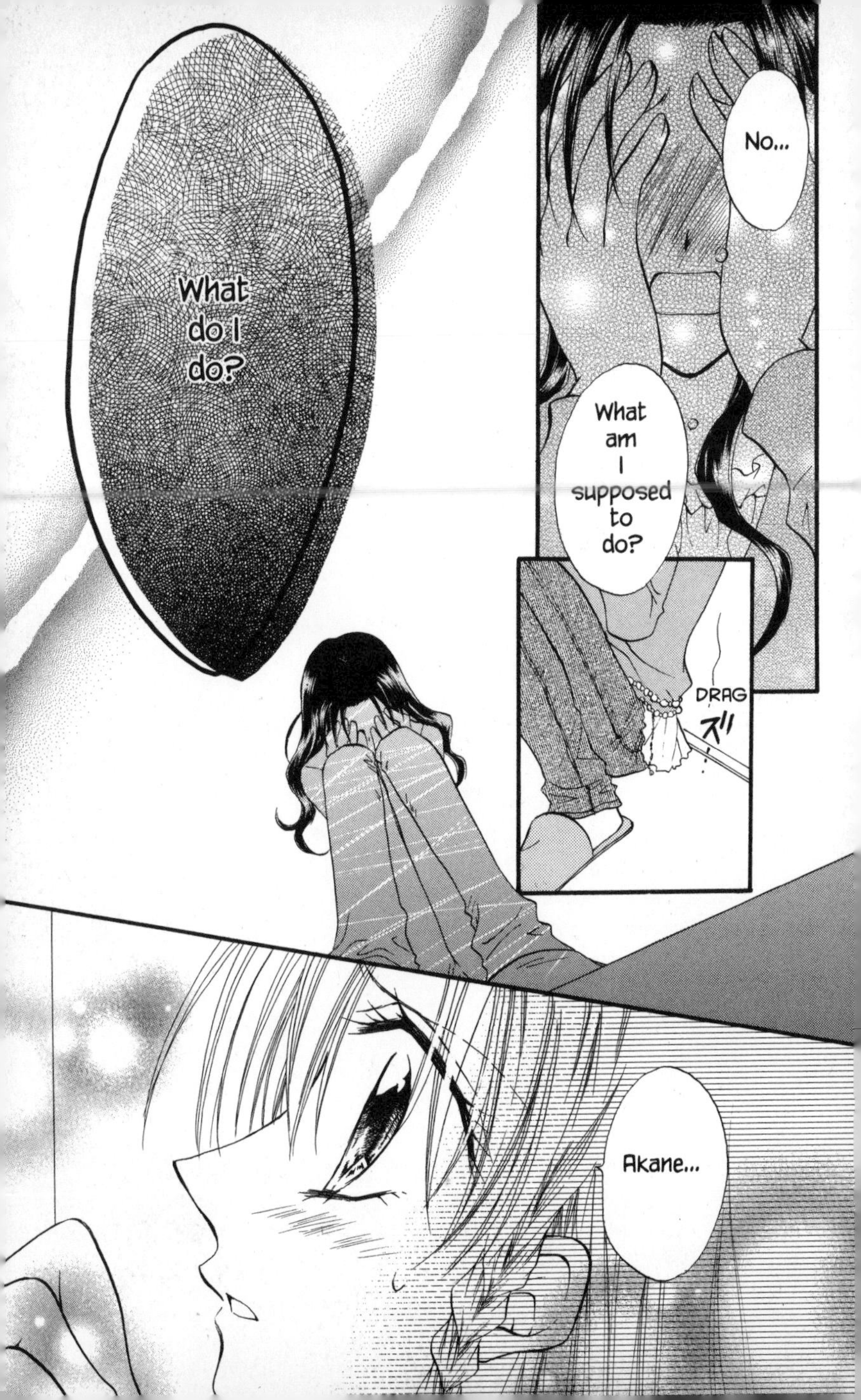
No...
What am I supposed to do?
DRAG
ズ
What do I do?
Akane...

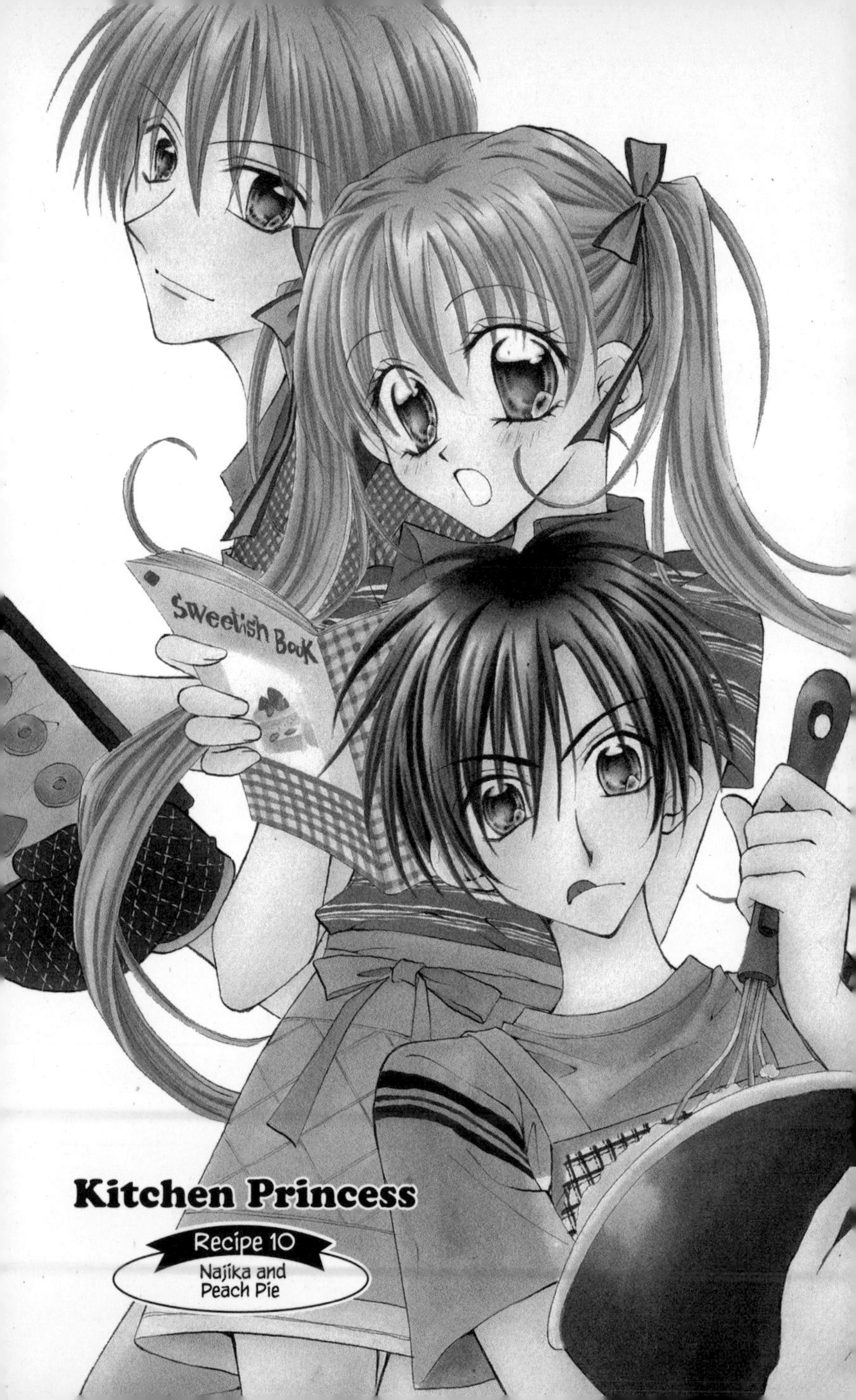

Sweetish Book
Kitchen Princess
Recipe 10
Najika and Peach Pie

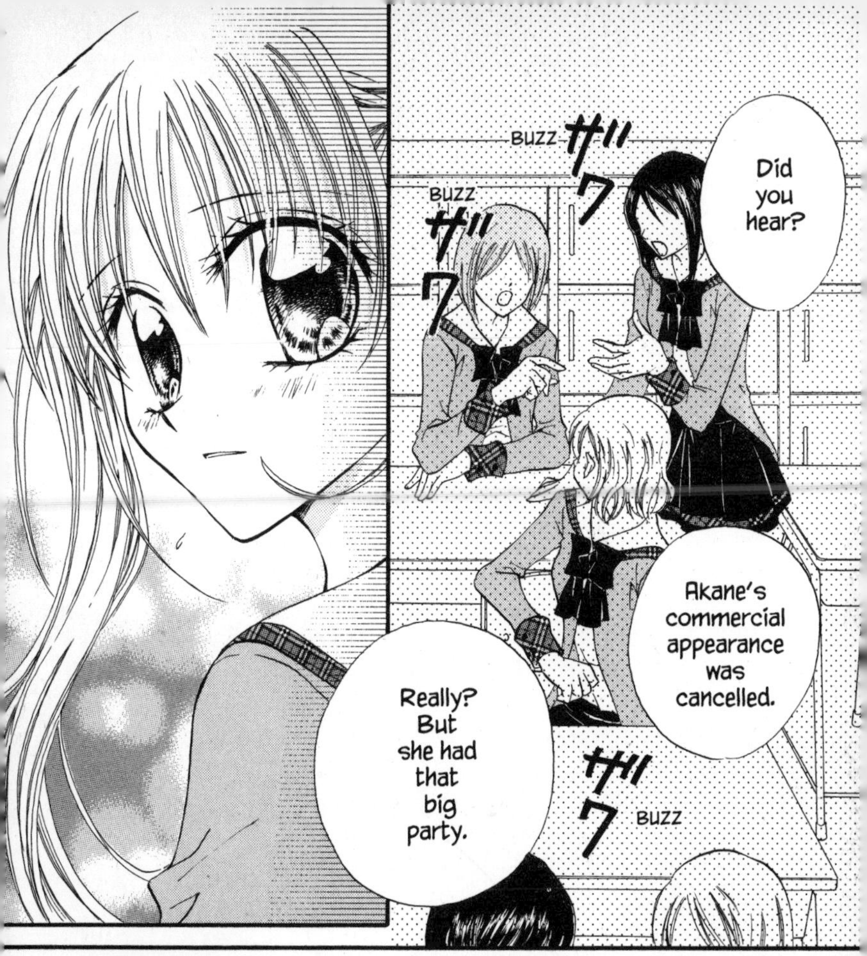
BUZZ ザワ
Did you hear?
BUZZ ザワ
Akane's commercial appearance was cancelled.
Really? But she had that big party.
ザワ BUZZ

About Recipe 10's Splash Page

This is the first splash page that I let someone else do the background on! But I did give them a polka-dot pattern and a general idea of what I wanted. I was really looking forward to seeing what it would turn out like. It came out really good, better than I imagined, and I am very happy. ♥

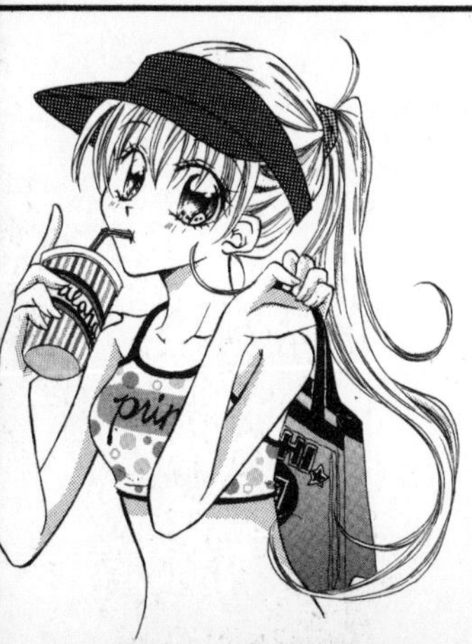

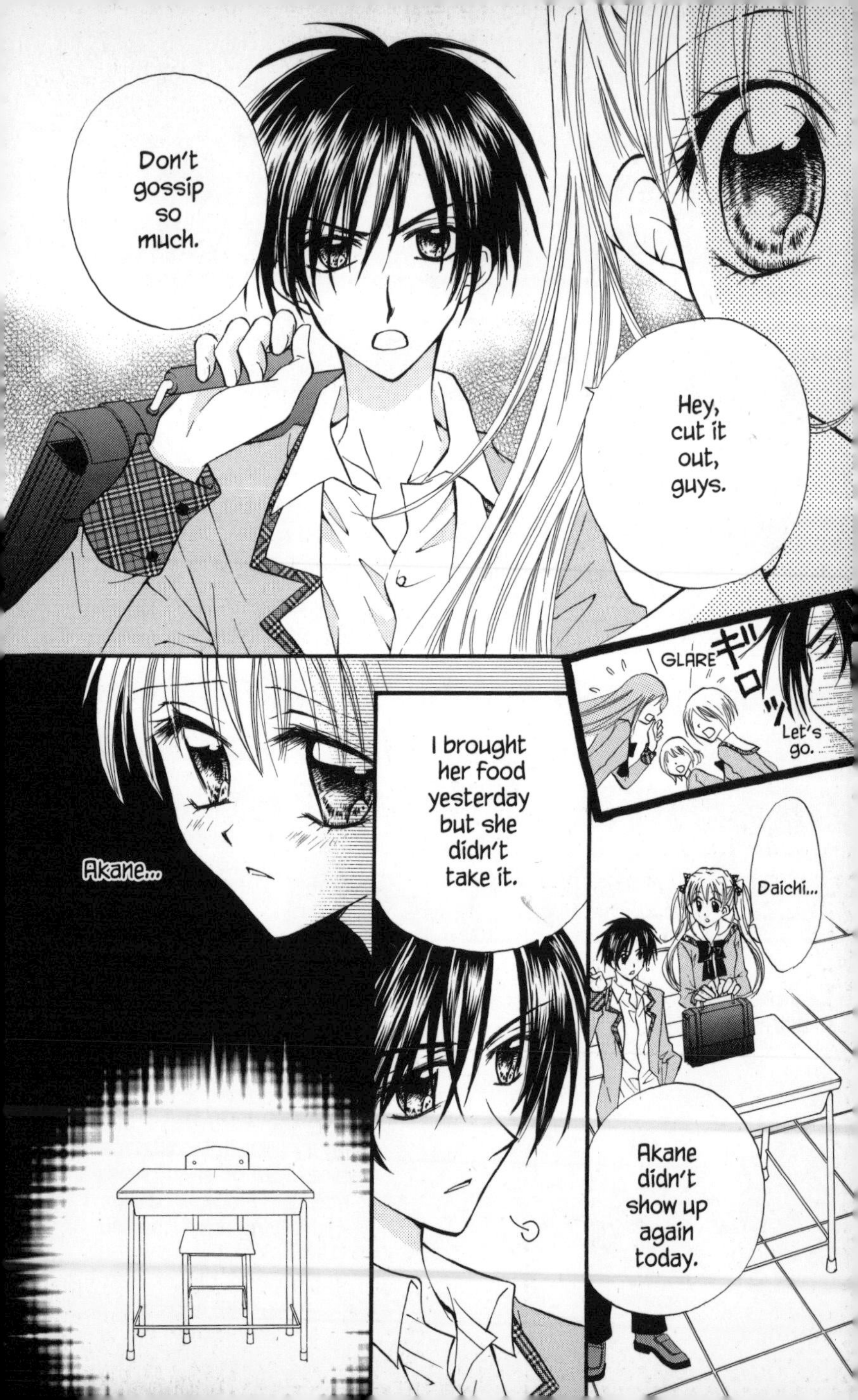
Hey, cut it out, guys.
Don't gossip so much.
GLARE
ギロッ
Let's go.
Daichi...
Akane didn't show up again today.
I brought her food yesterday but she didn't take it.
Akane...

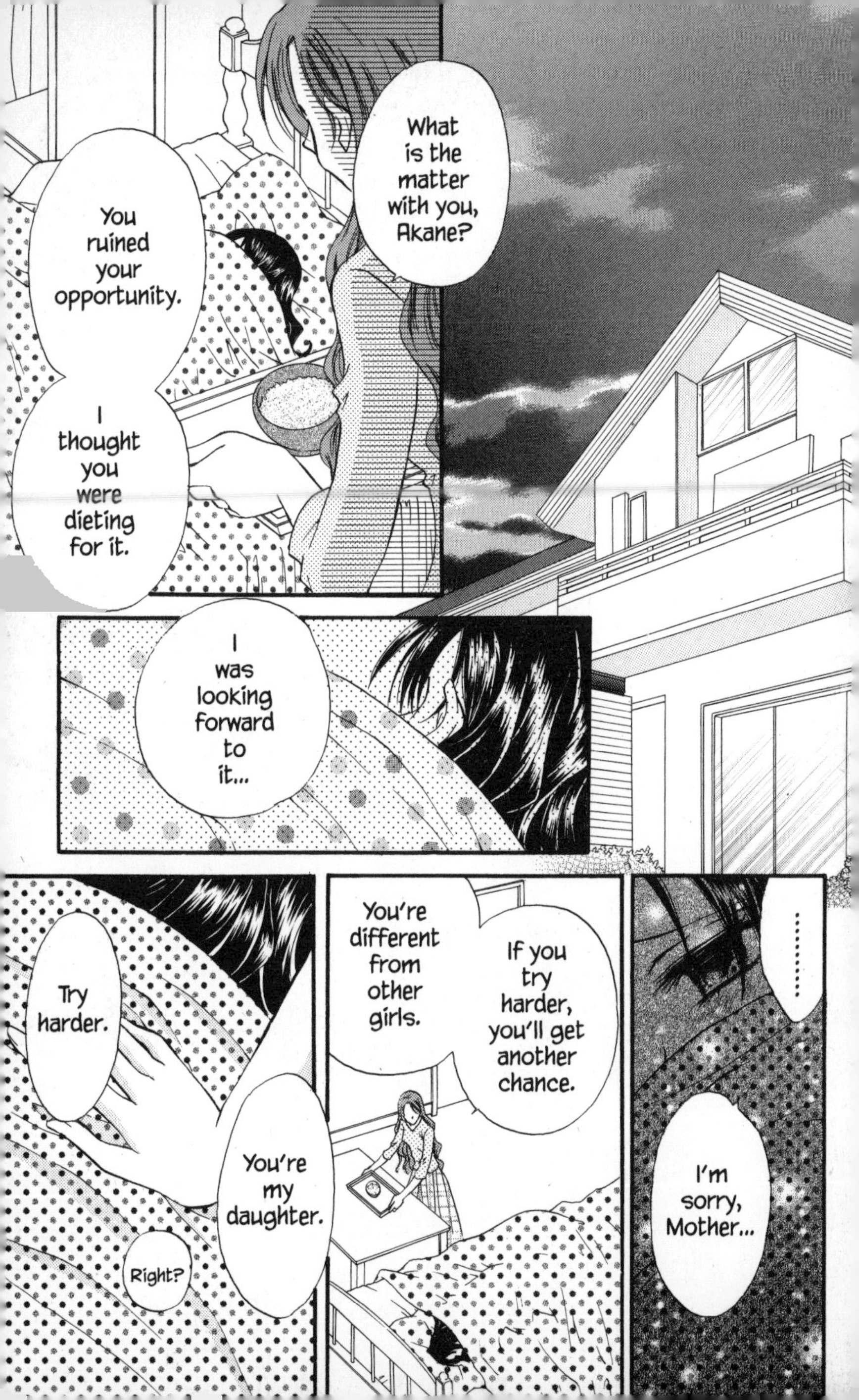
What is the matter with you, Akane?
You ruined your opportunity.
I thought you were dieting for it.
I was looking forward to it...
......
I'm sorry, Mother...
If you try harder, you'll get another chance.
You're different from other girls.
Try harder.
You're my daughter.
Right?

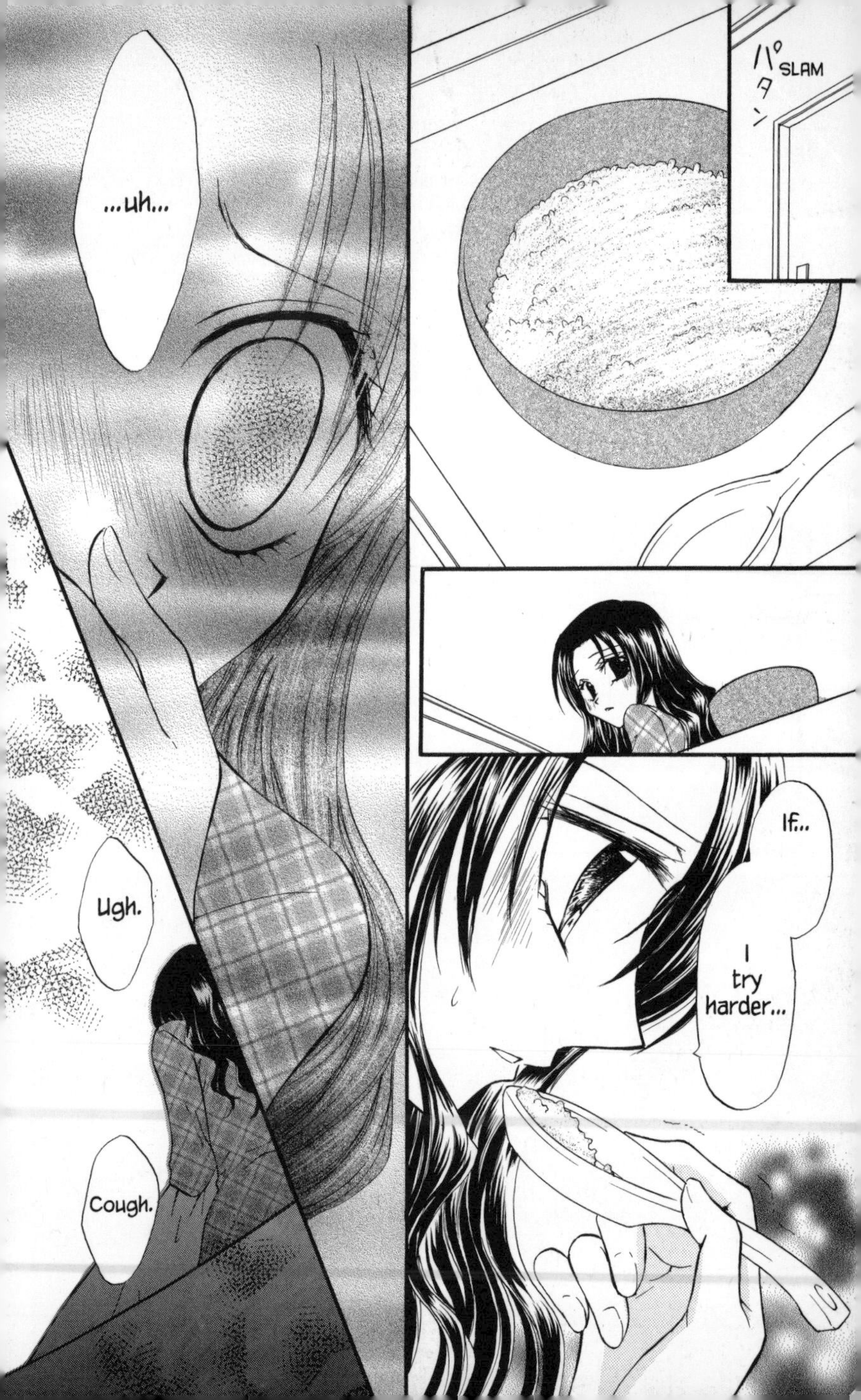
パタン
SLAM
If...
I try harder...
...uh...
Ugh.
Cough.

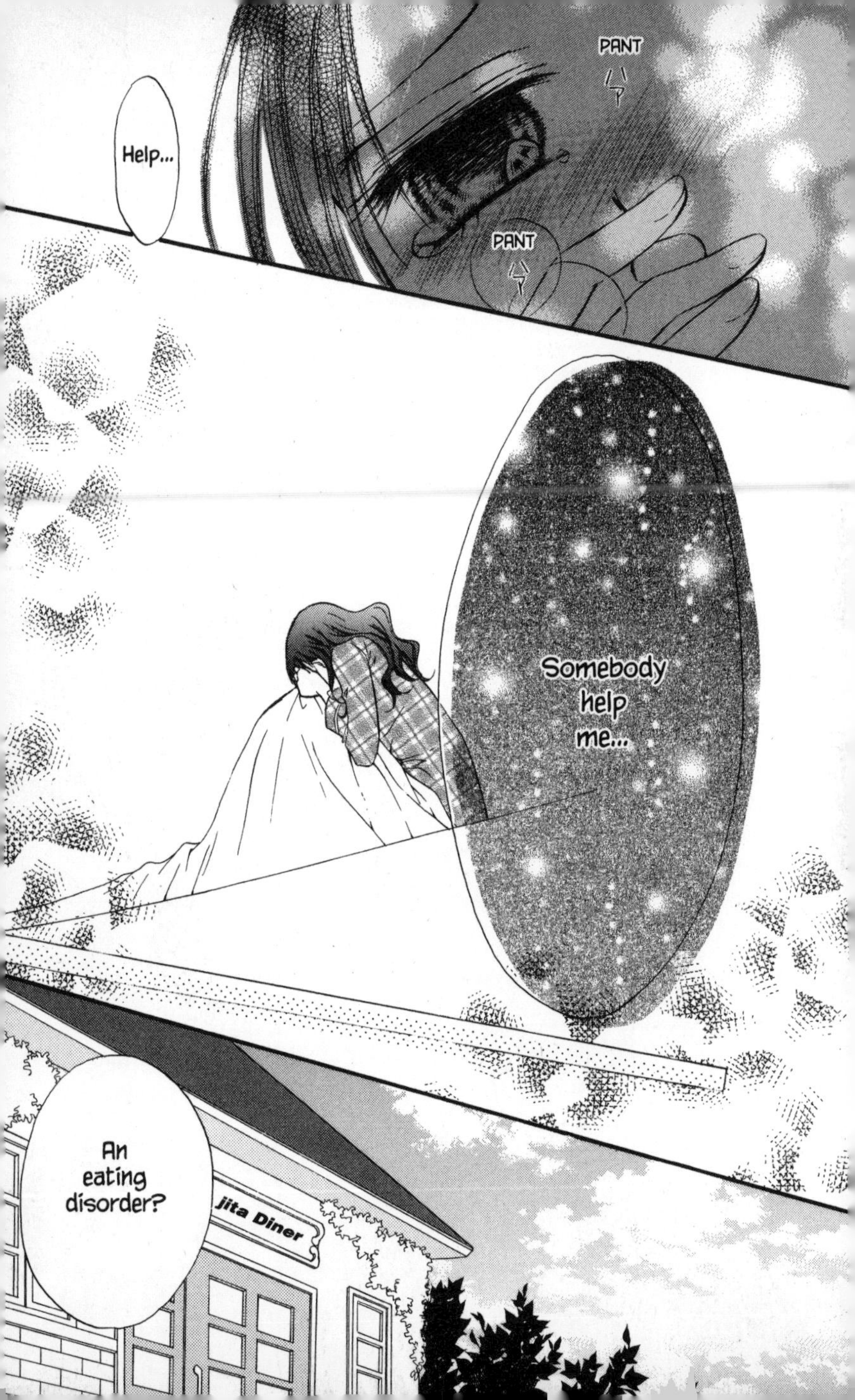
PANT
PANT
Help...
Somebody help me...
An eating disorder?
jita Diner

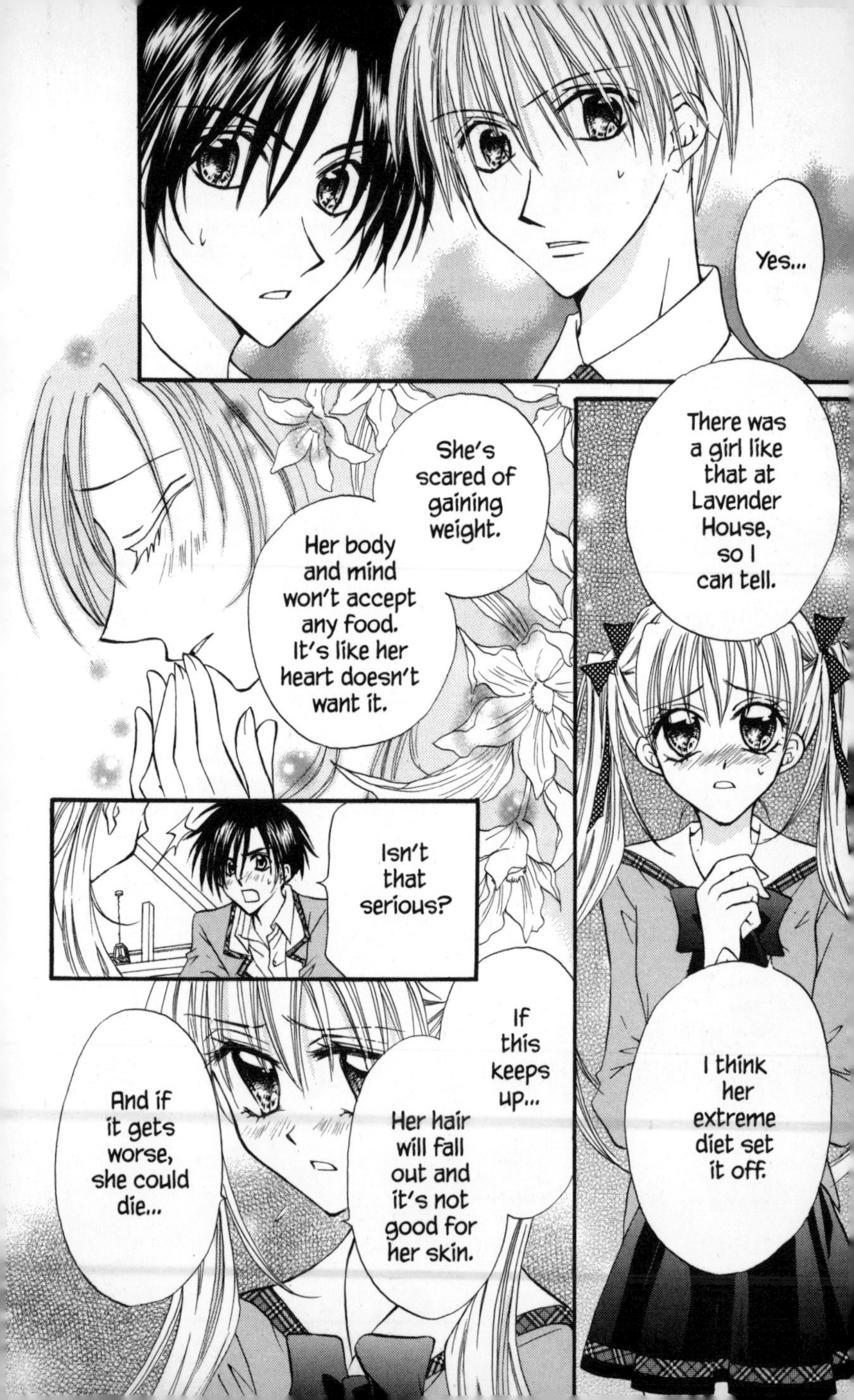
Yes...
There was a girl like that at Lavender House, so I can tell.
I think her extreme diet set it off.
She's scared of gaining weight.
Her body and mind won't accept any food. It's like her heart doesn't want it.
Isn't that serious?
If this keeps up...
Her hair will fall out and it's not good for her skin.
And if it gets worse, she could die...

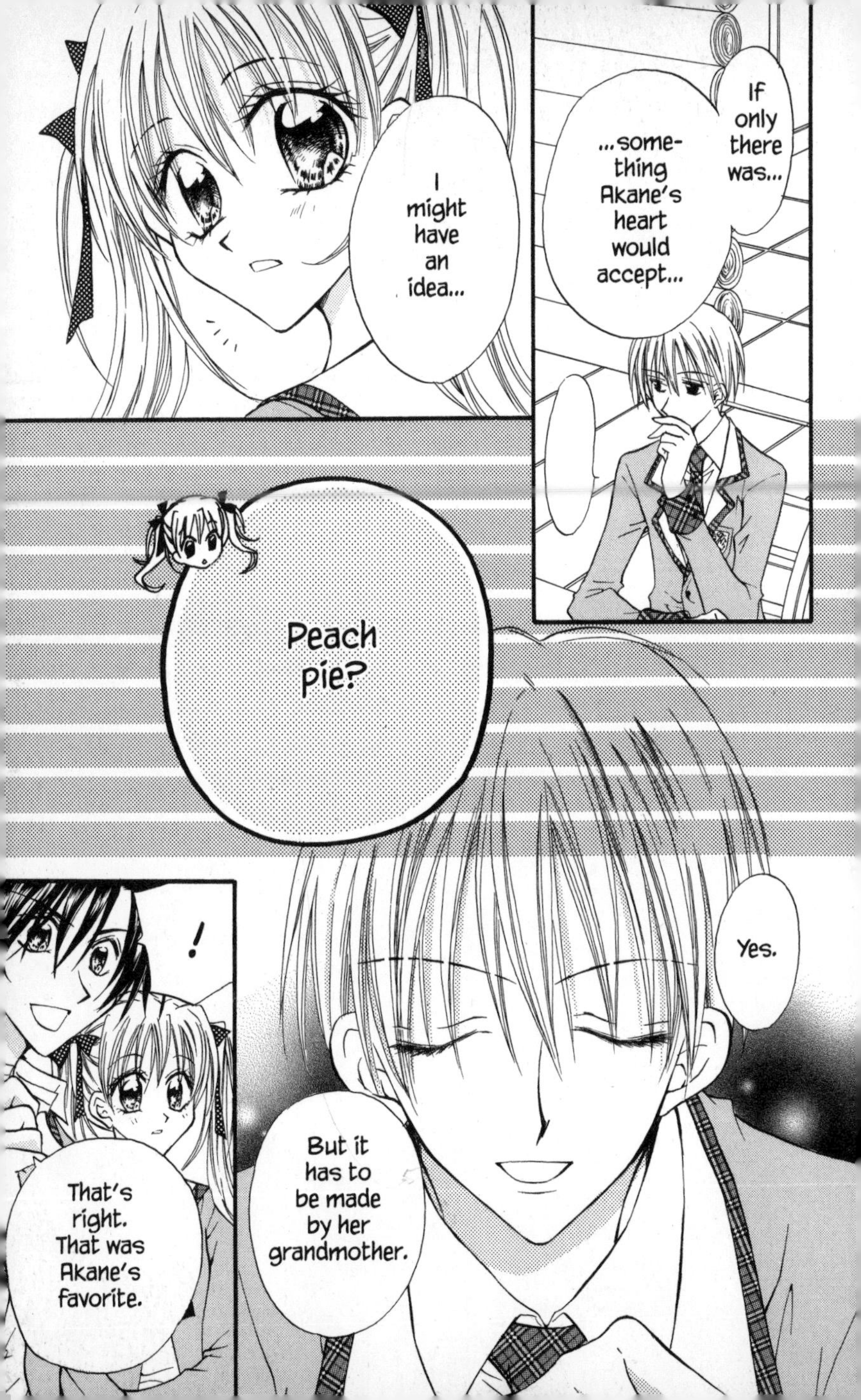
If only there was...
...something Akane's heart would accept...
I might have an idea...
Peach pie?
Yes.
But it has to be made by her grandmother.
!
That's right. That was Akane's favorite.

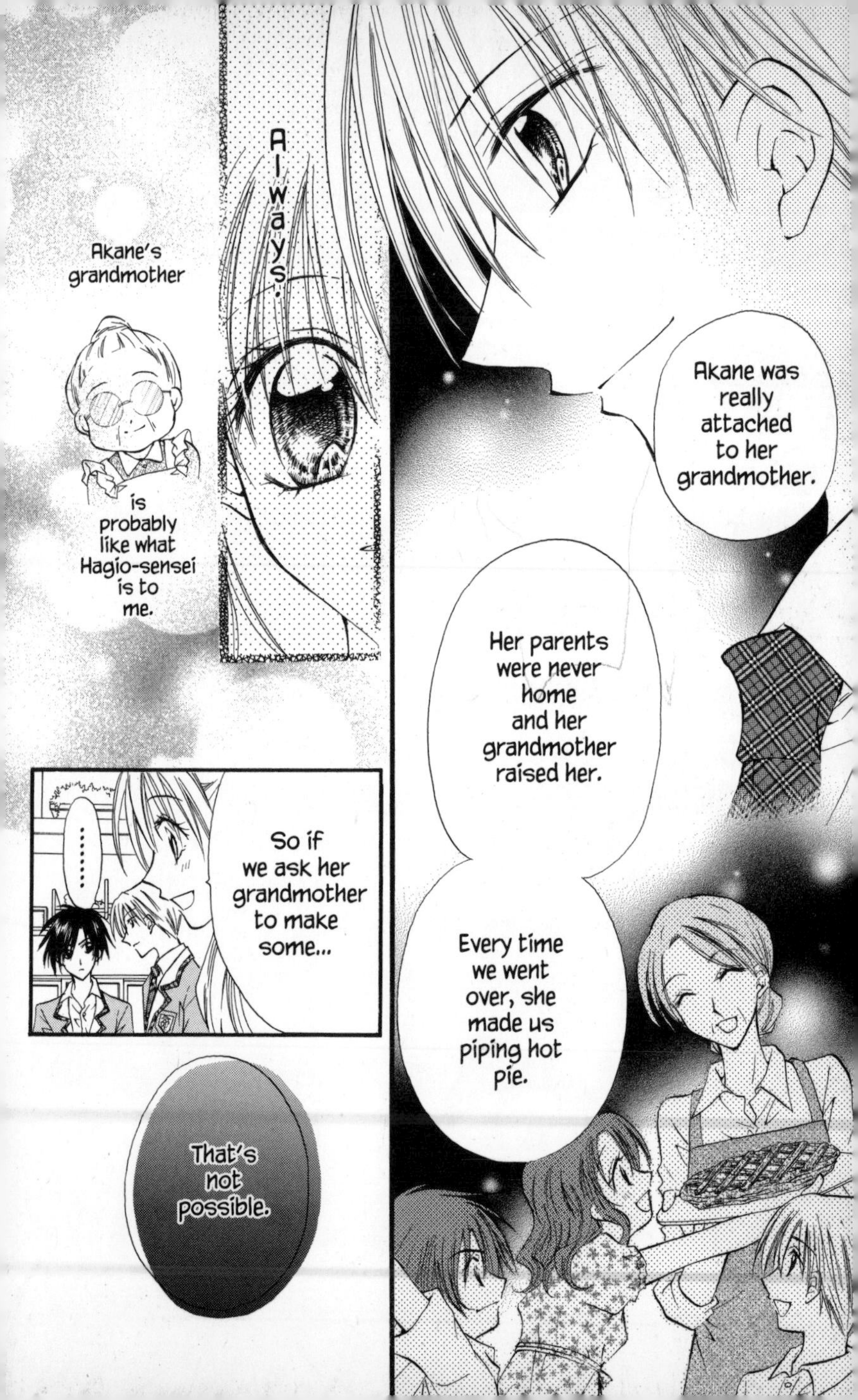
Akane was really attached to her grandmother.
Her parents were never home and her grandmother raised her.
Every time we went over, she made us piping hot pie.
Always.
Akane's grandmother
is probably like what Hagio-sensei is to me.
......
So if we ask her grandmother to make some...
That's not possible.

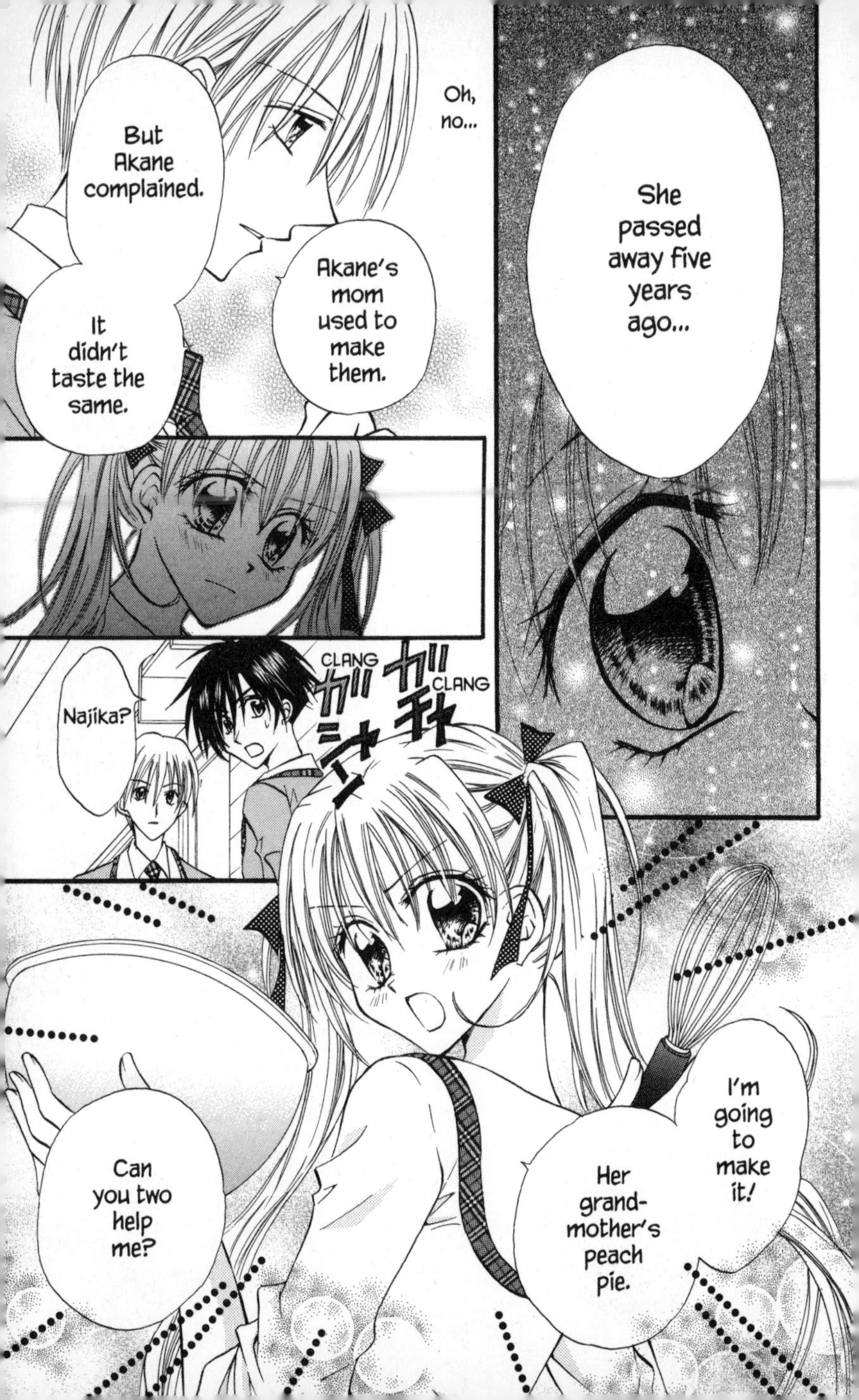
She passed away five years ago...
Oh, no...
Akane's mom used to make them.
But Akane complained.
It didn't taste the same.
CLANG
CLANG
Najika?
I'm going to make it!
Her grandmother's peach pie.
Can you two help me?

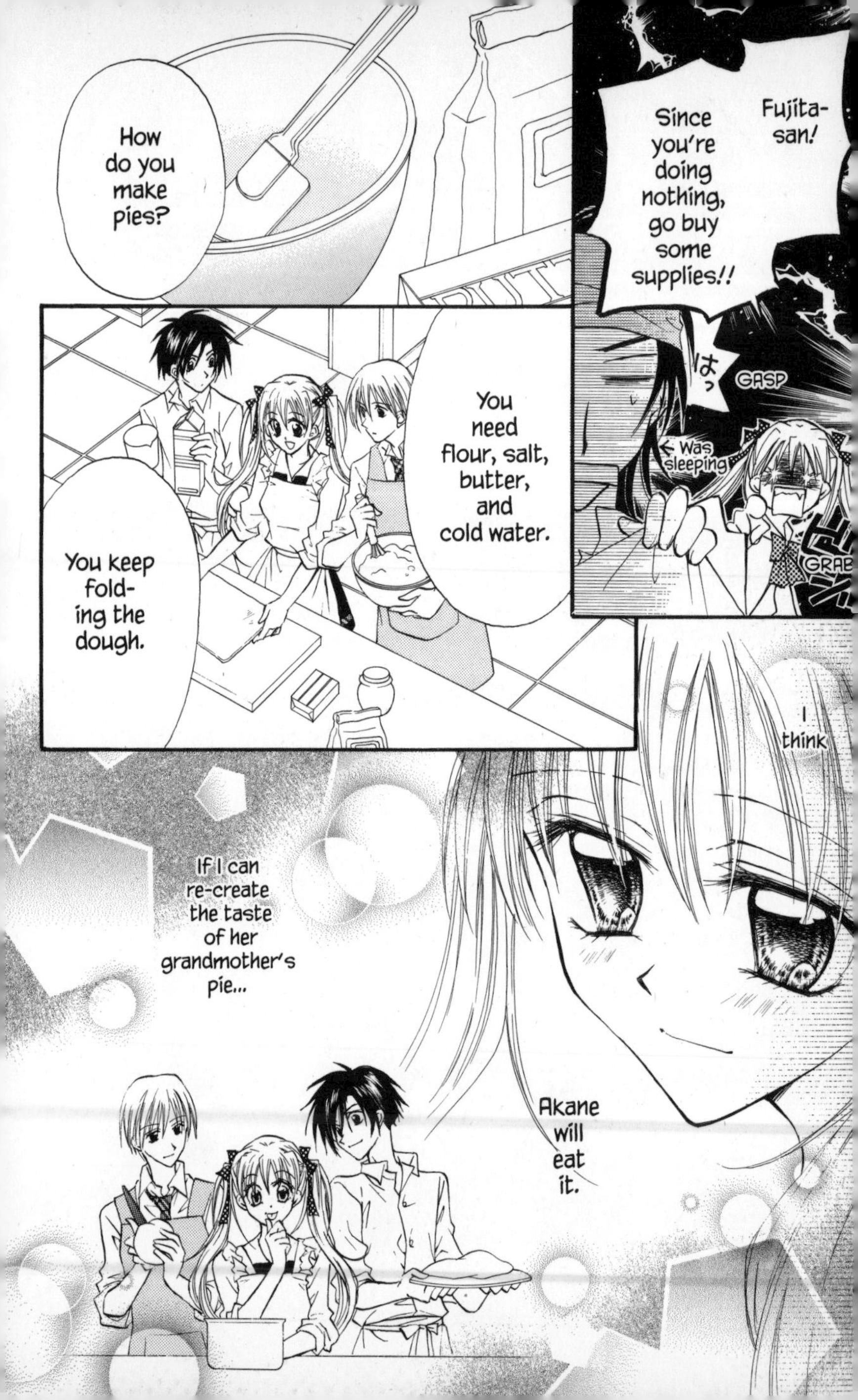

Fujita-san!
Since you're doing nothing, go buy some supplies!!
はっ
GASP
← Was sleeping
GRAB
How do you make pies?
You need flour, salt, butter, and cold water.
You keep folding the dough.
I think
If I can re-create the taste of her grandmother's pie...
Akane will eat it.

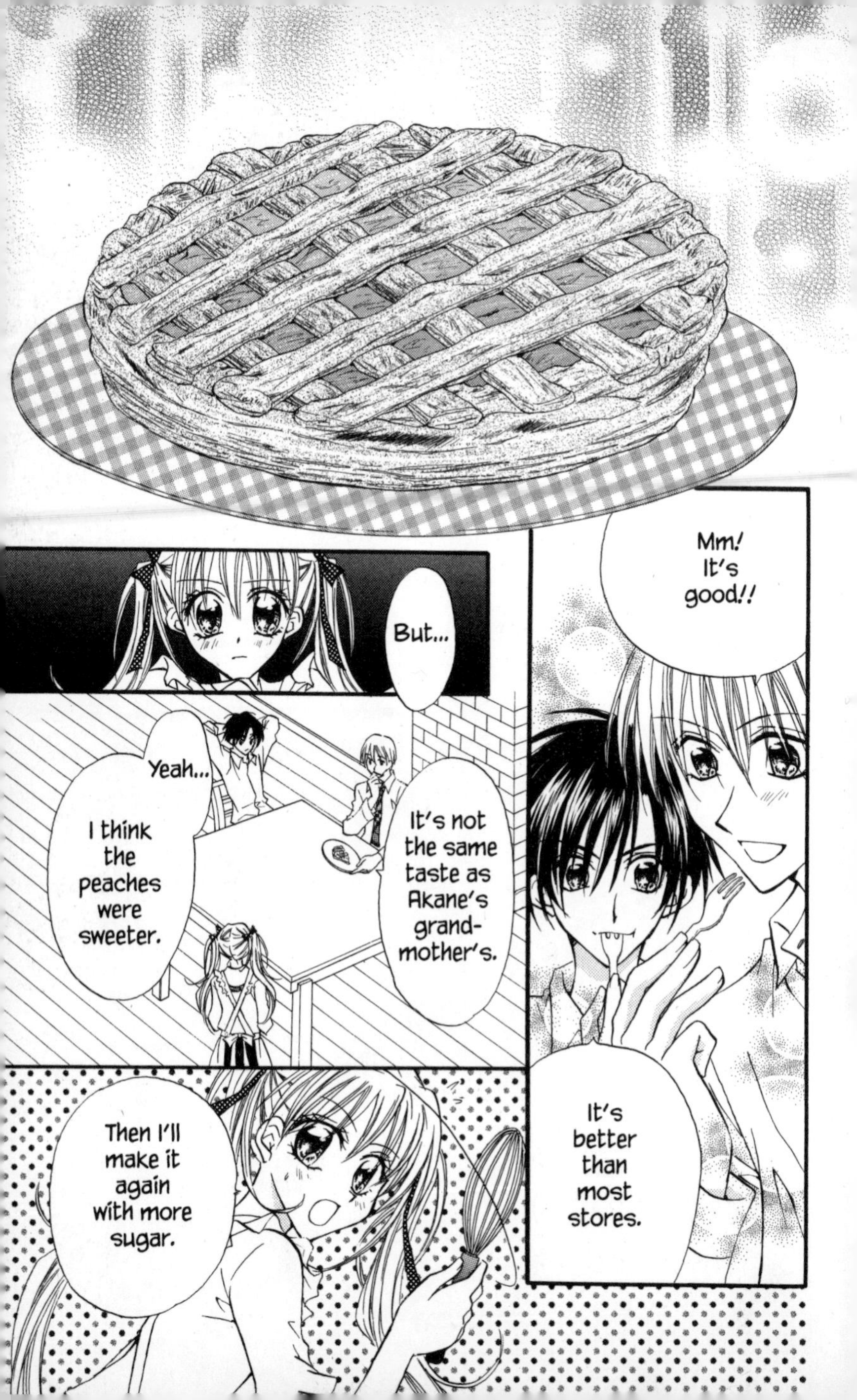
Mm! It's good!!
It's better than most stores.
But...
It's not the same taste as Akane's grand-mother's.
Yeah...
I think the peaches were sweeter.
Then I'll make it again with more sugar.

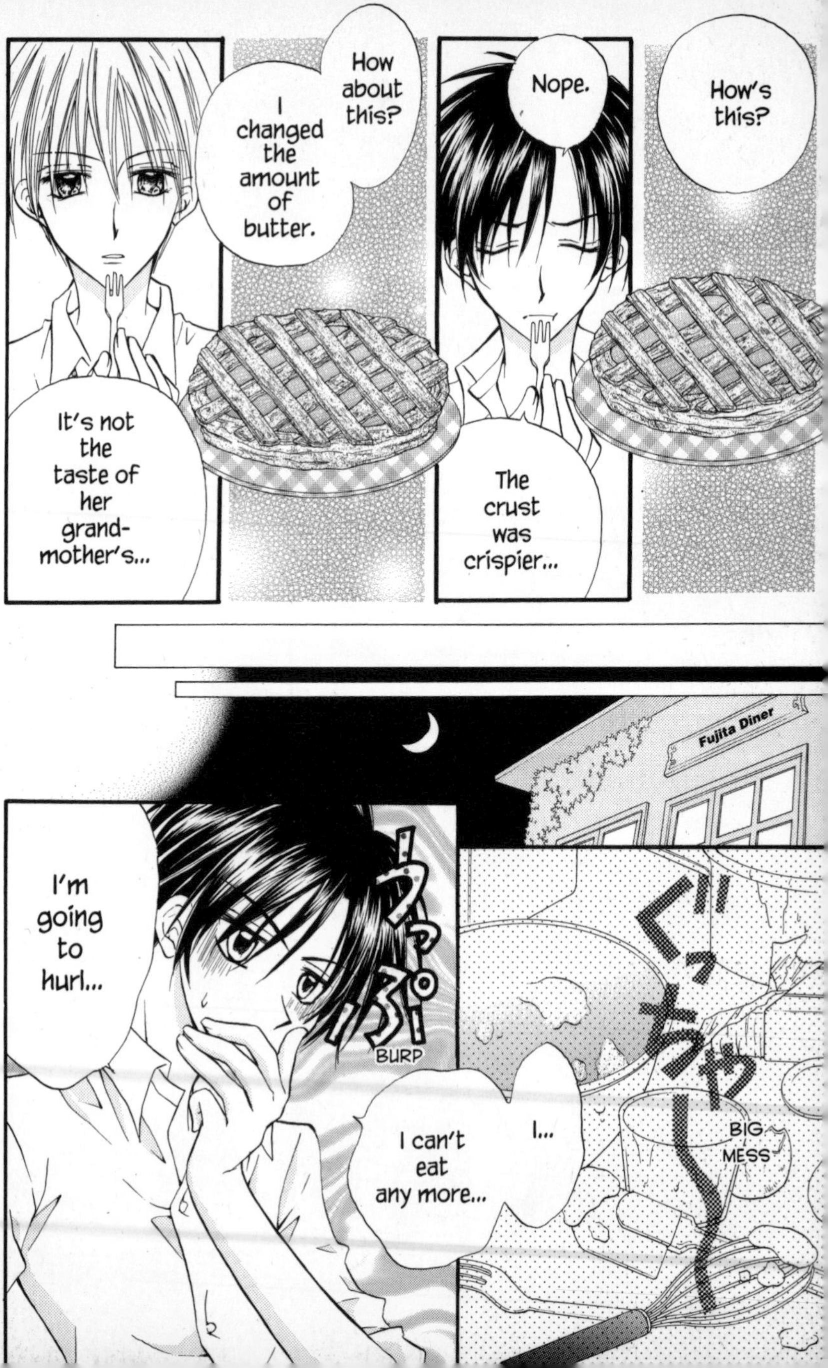
How's this?
Nope.
The crust was crispier...
How about this?
I changed the amount of butter.
It's not the taste of her grandmother's...
Fujita Diner
BIG MESS
I...
I can't eat any more...
BURP
I'm going to hurl...

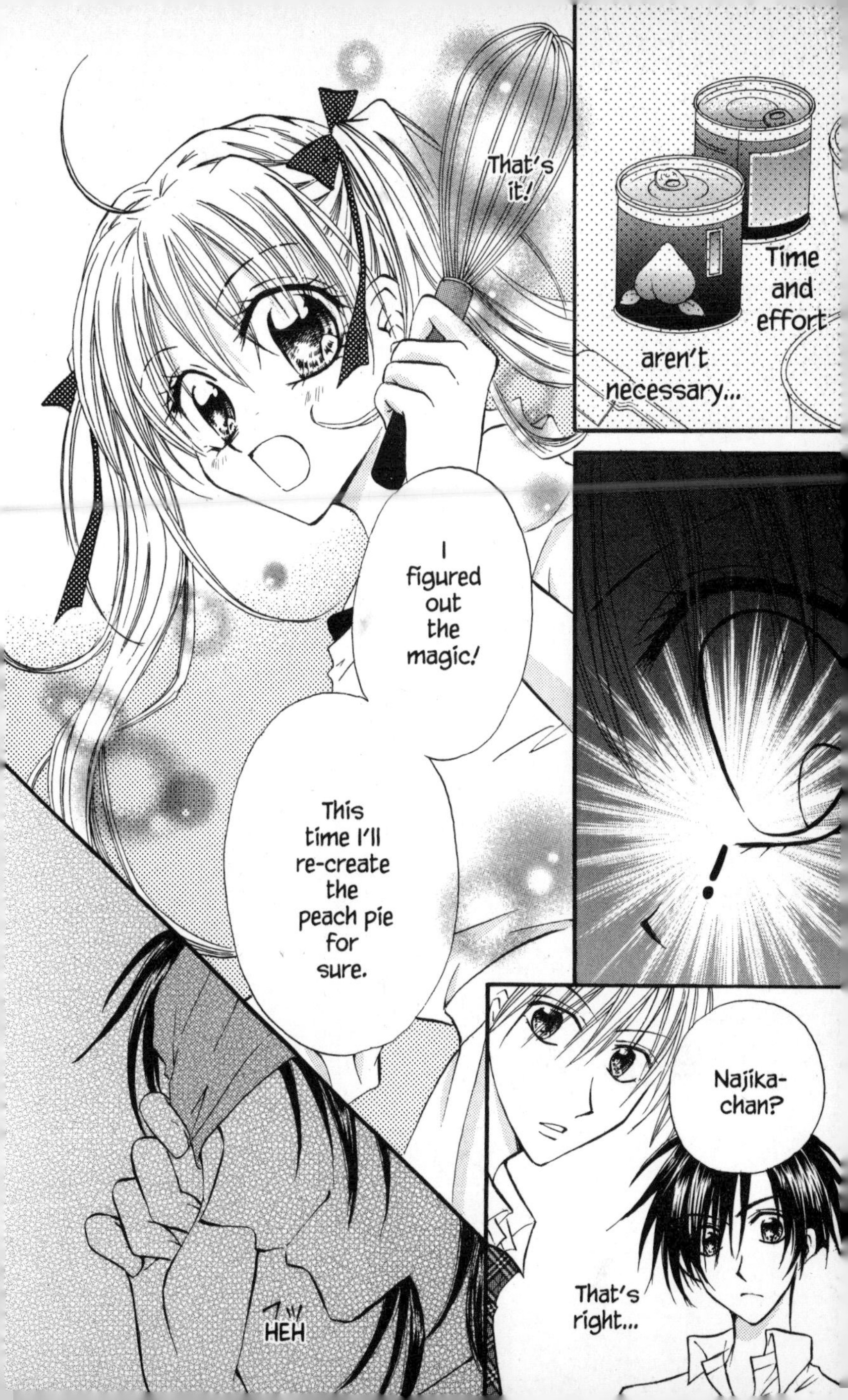
Time and effort aren't necessary...
!
Najika-chan?
That's right...
That's it!
I figured out the magic!
This time I'll re-create the peach pie for sure.
フッ
HEH

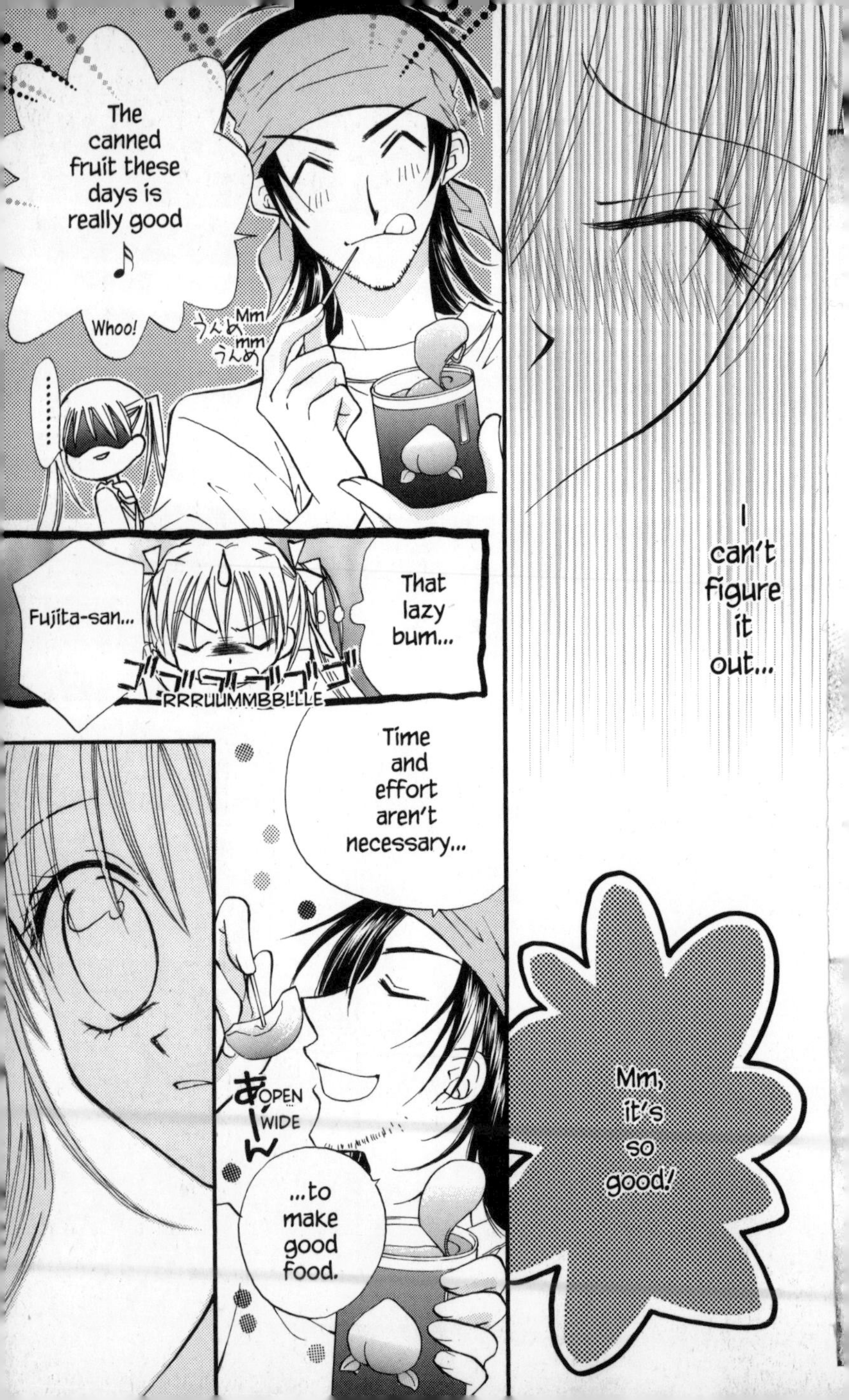
I can't figure it out...
Mm, it's so good!
The canned fruit these days is really good ♪
うんめ Mm
うんめ mm
Whoo!
......
That lazy bum...
Fujita-san...
ゴゴゴゴゴゴ
RRRUUMMBBLLLE
Time and effort aren't necessary...
あーん OPEN WIDE
...to make good food.

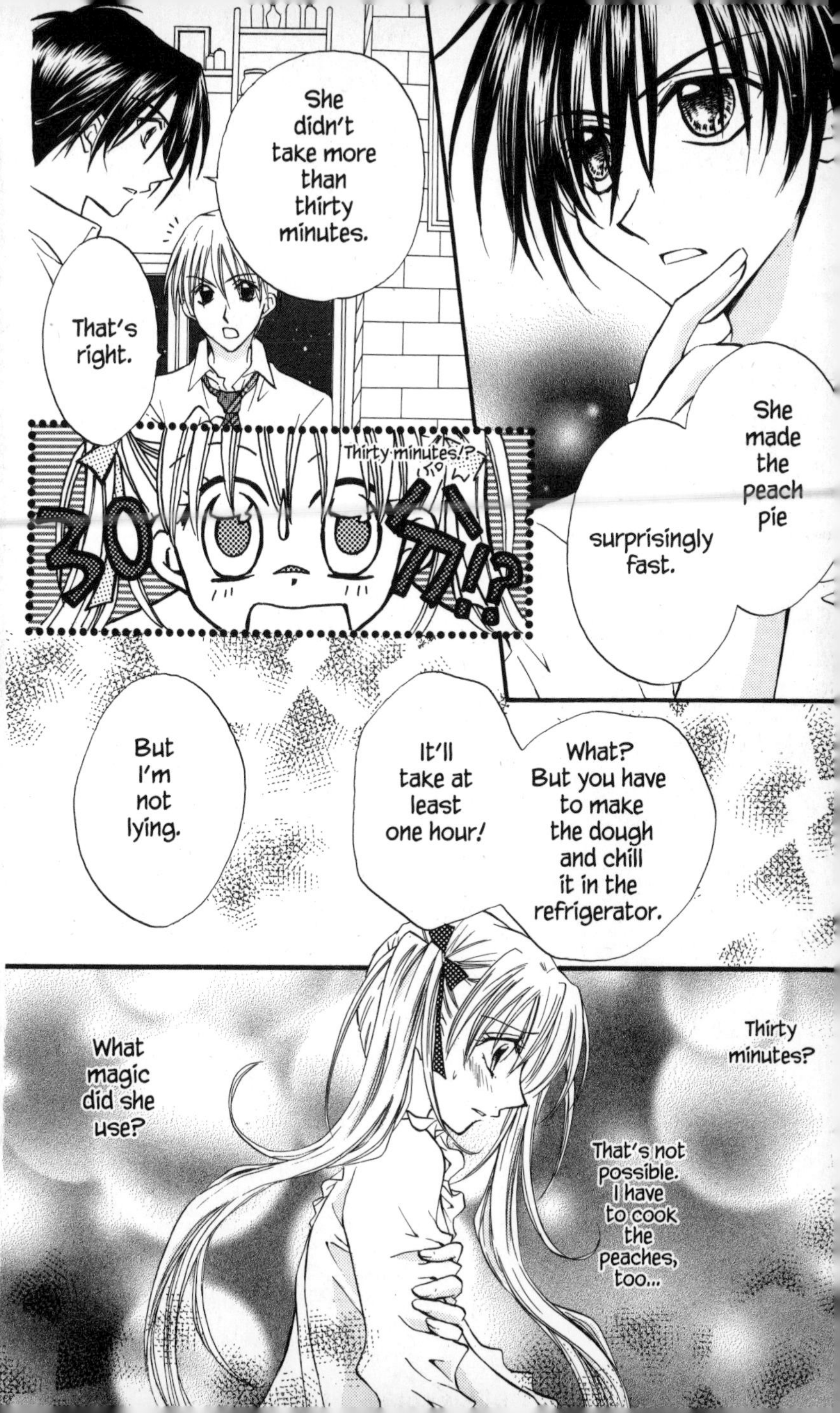
She made the peach pie
surprisingly fast.
She didn't take more than thirty minutes.
That's right.
Thirty minutes!?
What? But you have to make the dough and chill it in the refrigerator.
It'll take at least one hour!
But I'm not lying.
Thirty minutes?
That's not possible. I have to cook the peaches, too...
What magic did she use?

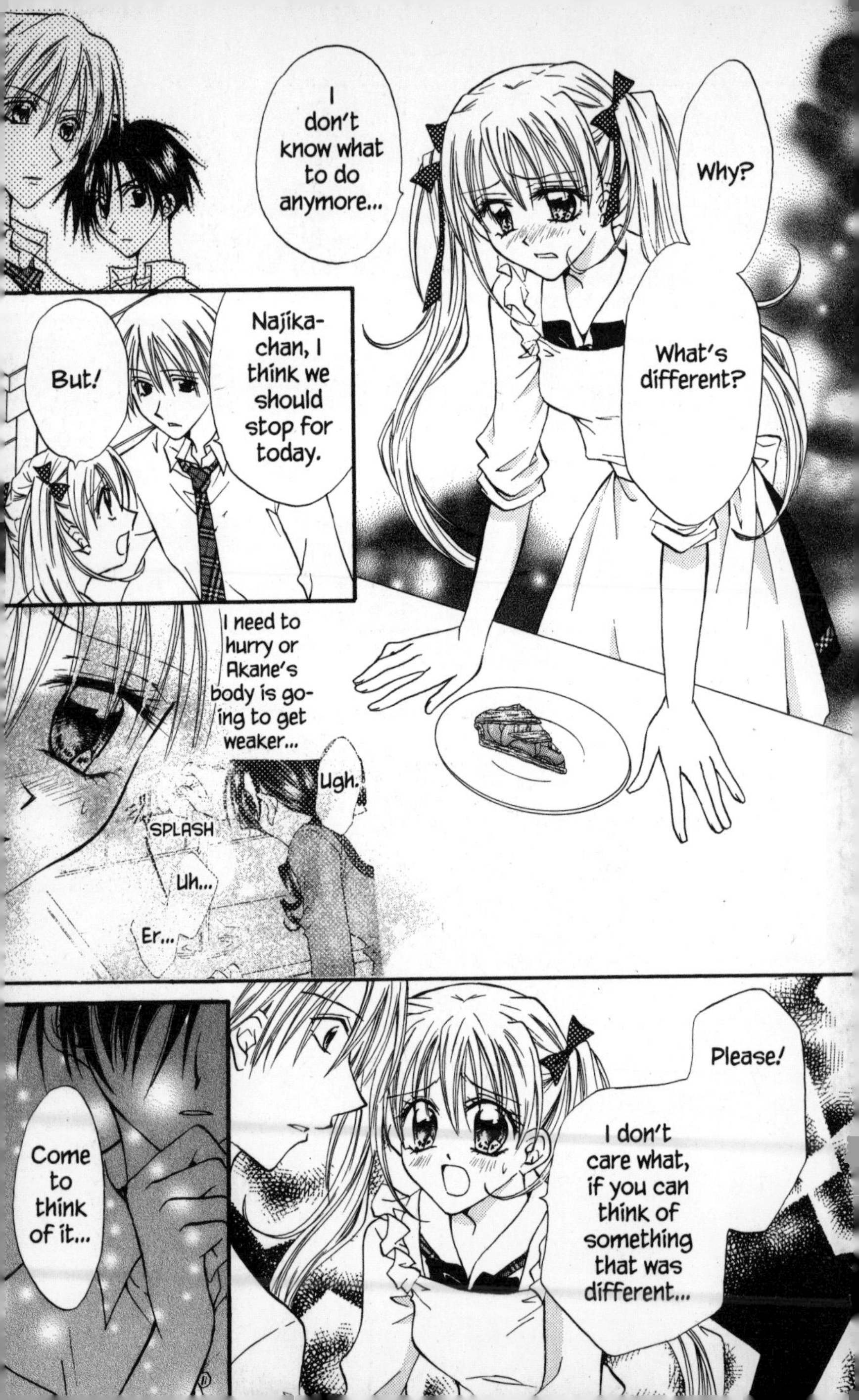
Why?
What's different?
I don't know what to do anymore...
Najika-chan, I think we should stop for today.
But!
I need to hurry or Akane's body is going to get weaker...
Ugh.
SPLASH
Uh...
Er...
Please!
I don't care what, if you can think of something that was different...
Come to think of it...

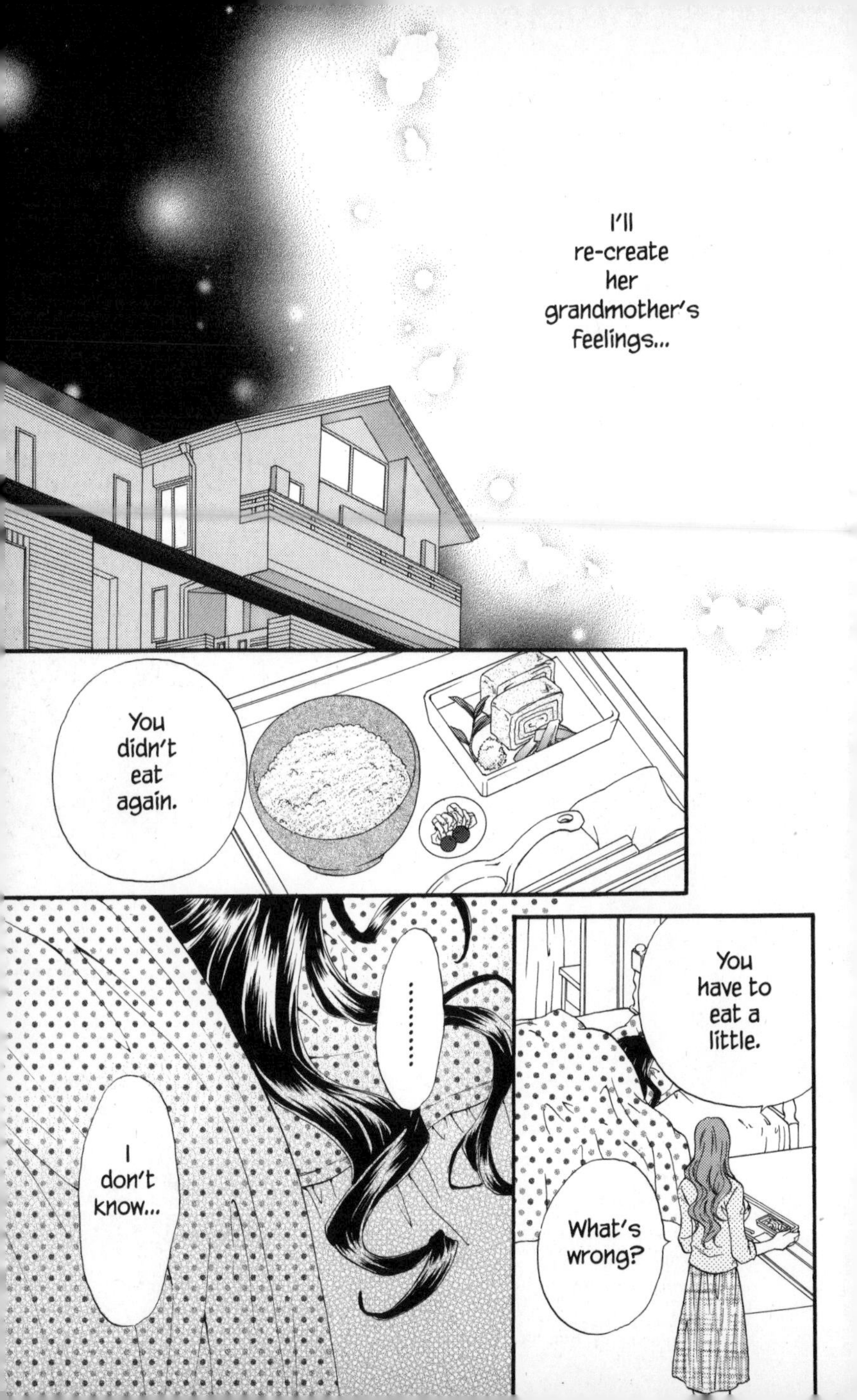
I'll re-create her grandmother's feelings...
You didn't eat again.
You have to eat a little.
What's wrong?
......
I don't know...

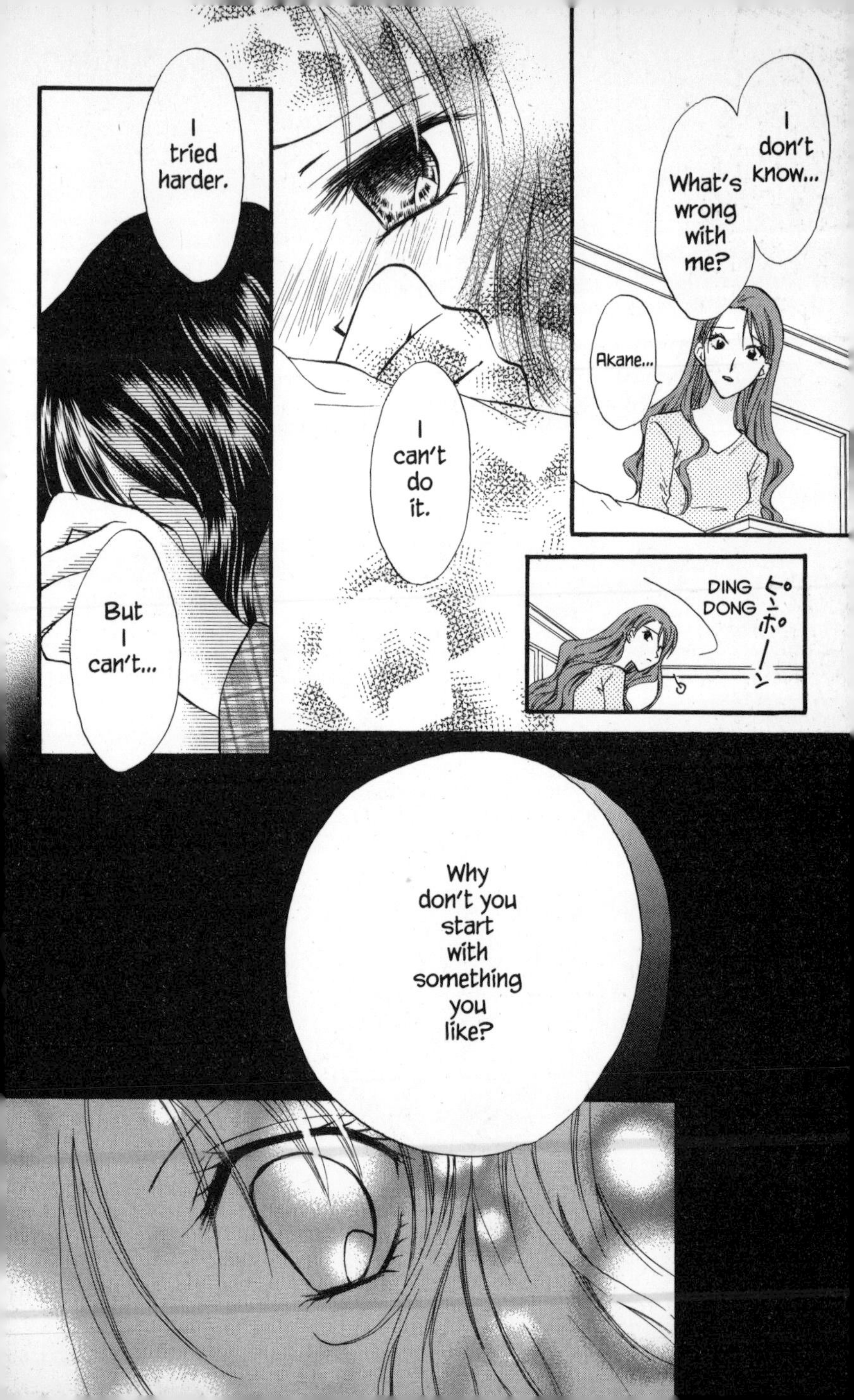
I don't know...
What's wrong with me?
Akane...
DING DONG
ピンポーン
I can't do it.
I tried harder.
But I can't...
Why don't you start with something you like?

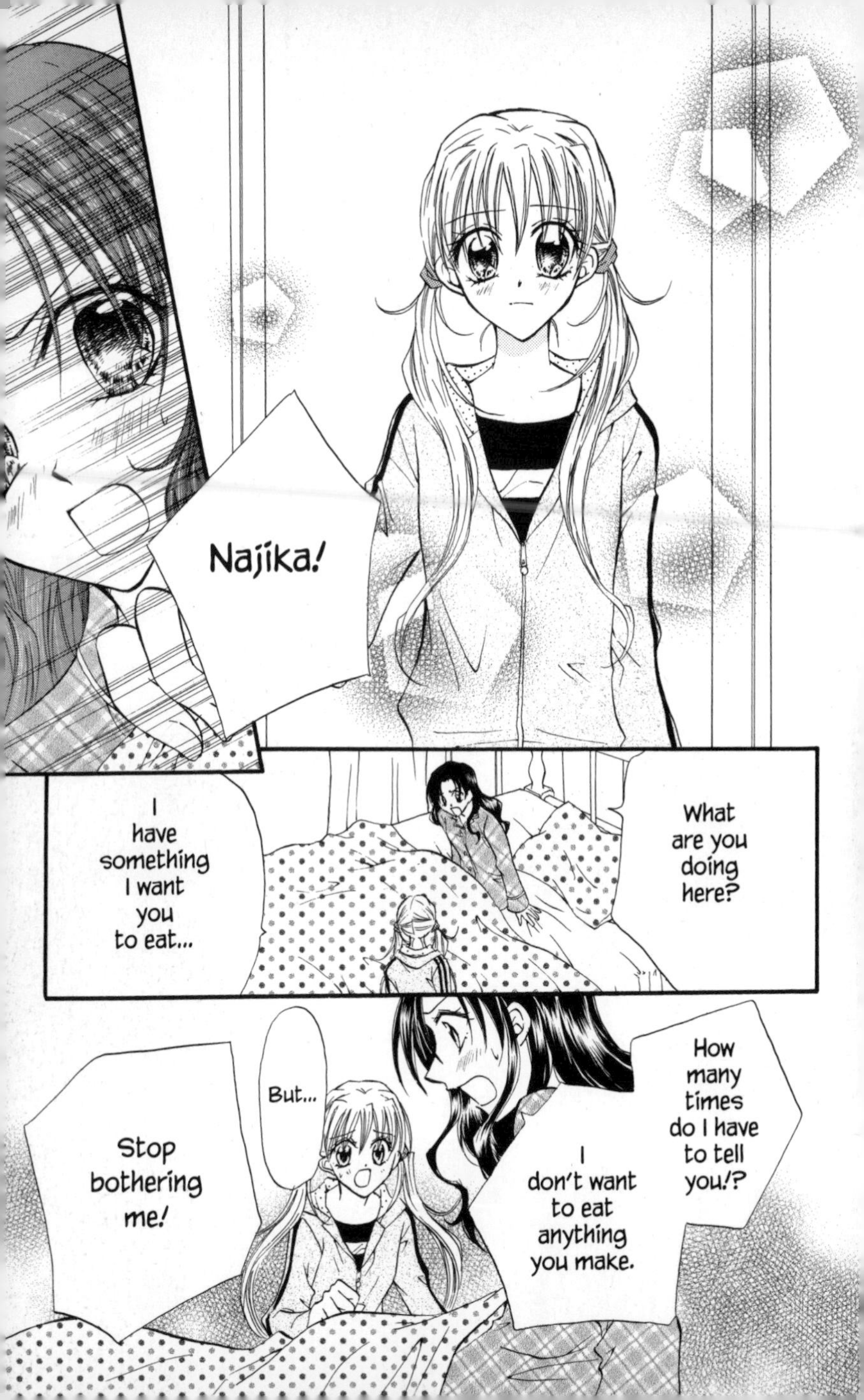
Najika!
What are you doing here?
I have something I want you to eat...
How many times do I have to tell you!?
I don't want to eat anything you make.
But...
Stop bothering me!

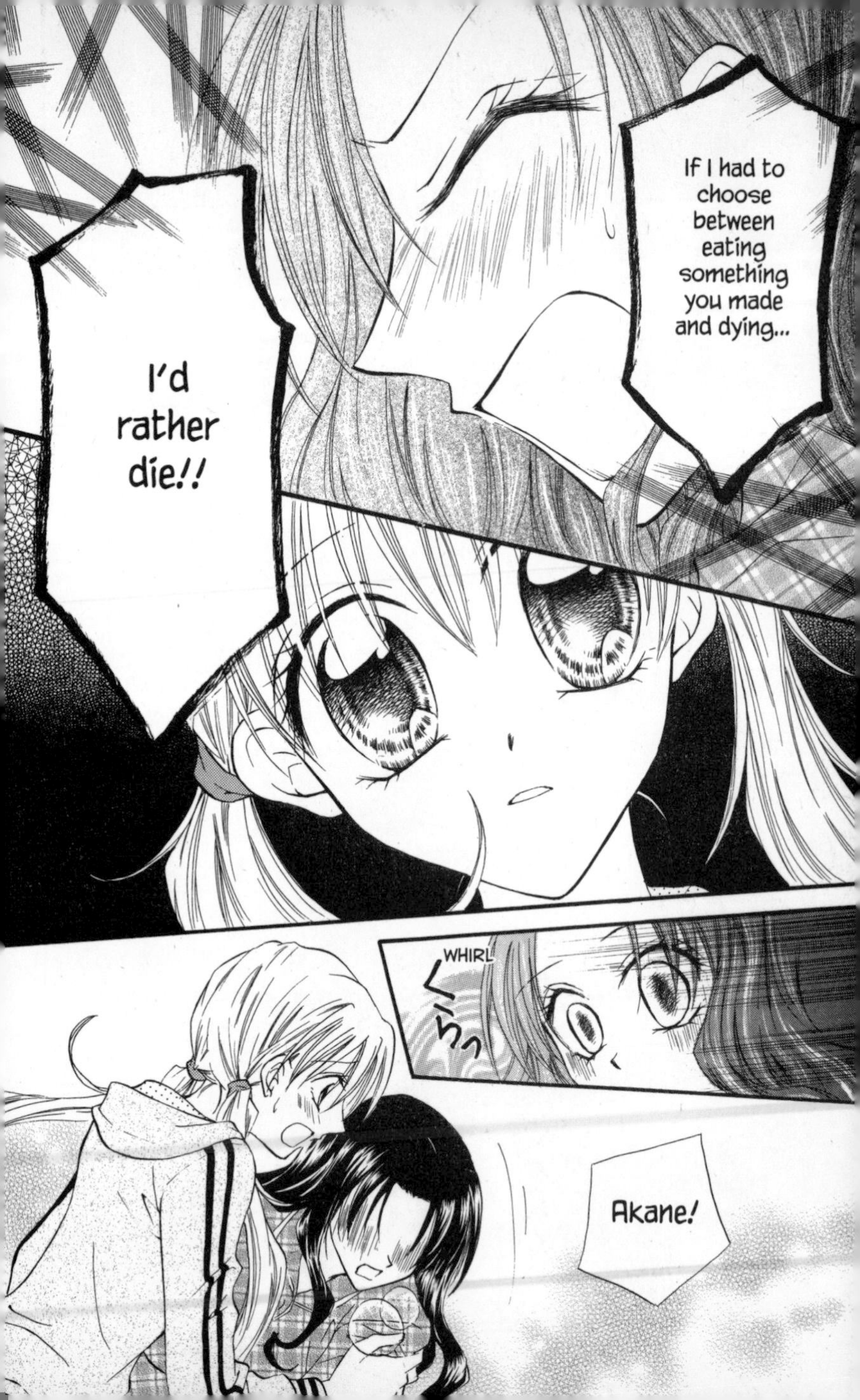
If I had to choose between eating something you made and dying...
I'd rather die!!
WHIRL
Akane!

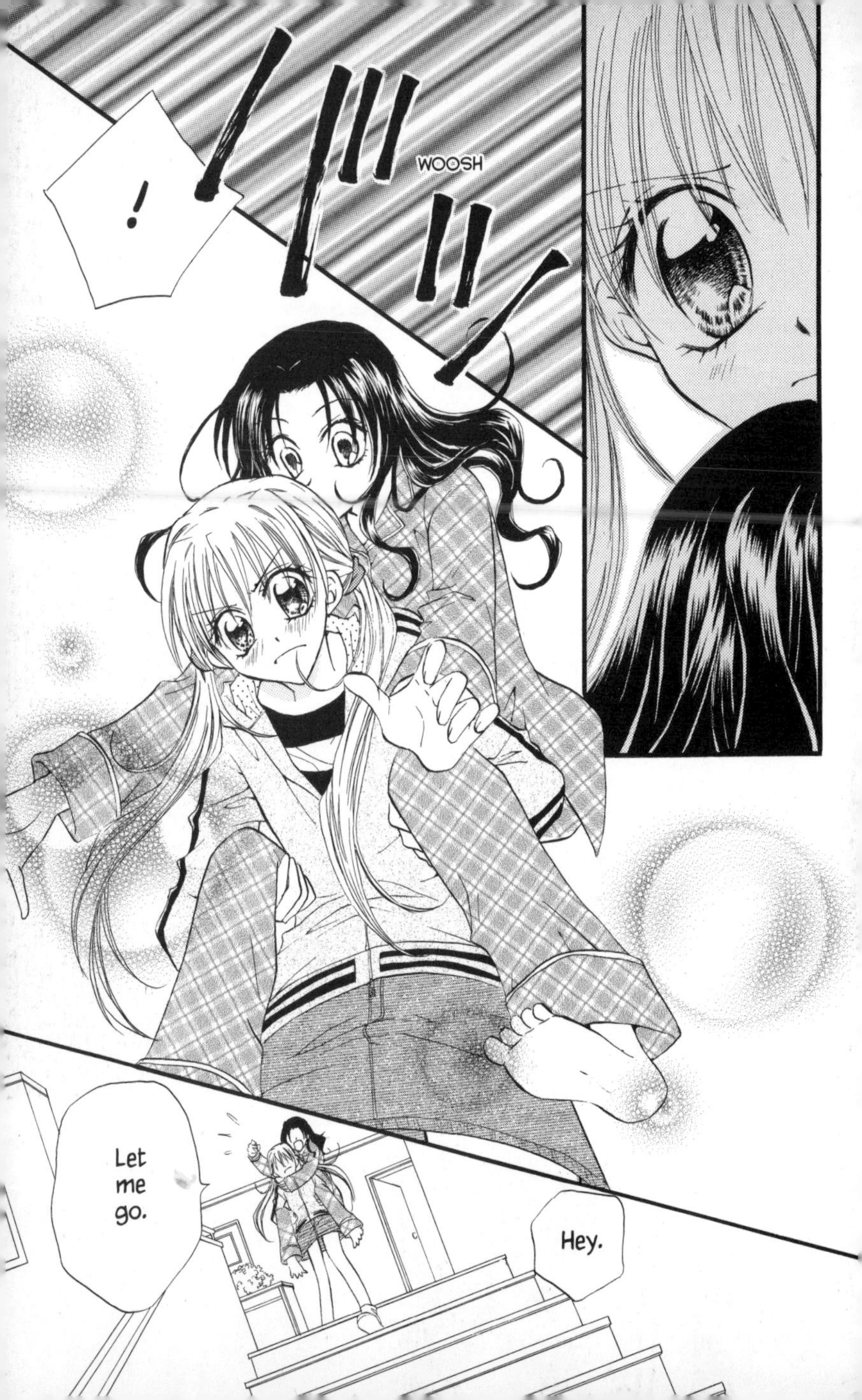
!
WOOSH
Hey.
Let me go.

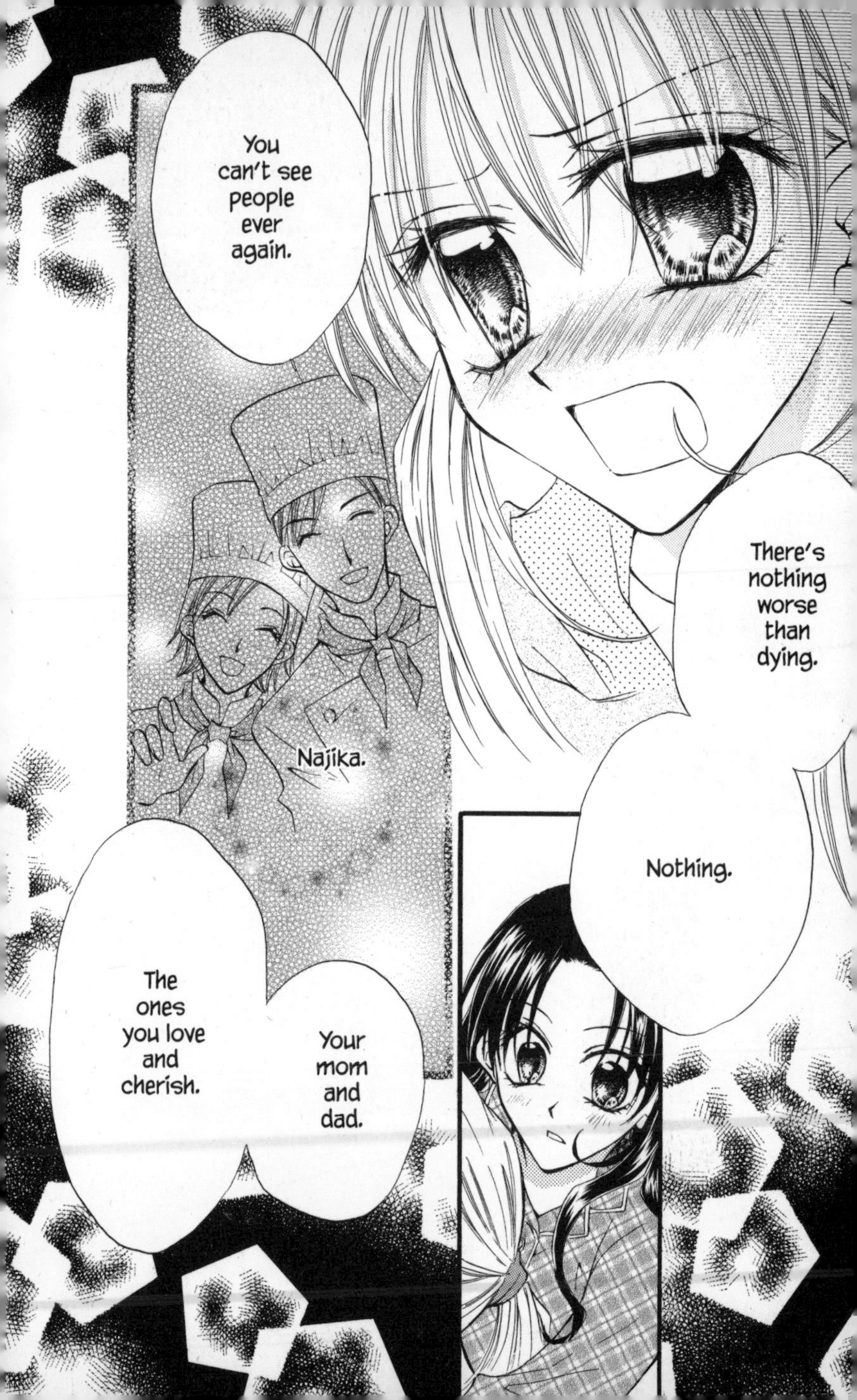
You can't see people ever again.
There's nothing worse than dying.
Nothing.
Najika.
Your mom and dad.
The ones you love and cherish.

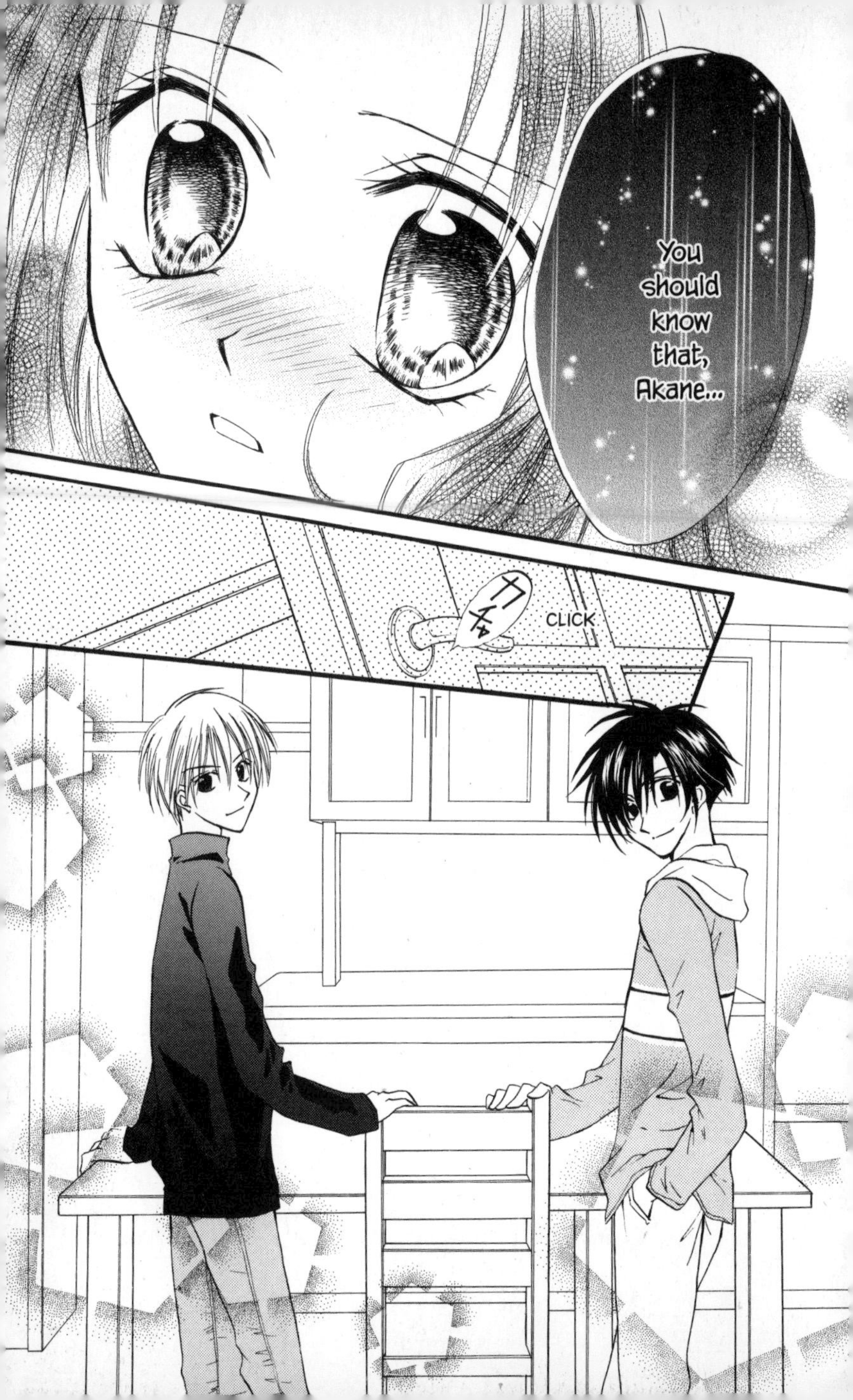
You should know that, Akane...
カチャ
CLICK

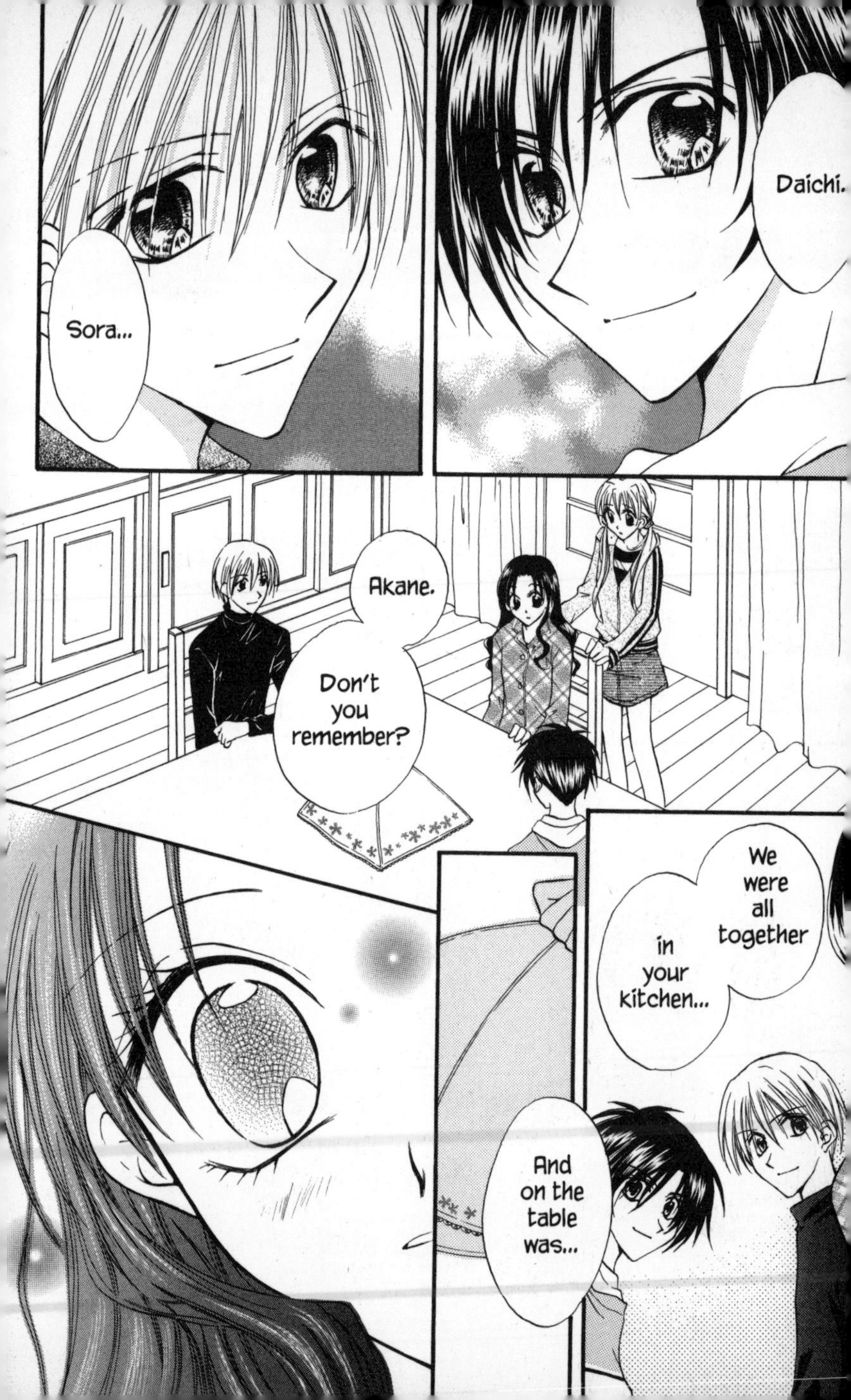
Daichi.
Sora...
Akane.
Don't you remember?
We were all together
in your kitchen...
And on the table was...

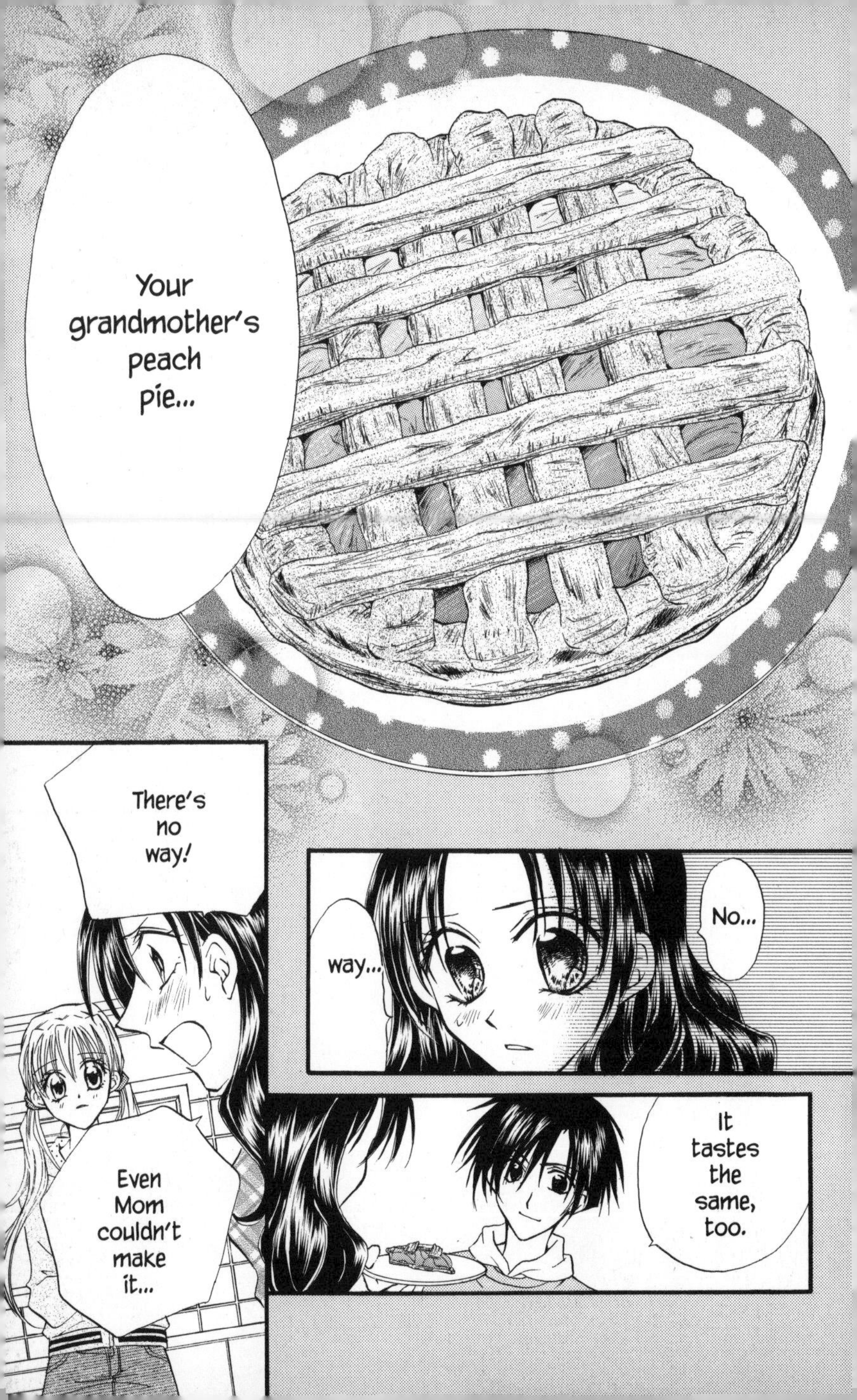
Your grandmother's peach pie...
No...
way...
It tastes the same, too.
There's no way!
Even Mom couldn't make it...

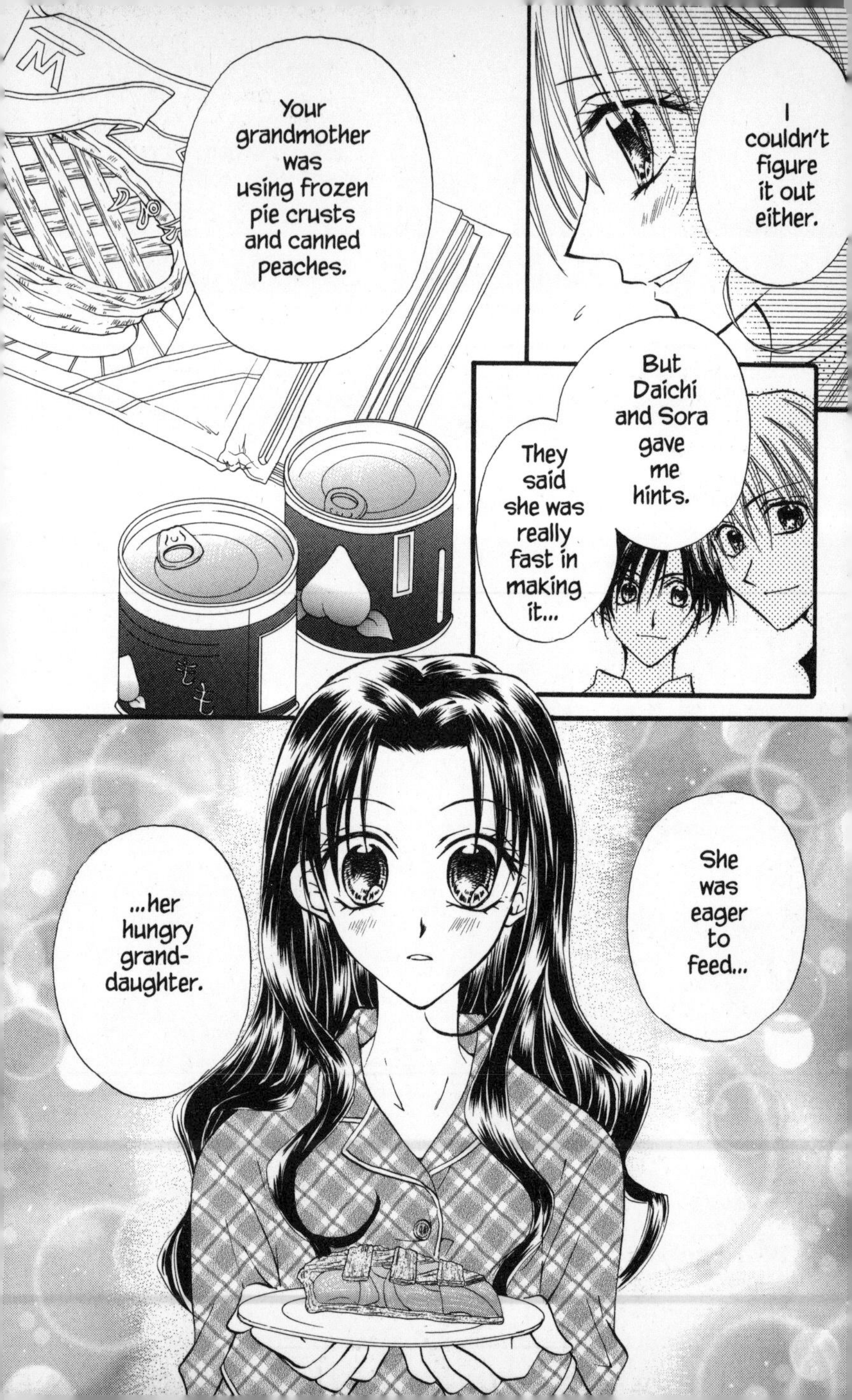
I couldn't figure it out either.
But Daichi and Sora gave me hints.
They said she was really fast in making it...
Your grandmother was using frozen pie crusts and canned peaches.
She was eager to feed...
...her hungry grand-daughter.

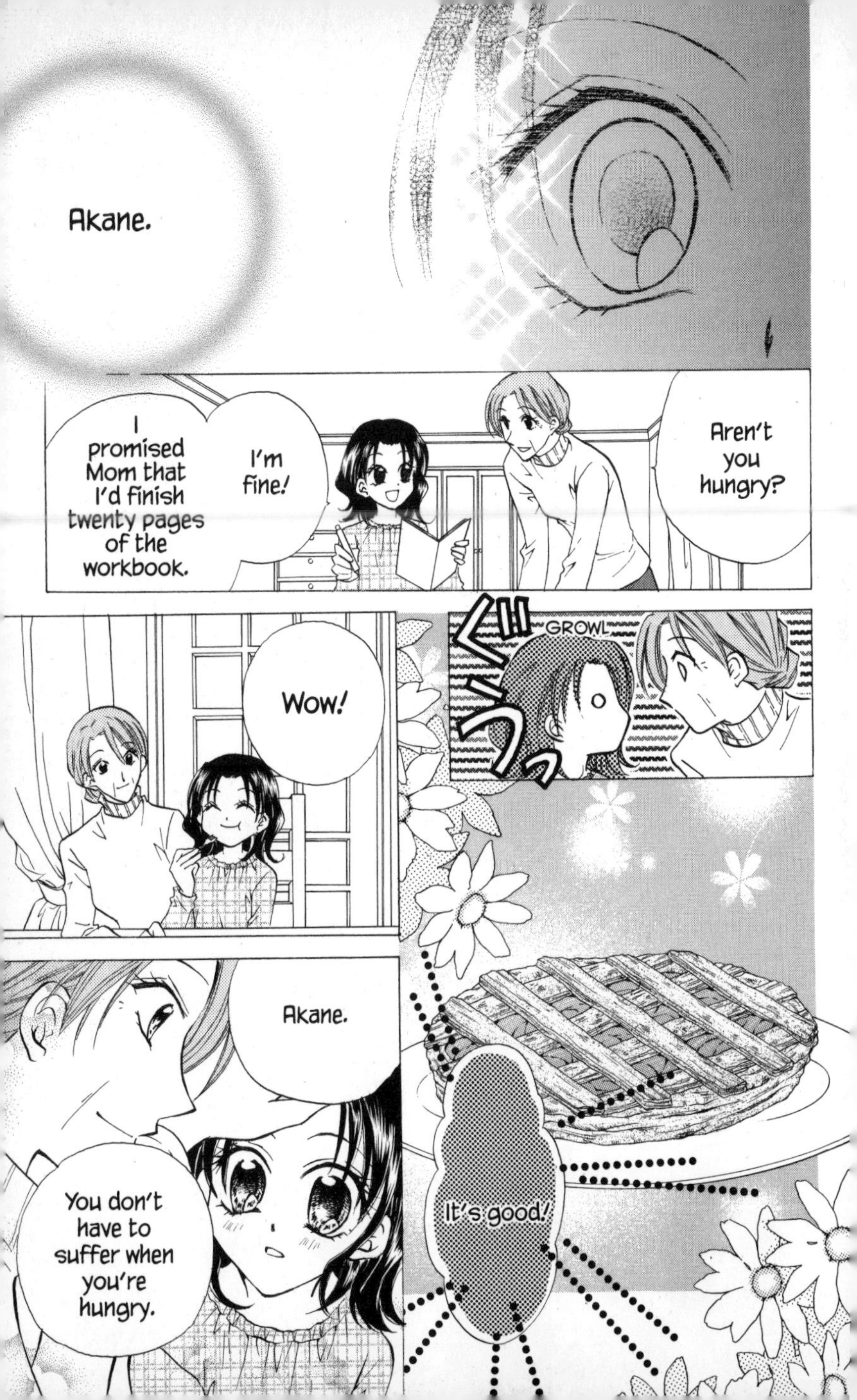
Akane.
Aren't you hungry?
I'm fine!
I promised Mom that I'd finish twenty pages of the workbook.
GROWL
It's good!
Wow!
Akane.
You don't have to suffer when you're hungry.

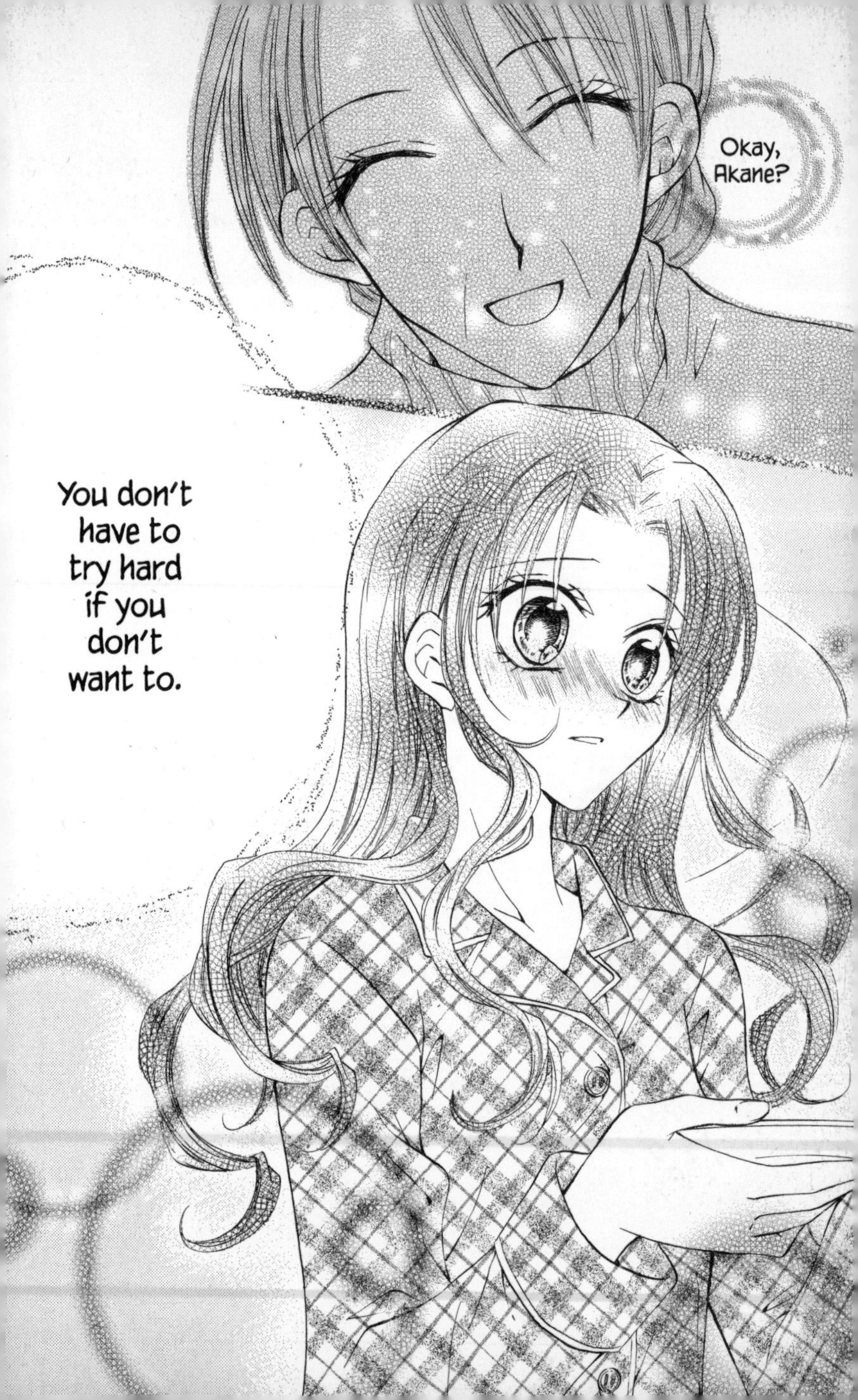
Okay, Akane?
You don't have to try hard if you don't want to.

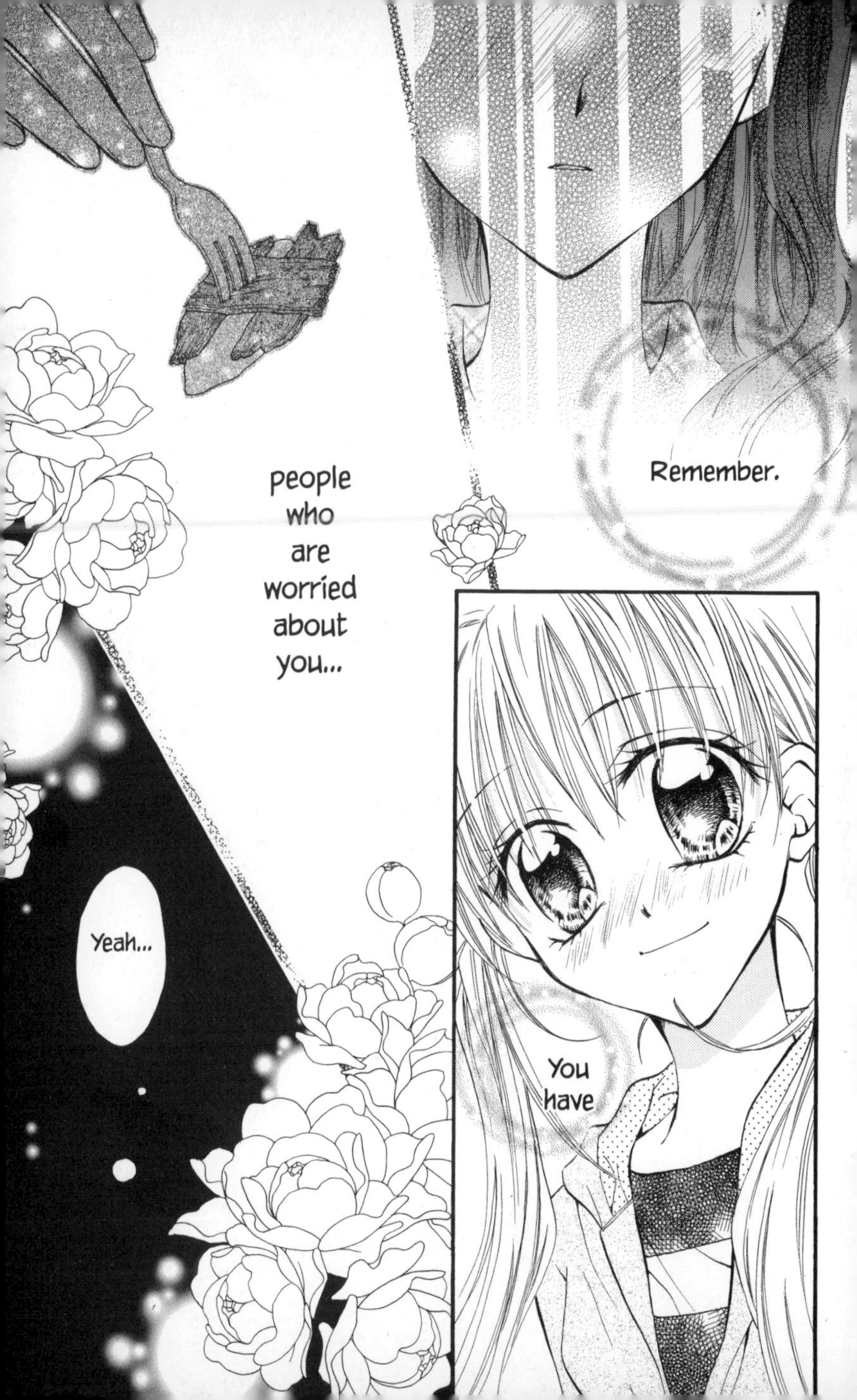

Remember.
You have
people who are worried about you...
Yeah...

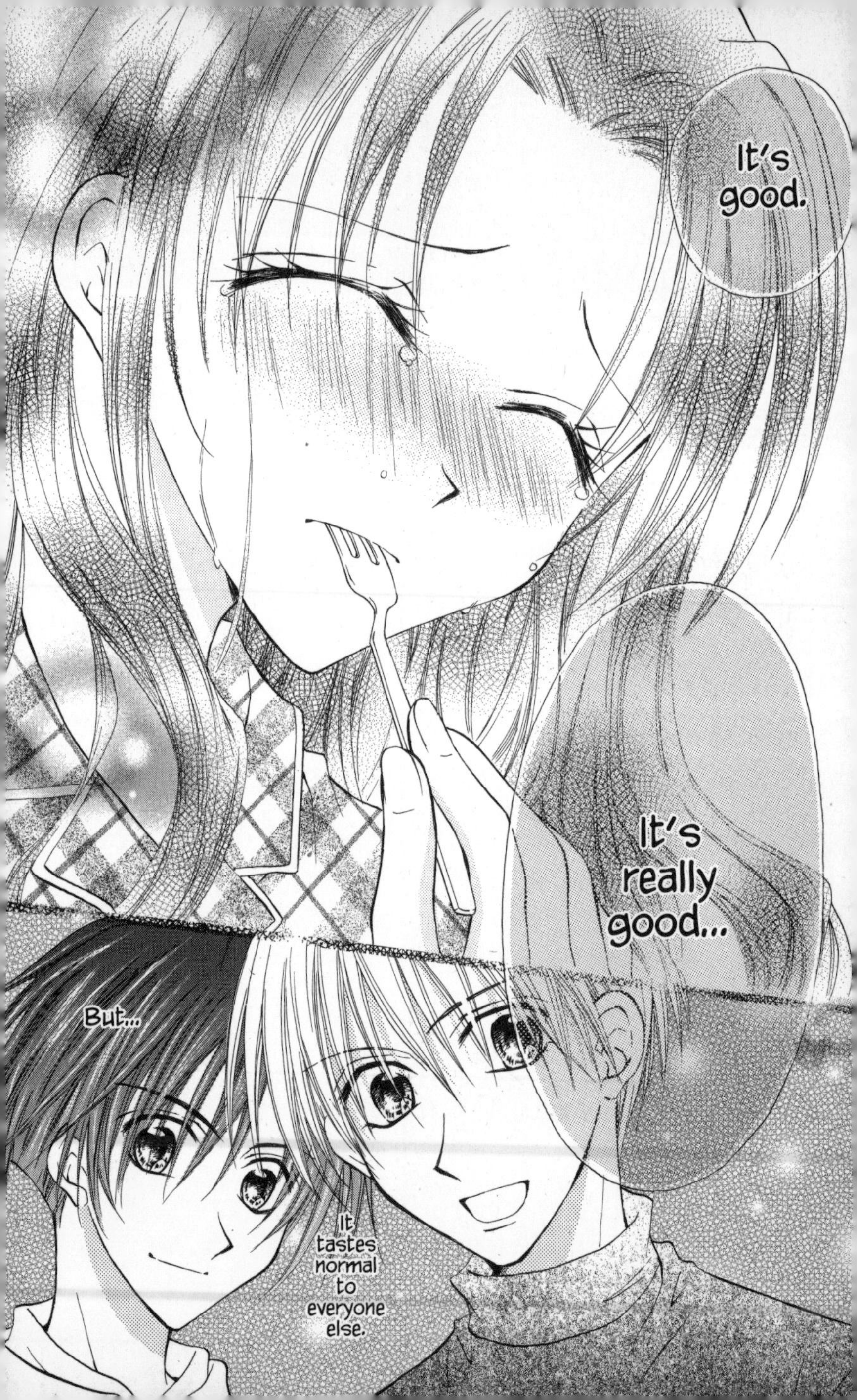
It's good.
It's really good...
It tastes normal to everyone else.
But...

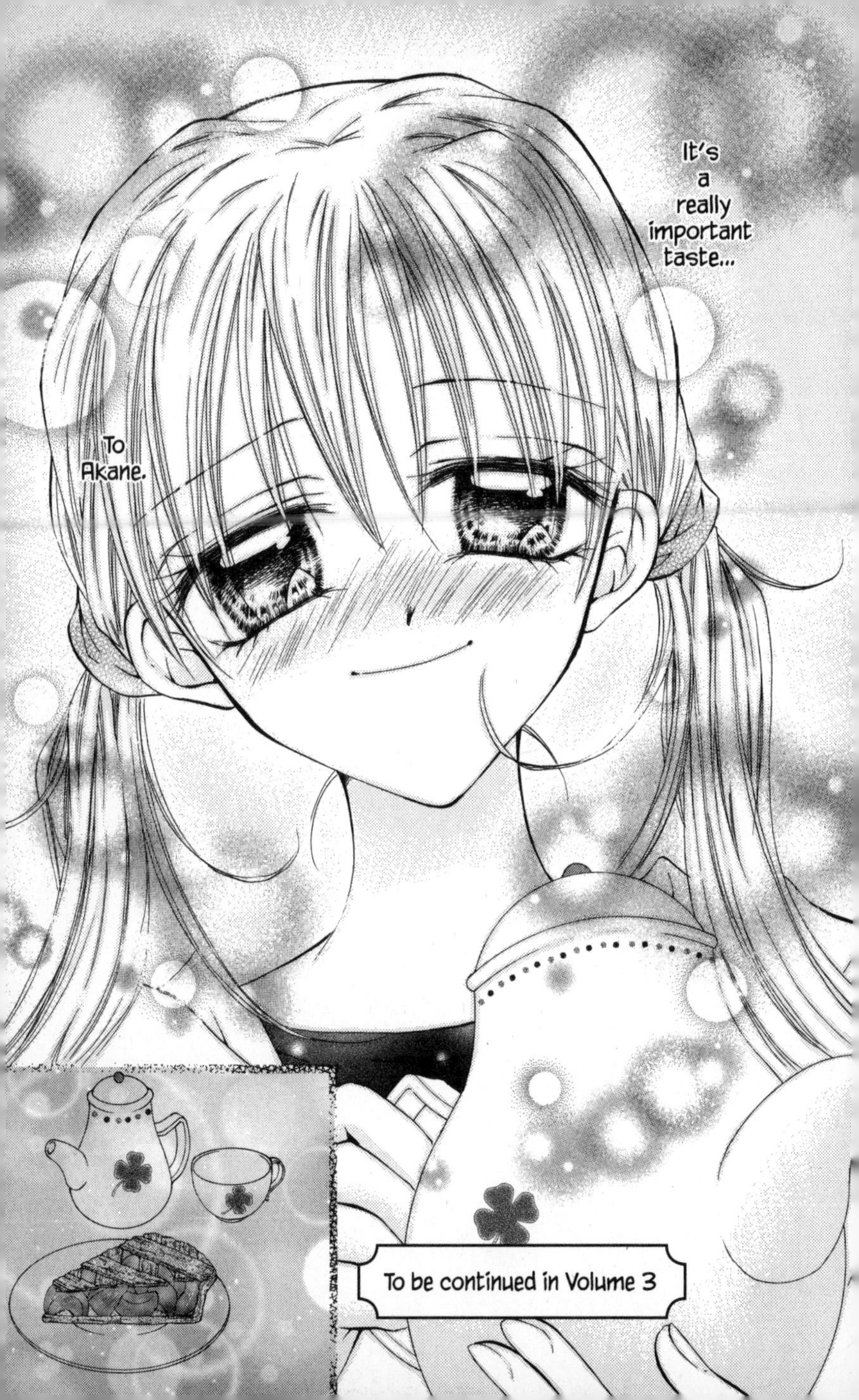
It's a really important taste...
To Akane.
To be continued in Volume 3

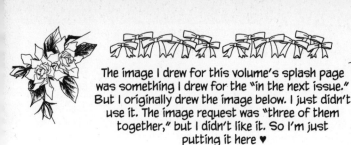

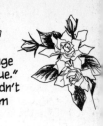

The image I drew for this volume's splash page was something I drew for the "in the next issue." But I originally drew the image below. I just didn't use it. The image request was "three of them together," but I didn't like it. So I'm just putting it here ♥

Please send letters to:
Nakayoshi Editorial Team
PO BOX 91
Akasaka, Tokyo 107-8652

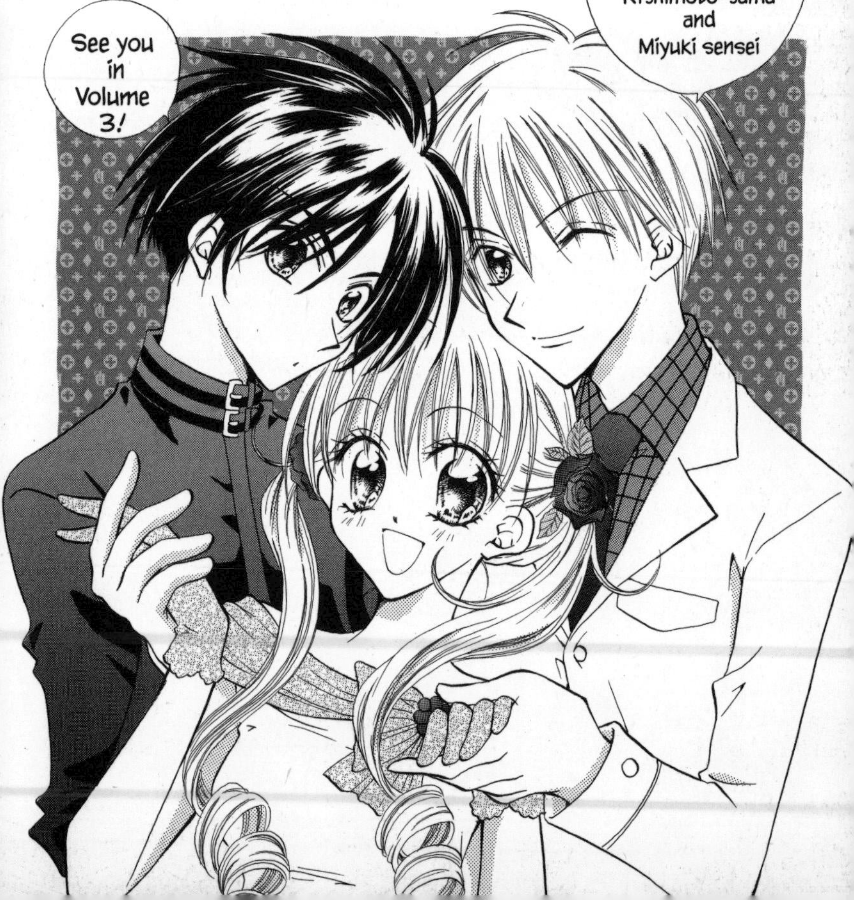

Thank you
Maruyama-sama
Shobayashi-sama
Marimo-sama
Kishimoto-sama
and
Miyuki sensei
See you in Volume 3!

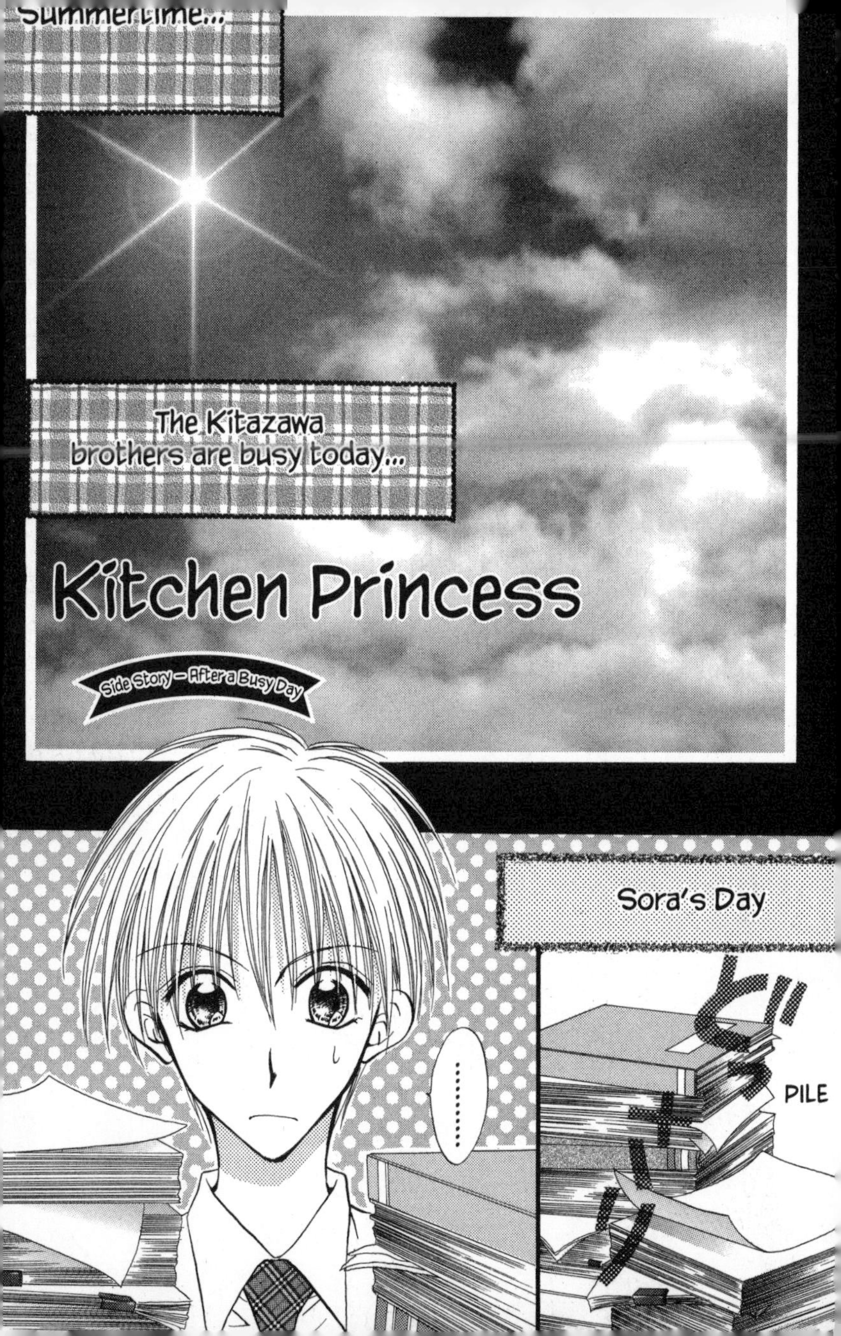
Summertime...
The Kitazawa brothers are busy today...
Kitchen Princess
Side Story – After a Busy Day
Sora's Day
PILE
....

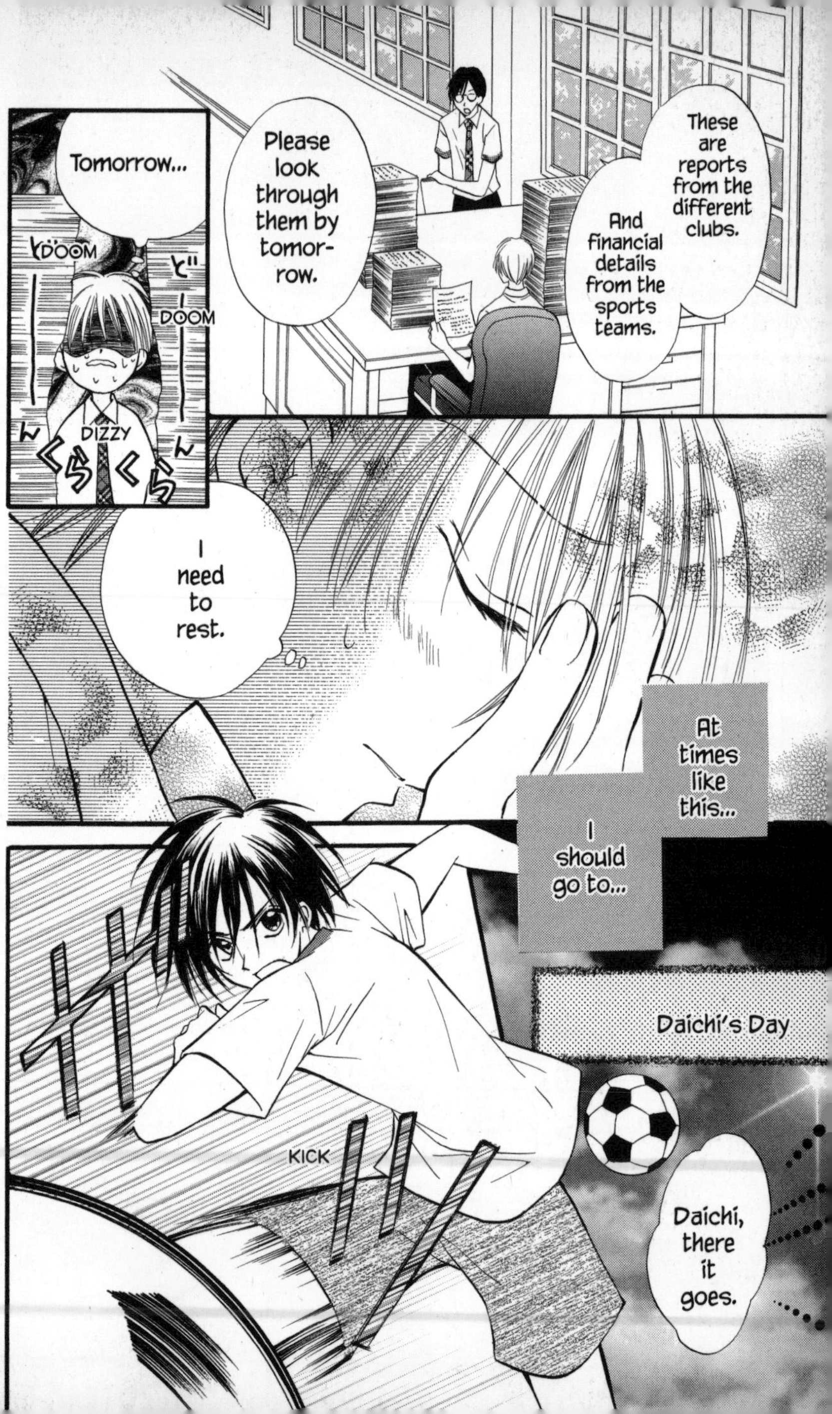
These are reports from the different clubs.
And financial details from the sports teams.
Please look through them by tomorrow.
Tomorrow...
DOOM
DOOM
DIZZY
くらくら
I need to rest.
At times like this...
I should go to...
Daichi's Day
Daichi, there it goes.
KICK

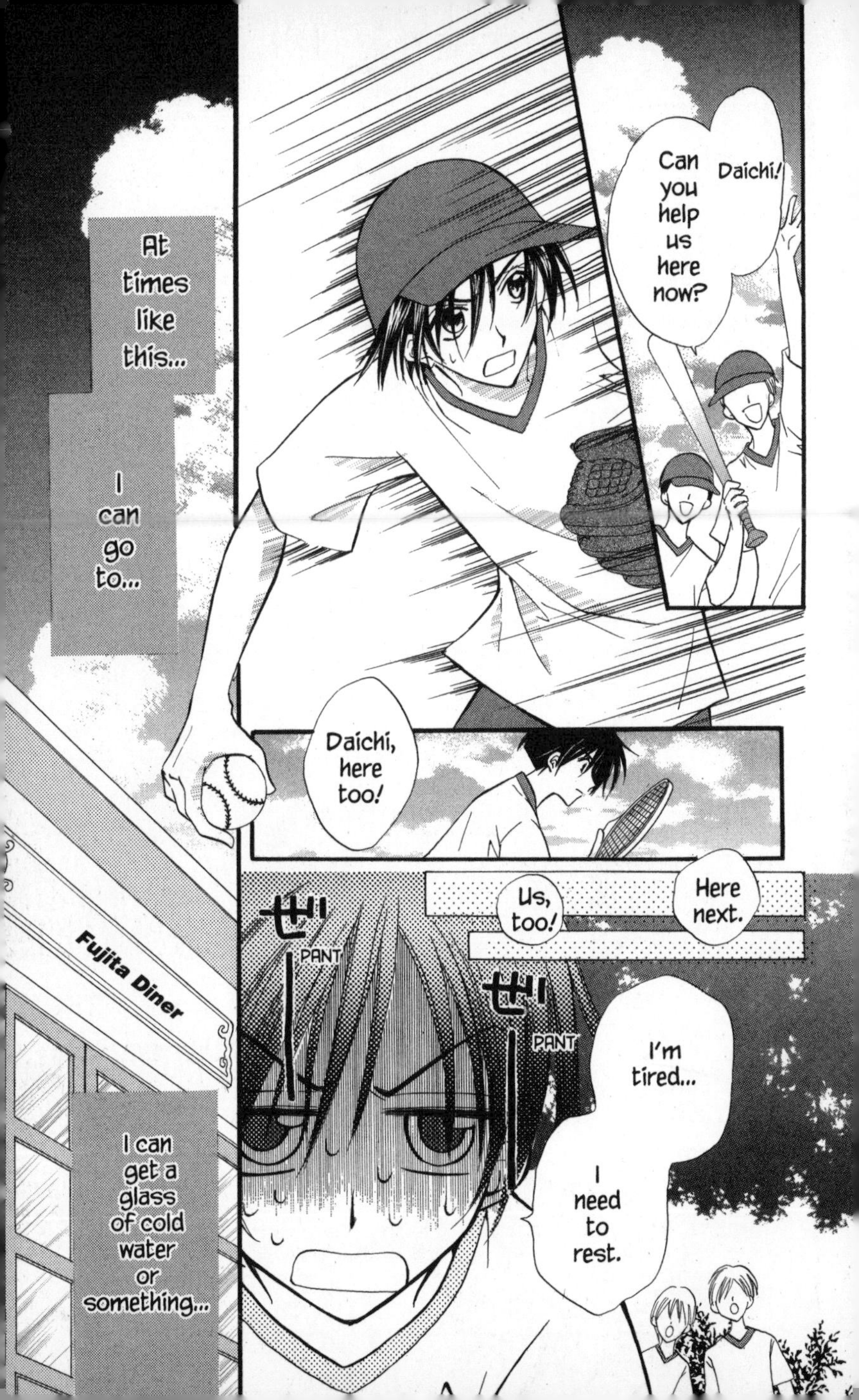

Daichi!
Can you help us here now?
Daichi, here too!
Here next.
Us, too!
ゼィ
PANT
ゼィ
PANT
I'm tired...
I need to rest.
At times like this...
I can go to...
Fujita Diner
I can get a glass of cold water or something...

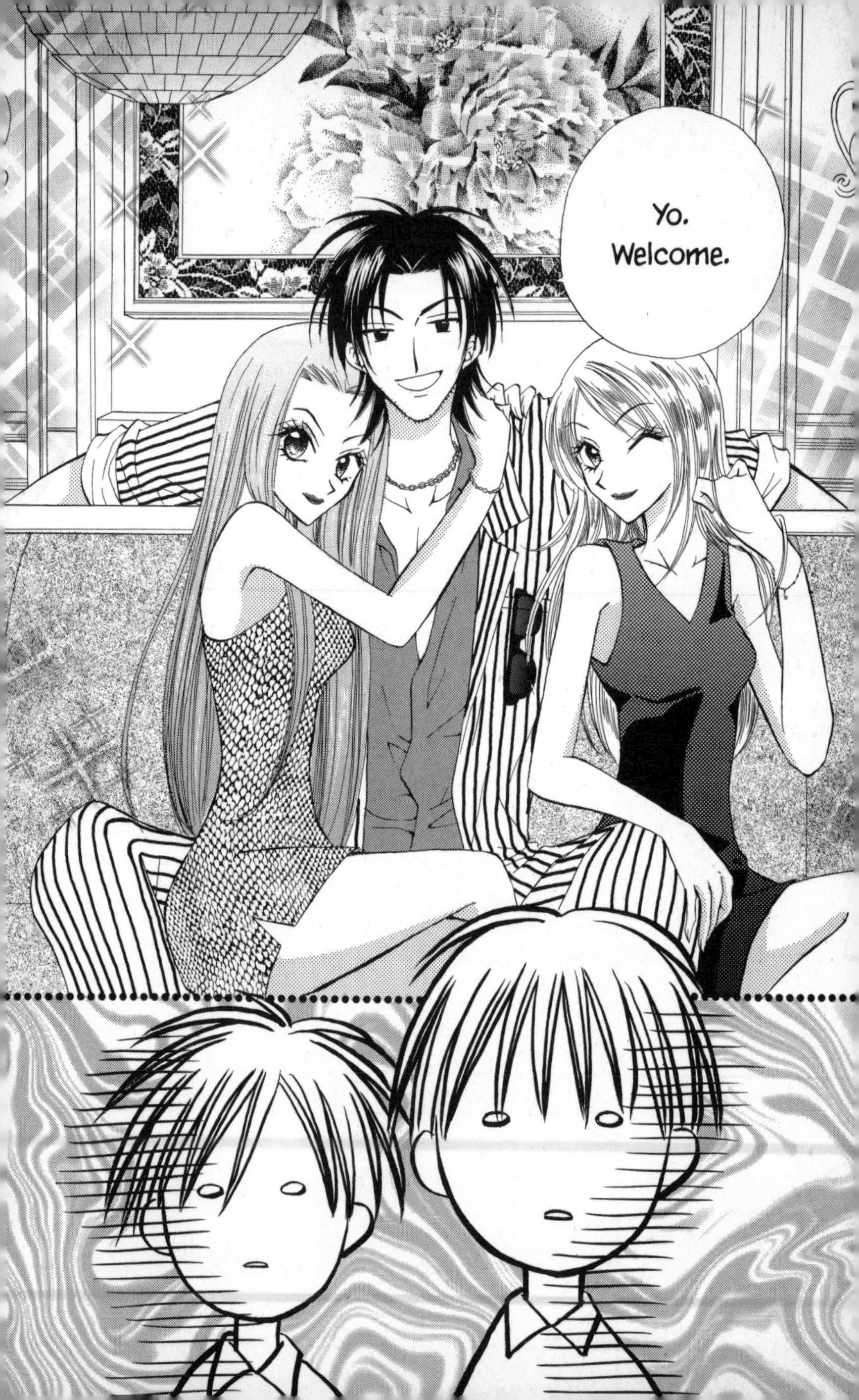
Yo. Welcome.

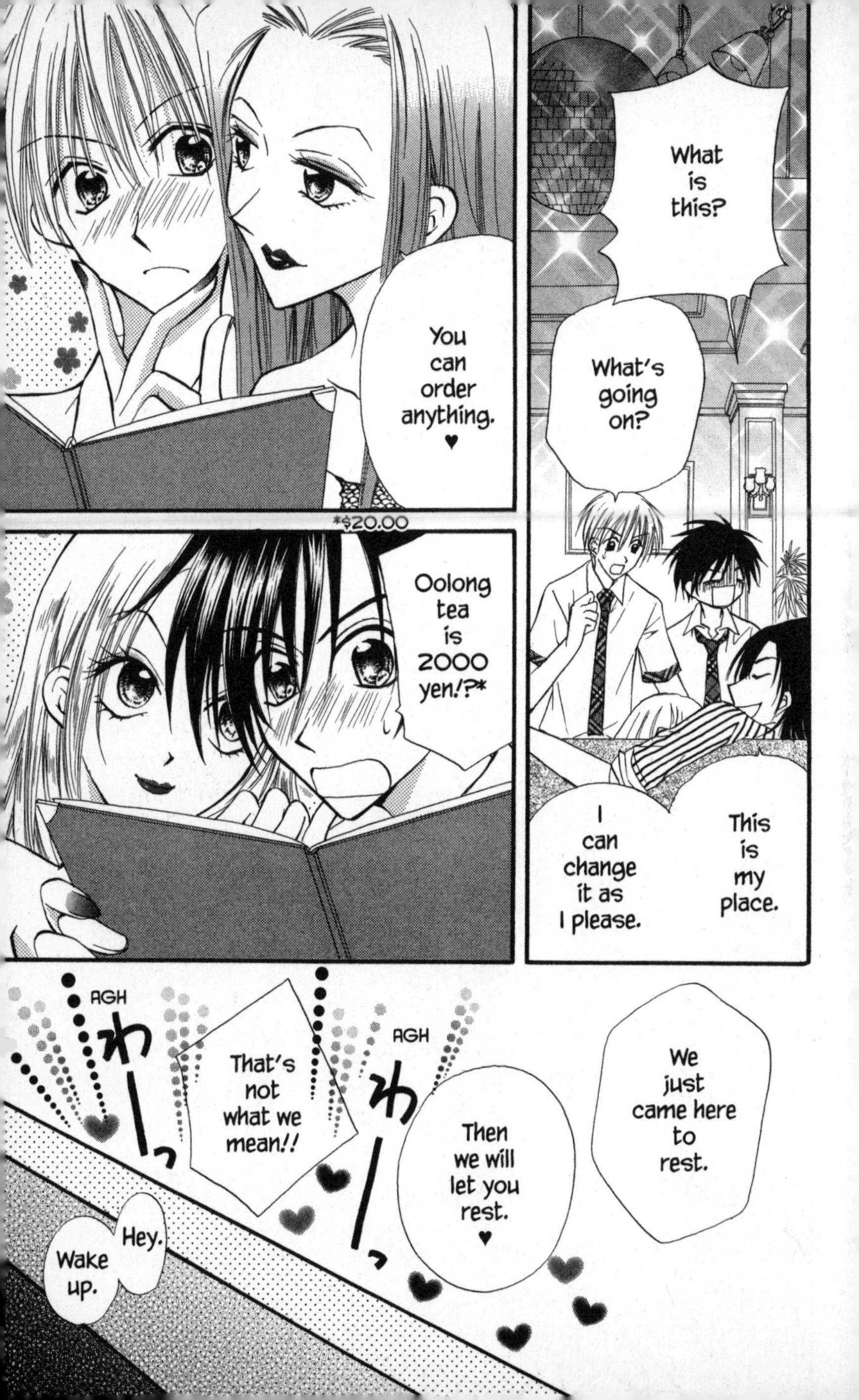

What is this?
What's going on?
This is my place.
I can change it as I please.
You can order anything. ♥
Oolong tea is 2000 yen!?*
*$20.00
We just came here to rest.
Then we will let you rest. ♥
AGH
That's not what we mean!!
AGH
Hey.
Wake up.

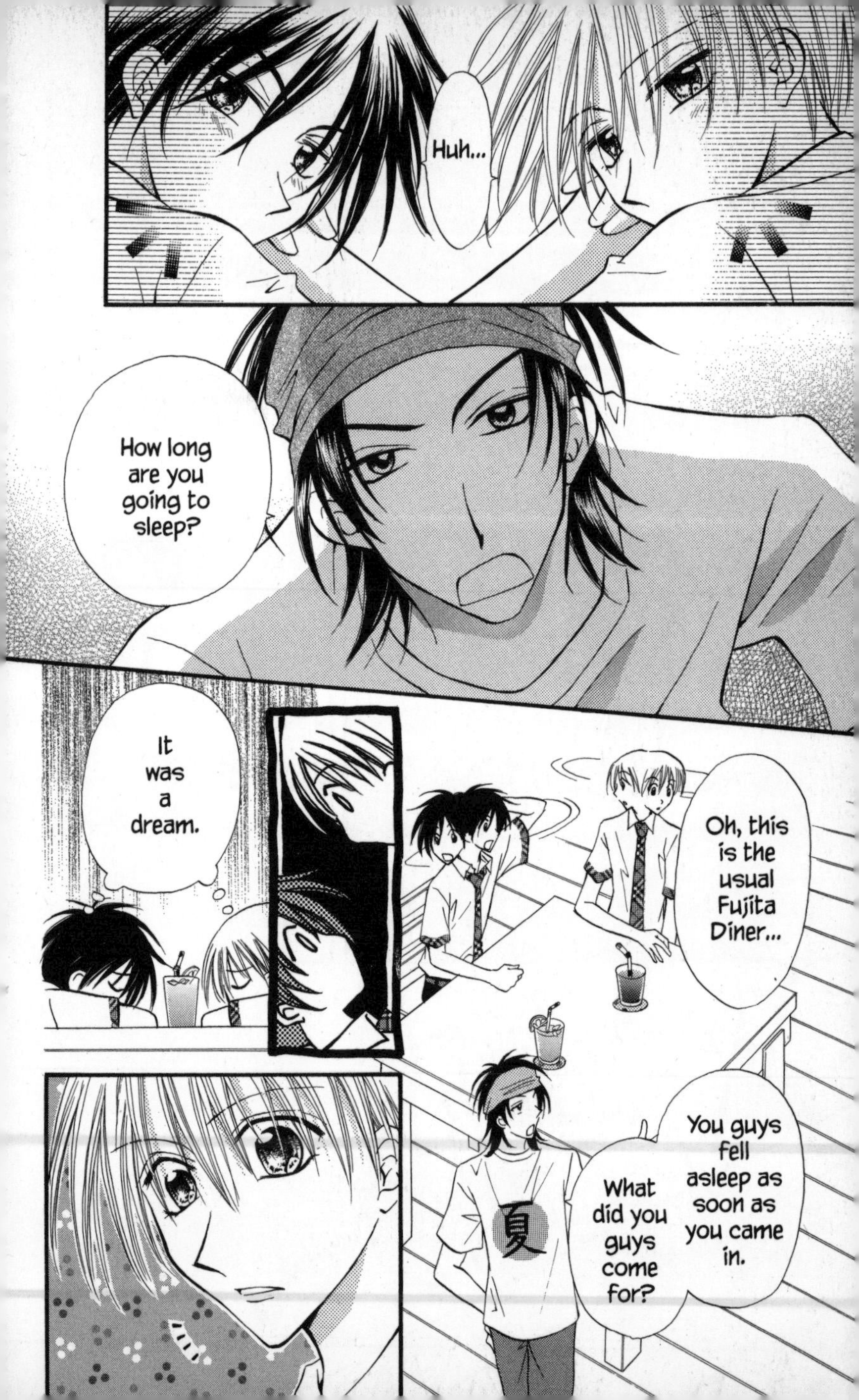
Huh...
How long are you going to sleep?
Oh, this is the usual Fujita Diner...
You guys fell asleep as soon as you came in.
What did you guys come for?
It was a dream.

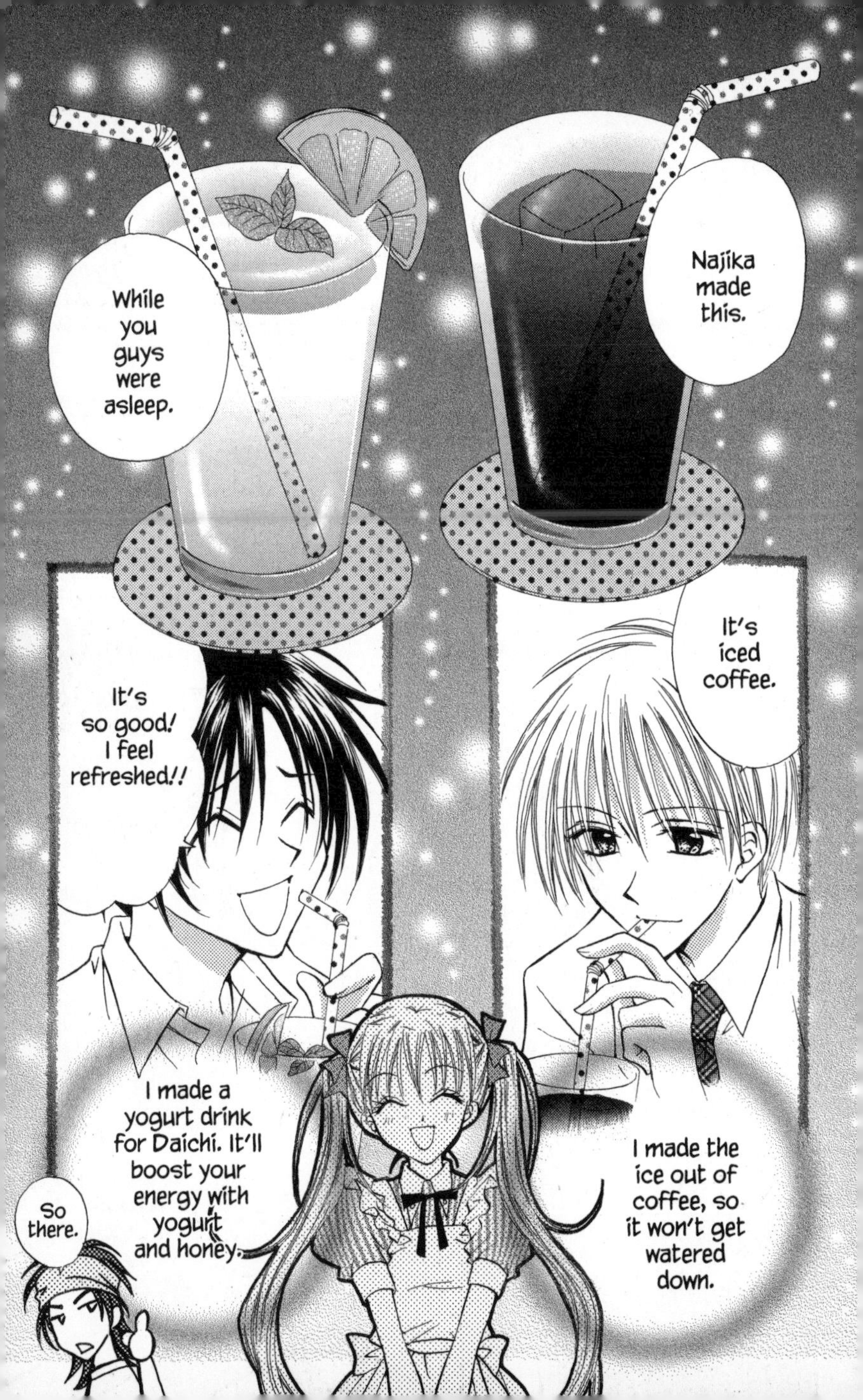
Najika made this.
While you guys were asleep.
It's iced coffee.
It's so good! I feel refreshed!!
I made the ice out of coffee, so it won't get watered down.
I made a yogurt drink for Daichi. It'll boost your energy with yogurt and honey.
So there.

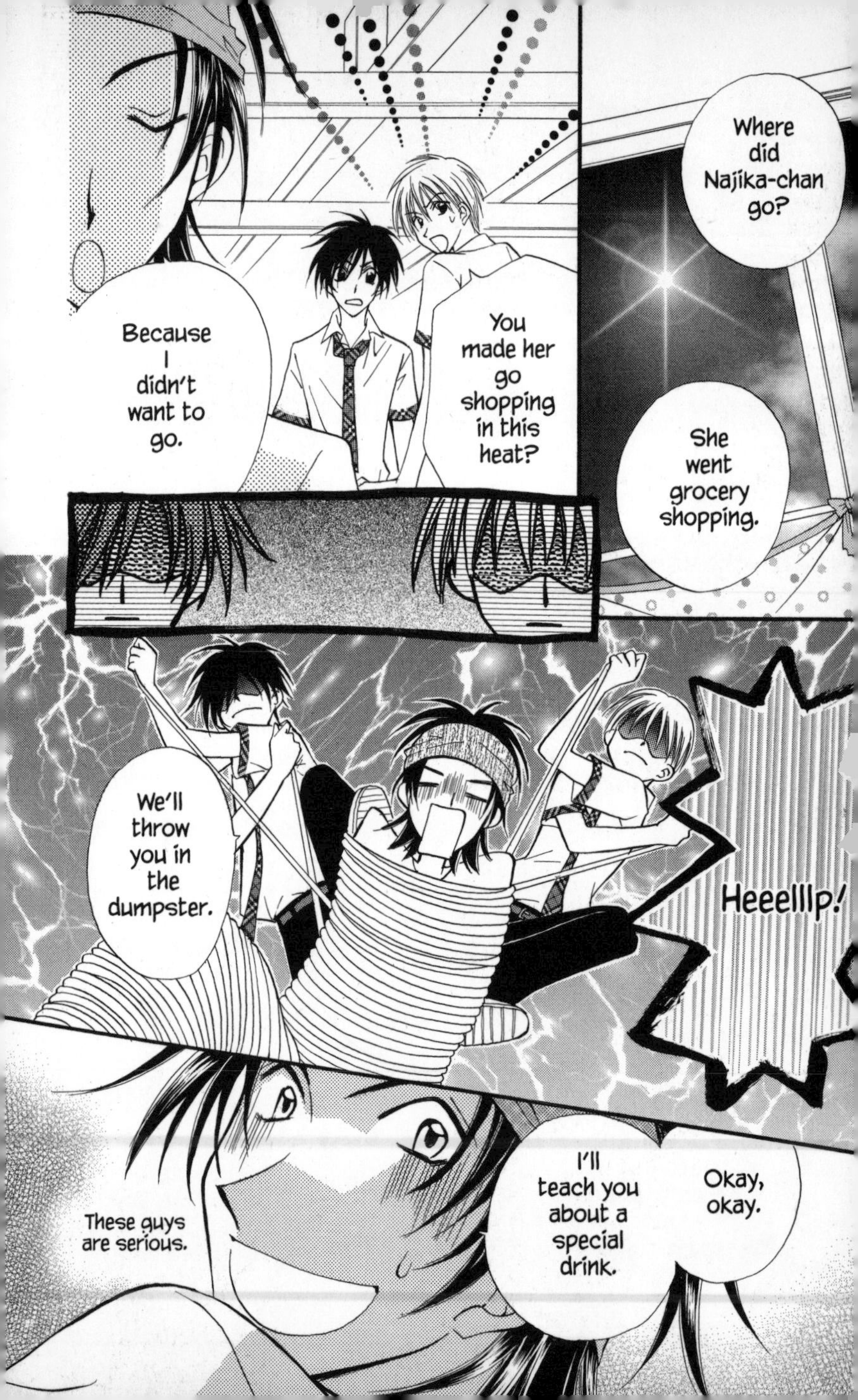
Where did Najika-chan go?
She went grocery shopping.
You made her go shopping in this heat?
Because I didn't want to go.
Heeelllp!
We'll throw you in the dumpster.
Okay, okay.
I'll teach you about a special drink.
These guys are serious.

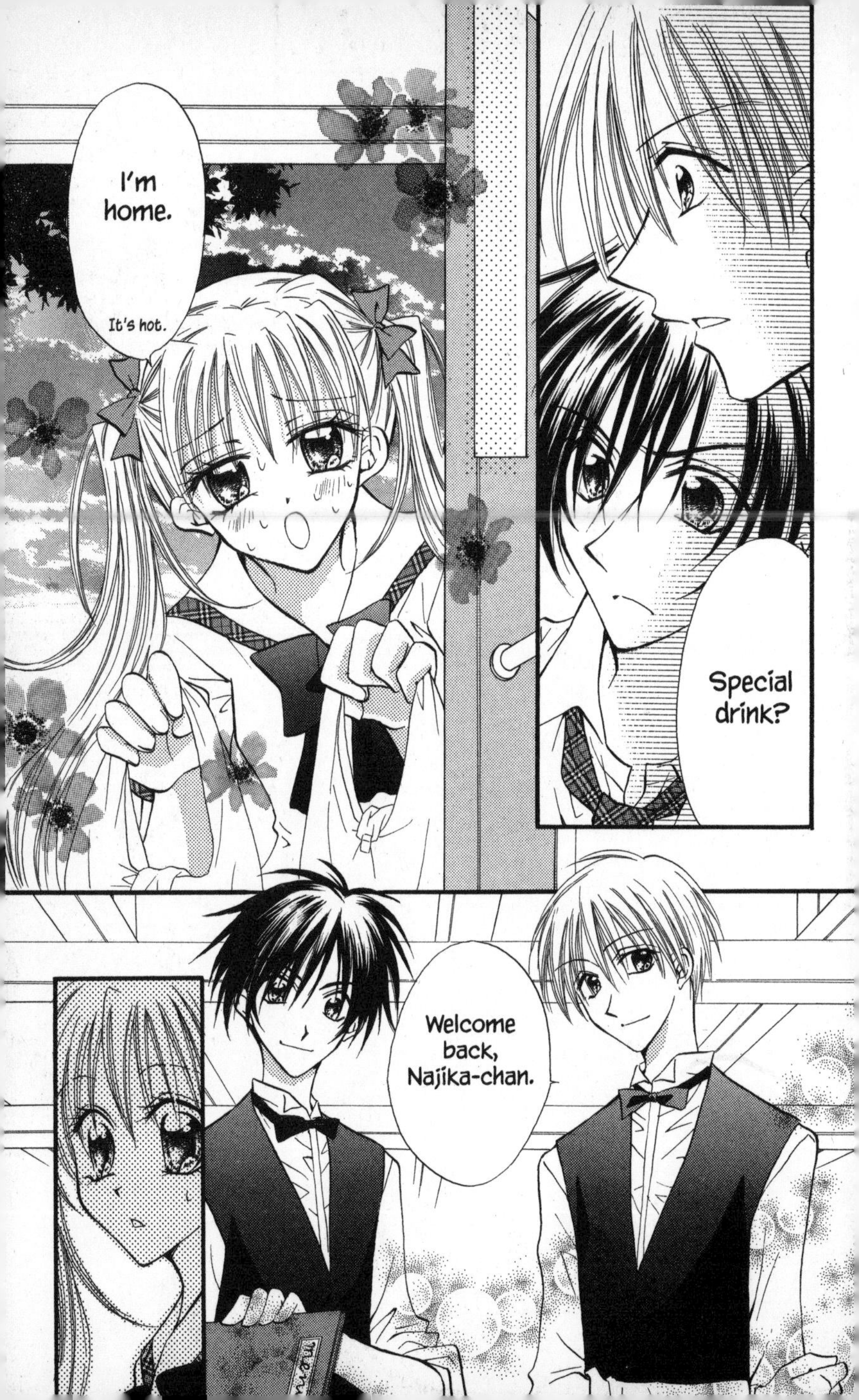
Special drink?
I'm home.
It's hot.
Welcome back, Najika-chan.

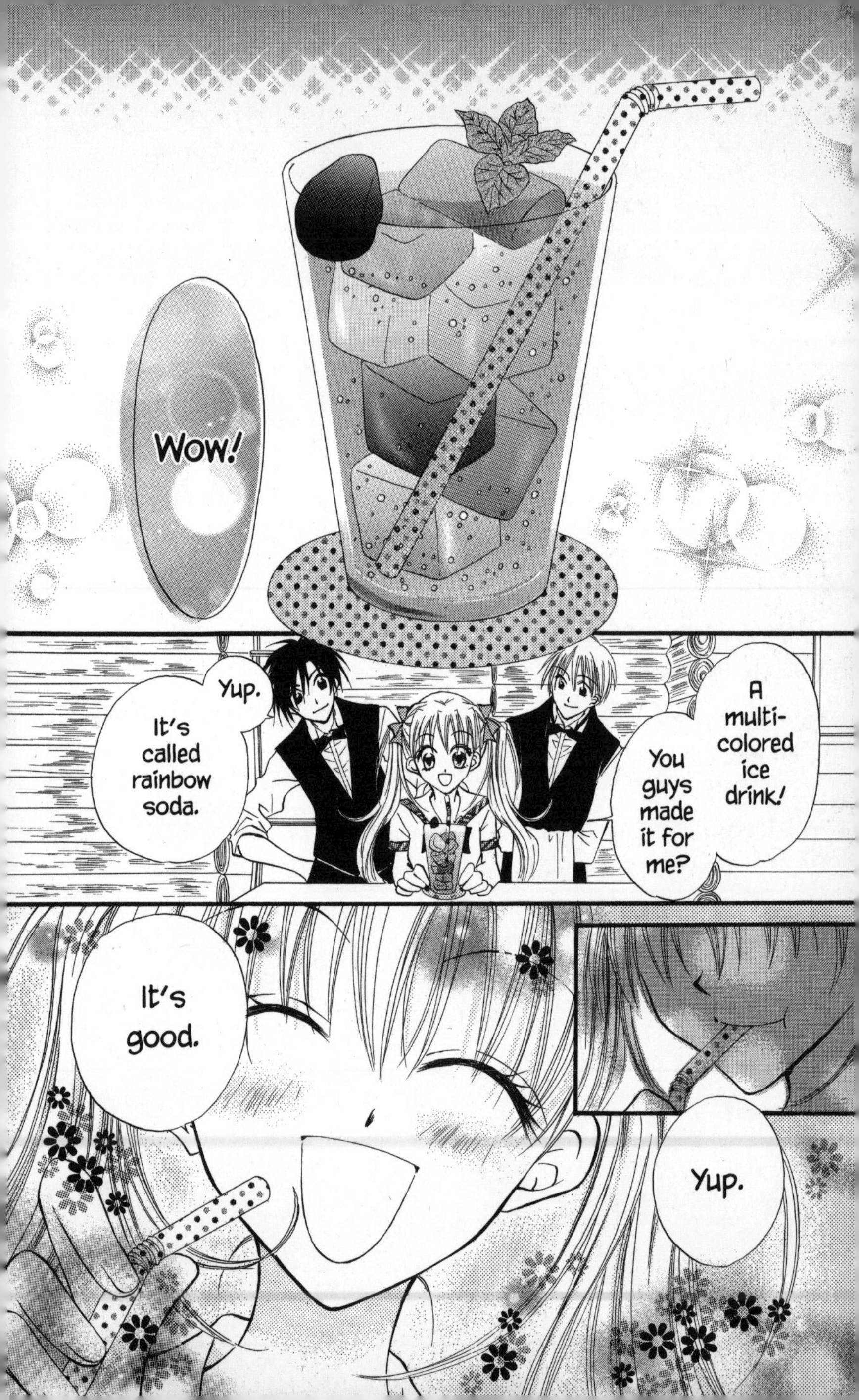
Wow!
A multi-colored ice drink!
You guys made it for me?
Yup.
It's called rainbow soda.
It's good.
Yup.

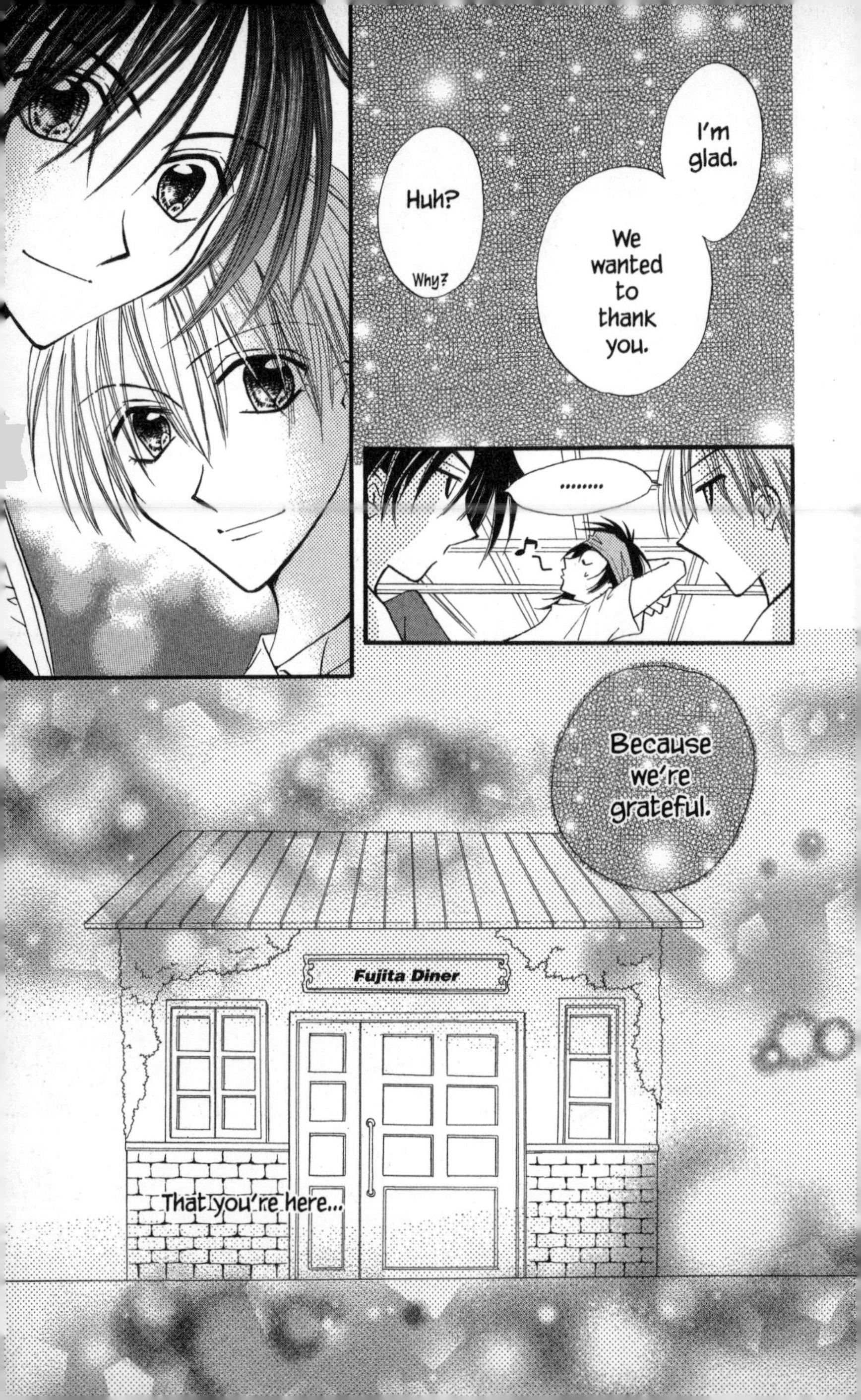
I'm glad.
We wanted to thank you.
Huh?
Why?
....
Because we're grateful.
Fujita Diner
That you're here...

Kitchen Palace

Did you enjoy *Kitchen Princess?*
In this section, we'll give you the recipes
for the food that Najika makes in the story.
Please try making them. ♥

Chocolate Macaroons

Tip from Najika.

It's also good if you substitute grated cheese for the cocoa!

Chocolate Macaroons

About 15 cookies.
70 g unsalted butter, 50 g soft flour, 50 g almond meal, 50 g corn starch, 4 tablespoons cocoa powder (no sugar), 3 tablespoons powdered sugar

How to make

1 Leave the butter at room temperature to soften it. In a bowl, whisk butter with a wooden spoon.

2 Sift all of the other ingredients into a separate bowl, and add to the first bowl. Make sure it is a little moist.

3 Roll the dough into balls of about 3 cm in diameter. If you take some dough and squeeze it in your fist, and then roll it with both of your hands, it'll come out good.

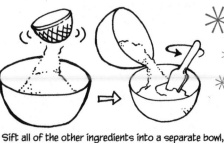

DONE ♥

4 Place the balls on a sheet of wax paper on a cookie sheet. Make sure to space them out 3-4 cm apart. Bake in oven for 15 minutes at 180 degrees Celsius (approx. 350 F).

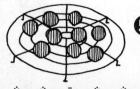

5 When done, take it out of the oven and cool.

This snack melts in your mouth and goes well with coffee or tea. You can wrap it nicely and give it away for Valentine's Day!

Strawberry Shortcake

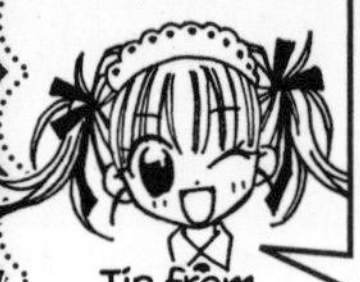

Tip from Najika.

The temperature of the oven depends on the make of the oven. So when you bake it, if the inside is still raw, try lowering the temperature and bake it longer.

Sponge Cake

One cake about 18 cm in diameter. 2 eggs, 1/3 cup sugar, 1/3 cup soft flour, 1 tablespoon unsalted butter. Frosting/Filling: strawberries, 3/4 cup whipped cream, 1 tablespoon sugar

How to make

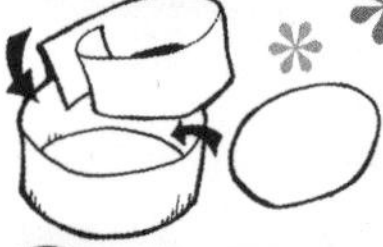

1. Cut out a piece of wax paper to match the cake, and put it in the bottom of the cake pan. Make sure to have all the ingredients measured out and ready. Microwave the butter for about 1 or 2 minutes. Preheat the oven to 160 degrees Celsius (approx. 320 F).

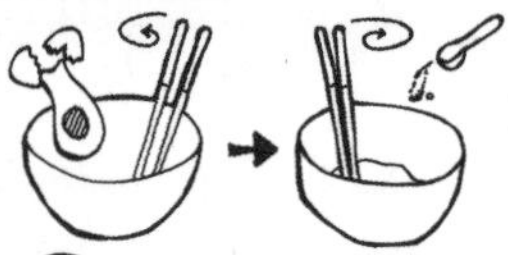

2. Crack the eggs in a bowl and mix. Then add sugar until it all melts.

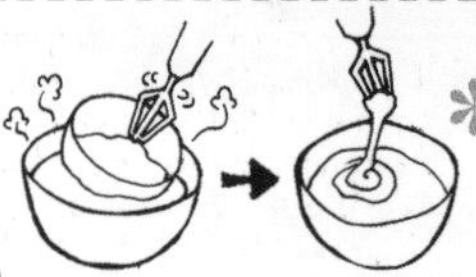

3. Put warm water (about 30 degrees C, 86 degrees F) in a big bowl. Place the bowl from step 2 inside and use a mixer to whip it up.

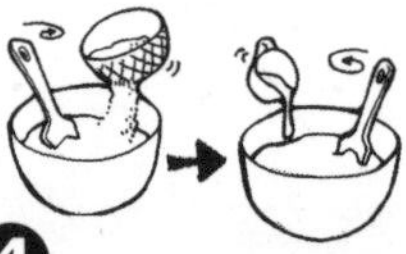

4. Sift soft flour into the bowl from step 3. After stirring, add the melted butter from step 1.

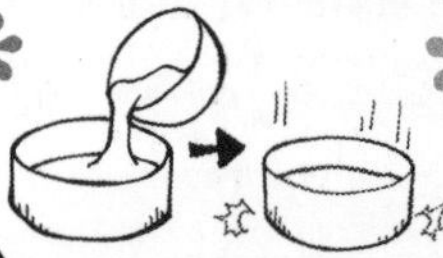

5. Pour the batter into the cake pan. Make sure to use both of your hands to tap the pan to take out any excess air. Then put the pan in the oven.

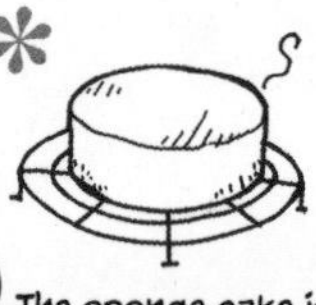

6. The sponge cake is ready when you stick a toothpick through it and it comes out clean! Once done, take it out of the pan and place it on a cake plate to cool.

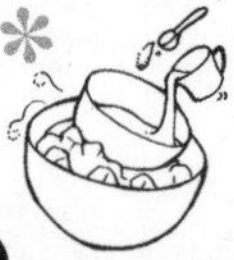

7. Put sugar in whipped cream, and place the bowl in a bigger bowl with ice water and use a mixer to whip.

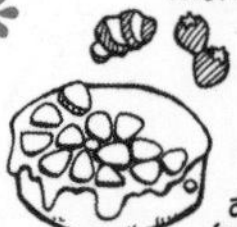

8. Wash the strawberries and cut off the stems. Cut them in slices and keep them aside. Cut the sponge cake in half and spread whipped cream on the bottom half. Place the strawberry slices on the whipped cream, and spread more whipped cream on top of that. Place the top half of the sponge cake on top of the bottom half.

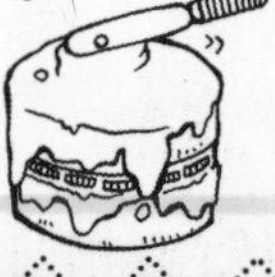

9. Spread whipped cream along the sides and the top evenly. Decorate the cake using strawberries and whipped cream and you're done!

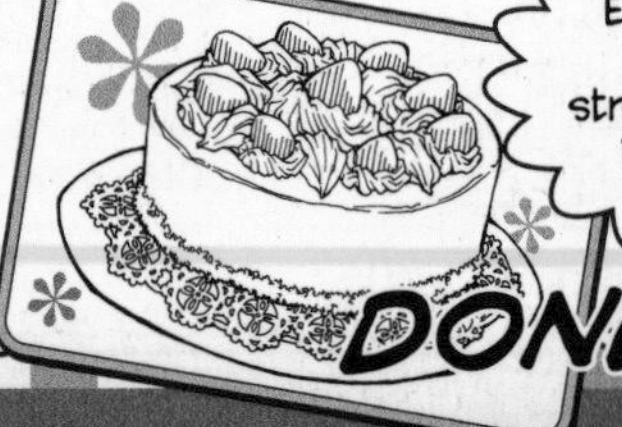

Everybody's favorite strawberry cake is so easy to make.

DONE ♥

Cake of Rice

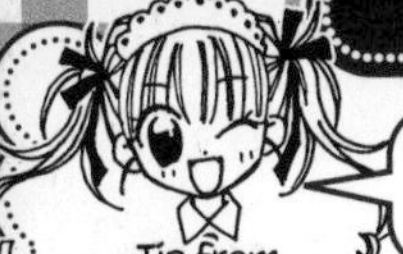

Make the rice ingredients first! You can choose your favorite things to put with the rice. ♥ You can also change the rice to sushi rice!

Tip from Najika.

How to make

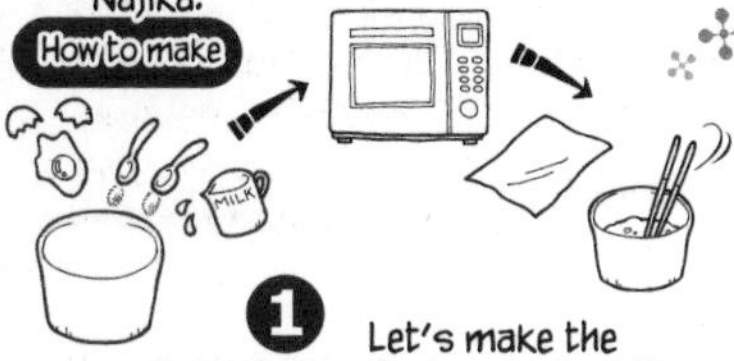

Cake of Rice

One cake about 15 cm in diameter. 4-5 bowls of rice, 3/4 cup salmon flakes, carrots 3 cm, a few daikon sprouts. Scrambled eggs: 2 eggs, 1 tablespoon milk, 1 tablespoon sugar, a little bit of salt. Flavored minced meat: 3 1/2 ounces minced meat, 3 tablespoons water, 2 teaspoons soy sauce, 2 teaspoons Japanese sake, 2 teaspoons sugar, a pinch of ginger

1 Let's make the scrambled eggs first. Put all of the ingredients in a microwave-safe bowl and stir. Wrap it with plastic wrap and microwave for 1 minute. Take it out and stir until scrambled. Since it's hard to burn the eggs, it'll come out pretty and yellow.

2 Wrap the carrot in plastic wrap and microwave it for 2 minutes. Once it cools down, peel it, wash it, and cut it into pieces.

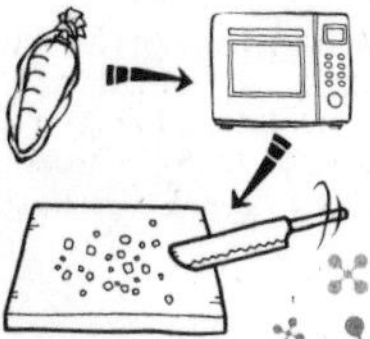

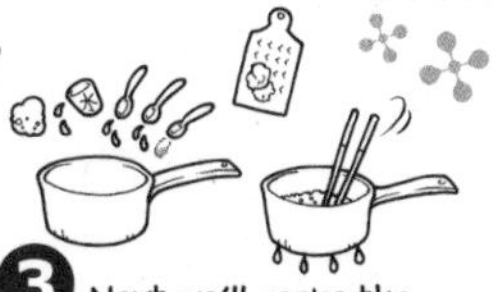

3 Next we'll make the flavored minced meat. First, grate the ginger. Put all the ingredients in a pan and stir well. Put it on medium heat and stir well until most of the juice evaporates. It is finished when the meat is a little moist.

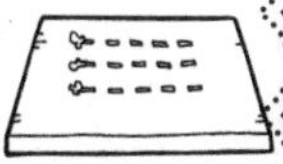

4 For the daikon sprouts, cut off the stems and cut the sprouts into short pieces.

5 Take out the base of the cake pan and replace it with plastic wrap. Put the scrambled egg in and lay it out so it is evenly distributed. On top of the eggs, put in 1 cm of rice. Use the base of the cake pan to push the rice down so it will stay in cake shape.

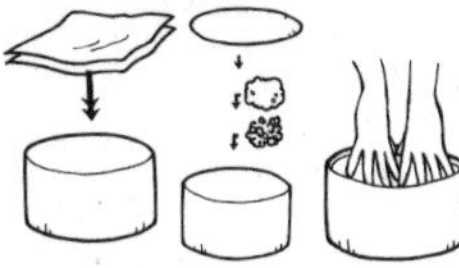

6 Remove the base and put in the following in order: salmon flakes, rice, minced meat, and rice. Make sure to push down each time you put in the rice! Leave in the cake pan for a few minutes, and when you think the shape is secure, remove the base.

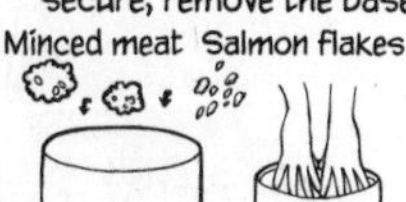
Minced meat
Salmon flakes

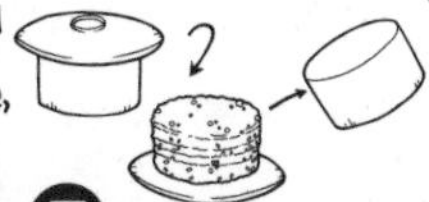

7 Place a plate facing down on top of the cake pan, and flip everything over. You should have the eggs on top. Remove the cake pan and the wrap on the sides.

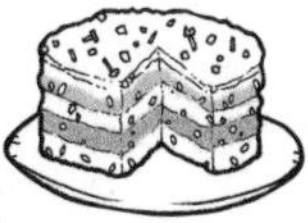

8 Sprinkle the carrots and daikon sprouts on top of the egg and you're done. Cut and eat it like a cake!

It's easy and looks very attractive, so it's perfect for a party!

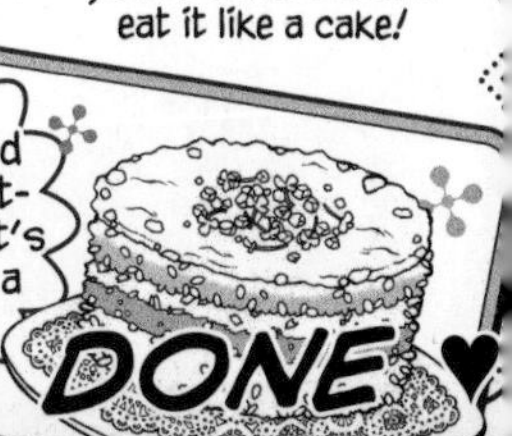
DONE♥

Yogurt Mousse

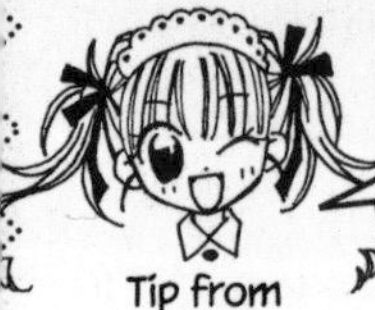

Tip from Najika.

Yogurt is made with fermented milk. Dairy bacteria is good for your stomach and intestines and works to regulate your system.

Yogurt Mousse

4 servings
1 cup plain yogurt, 3 tablespoons sugar, 1 cup whipped cream, 2 teaspoons gelatin, 3 tablespoons hot water

How to make

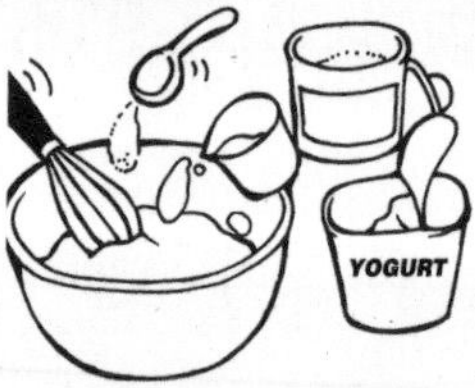
YOGURT

1. Mix the yogurt and sugar in a bowl.

do with mrs. Otero

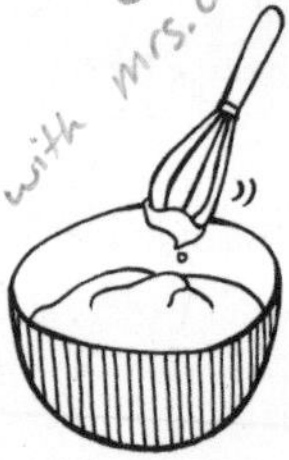

2. In a different bowl, pour whipping cream in and mix until it whips up. Make sure it has the same texture as the yogurt.

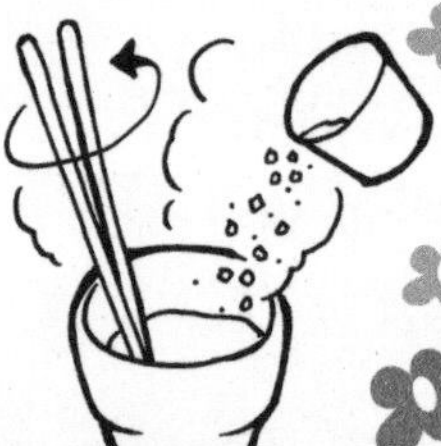

3. In a small bowl, put in hot water and pour the gelatin in. Stir as you are pouring the gelatin so it doesn't clump up. Stir until the gelatin is completely melted.

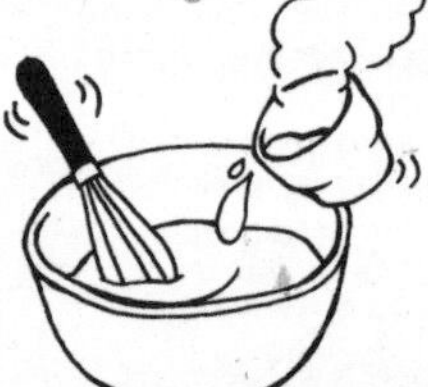

4. Put the hot water from step 3 in the yogurt and stir immediately. You have to be fast or the gelatin will clump up.

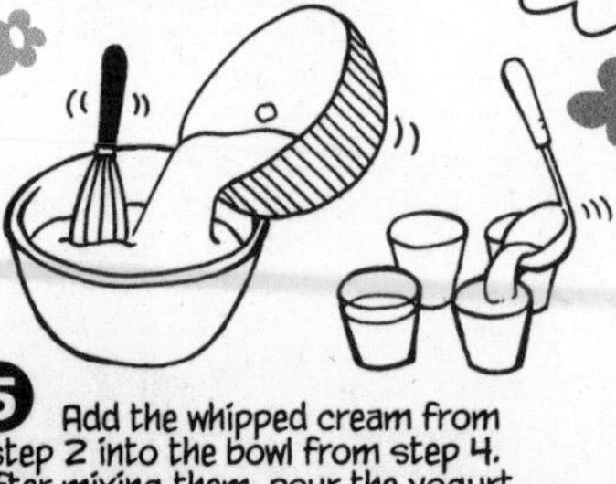

5. Add the whipped cream from step 2 into the bowl from step 4. After mixing them, pour the yogurt into glass cups and chill in the refrigerator for about an hour.

You can top it off with whipped cream and fresh fruit!

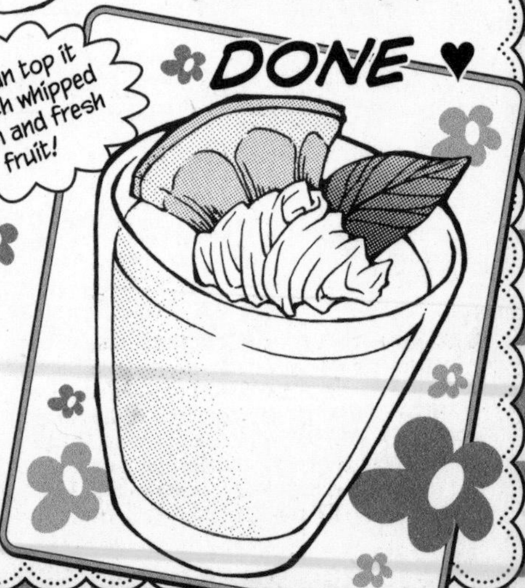
DONE ♥

Peach Pie

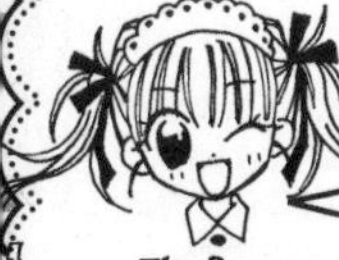

Tip from Najika.

Anyone can make delicious pie if you use frozen pie crust. You can make other pies using apples or pears, too!!

Peach Pie

One pie about 18 cm in diameter. 2 to 4 sheets frozen pie crust dough, 1 can peaches, 2 tablespoons sugar, 1 tablespoon lemon juice, egg

How to make

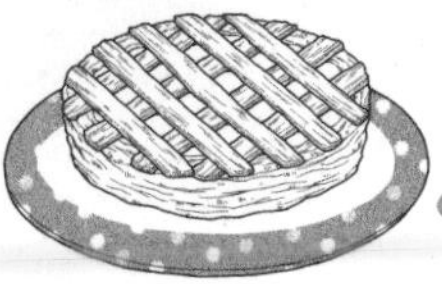

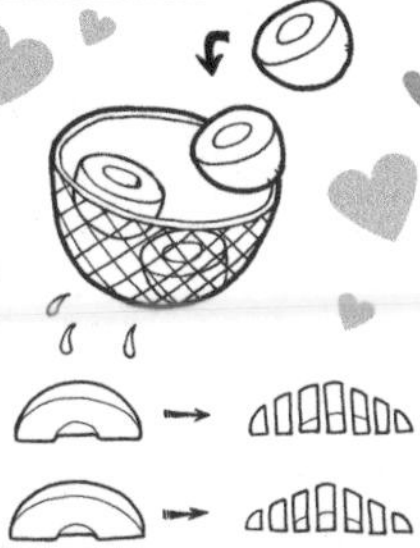

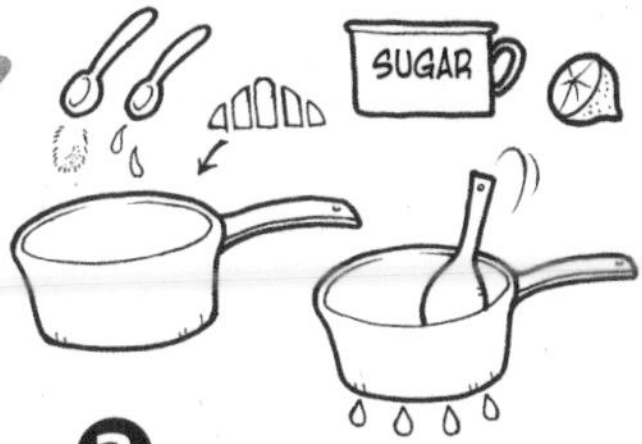
SUGAR

1. Take out the frozen pie crust dough from the freezer and thaw it at room temperature for about 10 minutes. *Depending on the brand, the thawing time may vary. Check the instructions on the package.

2. Open the peaches and drain in a strainer. Cut the peaches vertically in half, and cut those up in small pieces.

3. Put the peaches, sugar, and lemon juice in a pan. Heat on medium heat and stir with a wooden spoon until the water evaporates. This will take about 5 minutes. It is important to let the water evaporate or the pie will get soggy.

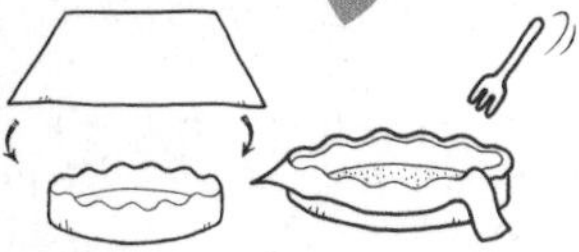

4. Lay the sheet of pie dough in a pie tin, and trim the excess dough. Poke holes in the base with a fork for air to go through.

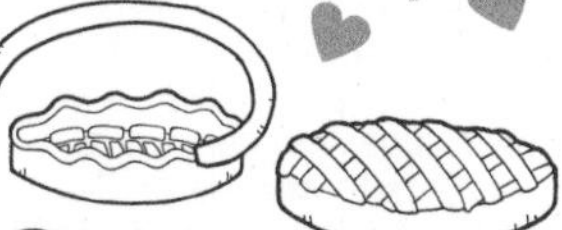

5. Place the peaches from step 3 flatly in the pie tin, and surround the outside of the tin with a pie sheet strip of about 1 cm. Place more on top, crossing the strips.

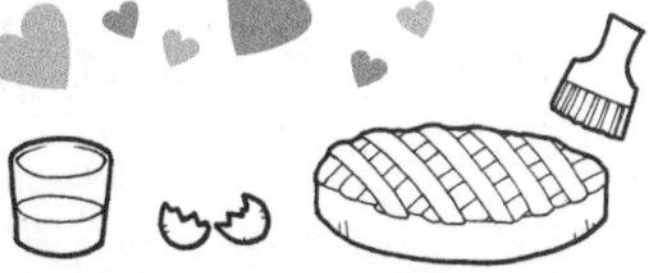

6. Brush some egg onto the surface. This is important, since it helps the crust turn a nice color during baking. Bake the pie at 190 degrees Celsius (approx. 375 F) for 20 to 25 minutes. *Depending on the oven, the amount of time may vary. Make sure to keep checking the pie so it doesn't burn.

You can make this in a short amount of time!

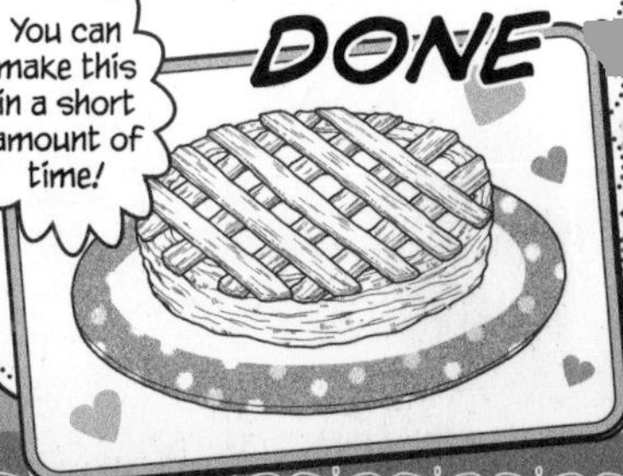
DONE

Side-Story Recipes

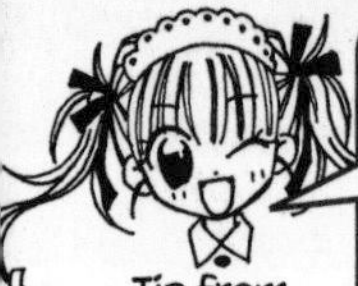

Tip from Najika.

Fight the heat with a cool drink! If you keep the glasses in the refrigerator, they'll be even cooler!

Cool Drinks

Yogurt Drink: 1/2 cup plain yogurt, 1 cup of milk, 1 tablespoon honey, 1 tablespoon lemon juice. Magic Iced Coffee: as much iced coffee as you like. Rainbow Soda: three or more types of juice (grapefruit, blueberry, cranberry, or anything you like), some cider

How to make

Rainbow Soda

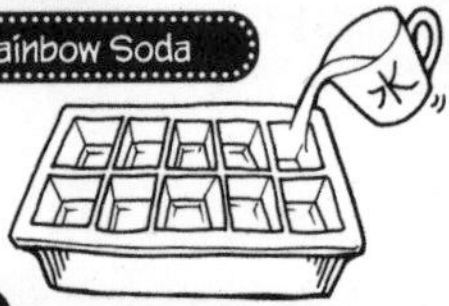

1. Fill the squares of an ice cube tray halfway up with water.

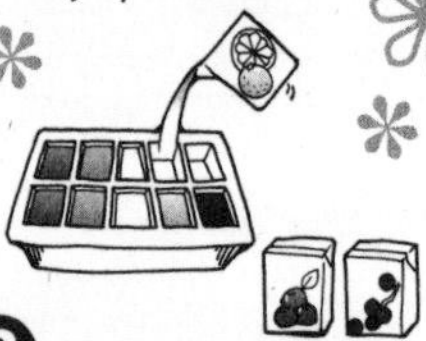

2. Add juice to each cube. As long as you are careful that they don't overflow into the next cube, you can make as many types as you want. It is important to mix it with water because if there is too much juice, it becomes sherbert-like and melts easily.

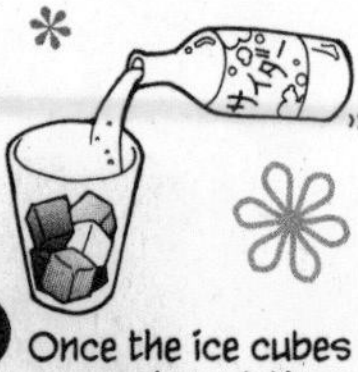

3. Once the ice cubes are ready, put them in a glass of cider.

Magic Iced Coffee

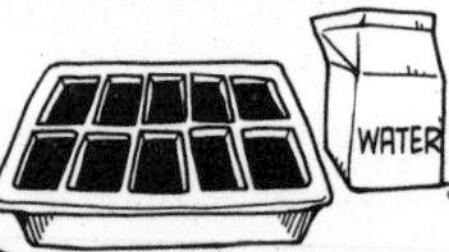
WATER

1. Put iced coffee in an ice cube tray.

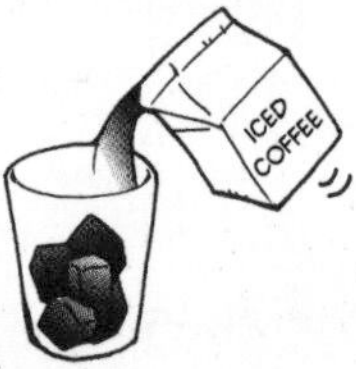
ICED COFFEE

2. Once the coffee ice cubes are frozen, put them in a glass. Pour iced coffee in the glass and you're done. This way, even if the ice melts, the taste won't change. You can do the same thing with iced tea.

Yogurt Drink

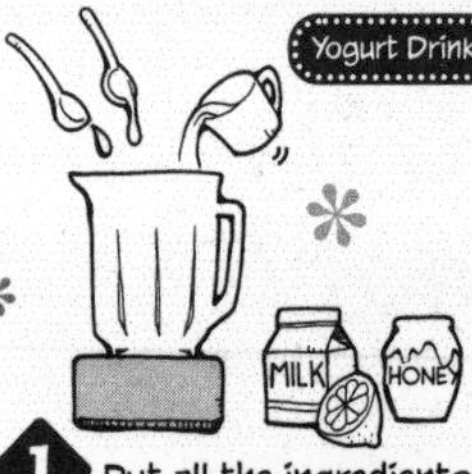
MILK
HONEY

1. Put all the ingredients in a blender and blend. If you don't have a blender, you can put them in a bowl and use an eggbeater.

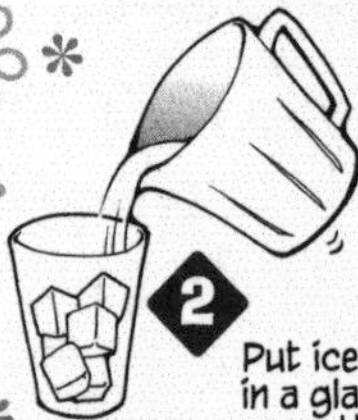

2. Put ice cubes in a glass and pour the mix from step 1.

You can top it off with a cherry or a lemon wedge to make it look cute! ♥

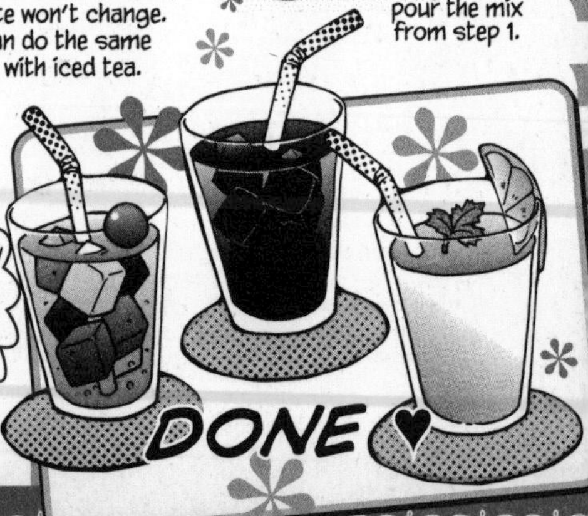
DONE ♥

Kitchen Princess

From the Writer

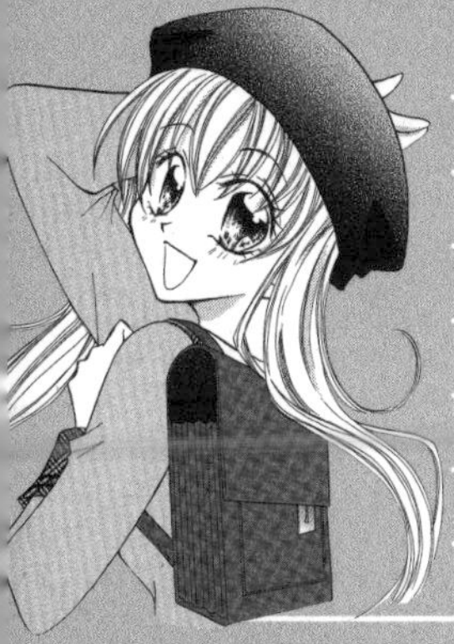

Thank you for reading Volume 2 of *Kitchen Princess.* I am the writer, Miyuki Kobayashi. In Volume 1, I explained Najika's, Sora's, and Daichi's names, but then I got questions asking about Akane's name. Everyone has a name referring to nature, so why is Akane's name a color? Why do you think it is? Najika's name makes me think of a bright cloudless sky after the rain. Shiny and colorful like a rainbow—that's the image I have. On the other hand, Akane's name makes me think of the setting sun. The sky is deep red, and that is where I got her name. Also, I am getting letters about who's more popular—Sora or Daichi. For now, Daichi is a little bit more popular. I sometimes get letters saying, "I like Fujita-san more than the boys!" Very funny (laugh). I would like to finish by saying thanks to Natsumi Ando-sensei, our editor Kishimoto-san, and editor-in-chief Nouchi-san. I will see you in the exciting Volume 3!

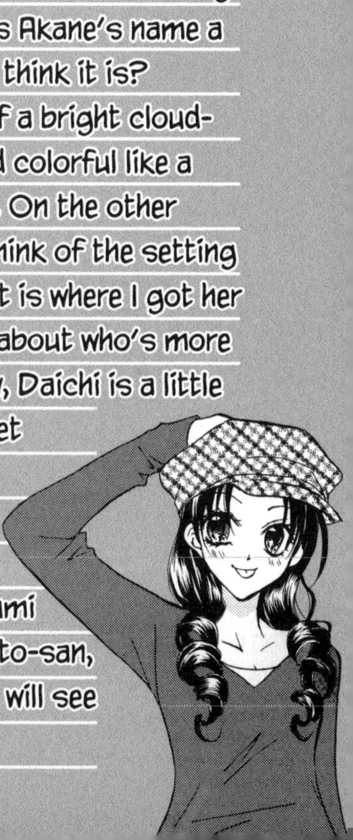

About the Creator

Natsumi Ando

   She was born January 27th in Aichi prefecture. She won the 19th Nakayoshi Rookie Award in 1994 and debuted as a manga artist. The title she drew was *Headstrong Cinderella.* Her other known works are *Zodiac P.I.* and *Wild Heart.* Her hobbies include reading, watching movies, and eating delicious food.

Translation Notes

Japanese is a tricky language for most Westerners, and translation is often more art than science. For your edification and reading pleasure, here are notes on some of the places where we could have gone in a different direction in our translation of the work, or where a Japanese cultural reference is used.

Hokkaido, page 11

Hokkaido is located in the northern part of Japan. It is the second largest island and the biggest prefecture.

Aniki, page 26

Aniki is the honorific term for "older brother," usually used by boys (or girls who are tomboys) starting in their younger teens. It is less honorific than *onii-chan* and *onii-san*.

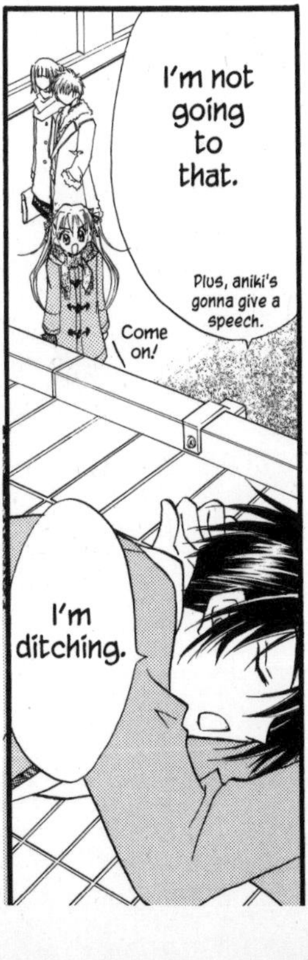
I'm not going to that.
Plus, aniki's gonna give a speech.
Come on!
I'm ditching.

Milkies, page 31

Milkies are a Japanese candy, similar to taffy. They are milky cream–flavored, hence the name. It is one of the signature candies of Fujiya, a major candymaker in Japan.

Akane, page 191

The character for Akane means "deep red" in Japanese.

Preview of Volume 3

We are pleased to present to you a preview from the next volume of *Kitchen Princess*. Volume 3 is available in English now!

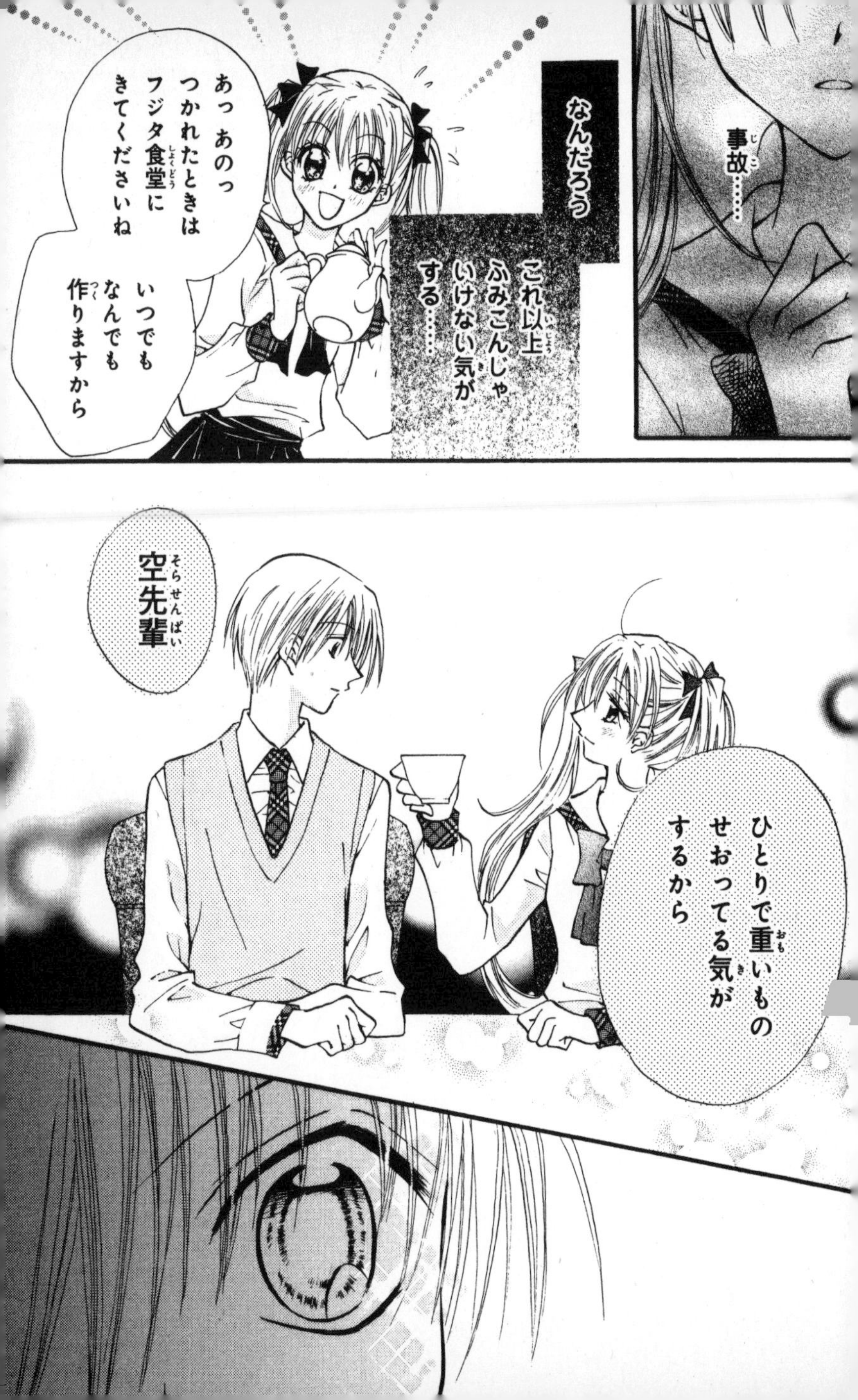
事故……
なんだろう
これ以上ふみこんじゃいけない気がする……
あっあのっ つかれたときはフジタ食堂にきてくださいね
いつでもなんでも作りますから
空先輩
ひとりで重いものせおってる気がするから

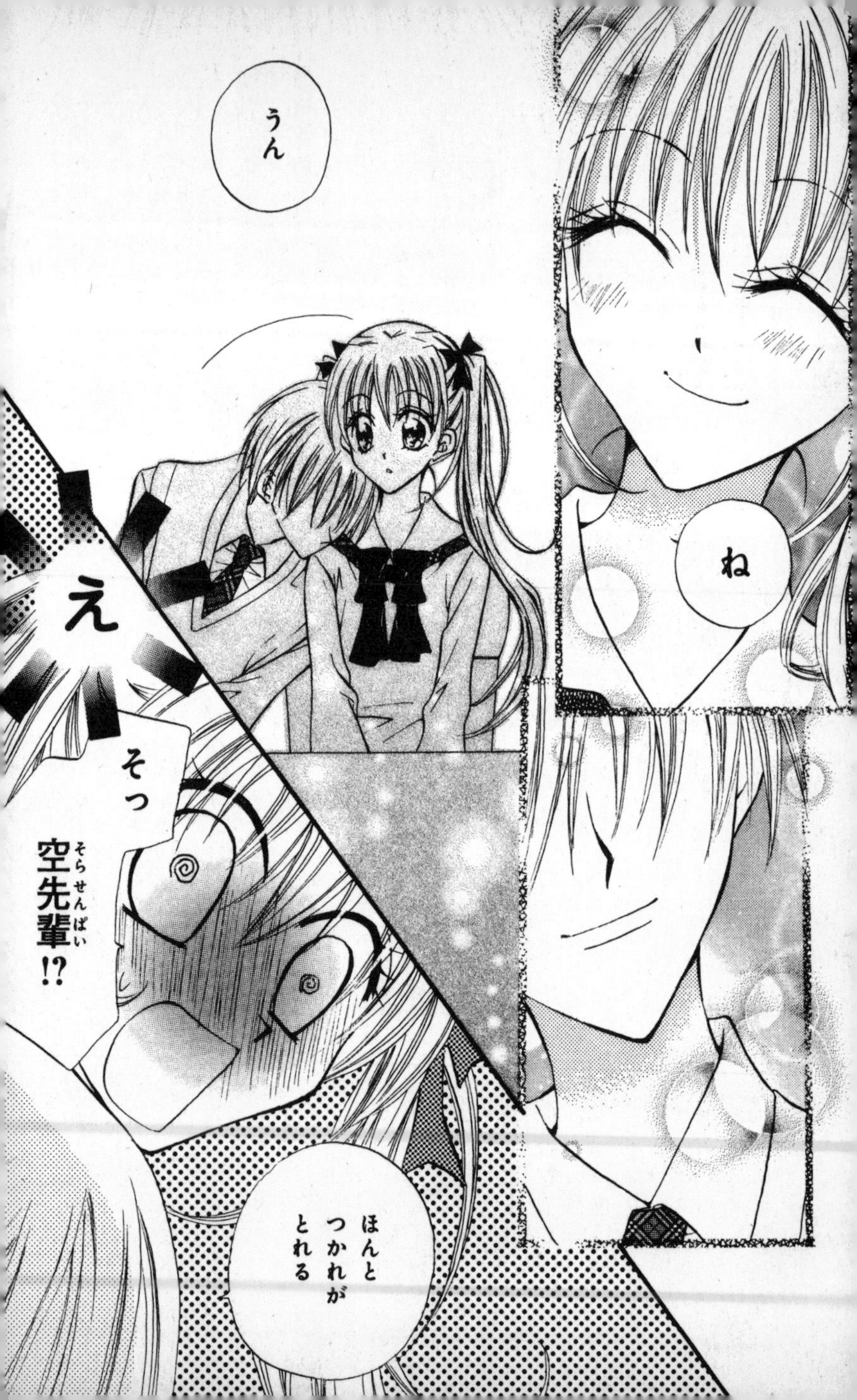
ね
うん
ほんと
つかれが
とれる
え
そっ
空先輩!?

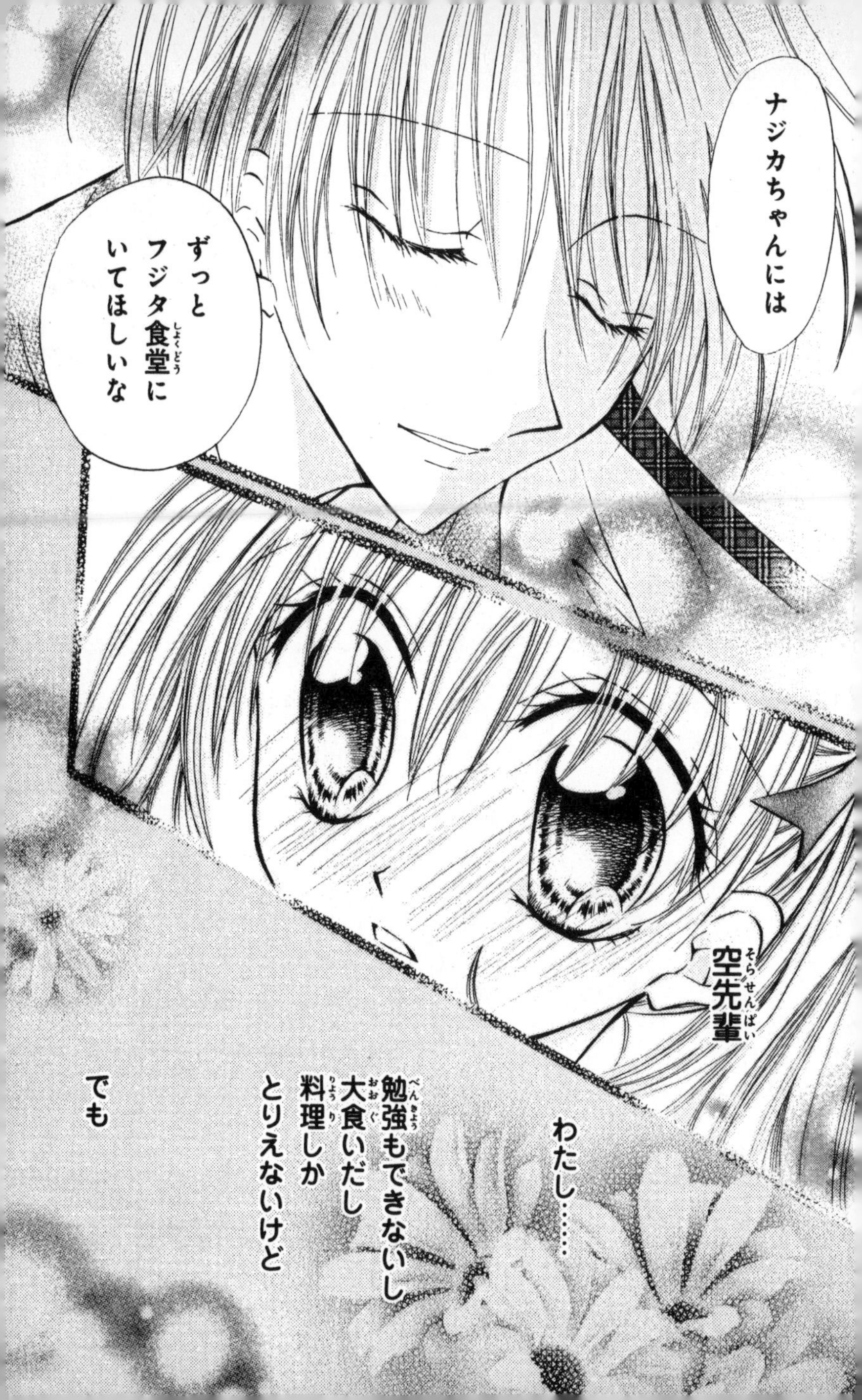
ナジカちゃんには
ずっとフジタ食堂にいてほしいな
空先輩
わたし……
勉強もできないし大食いだし料理しかとりえないけど
でも

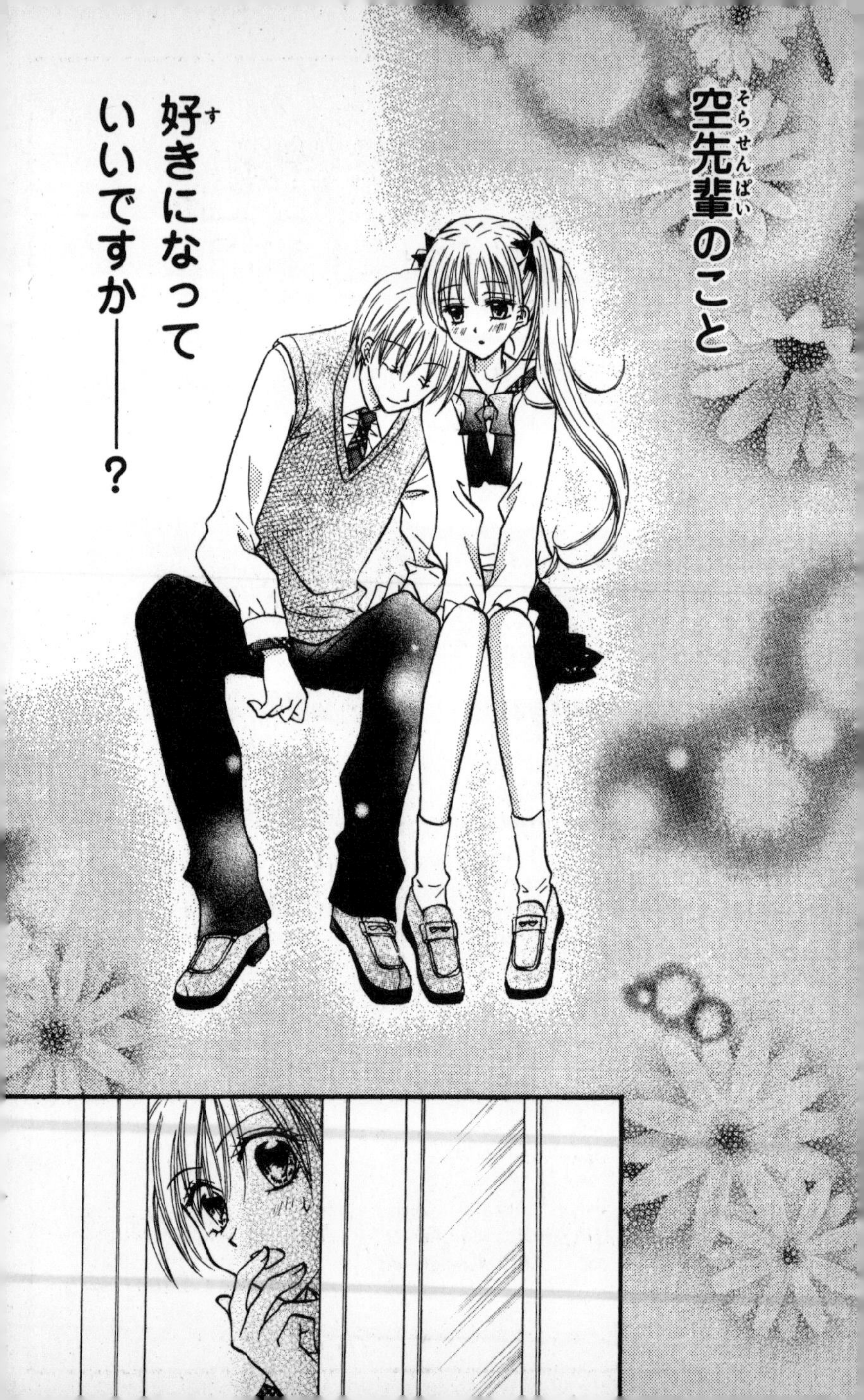
空先輩のこと
好きになって
いいですか――?

Mamotte! LOLLiPOP

MICHIYO KIKUTA

BOY CRAZY

Junior high schooler Nina is ready to fall in love. She's looking for a boy who's cute and sweet—and strong enough to support her when the chips are down. But what happens when Nina's dream comes true . . . twice? One day, two cute boys literally fall from the sky. They're both wizards who've come to the Human World to take the Magic Exam. The boys' success on this test depends on protecting Nina from evil, so now Nina has a pair of cute magical boys chasing her everywhere! One of these wizards just might be the boy of her dreams . . . but which one?

Michiyo Kikuta
1
Mamotte!
LOLLiPOP

Special extras in each volume! Read them all!

VISIT WWW.DELREYMANGA.COM TO:

- Read sample pages
- View release date calendars for upcoming volumes
- Sign up for Del Rey's free manga e-newsletter
- Find out the latest about new Del Rey Manga series

RATING T AGES 13+

DEL REY MANGA デルレイ

The Otaku's Choice

PEACH-PIT

Creators of *Dears* and *Rozen Maiden*

Everybody at Seiyo Elementary thinks that stylish and super-cool Amu has it all. But nobody knows the *real* Amu, a shy girl who wishes she had the courage to truly be herself. Changing Amu's life is going to take more than wishes and dreams—it's going to take a little magic! One morning, Amu finds a surprise in her bed: three strange little eggs. Each egg contains a Guardian Character, an angel-like being who can give her the power to be someone new. With the help of her Guardian Characters, Amu is about to discover that her true self is even more amazing than she ever dreamed.

Special extras in each volume! Read them all!

TOMARE!

止まれ

[STOP!]

You're going the wrong way!

Manga is a completely different
type of reading experience.

To start at the *beginning,*
go to the *end!*

That's right! Authentic manga is read the traditional Japanese way—
from right to left. Exactly the *opposite* of how American books are
read. It's easy to follow: Just go to the other end of the book, and read
each page—and each panel—from right side to left side, starting at
the top right. Now you're experiencing manga as it was meant to be!